The Frameworks of English

THE FRAMEWORKS OF ENGLISH

Introducing language structures

Third Edition

KIM BALLARD

First edition 2001
Second edition 2007
This edition 2013
Published by
PALGRAVE MACMILLAN

Palgrave Macmillan in the UK is an imprint of Macmillan Publishers Limited, registered in England, company number 785998, of Houndmills, Basingstoke, Hampshire RG21 6XS.

Palgrave Macmillan in the US is a division of St Martin's Press LLC, 175 Fifth Avenue, New York, NY10010.

Palgrave Macmillan is the global academic imprint of the above companies and has companies and representatives throughout the world.

Palgrave® and Macmillan® are registered trademarks in the United States, the United Kingdom, Europe and other countries

ISBN: 978–0–230–39243–4 hardback
ISBN: 978–0–230–39242–7 paperback

This book is printed on paper suitable for recycling and made from fully managed and sustained forest sources. Logging, pulping and manufacturing processes are expected to conform to the environmental regulations of the country of origin.

A catalogue record for this book is available from the British Library.

A catalog record for this book is available from the Library of Congress.

In memory of my grandparents

Ronald Elston Dell
&
Ivy Charlotte Dell

Contents

Part IV   Discourse Frameworks

List of Tables

List of Figures

Acknowledgements

The author would like to thank Clive Williamson, as well as the following former students, for permission to use their examples of spontaneous speech: Lucy Ambrose, Kelly Loughran, Nick Parry, Lucy Skinner, Clover Stevens, Zoe Walton.

The author would like to thank Harriet Constable and Rosie Sharratt for permission to use their exchange on Twitter.com.

The author would also like to thank Imogen Simmonds for the illustrations in Chapter 12.

Lastly, the author would like to thank Professor Jonathan Culpeper of Lancaster University for his helpful advice on several points of detail in the previous edition which have of course been retained in this new edition.

The extract from 'Gene involved in sperm-to-egg binding is key to fertility in mammals' is reproduced by kind permission of the University of Durham.

The extract by John Motson from the *Radio Times* 3–9 June 2006 is reproduced courtesy of *Radio Times* magazine.

The transcription of the commentary from the BBC's live coverage of the 2011 UCI Road World Championships appears by kind permission of the UCI and the BBC (and with thanks to the commentators themselves, Chris Boardman MBE and Hugh Porter MBE).

The extract from 'Cavendish is World Road Champion' by Eddie Allen is reproduced by kind permission of British Cycling.

The transcribed extract from the BBC Horizon documentary *Miracle in Orbit* (Horizon, 10 February 2000) is included by kind permission of the BBC.

The transcription from *Jools Holland: London Calling* is included by kind permission of the BBC and Mr Sterling Betancourt MBE.

SOURCES

The Art of Travel by Alain de Boton first published by Hamish Hamilton in 2002.

I'm the King of the Castle by Susan Hill first published in 1970 by Hamish Hamilton Ltd.

What you wear can change your life by Trinny Woodall and Susannah Constantine first published in 2004 by Weidenfeld & Nicolson.

Wonders of the Universe by Professor Brian Cox and Andrew Cohen first published in 2011 by Harper Collins.

Waterland by Graham Swift first published in 1983 by William Heinemann Ltd.

Extract from BBC *Focus* magazine April 2006 from an article by Robert Partridge.

Extract from the National Portal of India, www.india.gov.in, accessed 18 July 2012.

Part I
INTRODUCTION

1 Introduction

1.1 A VOYAGE AROUND THE ENGLISH LANGUAGE

In 1967, a science fiction film was released entitled *Fantastic Voyage*. In it, a team of scientists in a kind of space capsule are shrunk small enough to be injected into the human bloodstream and journey around the body exploring the lungs, stomach, heart and so on. The fascination of the film at the time was the way it showed the supposed workings of our anatomy from the inside, and the extraordinary perspective this gave on the human body. Human language is a subject of equal fascination and the aim of this book is to make a journey around the English language and get an inside view of how it works. Because language is something with which we are very familiar and which we are all very competent at using, it is easy to make the assumption that it is a relatively simple phenomenon. This is very far from the truth. Human language – be it English or any other tongue – is as complex in its own way as any of the biochemical and anatomical functions of the human body.

To take a relatively straightforward example, consider the following string of words: *whole scoffed the Kate cake greedy has*. They are clearly not a meaningful English sequence as they stand, although without any difficulty you could arrange them into *greedy Kate has scoffed the whole cake*. This might strike you as an extremely simple task, but in fact the knowledge about the English language which you would draw on in order to reorganise the words into a permissible sentence is highly complex. If you asked any number of other speakers of English to do this, they would all come up with the same response. This is not a coincidence. All native speakers of English share a set of mental rules which guarantee that they will know how to group the words into meaningful units – *greedy Kate / has scoffed / the whole cake* – not, for example, *Kate cake / whole the has / scoffed greedy*, and that these units have to be arranged in a particular order so that a combination such as *has scoffed greedy Kate the whole cake* would not occur. Not only do we employ knowledge about the rules of word order here, but we are also using knowledge about meanings (for example, knowing that *greedy* could describe *Kate* but not the *cake*). If you had heard these words read aloud instead of reading them on the page, you would need to use subtle information about the sounds of the language in order to distinguish between *Kate* and *cake*, which sound very similar.

Clearly, then, in order to make sense of that random string of words, you would need to employ specific knowledge about the English language. If you are reading this book, you are presumably interested in finding out how the English language works. Subconsciously you already know this because you are able to use the language effectively. However, your present knowledge about the patterns and rules which underpin English is **implicit**. In other words, you possess this knowledge, but only at a subconscious and instinctive level. The aim of this book is to help you make your knowledge **explicit**. In other words, to explain to you what exactly the nature of that knowledge is. Because you learn your first language instinctively from birth, it may come as a surprise later on to discover that you have mastered speaking it without consciously learning the rules on which it is based. This is one of the most extraordinary things about speech and language. But it is possible to distance yourself from your first language to see how it works and how it is structured: to take a voyage around it and understand it more closely.

1.2   FRAMEWORKS AND LEVELS

A framework is a structure which holds something together. Knowing the frameworks of a language enables you to understand how that language is structured and what rules operate to produce that structure. Without these patterns and rules, the language would be haphazard and would not be an effective means of communication.

This book is subdivided so that Parts II, III, IV and V each deal with a different aspect of the frameworks of English. Just as a book on the human anatomy might be subdivided into sections such as the skeleton, the nervous system, the digestive system and so on, in a similar way, this book is organised according to four different aspects of the language, namely

lexis	the words of the language
grammar	the way words are combined into sentences
discourse	the way sentences are combined into texts
phonology	the sounds and sound patterns of the language.

This voyage around the English language begins in Part II, Lexical Frameworks, with words, which may be regarded as the basic building blocks of language. We will look at ways of dividing words into family groups or **word classes** according to the features which characterise them and then move on to look at **morphology** – how English words are structured and the different strategies employed to create new words. Part III considers the way in which words can be combined – first into phrases, then into clauses and finally into sentences – and the way in which words are modified in certain situations by the addition of special endings or **inflections** (for example, by adding a plural ending to *cat* when we talk about *three cats*). The range of inflections and the principles of word order or **syntax** are together covered by **grammar**, so Part III deals with the grammatical frameworks of English. This is the most substantial part of this textbook. If you consider for a moment that there is an infinite number of possible sentences which we might compose in English (or any language, for that matter), then there must be a considerable range of ways to construct these sentences. It follows that there are many rules which ensure that the sentences we compose are both natural and meaningful. It is difficult to reduce a survey of these rules to anything much shorter, although it would be possible to go into even more detail on grammatical and other aspects of the language if the scope of this textbook were greater. The largest unit of construction in grammar is the sentence. Part IV, Discourse Frameworks, explores how we combine sentences into what is known as **text** or **discourse**.

While Parts II, III and IV cover the words of the language and the way they combine into larger and larger units, Part V, Phonological Frameworks, looks at English from a different angle by considering the sound system of the language. First, we will examine the set of distinct sounds which are used in English and then look at the way these sounds combine to form strings of sounds, including syllables, before moving on to what are known as the **prosodic** features of language which often operate across groups of words and which include aspects such as the **pitch** and **intonation** of our voices.

The different aspects of language which we are studying here are sometimes referred to as **levels of language**. So Part II, which deals with lexical frameworks, looks at language on a lexical level, Part III looks at language on a grammatical level and so on. We need to have a methodical way of exploring the language and we must therefore rely on the levels of language to map out our journey. However, these levels are not completely separate, as you will discover.

A further level of language not mentioned so far is the **semantic level**. **Semantics** is the study of meaning. It is a crucial aspect in that the purpose of language is to convey meaning. However, meaning is not an aspect of language which can be delimited in quite the same way as, for example, the lexis of the language. Meaning operates in a different dimension from the other levels and in conjunction with them all. For example, as far as the sounds of English are concerned, it may seem that individual sounds such as the '*b*' at the start of *bat* have no intrinsic meaning but there is a correlation between sounds and meanings in some words – beyond what can be considered coincidental. For instance, one dictionary lists the following words beginning with the *gru-* sound:

grub	*grubby*	*grudge*	*gruff*
grumble	*grumpy*	*grunt*	

It is not unreasonable to propose that, since five of these seven words carry suggestions of impatience or irritability, there is some semantic link between those negative associations and the sound *gru-* at the beginning of *grudge, gruff, grumble, grumpy* and *grunt*. It may even be that this meaning of *gru-* has come about because we clench our teeth when we feel irritated and *gru-* is a natural sound to produce in this position.

At the other extreme, we can see how sentences can colour the meaning of adjoining or associated sentences. Consider, for example, *My best friend has just played a trick on me*. If you heard or read this sentence in isolation, you are likely to assume that the trick in question was a harmless prank of some kind. You would think this, first, because the expression *play a trick* suggests this kind of playfulness and, second, because you are told that the person playing the trick is the speaker's best friend and you wouldn't expect a best friend to do something unkind. If the sentence were followed with a further comment such as *I laughed so much I cried*, then you would be confirmed in your initial assumption. However, if the follow-up comment to *My best friend has just played a trick on me* were something like *A dirty, rotten trick*, then you would have to rethink your interpretation of the first sentence since the trick in question was clearly far from harmless.

The above is an example of how meaning is constructed and reconstructed as more information is received, and how this happens using large linguistic building blocks, namely sentences. You can see that meaning is not a unit of construction in the same way as other aspects of language are. Furthermore, meaning is often dependent on context. We may not be able to interpret something accurately or appropriately unless we know the context in which it is spoken or written. For example, if a person you meet at a business occasion introduces someone else as their partner, you would assume a professional relationship between these two people. On the other hand, if you were introduced to someone's partner at a social occasion, you would probably assume a more personal relationship.

Semantics, then, is an aspect of language which is very diverse in that it operates at all linguistic levels. Because of this, and because meaning can be constructed either by language which is relatively free from contextual consideration or by having to consider closely the context or situation in which language is used, semantics would prove an extremely demanding area to classify or describe comprehensively within the scope of this book. As mentioned before, explaining meaning is not the same kind of process as describing the frameworks on which a language is constructed. On the other hand, it is impossible to look at the frameworks of English without frequently making reference to meaning. For this reason, rather than presenting semantics as a separate topic or chapter, meaning is discussed at various points throughout this book where it is relevant to a full understanding of the frameworks. Inevitably, this will be frequently, but often the exploration of meaning is implicit to the discussion rather than a separate part of it.

1.3   SPEECH AND WRITING

Language can be spoken or written. (Some users also employ signing as a mode of communication.) Speech is the primary mode of communication. This is because all humans learn to speak as part of their natural biological development. Learning to speak is not something we choose to do: it is an instinctive process. By contrast, we have to make a conscious effort if we are to acquire the ability to write our language, and not all language users develop the same facility for doing this. In our society, writing is highly valued for a variety of reasons including its permanence and the way it embodies our social and cultural codes, such as our laws and our literature. However, other cultures do not depend so heavily on the written language as we do, and there are many people in the world who have not learnt to write.

This book is about the frameworks of English and to a large extent it is irrelevant whether we are talking about the language in its spoken or written form. Although we employ special conventions for writing our language (namely, using an alphabet, a standardised system of spelling and a set of punctuation marks), the vocabulary and the grammatical structures we use for speaking and writing are essentially the same even though speech will often exhibit more signs of spontaneity than writing. However, there are some lexical and grammatical choices which are more typically selected in informal speech and others which are more likely to be found in writing. When we explore the lexis and grammar of English in Chapters 2 to 7, the material covered will be largely applicable to both the spoken and written modes of language. In Chapter 8, which deals with discourse, some of the differences between spoken and written modes will be discussed, as will the relationship of electronically mediated language to both speech and writing. Exclusive attention is then given to speech and speech production in Chapters 9 to 11.

1.4 WHICH ENGLISH?

When we talk about the frameworks of English, we think of English as a specific language as opposed to the French language or the German language and so on. So far, this introduction has simply referred to 'English' on the assumption that the reader knows what is meant by this term. However, you are doubtless already aware that English can take many different forms. For example, the English spoken in America varies in several ways from the English spoken in Britain. And within Britain, there are many regional variations in the pronunciation, vocabulary and grammar of English, just as there are variations in America.

When analysing the lexical and grammatical frameworks of English, linguists find it helpful to use just one variety in order to find out what typifies or characterises the language. They can also use that variety as a yardstick or model with which to compare other varieties. It is perhaps unfortunate that there has to be such a yardstick, as this can mislead people into thinking that the selected variety of English is in some way intrinsically better as a means of communication than all the other varieties. This is not the case, but it is nevertheless valuable to have the set of reference points that the chosen variety provides. The 'yardstick' variety which linguists use – and therefore which is used in this textbook – is **Standard English** and, because this book is designed primarily for readers living in the British Isles, it is specifically **Standard British English** which is used. Although you may not speak Standard English yourself, you are certain to be familiar with it as it is the English of newspapers, of news broadcasting on television and radio, and the English which is used in public documents and in textbooks. Standard English is also the variety of English which foreigners learn (which adds weight to the notion that it in some way represents or typifies the language).

Standard British English is a **dialect**. By dialect, we mean the lexis and the grammar of a particular language variety. (This is in contrast to pronunciation or **accent**, an aspect which is considered in Part V.) A dialect may be spoken or written. Whereas a relatively small percentage of the British population speak Standard English (possibly as few as 10 per cent), virtually everyone is aware of the standard variety because it is used so widely in the written mode as well as in national broadcasting.

Another important point to make when defining exactly which English is being described here is that we are only concerned with contemporary English – English as it is spoken at the start of the new millennium. The frameworks of any living language do not remain the same over a period of time but change in a variety of ways, some of these changes taking place slowly, others more rapidly. It is beyond the scope of this book to chart such changes – a full comparison of English in the year 2000 with, say, Shakespeare's English of 1600 would be an enormous task – but we will occasionally touch on the history of the language when this has some bearing on what English is like today.

The business of this book, then, is to describe those features and patterns of the language which characterise English as it is currently used. Simply because this book describes the grammatical rules of Standard English, it does not mean that the grammatical rules (or the lexis) of other varieties such as the Yorkshire dialect are inferior or incorrect. The term 'rule' can be misleading. It is essential to understand 'rule' as referring to a principle of construction rather than a way of judging correctness. This book, then, takes a **descriptive** rather than a **prescriptive** approach. This is important because we want to avoid being judgemental about language varieties. For instance, a Standard English speaker will say I _never_ did _anything_ to upset her while speakers of some non-standard dialects will say I _never_ did _nothing_ to upset her, using what is known as **multiple negation** in order to construct the sentence. An observer who tends towards a prescriptive approach to language will typically regard the use of multiple negation in this way as incorrect or sub-standard English and may even go so far as to label the speaker who uses it as ignorant or stupid. A descriptive linguist, on the other hand, will see this usage as a significant grammatical difference between Standard English and some non-standard varieties, and will even recognise the value of multiple negation in being able to emphasise meaning.

Many readers of this book will want to study dialects other than Standard British English and accents other than **Received Pronunciation**, the representative accent which is used in Part V. Part VI is therefore designed to give those readers some guidelines as to how varieties of English might differ from the dialect and accent described in Parts II to V, along with some examples of how to analyse these differences.

1.5   USING THIS BOOK

Section 1.2 above explained how this book is divided up according to four levels of language, Part II dealing with lexis, Part III with grammar, Part IV with discourse and Part V with phonology. Part VI then draws all these levels together to consider variation across different varieties of English. At the end of each part you will find some exercises, and there are also some suggestions for further reading as well as the addresses of some useful websites. The answers to the exercises are at the back of the book. Also at the back, you will find a reference section which contains a list of phonetic symbols and a glossary. Phonetic symbols (which are shown primarily between slant brackets) are used as a way of referring in writing to particular sounds of the language. It is easy to tell which sounds many symbols refer to: /b/ for example refers to the sound at the start of *bat* and /z/ to the sound at the start of *zip*. However, others are less transparent, such as the /æ/ at the start of /ænd/ (*and*). Although the phonetic symbols are explained fully in Chapter 9, other chapters do make use of them and you can check the sounds which they represent by referring to the list at the back.

The glossary contains an alphabetical list of all the linguistic terminology used in this book, with a definition for each term. When a new term is introduced in the text, it is in bold print. This also indicates that it is one of the terms listed in the glossary. At the end of some sections, you will find entries such as the following:

□ **connected speech** ⇨ 10.6

What this means is that the topic of connected speech has been touched on in another section and to find out more you should turn to Section 6 of Chapter 10. These cross-references are designed to help you make links across the frameworks.

There are a range of other symbols which are used in this book. An asterisk (*) placed in front of an example, be it a word, phrase or sentence, indicates that the example would not normally or naturally occur in English. A question mark (?) at the beginning of an example indicates that it might occur, but it may not be accepted by all speakers. The null sign Ø indicates that a word or phrase has been omitted but is understood, as in

Fred went to the shops and Ø bought a loaf of bread

where Ø stands for *Fred*.

Various types of bracket are used. Phonetic symbols (representing speech sounds or **phonemes**) are contained within slant brackets / /, angled brackets < > are used for letters of the alphabet, and square brackets [ ] are used to mark out phrases in grammatical analysis or for detailed phonetic transcriptions.

In a study of this kind there has to be a degree of selection and simplification. This is a concession to the sheer complexity of the language. It is not impossible that you will come across some differences in the way the frameworks are described if you look at other textbooks. This kind of variation is inevitable when the subject matter is so vast and complex: it is unlikely that any two linguists will agree totally on how to describe English – or any other language for that matter. The aim is to give you as clear and coherent a description as possible: you will find that other textbooks you consult will concur with this one on the majority of points. If you encounter differences, you need to make up your own mind which description or interpretation you find most appropriate.

If you are a student taking a course in English language or linguistics, you may initially find the content of this book somewhat overwhelming because, of necessity, it is fairly dense with linguistic terminology and with detailed explanations of how the language works. However, there is no need to panic! Tackle the content a little at a time and make sure you are building up a clear picture of how the language is structured by keeping the levels of language firmly in mind. You may also find it helpful to make a separate note of the key points. The exercises will help you check your knowledge, but you could also do this by identifying examples of your own, such as by finding further instances of specific word formation processes after reading Chapter 3. Another good strategy is to take a piece of text (such as a short newspaper report) and look for specific features in that text. For instance, you could check that you can label all the word classes in the first couple of sentences, or you could scan the whole text to look for structures such as complex sentences or passives.

As for the terminology, again it is better to learn a few terms at a time. Many of the terms introduced are used in more than one section, so you may find you learn the terms through seeing them applied and used in other contexts. Although there is a glossary at the back of this book, students often find it helpful to compile their own glossaries as a record of what they have covered. An effective way to do this is to put each term on a separate index card, and to add a couple of examples as well as the definition. Alternatively, you could create some kind of electronic record or database.

Part II
LEXICAL FRAMEWORKS

2 Word Classes

2.1 WORDS: THE BUILDING BLOCKS OF LANGUAGE

If you were to ask someone what they considered language to consist of, the most likely answer you would receive is 'words'. Most of us, whether or not we have made a close study of language, perceive words as the building blocks of language. Often, when we talk about language, we talk about it in terms of words – 'actions speak louder than words', 'mark my words', 'in other words' and so on. Of course, there is much more to studying a language than simply studying it on a **lexical** (or 'word') level. We can look at the units which make up words and which are therefore smaller than words, and we can look at larger units by exploring how words are grouped together in strings to form phrases, clauses and sentences and much longer texts too. Nevertheless, words are a very good place to start when studying a language and this is where we will therefore begin.

There is no doubt that the concept 'a word' has psychological reality for all users of the English language. Any definition of 'word' has to be, in some respects, specific to a particular language because words do not behave in the same way in all languages. This is often noticed when you try to translate from one language to another. If you were translating from Russian into English, for example, you would find that many single words in Russian can only be translated using several English words.

In some respects, defining 'word' in English appears to be a relatively straightforward task because we can make recourse to the written language in order to clarify what we mean by a word. For example, speakers of English will agree that the following sentence contains ten words:

Old fat cats like to sleep in quiet sunny places

The reason why identification of words seems straightforward here is because in writing we normally leave a space between them. It is therefore possible to count the number of words in a sentence or text. For many speakers, their concept of 'word' is reinforced by the written conventions of their language.

Nevertheless, there are some problems with word identification or word definition which cannot be solved simply by stating that a word is a linguistic item which is written with a space on either side. One of these concerns **compound words**. These are words such as *world-class* (as in *world-class cricketer*) or *world power* made up of two existing words, which might be written with a hyphen or with a space between them. In the case of *world power,* most speakers think of it as a single lexical item despite the way it is written. In English there are also many verbs (known as **multi-word verbs**) which consist of more than one element. They can normally be defined with a single alternative word. Examples include *put off* (meaning either *deter* or *postpone*), *run up* (meaning *incur* or *make*) and *take on* (meaning *employ* or *challenge*). Again, speakers instinctively feel that although these multi-word verbs consist of more than one element, in terms of meaning they are a single unit.

This idea can be taken one step further when we consider **idioms**. Idioms are little groups of words whose meaning is not retrievable from the individual parts which make up the idiom. In a sense, the multi-word verbs we have just mentioned are idioms (*run up* in *run up a debt,* for example, does not have the literal meaning it has in *run up a mountain*), but there are many more groups of words in the language which, as a fixed expression, have a distinct meaning. An example of this is the expression *to pay through the nose*. This does not literally mean that money is passed down the nostrils when paying for something. This is clearly ridiculous, but it is impossible for a speaker to deduce without some contextual clues that *to pay through the nose* means 'to pay an excessive amount of money for something'. Another interesting feature about idioms, and another reason to treat them as single entities, is that they are fixed expressions. *To pay through the nose*, for example, could hardly be adjusted to *to pay <u>down</u> the nose* or *to pay through the <u>nostril</u>*. This fixedness lends weight to the notion that although we might be dealing in these idiomatic examples with two or more words, we are nevertheless dealing with single items of meaning.

Despite the problem just outlined, and despite the fact that ultimately there is no watertight definition of 'word', there are some features of words which we can regard as fairly typical and which go beyond the initial observation that words are linguistic items written with a space either side of them. For one thing, a word can typically occur as a **minimal free form**. What this means is that a word in isolation can be a complete utterance. Some examples include:

Stop!
Here!
No
Possibly

Often these items are uttered in response to a question or other comment. For example, *possibly* might be uttered as a response to *Can you come to the cinema on Saturday?* Nevertheless, it is difficult to imagine some words – such as *the*, *by* and *their* – occurring in isolation in this way.

A further approach by which we might consider words as free-standing units is by considering the ability of one word to be substituted by another word, but not by anything less than a word. Thus we could replace *feeling* in the first example below with *premonition* but not with *pre-*:

> She had a *feeling* that there would be an accident
> She had a *premonition* that there would be an accident
> *She had a *pre-* that there would be an accident

In these examples, *pre-*, while having a discernible meaning (namely 'before' as in *preview* or *prejudge*), can neither replace a word nor can it be a free-standing and complete linguistic item. We accept that *pre-* can only be part of a full word.

Another feature typical of words is that, in addition to being free-standing, they also have a mobility which parts of words do not have. Compare these two examples:

> I can't stand hypocrisy
> Hypocrisy, I can't stand

It is possible to rearrange the first sentence by moving *hypocrisy* to the beginning. Similarly, we can place additional words between existing words:

> I admire the poetry of T. S. Eliot
> I <u>really</u> admire the poetry of T. S. Eliot

However, in both cases, it would be impossible to carry out these operations on parts of words:

> * I can't hypo <u>stand</u> crisy
> * I ad <u>really</u> mire the poetry of T. S. Eliot

Words are typically minimal free-standing units which cannot be interrupted. When dealing with combinations such as *world-class* and *world power* which we mentioned earlier, this basic principle will often still apply:

> * I thought he was a world <u>impressive</u> class cricketer
> * There was no doubt the country was a world <u>giant</u> power

However, this is a more problematic area given that there are other constraints on the order in which some items can occur and given that items such as multi-word verbs can be divided:

> Dave _put off_ the meeting until the following week
> Dave _put_ the meeting _off_ until the following week

Both these examples are acceptable, and seem to partly contradict our sense that words are uninterruptible. Nevertheless, we would still instinctively wish to signal the existence of multi-word verbs as identifiable items which merit a separate definition.

This takes us a little nearer to a solution to our problem. Just as we might treat _put off_ in the sense of 'postpone' as a separate item so, conversely, we are unlikely to treat _cats_ in our much earlier example of _Old fat cats like to sleep in quiet sunny places_ as a separate word from _cat_. _Cats_ is plural while _cat_ is singular. Most speakers would accept that _cats_ is simply a variant form of _cat_. This leads us to the notion that many items of the kind we have been discussing have both an abstract, representative form and an actual spoken or written form. For example, _cat_ is an abstract form for both _cat_ singular and _cats_ plural, while _put off_ is an abstract form meaning 'postpone' whether that form occurs as two consecutive elements (_put off_ the meeting) or not (_put_ the meeting _off_). At this point, it is helpful to posit the existence of abstract forms which can encompass single words as well as combinations such as _put off_ and _pay through the nose_. These abstract forms are known as **lexemes**.

The distinct advantage of bringing lexemes into the picture is that it solves our problem of how to account for items which are made up of more than one word, but which we feel are sufficiently distinct to merit entry in a dictionary. In fact, the forms which are given in dictionaries (what are known as **citation forms**) are in a sense lexemes, although a lexeme is an abstract entity. Nevertheless, we need to be able to classify the lexemes in our language and dictionary citation forms are the closest we can come to doing this. That is why a dictionary will have _cat_ as an entry but not _cats_: the citation form (together with the information that _cat_ is a noun) is sufficient indication that there is a lexeme _cat_ which could also have a plural form _cats_.

Further factors about lexemes are usually reflected in the way that entries in dictionaries are organised. If, for example, you look up _host_ in the dictionary you will see that _host_ can mean someone who is holding a party of some kind, or a large number (as in _a host of angels_) or the bread used in the Christian church to signify the body of Christ. However, these three meanings are unrelated to one another and it is appropriate that each meaning should have a separate entry in the dictionary. In other words, there are three separate lexemes which are represented by the **word-form** *host*. This is an example of **homonymy**: a **homonym** is a word-form which just happens to be the same as another word-form even though their meanings are unrelated. By contrast, some lexemes have more than one meaning. A good example of this is *mouse*. First and foremost, *mouse* is defined as 'a small rodent', but we are also familiar with *mouse* as an item of IT hardware. Since the latter meaning is clearly derived from the former (a computer mouse supposedly resembles an actual mouse), we are unlikely to claim that *mouse* and *mouse* are separate lexemes. Instead we would probably suggest that they are related meanings of the same lexeme. This is an example of **polysemy**: in other words, one lexeme has two or more related meanings.

There is a value then in positing an abstract form, the lexeme, which helps us to get round some of the difficulties of defining 'word'. Later we will see how there are similar abstract concepts for looking at the smaller units which make up words and those units of speech which make up the sound system of the language. From now on, 'lexeme' is used if this term is appropriate, but 'word' is used for convenience and when it is unlikely to cause any misunderstanding.

Before we progress any further, it may be valuable to explain other terms used for discussing words in general. We use the term **vocabulary** to talk about words collectively. For example, we may say of someone that they have a large vocabulary or we may have to learn some vocabulary to develop our knowledge of a foreign language. In linguistics, a term which is often used in preference to vocabulary is **lexis**. Lexis is a collective term for words in general or for the vocabulary of a specific language. You may also come across the term **subject-specific lexis** (a set of specialised words relating to a particular topic) or you may find instances of 'lexis' being modified in some way: for example, 'polysyllabic lexis' or 'scientific lexis'. When we examine language in relation to its lexis, we are examining it on a **lexical level** (a term already used at the beginning of this chapter). A **lexical item** is an alternative way of referring to a lexeme and a **lexical set** is a group of closely related words of the same word class (for instance, the names of fruits form a lexical set). You may also encounter the term **lexicon**, which refers to the vocabulary of a language (for example, the English lexicon) but is sometimes used to refer to a type of dictionary.

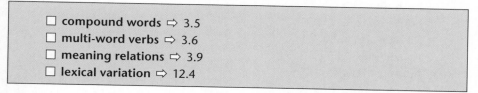

☐ **compound words** ⇨ 3.5
☐ **multi-word verbs** ⇨ 3.6
☐ **meaning relations** ⇨ 3.9
☐ **lexical variation** ⇨ 12.4

2.2   WORD CLASSES

The previous section has shown us that in talking about words the concept of a lexeme is a very useful one in that it covers items which are not typical words and therefore goes some way to solving any problems involved in defining 'word'. Another aspect which we need to consider when discussing words (or lexemes) is that all words belong to a particular grammatical category. Many people know that a particular linguistic item is, say, a noun or a verb, although they may not be aware of the full range of categories into which words can be subdivided. These categories are known as **word classes**. There are nine major word classes and two minor ones. The major ones are **nouns, verbs, adjectives, adverbs, pronouns, determiners, auxiliaries, prepositions** and **conjunctions**. These classes are useful because they group words together according to particular characteristics which they share and give us more precise labels to use when referring to certain words or lexemes.

There are two minor word classes and they require a brief mention. The first of these is the class of **interjections**. These are the little exclamations such as *ouch, phew* or *wow* with which spoken language is peppered. The reason, however, that interjections are only a minor word class is that they do not enter into grammatical structures, unlike words of the classes listed above. They are often, in fact, uttered in isolation as a response to a comment, question or event. The other minor class is the group of **particles**, of which the most notable are the particle *to* as in *to be or not to be*, and the negative particle *not*.

One group of words which is treated in different ways by linguists is the group of **numerals**. It includes both **cardinal numerals** – *one, two, three* and so on – and **ordinal numerals** such as *first, second*, and *third* as well as **fractions** such as a *quarter, two-thirds* and *five-eighths*. Sometimes numerals are treated as a separate word class and sometimes they are seen as subsets of the major classes of pronouns and determiners. The latter approach is adopted here.

☐ **nouns** ⇨ 2.4
☐ **verbs** ⇨ 2.5
☐ **adjectives** ⇨ 2.6
☐ **adverbs** ⇨ 2.7
☐ **pronouns** ⇨ 2.8
☐ **determiners** ⇨ 2.9
☐ **numerals** ⇨ 2.8, 2.9
☐ **auxiliaries** ⇨ 2.10
☐ **prepositions** ⇨ 2.11
☐ **conjunctions** ⇨ 2.12

2.3   OPEN AND CLOSED CLASSES OF WORDS

One question which students sometimes ask is, how many words are there in the English language? If we're used to using dictionaries, we probably have a notion that it is possible to count how many words there are in our language. Dictionaries usually proclaim how many entries they contain and it is tempting to believe that if we possessed the largest dictionary we would be in possession of all the words in the language. However, it is impossible to know precisely how many words there are in the language or to produce a comprehensive and accurate list of them. For one thing, the language is constantly changing: new words enter the language and other words become obsolete all the time so even the most recent dictionary (be it in book form, or electronic form) is out-of-date the moment it appears. Then, it is arguable whether obsolete words, which exist in texts such as the plays of Shakespeare (which are still performed of course), should be included in the count or not. A further problem is when to include new words, especially if they are slang (words which tend to have a short linguistic shelf-life) or from a foreign source. Should very specialised medical and scientific words be counted? Additionally, old words are given new meanings. At what point can we say that an additional or alternative meaning for an existing word has resulted in a new word or the replacement of an old one? The problems involved in 'measuring' the lexicon seem endless.

What we can do, however, is tackle the question in a different way in order to achieve something approaching a satisfactory answer. We have seen above that we can label all words in terms of the word class they belong to. Clearly, this means that the words in each class possess particular characteristics and properties which differ partly or totally from those of words in other classes. One observation that we can make in fact is that it is much easier to come up with a fairly accurate total number of words in some classes than in others.

Look carefully at the following random collection of words, which are drawn from all nine major word classes:

pig	*autumn*	*me*	*explain*
they	*which*	*sing*	*suddenly*
from	*today*	*biology*	*and*
truth	*could*	*the*	*extraordinary*
since	*hot*	*announce*	*in*

Now divide these words into two separate groups. (These will not necessarily be of equal size.) It is probably best to be guided by your instinct in making this division: don't worry about trying to explain your rationale in deciding which word goes into which group.

When asked to do this same experiment, speakers most typically and without any prompting or assistance divide the words as follows:

> group one
> *pig, autumn, explain, sing, suddenly, today, biology, truth, extraordinary, hot, announce*

> group two
> *me, they, which, from, and, could, the, since, in*

The words in the first group appear to be different from those in the second group in a number of ways. First, the words in the first group are longer on average than those in the other group (not just in terms of letters but more significantly in terms of syllables as well as units of construction such as in *suddenly* which consists of *sudden* + *ly*). Second, they are far more specific in meaning than those in group two. For example, *hot* has a specific and imaginable meaning in the way that an item such as *the* definitely does not. Third, words in group one could be linked together to make what would be a rather odd but nevertheless meaningful string such as *today autumn hot extraordinary* or *pig announce truth*, whereas the items in group two allow no such process, since the words in this group have little meaning except in relation to other words of the group one variety.

The words in group one are all either **nouns** (*pig, autumn, biology, truth*), **verbs** (*explain, sing, announce*), **adjectives** (*extraordinary, hot*), or **adverbs** (*suddenly, today*). Nouns, verbs, adjectives and adverbs are **open class** words. The words in group two consist of **pronouns** (*me, they, which*), a **determiner** (*the*), an **auxiliary** (*could*), **prepositions** (*from, in*) and **conjunctions** (*and, since*). Pronouns, determiners, auxiliaries, prepositions and conjunctions are **closed class** words. The reason for these particular names is that the open classes form an extremely large group and it is the extent of the open classes which makes it virtually impossible to count the number of words in the language, especially since the words in this group are constantly changing. By contrast, the closed classes form a much smaller group and it is possible to make a finite list of its members. The words in closed classes change very slowly: new words rarely enter these classes while existing words rarely change their form or meaning, or become obsolete.

The words in the open classes are known as **lexical words** or **content words** and those in the closed classes as **grammatical words** or **function words**. We noted that the lexical words in our earlier list were longer than the grammatical words. This is not a coincidence: lexical words may be **monosyl-labic** but they are equally likely to consist of two, three or even more syllables. (The term **disyllabic** refers to a word of two syllables and **polysyllabic** to one of three or more.) Grammatical words, on the other hand, typically contain just one or two syllables. In addition, the lexical words are drawn from a very wide range of languages which have influenced English. These include Latin, Greek, French and many more, probably over a hundred. Although some lexical words have been in English since its earliest stages, new lexical words have entered the language throughout its history and of course still do so. The vast majority of grammatical words are of either Old English or Old Norse origin. If they derive from Old English, they have been part of the language from the outset. Old Norse had a very strong influence on English in its early centuries and there are a few grammatical words derived from this language of the Viking invaders, so these have existed in English for a very long time, most of them appearing in written form before the year 1100.

Another striking difference between lexical and grammatical words is the frequency with which we use them. Whereas there may be some lexical words which we will only use very occasionally, hardly an utterance goes by without using little grammatical words like *the* or *and*. You might think that such frequency of usage would jar on a listener but we give very little sentence stress to grammatical words when we speak and in some respects listeners barely notice them.

So, to answer the question of how many words there are in the English language, we might give the following response. The open classes are very extensive and contain hundreds of thousands of words. Not only this but, because language change affects these classes much more than it affects the closed classes, it is impossible to count the number of words in the open classes. By contrast, the number of words in the closed classes is far fewer and change is very slow. It is therefore possible to count the number of words in the closed classes, which contain only several hundred words.

In the following sections, we will work through the word classes, beginning with the open classes, and look at the features which characterise them and at ways of determining which class any individual word belongs to. Sections 2.4 to 2.7 explain how to identify words which belong to any of the open classes. As far as possible, these sections show you how to assign words to the correct category chiefly by looking at their grammatical properties – where they occur or how they combine with other words. When we move on to the closed classes (Sections 2.8 to 2.12), fairly comprehensive lists and tables of the words in each class are provided (something which would be impossible for the open classes) although there will also be some exploration of the functions of the various groups. If you are ever in doubt as to which word class a particular item belongs to, then you can check this in a dictionary. The word class is usually given in an abbreviated form (such as n. for noun) but there will be a key to these abbreviations, probably at the front of the dictionary. It is possible for a word to belong to more than one word class – *access*, for example, can be both a noun and a verb – but you can check a category by considering the word in its grammatical context.

2.4 NOUNS

Sometimes, speakers know a simplistic and traditional definition of a noun, which is that it is a naming word. In one sense, this is an appropriate way to define a noun. In fact, 'noun' derives from the Latin word for a name, which is *nomen*. Nouns make up one of the most central categories of all word classes (the other being verbs). What we mean by 'central' is that nouns and verbs are the most useful elements in constructing a very basic sentence such as:

noun	verb	noun
cats	*like*	*cream*

It is significant that children normally learn several nouns before they learn any other words, and that about 75 per cent of a child's first 50 or so words will be nouns.

The simplest way to test whether a word is a noun (and far more reliable than asking yourself if the item in question is a naming word) is to isolate it and then see if it is possible to place *the* (the **definite article**) in front of it. For instance you might want to test your judgement that the underlined words in the following sentences are nouns, because they are both naming something (an animal and a place respectively):

Much to my amazement a large fat <u>cat</u> was sleeping in our <u>garden</u>

You can isolate *cat* and *garden* to see if the definite article test works. It is perfectly possible to say *the cat* and *the garden*, so this tells us that they are indeed nouns. Other nouns name things less concrete than *cat* and *garden*. In the above example, *amazement* is also a noun (*the amazement* is again perfectly possible, as in *the amazement I felt at that moment was obvious*), although it refers to something intangible and rather more abstract than *cat* or *garden*. Even though *cat* and *garden* are concrete and *amazement* is abstract, all nouns of this kind which can be preceded by *the* are known as **common nouns**. These can be subdivided into **concrete nouns**, which refer to measurable or tangible objects, and **abstract nouns**, which refer to concepts and things which have no material existence.

In contrast to common nouns there is a group of **proper nouns**. The difference between common and proper nouns is that proper nouns name something or someone unique. They are the nouns which in writing we would write with a capital letter and which are the names of places, people, pets, rivers, months, days of the week and so on. Examples of proper nouns might include *London* (the name of a unique place), *Jane* (the name of a specific person – although of course there will be more than one person called *Jane*) and *Monday* (the name of a particular day). The way in which proper nouns differ most obviously from common nouns is that the definite article test doesn't really work on them:

common noun	proper noun
the city	** the London*
the woman	** the Jane*
the day	** the Monday*

However, there is the possibility of *the* preceding these nouns in certain contexts. For example:

> <u>*The Jane*</u> *I know is the one with blonde hair*
> <u>*The London*</u> *my father remembers was a much cleaner place*
> <u>*The Monday*</u> *I mean is the one just before Christmas*

(And in fact there are lots of proper nouns that have *the* as part of their name and do not normally occur without it. Examples include *The Thames*, *The Hague* and *The Bank of England*.) More importantly, proper nouns such as these occur in the same positions in phrases and sentences in which common nouns occur:

> <u>*The cat*</u> *is my best friend*
> <u>*Jane*</u> *is my best friend*
> *The man was lost in* <u>*the maze*</u>
> *The man was lost in* <u>*London*</u>

The position in which members of a word class occur in a sentence is one of the key factors which characterises them. We will look more closely at the grammatical context in which nouns occur in Part III.

- ☐ **definite articles** ⇨ 2.9
- ☐ **meanings of common nouns** ⇨ 3.9
- ☐ **singular and plural nouns** ⇨ 4.3
- ☐ **noun phrases** ⇨ 5.2

2.5   LEXICAL VERBS

Verbs, like nouns, are of central importance as a class of words. They could in fact be considered the most important aspect of language because of their central role in constructing sentences and the influence they exert over other elements in a sentence. 'Verb' derives from the Latin *verbum* which means 'word' and this is an appropriate indication of the importance of this word class.

Verbs are sometimes notionally defined as 'doing words' but this is not a very accurate way of identifying them. For one thing, verbs do not always refer to actions: they can also refer to states. Consider the verbs in the following sentence:

Jane strolls into the park where she relaxes and feels content

Whereas *strolls* clearly refers to a deliberate physical activity, *relaxes* is less obviously an action (although still a physical process) while *feels* refers not to an action of Jane's but to her state of mind. Verbs which refer to physical processes, such as *stroll* and *relax*, are referred to as **dynamic verbs** in contrast to **stative verbs** which refer to states and conditions.

A more watertight (and grammatical) way to check if a word is a verb is to look for a property that only verbs possess (as we did with nouns). This is the ability to make a contrast between **present tense** and **past tense**. If we isolate the verbs underlined in the above sentence, we see that it is possible to form them in both the present tense and the past:

present tense	past tense
stroll(s) (I stroll / she strolls)	*strolled (I strolled / she strolled)*
relax(es)	*relaxed*
feel(s)	*felt*

To reiterate an earlier point, many word forms exist as members of more than one word class, and this is particularly true of nouns and verbs. An example of this from the given sentence is *park*. In the example, *park* is clearly a noun – it is preceded by *the* (and it is naming something – in this case a place). However, it is also possible to use *park* as a verb where contrasts of tense can be employed:

| *Kathy parks the car* | (present tense) |
| *Kathy parked the car* | (past tense) |

Different word classes take up different positions within the structure of a sentence: we will come to this more fully later but we will use this approach to some extent in our discussion of words in the remaining classes.

The heading at the top of this section refers to **lexical verbs** rather than simply 'verbs'. Lexical verb is a term which is sometimes used to distinguish verbs like *stroll*, *relax*, *feel* and *park* from **auxiliaries** or **auxiliary verbs** which make up a very small closed class of words. Auxiliaries are added to the lexical verb for various purposes. For example, the following sentence uses the auxiliary *has* to indicate that the process the lexical verb *finished* refers to is complete and that this fact is still of some relevance:

> Ian *has finished* the book (so I can borrow it next)

Although *has* provides a useful shade of meaning in this example, it is *finished* which denotes exactly what Ian has done (it might be contrasted with *Ian has burnt* the book, for example) and it is this specificity of meaning which is indicated when we say *finished* is a lexical verb. Lexical verbs are also sometimes known as **full verbs** or **main verbs** but it is acceptable to refer to them as verbs provided there is no need to distinguish between them and auxiliaries.

- ☐ **auxiliaries** ⇨ 2.10
- ☐ **verb meanings** ⇨ 3.9
- ☐ **verb inflections** ⇨ 4.4
- ☐ **tenses** ⇨ 5.3

2.6 ADJECTIVES

Adjectives, while not as central as nouns and verbs in the basic structure of sentences, are nevertheless an important and relatively distinctive open class. Although they are traditionally defined as describing words, this is not the basis for accurate identification of adjectives since words of other classes also have descriptive properties. We can identify adjectives by reference to each of two features – first, the positions in which they appear in sentences and, second, their ability to be graded.

Central adjectives are able to appear in two positions. First, they can occur before a noun, as in *the extraordinary boy* or *lucky Jim*. In this position their function is **attributive**. In other words, they give us information about an attribute of the noun. Second, they can occur after certain verbs like *be* and *appear* (what are known as **copular verbs**) as in *the boy is extraordinary* or *Jim appears lucky*. In this position their function is **predicative**. In other words, they occur in the **predicate** – the part of a clause which consists of the verb and the items which follow it. Central adjectives, then, are found in both attributive and predicative position. However, there are some adjectives which only appear in one of these two positions:

predicative only
the child is <u>afraid</u>   * *the <u>afraid</u> child*

attributive only
the <u>chief</u> mourner   * *the mourner is <u>chief</u>*

Adjectives such as *afraid* and *chief* are clearly less central than adjectives which occur in both attributive and predicative position. Like adjectives, nouns can also occur in these positions. Nouns, however, are highly unlikely to be able to occur in both positions in a comparable way to adjectives:

position	adjective	noun
attributive	*the <u>extraordinary</u> boy*	*the <u>newspaper</u> boy*
predicative	*the boy is <u>extraordinary</u>*	* *the boy is <u>newspaper</u>*
predicative	*Jim is <u>lucky</u>*	*Jim is <u>boss</u>*
attributive	*<u>lucky</u> Jim*	* *<u>boss</u> Jim*

Although nouns are likely to be far less flexible than adjectives in their ability to appear in both these positions, it is helpful to have another characteristic to identify in adjectives in order to assign them to the correct class. This is the fact that most adjectives are **gradable**. In other words, we can indicate to what extent the quality referred to by an adjective applies. For example, a person may be *lucky*, or they may be *<u>very</u> lucky*, *<u>fairly</u> lucky*, *<u>extremely</u> lucky* and so on. **Intensifiers** like *very*, *fairly* and *extremely* precede adjectives but not nouns (although some adverbs can also be graded in this way). Combinations such as **very newspaper* and **fairly boss* are clearly not permissible. There are one or two adjectives like *perfect* and *unique* which it might be unusual to grade since their meaning is absolute. In actual fact, though, you may come across these 'ungradable' adjectives being graded as in *a most perfect day* and *an extremely unique gift*.

In conclusion, central adjectives can be identified by their ability not only to occur both attributively and predicatively but also to be preceded by intensifiers. A handful of adjectives don't meet all these criteria, but if you're uncertain whether a word is an adjective or a noun you can apply the definite article test which we used to identify nouns.

☐ **meanings of adjectives** ⇨ 3.9
☐ **other ways to grade adjectives** ⇨ 4.5
☐ **position of adjectives** ⇨ 5.2, 5.4
☐ **copular verbs** ⇨ 6.6

2.7 ADVERBS

Just as adjectives are less central than nouns and verbs, so adverbs are less central than the other three open classes. In fact, they are a very diverse group and this can make them difficult both to define and to identify. We have to identify adverbs by looking at several features which characterise them – although not all these features will apply to all adverbs. Like adjectives, many adverbs have a describing purpose in a sentence and adverbs have other features in common with adjectives too. You can check whether a word is an adjective or adverb by seeing which position it can appear in. If the word cannot appear in **attributive** position then it is an adverb:

the <u>lovely</u> hotel	adjective
the <u>careful</u> person	adjective
* the <u>carefully</u> person	adverb

Adverbs have the ability not only to give information about, amongst other things, how, where and when, but also to allow you to comment on whole utterances. For instance:

<u>Fortunately,</u>	<u>today</u> the dog has eaten his food	<u>quietly</u>	<u>outside</u>
comment	when	how	where

You will see that two of the adverbs in this sentence – *fortunately* and *quietly* – end in *-ly*. This typifies many adverbs particularly of the 'comment' and 'how' types.

In the example *Fortunately today the dog has eaten his food quietly outside*, you may notice that adverbs seem to be less central elements in a sentence. If you stripped the adverbs away from the example, the essence of the sentence – *the dog has eaten his food* – still remains. Only occasionally are adverbs crucial to the completion of a sentence's meaning.

Adverbs can be divided into three subclasses – **adjuncts, conjuncts** and **disjuncts**. (In Chapter 7 we will, however, extend the use of these terms to include units larger than single adverbs but which function like adverbs.) The first subclass, adjuncts, is by far the largest.

Adjuncts have a certain amount in common with adjectives and might be considered their first cousins:

The <u>careful</u> surgeon completed the operation	adjective
The surgeon completed the operation <u>carefully</u>	adverb (adjunct)

What *careful* and *carefully* have in common in these two examples is their ability to provide more information – about the surgeon in the first example and about how the surgeon performed the operation in the second example. The meanings of these two sentences are clearly closely linked (we would expect a *careful* surgeon to operate *carefully*) but not identical. Further, an important difference between the adjective in the first sentence and the adverb in the second is that the adjective *careful* can only appear in this sentence in its given position preceding *surgeon* whereas the adverb *carefully* could appear in any one of several positions:

> *The surgeon completed the operation <u>carefully</u>*
> *<u>Carefully</u>, the surgeon completed the operation*
> *The surgeon <u>carefully</u> completed the operation*
> *? The surgeon completed <u>carefully</u> the operation*

An adverb such as *carefully* is typical of many adverbs in the adjunct subclass in that it modifies information given by one or more of the other elements.

In terms of their meaning, adverbs which are adjuncts provide us with information about how, where, when and to what extent. Adverbs which tell us how are **adverbs of manner**:

> *The surgeon completed the operation <u>carefully</u>*
> *<u>Silently</u>, Arusha observed what Dave was doing*

Adverbs of place indicate location or direction:

> *Put the parcel <u>here</u>*　　　　location
> *She turned the key <u>clockwise</u>*　　direction

Adverbs of time denote when something happened, how long it lasted or how often it happened:

> *Someone saved my life <u>tonight</u>*　　when
> *The symphony lasted <u>forever</u>*　　　how long
> *He telephoned her <u>nightly</u>*　　　　how often

Adverbs of degree indicate extent, including whether a piece of information applies to more than one item:

> *She found her job <u>particularly</u> difficult in the winter*
> *She ignored him at the party <u>simply</u> to make a point*
> *She loved him, and he loved her <u>too</u>*

Some of the adverbs of degree form a further subset of **intensifiers**. The adverb *particularly* in the set of examples above is an intensifier: it indicates a point on an imagined scale and can therefore be contrasted with other intensifiers:

> *She found her job particularly / somewhat / fairly / slightly difficult...*

You can see from the examples of the different types of adjuncts that adverbs can appear both before and after items which they qualify, although there are restrictions on this. Conjuncts and disjuncts often have more flexibility of position than many adjuncts as their functions are essentially different.

Sometimes adjuncts are **wh-words**. A *wh*-word is – unsurprisingly – one which begins with *wh-* although *how* and *however* are also included in the *wh*-group. Examples of *wh*-adverbs include *how, when, where* and *why*. They often take the place of a regular adverb in a question, although they can occur in other constructions. In addition to replacing simply another adverb, they can also take the place of a larger unit such as a phrase or a clause:

The surgeon performed the operation <u>carefully</u>	adverb
The surgeon performed the operation <u>with great care</u>	phrase
<u>How</u> did the surgeon perform the operation?	
He telephoned her <u>nightly</u>	adverb
He telephoned her <u>every night</u>	phrase
<u>When</u> did he telephone her?	
<u>How often</u> did he telephone her?	
She fell asleep <u>outside</u>	adverb
She fell asleep <u>on the sofa</u>	phrase
<u>Where</u> did she fall asleep?	
She went to France <u>to buy some champagne</u>	clause
<u>Why</u> did she go to France?	

Further uses of *wh*-adverbs, as well as larger units such as phrases and clauses, are explored in Part III.

Adverbs which are adjuncts give additional information either about a particular element of a sentence or about the event referred to in a sentence. In this respect they contrast with disjuncts and conjuncts which relate only to complete sentences and do not give information as such. One function of disjuncts is to comment on what is being said:

> *<u>Obviously</u>, I should have told her what happened*
> *(It is obvious that I should have told her ...)*
> *<u>Probably</u>, I should have told her what happened*
> *(It is probable I should have told her ...)*

A further function of disjuncts is to indicate the 'voice' in which something is said:

> <u>*Frankly*</u>, *I should have told her what happened*
> *(I am being frank when I say I should have told her what happened)*
> <u>*Confidentially*</u>, *I think she will lose her job*
> *(I am being confidential when I say I think she will lose her job)*

Whereas disjuncts relate to the sentence in which they occur (or possibly to just part of it if it is a complex sentence), conjuncts relate one sentence or one part of a sentence to another. They include adverbs such as *moreover, therefore, however* and *nevertheless*. If one of these conjuncts appeared in an isolated sentence it would seem slightly strange:

> *They decided to go for a picnic <u>nevertheless</u>*

The presence of *nevertheless* here implies the existence of a previous statement indicating that a picnic was not a good idea:

> 1. *It looked as if it might rain*
> 2. *They decided to go for a picnic <u>nevertheless</u>*

A conjunct therefore has the property of linking two sentences together. It could also link two parts of the same sentence:

> *She wasn't free to go to New York at Christmas and <u>besides</u> she couldn't afford it*

The adverbs here are not central to the structure of the sentence. Only occasionally are adverbs crucial to the completion of a core sentence.

2.8 PRONOUNS

We move now to the closed class words and how to identify them. Since the closed classes form a much smaller groups of words than nouns, verbs, adjectives and adverbs, it will be possible to list them fairly comprehensively. We will also consider what characterises the closed class words and the functions they perform.

We will begin our survey of closed class words by looking at pronouns. There is a close relationship between pronouns and determiners and we will look at this in Section 2.9. When we were looking at the words of the open classes, notional definitions of word classes – such as 'a noun is a naming word' – were sometimes mentioned. We saw that these definitions were helpful in some respects but misleading in others. The same is true of the notional definition of a pronoun which is that it 'takes the place of a noun'. In reality, the picture is far more complex than this. It is certainly true that pronouns can function as substitutes for nouns. In the following example, the personal pronoun *she* acts as a substitute for the proper noun *Michelle*:

> <u>Michelle</u> was offered an exciting new job and <u>she</u> decided to take it

Here, the pronoun *she* is used to avoid a clumsy repetition of *Michelle*. In the following example, however, the pronoun – this time *them* – replaces not a single noun but a noun together with some other words which are dependent on it (namely a **noun phrase**):

> Annette left <u>some fresh jam doughnuts</u> on the table and Ashley
> came in and scoffed <u>them</u>

Here, the pronoun *them* replaces not the plural noun *doughnuts* but the noun phrase *some fresh jam doughnuts*. It is also possible for a pronoun to replace part of a phrase:

> Sarah chose <u>a Kenyan safari</u> but Martin preferred <u>a South African one</u>

In this example, *a Kenyan safari* is a noun phrase. What Martin actually preferred was *a South African safari* (another noun phrase which parallels *a Kenyan safari*) but part of the phrase – the noun *safari* – has been replaced by the pronoun *one*.

As well as performing this substitution role to avoid unnecessary repetition of both single nouns and longer phrases, some pronouns are used not in a substitutional function but in order to refer to what is unknown:

> <u>Somebody</u> has stolen my chocolate muffin
> I looked, but there was <u>nothing</u> in the cupboard

In these two examples, we could not claim that *somebody* and *nothing* are replacing specific nouns or noun phrases.

Table 2.1   The primary pronouns of English

		Personal pronouns		Possessive pronouns		Reflexive pronouns
		subjective form	objective form	dependent form	independent form	
singular	**1st person**	I	me	my	mine	myself
	2nd person	you	you	your	yours	yourself
	3rd person	he	him	his	his	himself
		she	her	her	hers	herself
		it	it	its	(its)	itself
		they	them	their	theirs	themself
plural	**1st person**	we	us	our	ours	ourselves
	2nd person	you	you	your	yours	yourselves
	3rd person	they	them	their	theirs	themselves

So far, we have considered just a few examples of pronouns: *she, them, one, somebody* and *nothing*. Pronouns can be divided into several subclasses of which the most central are the **primary pronouns**. These are shown in Table 2.1. The most significant feature of the primary pronouns is that they are not a random group but a systematic one, as Table 2.1 shows. First, there is a basic distinction of **number**: primary pronouns, like most nouns, are either singular or plural. There is a further distinction of **person** – first, second or third. This distinction is closely linked with the form which verbs take, although this is far more noticeable in many other languages than it is in English. However, we do make a distinction in English in the present tense between third person singular and, say, first person singular: in other words *she laughs* contrasts with *I laugh*. All the primary pronouns occur in several forms as **personal pronouns**, as **possessive pronouns** and as **reflexive pronouns**. The personal pronouns are subdivided again into the **subjective** form and the **objective** form. This distinction relates to the position in which the pronouns occur. The subjective form is used when the pronoun is in the subject position in a sentence – namely before the verb – whereas the objective form is used when it is in the object position after the verb:

> They love football
> * Them love football
> Richard telephoned me
> * Richard telephoned I

Some flexibility exists in the use of subjective and objective forms, however. In informal usage, for example, *me* might occur in subject position:

Me and Julian went to the cinema last night

The possessive pronouns take either a **dependent** or an **independent** form. The independent form acts as a replacement for a complete noun phrase:

This house is <u>the doctor's (house) and her husband's (house)</u>
This house is <u>theirs</u>

By contrast, the dependent form precedes a noun which it qualifies:

This is <u>Janet's</u> house
This is <u>her</u> house

Dependent possessive pronouns may also be classified as determiners and in many respects they are more typical determiners than they are pronouns. However, for the sake of completeness they are included in the set of primary pronouns. **Reflexive pronouns** can be used for emphasis as in the first example below, but they are usually used to refer back to someone or something mentioned previously:

Gregory <u>himself</u> has been to Lambeth Palace
<u>Gregory</u> went to Lambeth Palace by <u>himself</u>
I fell down the stairs and (<u>I</u>) hurt <u>myself</u>
* <u>I</u> fell down the stairs and the splinters hurt <u>myself</u>

The ungrammaticality of the last example above shows that there are restrictions on the referential scope of reflexive pronouns.

Table 2.1 shows that the set of *they* pronouns occurs as both a plural and a singular set. We have already noted that changes to closed classes of words happen very slowly but the acceptance of the *they* set as singular pronouns is an example of a recent development, especially in writing. As users have become more conscious of gender issues in the language, they have looked for a way of avoiding references which are intended to be non-gender-specific but which actually suggest the male of the species. For example, in a sentence such as A *human being is unique among mammals in that he has speech* the pronoun *he* is, in theory, meant to refer to any human, male or female. However, when speakers encounter *he* in a context such as this, they often assume maleness. Sometimes speakers try to get round this difficulty by using *he or she*:

If any student would like a parking permit <u>he or she</u> should go to reception

The frequent use of *he or she* can seem rather clumsy so *they* is often used instead (albeit with the plural form of the verb) when the gender of a single referent is unknown. Further evidence that speakers treat *they* as a singular pronoun is the use of the reflexive form *themself* (for example, *Someone fell off the roof and they hurt <u>themself</u> very badly*) which is in contrast to the plural *themselves*.

The independent form of *it*, namely *its*, is bracketed in Table 2.1. This is because there is no actual reason why that form should not exist but in practice speakers are unlikely to use it:

> *This is the dog's dinner*
> *This is <u>its</u> dinner*
> *? I will have my dinner while the dog has <u>its</u>*

Most speakers would probably say that this last example sounds clumsy but we could use it without being ungrammatical.

A further pronoun which could be included in the table of primary pronouns is the **generic pronoun** *one*. This is used in the third person singular (for example, *<u>One</u> needs to take care of <u>oneself</u>*) but is becoming increasingly rare, particularly since it is considered very formal. The generic pronoun *one* is distinct from the **substitute pronoun** *one* which we saw in an earlier example (*Sarah chose a Kenyan safari and Martin chose a South African one*). Here, *one* is functioning as a substitute for *safari* and clearly not as a way of referring to an unspecified person.

Having looked at the primary pronouns of English, we will now look briefly at the other subclasses of pronoun. First, there are several **wh-pronouns** and these, like the primary pronouns, can be divided into subclasses:

> interrogative pronouns
> *who, whom, whose, what, which*
>
> relative pronouns
> *who, whom, which, that*
>
> nominal relative pronouns
> *who, whoever, whom, whomever*
> *which, whichever, what, whatever*
>
> conditional pronouns
> *whoever, whomever, whichever, whatever*

Many of the forms listed above have more than one function. *Who*, for instance, can be an interrogative pronoun, a relative pronoun, and a nominal relative pronoun. **Interrogative pronouns** are used to ask questions:

> *Liz* has a flat in Majorca
> *Who* has a flat in Majorca?

Relative pronouns are used to introduce relative clauses. Similarly, **nominal relative pronouns** introduce nominal relative clauses, while **conditional wh-pronouns** introduce *wh*-conditional clauses. These three types of *wh*-pronouns and their associated clauses are considered in detail in Part III but here are examples of each type within the context of a sentence:

relative *wh*-pronoun	*This is the car* *which* *I want to buy*
nominal relative *wh*-pronoun	*Who* *to ask was something of a problem*
conditional *wh*-pronoun	*Whatever* *happens, I'm leaving*

Wh-pronouns such as *whoever* can also take the form *whosoever*. This is a slightly more formal usage but it can also be used for emphasis. The pronoun *whom* is the objective form of *who* but again it is rather formal and most speakers rarely use it now, if at all.

The next group of pronouns is the **indefinite pronouns**. The main ones are:

some	*any*	*none*	*all*
someone	*anyone*	*no one*	*everyone*
somebody	*anybody*	*nobody*	*everybody*
something	*anything*	*nothing*	*everything*

More often than not, these pronouns do not have an identifiable referent and are not therefore functioning as noun or noun phrase substitutes as such. The pronouns *either, neither, both* and *each* in addition to *enough, much, many, more, most, few, little, several* and *another* are also classified as indefinite pronouns.

Finally, there are the four **demonstrative pronouns**. These are:

this	*that*
these	*those*

This and *that* are singular and have plural counterparts in *these* and *those*. The demonstrative pronouns, like the primary pronouns, are **deictic**. This means that their meaning is relative to the speaker or the context. In the sentence *I want these not those* where the speaker is referring to two boxes of chocolates, we would infer that the box of chocolates the speaker wants is whichever one is nearer to them. We will look more closely at **deixis** in Chapter 8.

To summarise, we have so far identified four subclasses of pronouns, some of which we have subdivided again:

primary pronouns
>   personal pronouns
>   possessive pronouns
>   reflexive pronouns

wh-pronouns
>   interrogative *wh*-pronouns
>   relative *wh*-pronouns
>   nominal relative *wh*-pronouns
>   conditional *wh*-pronouns

indefinite pronouns

demonstrative pronouns

You can see that although pronouns make up a relatively small set of words, they fulfil a considerable range of functions.

One final subclass of pronouns which we need to consider briefly is the subclass of numerals. Numerals subdivide into cardinal numerals (*one, two three* ...), ordinal numerals (*first, second, third* ...) and fractions (*a quarter, two-thirds, five-eighths* ...). We have already seen how the substitute pronoun *one*, which is a cardinal numeral, operates. Here is a further example containing this particular pronoun:

>   *Terry wanted a new piano and Clive wanted <u>one</u> too*

Here, *one* is a substitute for *a new piano* and is a means of avoiding a clumsy repetition of this phrase. The other cardinal and ordinal numerals can function in a comparable way by making language more economical:

>   *<u>Seven</u> turned up for the rehearsal*
>   *Aidan made three wishes on his birthday: the <u>first</u> was for his brother*

In the first example above, *seven* stands for all the various individuals who turned up (making it unnecessary to list them) while in the second example *first* refers to one of the *three wishes*. Arguably, cardinal numerals could be classified as a subclass of nouns since in certain contexts they can be made plural – a central characteristic of nouns:

>   *They arrived at the party in <u>twos</u> and <u>threes</u>*

Furthermore, they appear in comparable positions to head nouns:

They were an experienced and skilful <u>team</u>   concrete noun
They were an experienced and skilful <u>eleven</u>   numeral

Numerals are a slightly problematic group to classify. However, the fact that they share similarities in different contexts with nouns, pronouns and determiners is a reason to classify them within these classes rather than as a word class in their own right.

☐ **nouns** ⇨ 2.4
☐ *wh*-**words** ⇨ 2.13
☐ **subjective and objective forms** ⇨ 4.6
☐ **noun phrases** ⇨ 5.2
☐ **nominal relative clauses** ⇨ 6.14
☐ **interrogative sentences** ⇨ 7.4
☐ *wh*-**conditional clauses** ⇨ 7.11
☐ **deixis** ⇨ 8.6

2.9 DETERMINERS

Determiners are only found in noun phrases, although they are not an obligatory element of this structure. A noun phrase is a noun plus any other elements which belong to or depend on that **head noun**. Determiners only occur at the beginning of a noun phrase (although some determiners can be qualified by an intensifier). Adjectives (and other nouns) can also occur before the head noun but they come after any determiners. They do not function in the same way as determiners and they possess different grammatical properties so there is no sound argument for treating determiners as a subclass of adjectives.

We will consider noun phrase structure in detail in Section 5.2, but the following example shows the position of determiners in the context of a noun phrase:

determiners	premodification	head noun	postmodification
all these	*large sugary*	*doughnuts*	*filled with jam and cream*

Determiners subdivide as a group into **predeterminers**, **central determiners** and **postdeterminers**. Table 2.2 illustrates the main types of determiner. One way in which determiners differ from adjectives is that there are restrictions on the number (and type) of determiners which can occur in any noun phrase whereas, in theory at least, there is no restriction on the number of adjectives. There may be a predeterminer, a central determiner and a postdeterminer but (with very few exceptions) there can be no co-occurrence of any of these types.

Table 2.2   Determiners

	Predeterminers	Central determiners	Postdeterminers
articles	**definite article**	the	
	indefinite article	a/an	
possessive determiners		my	
		your	
		his	
		etc.	
***wh*-determiners**	**interrogative**	*whose*	
		what	
		which	
	exclamative	what	
		such	
	relative	*whose*	
		which	
	nominal relative	*what*	
		what(so)ever	
		which	
		which(so)ever	
	conditional	*what(so)ever*	
		which(so)ever	
indefinite determiners	*all* (of)	*some*	*many/more/most*
	both (of)	*any*	*few/-er/-est*
		no	*little/less/least*
		(n)either	*several*
		each	
		every	(every)
		enough	
		much	
		another	
		other	lot of, load of etc
demonstrative determiners		*this*	
		these	
		that	
		those	
numerals	**cardinal**		*one, two, three...*
	ordinal		*first, second, third...*
			next, last
	fractions	*half* (of)	
		a third (of)	
		three-fifths (of)...	
	multipliers	once, twice...	
		double...	
		three times...	

In other words, a noun phrase which included the central determiner *these* could not also contain the central determiner *some*:

> * *some these delicious chocolates*

The restrictions on co-occurrence of determiners is the principle by which determiners are assigned to either the pre-, post- or central determiner groups. It is not the case, however, that any central determiner can occur with any pre- or postdeterminer. Central determiners are identified primarily on the basis that they cannot occur with each other. You will see from Table 2.2 that there are relatively few pre- and postdeterminers. The exclamatives *what* and *such* normally only occur before the central determiner *a/an* as in <u>*What*</u> *a lovely day it is*. By contrast, the indefinite predeterminers can occur with a much wider range of central determiners as in <u>*all (of)*</u> *these good ideas* or <u>*both (of)*</u> *your sisters*. Fractions and multipliers are also included as predeterminers (<u>*one third (of)*</u> *the price*) since they function in a similar way to *all* and *both*. The determiner *every* can be a central determiner preceding a postdeterminer such as a numeral – <u>*every*</u> *third day* – but *every* can also be used as a postdeterminer when its function is emphatic: *he ignored my* <u>*every*</u> *wish*.

Postdeterminers and predeterminers do not have to occur with a central determiner. However, whatever determiners do occur have a prescribed sequence. It is possible to have a predeterminer, a central determiner and a post determiner in one noun phrase although there are many restrictions on these combinations:

determiners			head noun	
pre-	central	post-		
all	*your*	*many*	*ideas*	*(were useless)*

Many of the determiners in Table 2.2 are italicised. These are the forms which are also pronouns. Determiners, however, will always be followed by a head noun (although there may be some premodifying element such as an adjective between the determiner and the head noun):

<u>*Which*</u> *is the best way to London from here?*	pronoun
<u>*Which*</u> *route is the best way to London from here?*	determiner
I really have had <u>*enough*</u>	pronoun
I really have had <u>*enough*</u> *greasy chips*	determiner

In the above examples, the pronouns *which* and *enough* are in contrast to the determiners *which* and *enough* which occur with *route* and *greasy chips* respectively.

☐ **noun phrase structure** ⇨ 5.2
☐ **exclamative sentences** ⇨ 7.6

2.10 AUXILIARIES

Auxiliaries or **auxiliary verbs** are a very small group of verbs and they only occur in **verb phrases**. Like determiners in noun phrases, they will occur at the start of the phrase, before the **lexical verb**. Although they are optional phrase elements, they are used extensively and for a number of purposes. The term 'auxiliary' comes from the Latin *auxilium* which means 'help' or 'assistance'. There are two types of auxiliary verbs, **primary auxiliaries** and **modal auxiliaries**:

> primary auxiliaries
> *have, be, do*
>
> modal auxiliaries
> *can, could, shall, should, will, would, may, might, must*

Both types have a range of functions, but they are distinct for each type. The primary auxiliaries *have* and *be* are chiefly used to create different **aspects**. Aspects indicate whether the action or state of a verb is complete or on-going. Here are two examples to show this:

> Phil *has composed* his first symphony
> Liz *is looking after* the children

We will look at the construction of the full range of verb aspects in Chapter 5.

The primary auxiliaries are also important in the construction of questions and for negation. In questions, if a primary auxiliary is present, it may change position. If no primary is present, then *do* is used:

> Phil *has* composed his first symphony
> *Has* Phil composed his first symphony?
> Phil composed his first symphony
> *Did* Phil compose his first symphony?

In negation, the negative particle is positioned after the first auxiliary. Again, *do* is used if no auxiliary is present:

Phil <u>has</u> composed a symphony
Phil <u>has not</u> composed a symphony
Phil composed a symphony
Phil <u>did not</u> compose a symphony

The primary auxiliary *do* can also be used for emphasis:

Liz <u>does</u> enjoy looking after the children

The primary auxiliary *do* therefore has a slightly different role from the primary auxiliaries *be* and *have*.

The modal auxiliaries, like their primary counterparts, have a range of functions, mainly in providing shades of meaning relating to the lexical verb. Sometimes they do this by expressing the degree of certainty associated with the lexical verb (their **epistemic** function) and sometimes by expressing the degree of obligation (their **deontic** function). They also have a **dynamic** function when stating facts, often referring to past action. Table 2.3 illustrates the range of meanings modal auxiliaries can express.

Table 2.3 Modal auxiliary functions and meanings

Function	Examples	Expressing...
expressing degree of certainty (epistemic function)	I <u>will/shall</u> take a holiday in August I <u>should</u> be able to take a holiday next year I <u>may/might</u> take a holiday in August	intention probability possibility
expressing degree of obligation (deontic function)	Now I've left work, I <u>can/could</u> take a holiday My boss said I <u>can/could/may/might</u> take a holiday I <u>must/should</u> take a holiday or I'll make myself ill	ability permission obligation
making factual statements (dynamic function)	In the past I <u>would</u> take a holiday every autumn As a student, I <u>could</u> always find time for a holiday She <u>can</u> holiday in France whenever she likes	habit past ability present ability

These are the main semantic functions of the modal auxiliaries, the differences between them sometimes being very subtle. There are also a few marginal auxiliaries such as *have to*, *need to* and *ought to* which express similar meanings to *must* and *should*: for example, *I <u>ought to</u> take a holiday* is comparable in meaning to *I <u>should</u> take a holiday*. The marginal auxiliary *used to* expresses something habitual or continuous in the past: *I <u>used to</u> like swimming but I'm not so keen now.*

The order of auxiliaries, like the order of determiners, is prescribed. Auxiliaries always precede the head verb. Modal auxiliaries precede primary ones and the primary auxiliary *have* will precede the primary auxiliary *be* if both occur. All these points are explored further in Chapter 5.

☐ **verb phrases** ⇨ 5.3
☐ **negative clauses** ⇨ 6.15
☐ **question structures** ⇨ 7.4

2.11 PREPOSITIONS

Prepositions are a moderately large group as far as grammatical words go. We will identify a considerable number here in order to have a representative sample of this word class. Prepositions are used to show the relationship between two elements, although again this is a notional definition which is not grammatically watertight. Consider these examples:

> *The dog ran <u>under</u> the table*
> *The dog ran <u>round</u> the table*
> *The dog ran <u>into</u> the table*

In all three examples, a preposition is used to indicate the relationship between *the dog ran* and *the table*. Of course, prepositions are not the only word class which can express the relationship between one thing and another. For example, the verb *loves* expresses a relationship between *Debra* and *Sam* in the sentence *Debra loves Sam*. If we are to identify a feature of prepositions which is grammatical rather than semantic, then it is that prepositions are normally followed by noun phrases (such as *the table*) with which they form a **prepositional phrase**.

Prepositions most typically express relationships of time and place, although other relationships may be expressed too. Prepositions may be **simple** or **complex**. A simple preposition is a single word such as *under*, *round* and *into* while a complex preposition consists of two or three words. Examples include *according to*, *on behalf of* and *with regard to*. Here is a selection of both simple and complex prepositions. Those which express time or place have been listed separately. Others, which express a range of aspects such as cause and purpose, have been grouped together:

prepositions of time
about, after, at, before, between, by, during, from, in, out of, past, post, prior to, since, towards, until

prepositions of place
about, above, across, against, along, among, at, away from, behind, below, beneath, beside, between, beyond, by, by way of, close to, down,

from, in, inside, into, near, off, on, onto, outside, over, past, round, through, towards, under, within

prepositions of cause, purpose, association, attitude and so on
about, according to, anti, apart from, because of, besides, by, concerning, contrary to, despite, due to, except, for, in return for, instead of, of, regarding, with, with regard to, without

Some prepositions have more than one semantic function. *About*, for example, can express time, place and association:

She arrived about noon	time
She walked about the shopping centre	place
She was concerned about her health	association

We saw earlier that there is a close relationship between pronouns and determiners and that many words of these classes take the same form. A comparable relationship exists between prepositions and adverbs:

She walked about the shopping centre	preposition
She walked about	adverb (of place)

☐ **noun phrases** ⇨ 5.2
☐ **prepositional phrases** ⇨ 5.5

2.12 CONJUNCTIONS

Conjunctions, as their name suggests, are used to join linguistic elements. They can be subdivided into **coordinating conjunctions** (or **coordinators**) and **subordinating conjunctions** (or **subordinators**). Essentially, there are only three coordinating conjunctions. These are *and*, *but* and *or*. More marginal coordinators are *nor*, which is the negative counterpart of *or*, and *for*. Coordinators join words, phrases and clauses of a similar status. Their role is explored in detail in Section 7.9.

Subordinating conjunctions, by contrast, form a much larger group. Subordinating conjunctions mainly join clauses together, although they do this in a rather different way from coordinating conjunctions. Like prepositions, they can be simple or complex. Here is a selection of subordinating conjunctions:

after, although, as, as far as, assuming that, because, before, if,
in case, in order that, provided that, since, that, unless, until,
when, whereas, while

Subordinating conjunctions occur at the beginning of clauses: when a subordinating conjunction introduces a clause in this way it has the effect of making that clause **subordinate** to another clause in the same sentence (and the sentence will be **complex**).

We noted earlier that many prepositions share the same forms as adverbs. Similarly, some prepositions share the same forms as subordinating conjunctions. However, whereas prepositions normally introduce a noun phrase, a subordinating conjunction introduces a clause (a grammatical unit which contains a verb element). The following examples show how *since* can be either a preposition, an adverb or a subordinating conjunction:

I haven't eaten <u>since lunchtime</u>	preposition
I ate at lunchtime and haven't eaten <u>since</u>	adverb
I haven't eaten <u>since Sue arrived</u>	subordinating conjunction
<u>Since the cupboard is bare</u>, I haven't eaten	subordinating conjunction

☐ **coordination of phrases** ⇨ 5.7
☐ **clauses** ⇨ 6.1
☐ **compound sentences** ⇨ 7.9
☐ **complex sentences** ⇨ 7.10

2.13   *WH*-WORDS

There are three word classes which include a subset of items beginning with *wh*-, namely adverbs, pronouns and determiners. Items which begin with *wh*- are *wh*-words, although *how* and *however* are also included in this group. Collectively, *wh*-adverbs, *wh*-pronouns and *wh*-determiners perform similar grammatical functions. Table 2.4 shows you the complete set of *wh*-words and indicates the different functions they perform.

Table 2.4 also gives examples of each of the *wh*-word types in the context of a clause or sentence. (Some of the examples are repeated from earlier sections in this chapter.) While it is helpful to understand how *wh*-words work as a group, at the same time it is important to maintain the distinction between those of the adverb class, those of the pronoun class and those of the determiner class.

Table 2.4 *Wh*-words

Function	Type		
	wh-**adverb**	*wh*-**pronoun**	*wh*-**determiner**
introducing an interrogative clause or sentence	how when where why	what which who whom whose	what which whose
examples	When did he telephone her?	Who has a flat in Majorca?	Which book did you choose?
introducing an exclamative clause or sentence	how		what
examples	How irritating that person is		What a nuisance this person is
introducing a relative clause	when where why	which who whom	which whose
examples	This is a place where everyone has fun	This is the car which I want to buy	This is the person whose car I'm buying
introducing a nominal relative clause	how when where why	what, what(so)ever which, which(so)ever who, who(so)ever whom, whom(so)ever	what which
examples	Where to go was quite a problem	Who to ask was quite a problem	Which option to select was quite a problem
introducing a *wh*-conditional clause	whenever wherever however	whatever whichever who(so)ever whom(so)ever	whatever whichever
examples	Wherever you go, be careful	Whatever happens, I'm leaving	Whichever choice you make, think about it carefully

- ☐ *wh*-adverbs ⇨ 2.7
- ☐ *wh*-pronouns ⇨ 2.8
- ☐ *wh*-determiners ⇨ 2.9
- ☐ clauses ⇨ 6.1
- ☐ relative clauses ⇨ 6.13
- ☐ nominal relative clauses ⇨ 6.14
- ☐ sentences ⇨ 7.1
- ☐ interrogative sentences ⇨ 7.4
- ☐ exclamative sentences ⇨ 7.6
- ☐ *wh*-conditional clauses ⇨ 7.11

3 Word Formation

3.1 SIMPLE AND COMPLEX WORDS

In this chapter, we will be looking closely at the internal structures of the words in the English language. The area of linguistics which is concerned with the internal structure of words is **morphology**. Morphology is normally divided into two branches – **lexical morphology** (sometimes known as **derivational morphology**) and **inflectional morphology**. Inflectional morphology deals with the way words are adapted in different grammatical contexts (such as making a noun plural), an aspect which is examined in Chapter 4. In this chapter we will be concerned with lexical morphology. In other words, we will be exploring the means by which existing words have been constructed and by which new words – **neologisms** – might be constructed.

When considering word formation, we can divide words into two broad categories – **simple words** and **complex words**. Simple words are those which cannot be analysed into smaller units of meaning. Examples might include *cat, paper, fear* and *rubbish*. Complex words, on the other hand, can be subdivided into smaller units of meaning. Here are some examples:

printer	*print + er*
unfortunately	*un + fortun(e) + ate + ly*
dispel	*dis + pel*

We know intuitively that the above examples are made up of smaller units because we have many other words in our mental lexicons that follow similar patterns. For instance, there are many nouns which end in *-er* where this ending denotes the performer of the action to which it is attached. So a *print-er* is someone who prints, a *teach-er* is someone who teaches, a *sing-er* is someone who sings and so on. Similarly, we know of many instances where *un-* at the beginning of a word has the effect of oppositeness (as in *happy/unhappy* or *successful/unsuccessful*) and we can form new words by using the same pattern: *funny* has now given rise to *unfunny*. The *-ate* element in *unfortunately* is found on the end of several adjectives – *temperate, immaculate, delicate* and so on – and many adverbs are formed by adding *-ly* to an existing adjective. We are able to subdivide *dispel* into *dis* + *pel* not because we necessarily know that *-pel* comes from the Latin root meaning 'to drive' or 'to force' (consider *compel, expel* and *repel*) but because we know that *dis-* occurs at the start of many words with the meaning of 'away from' or 'the reverse of' as in *dismiss, disconnect, disagree* and *displease.*

Sometimes, however, it will not be clear to us whether a word is simple or complex. If we are unaware of a word's origins in another language such as Latin or Greek, then we would not necessarily identify it as a complex word. Examples of such words might indeed include *repel* or words such as *magic* or *usual.* This is not a difficulty here because we are not concerned with the historical origins (or **etymology**) of words. The focus of this chapter is on identification of the strategies which are used in English to form words, partly with the aim of identifying how new words are likely to be formed.

Words which belong to open classes (nouns, verbs, adjectives and adverbs) form a huge group of words which it is impossible to count. In exploring word-formation strategies, we will only consider the open classes of words. There are two reasons for this. The first is that members of the closed classes are largely simple words – consider determiners such as *the, a/an, each, both, every* and so on – with relatively few being divisible into smaller units (examples include the conjunction *because* and the pronouns *myself, everyone*). The second reason is that our interest in word formation is very much in identifying how new words are formed and may be formed and of course the closed classes of words very rarely admit new members.

☐ **open and closed classes of words** ⇨ 2.3

3.2 SOME TERMS AND CONCEPTS

There are several important and useful terms for discussing the morphology of words. One of the aspects of word construction which we will frequently be considering is the position of particular units of construction. This is important because some units only occur at the beginning of a word (for example, the *un-* of *unfortunately*) and others only at the end (such as the *-ly* of *unfortunately*). When discussing the beginning of a word, we can say that an element is **word-initial** and, by contrast, an element at the end of a word is **word-final**. Very occasionally, we may wish to refer to an element positioned within the word and we would refer to this as **word-medial**.

Many words are complex in their construction and can therefore be broken down into smaller units of meaning. The smallest unit of meaning in a word is a **morpheme**. Therefore a word like *printer* given above, which is made up of *print + er*, is constructed from two morphemes while *un + fortun(e) +ate + ly* consists of four morphemes. Words which are indivisible into smaller elements of meaning such as *cat* and *rubbish* comprise a single morpheme only. Morphemes themselves can be subdivided into two types: **free morphemes** and **bound morphemes**. A free morpheme is one that can stand alone as a word in its own right. Thus *cat* and *rubbish* are free morphemes and so too are the *print* and *fortun(e)* elements of *printer* and *unfortunately*. Any morpheme which cannot stand alone is a bound morpheme. The *-er* of *printer,* and the *un-, -ate* and *-ly* of *unfortunately* are all bound morphemes.

In Section 3.1 we divided words in terms of their structure into simple and complex words. Sometimes, however, it is helpful to make a three-way distinction between simple words, **compound words** and complex words, with a compound word being constructed from two free morphemes while a complex word is constructed from a root morpheme (free or bound) plus at least one bound morpheme. Here are examples of the three types:

simple word	*sketch*	
compound word	*sketchpad*	*sketch + pad*
complex word	*sketchy*	*sketch + -y*

The beauty of this three-way distinction is that it mirrors the three basic structural possibilities for sentences, which can also be simple, compound or complex. This is not just a matter of terminology, however: there is a genuine similarity between the internal structures of words and those of sentences.

We considered in Chapter 2 how all words might be said to have a kind of abstract existence – a form which is known as a lexeme. Morphemes are similarly abstract. Consider the word-initial bound morphemes in the following examples:

inelegant	*in + elegant*
impolite	*im + polite*
illegal	*il + legal*
irregular	*ir + regular*

These four examples (*in-, im-, il-* and *ir-*) are used to express the opposite of what follows – *inelegant* is the opposite of *elegant* and so on. If we had a much fuller range of examples, we would see that *il-* only occurs when the following morpheme begins with /l/ (*illicit, illegible*) and *ir-* only occurs when the following morpheme begins with /r/ (*irreverend, irresponsible*), while *im-* only occurs before /b/ (*imbalance*), /m/ (*immature*) and /p/ (*impolite*), the reason being that /m/, /b/ and /p/ are all sounds made with the lips. All other comparable opposites are formed using *in-*. What this shows is that *in-*, *im-* *il-* and *ir-* are not four distinct morphemes but different forms of the same bound morpheme, the actual form used depending on the phonological (or pronunciation) environment in which it occurs. This is a sound argument for the existence of abstract forms or morphemes which are then realised by different **allomorphs**.

Two further terms which are useful when studying morphology are **root** and **base**. The root or **root morpheme** is the part of a complex word which is at the heart of the word's construction and its meaning. Roots can often be used to identify families of words. For example, we saw above that *impel*, *expel, compel* and *repel* all share the root *-pel*. The morpheme *-pel* is the root because it is at the heart of the construction of all these examples and its original meaning from Latin of 'drive' or 'force' is also central in semantic terms. Similarly, *original, originality, originate* and *originally* all share the root *origin,* although there is a contrast here with the *-pel* root in that *origin* is a word in itself (and a free morpheme) whereas *-pel* clearly is not (and is therefore a bound morpheme). A base is a unit to which other morphemes may be added to create a new word or words. In the example just given, the root *origin* provides the base for the adjective *original*. This in turn provides the base for both the noun *originality* and the adverb *originally*.

> ☐ **lexemes** ⇨ 2.1
> ☐ **simple sentences** ⇨ 7.8
> ☐ **compound sentences** ⇨ 7.9
> ☐ **complex sentences** ⇨ 7.10

3.3 WORD-FORMATION STRATEGIES

It is clear from our discussion so far that many words of the open classes have complex structures. In the following sections, we will look at the full range of strategies which are used in modern English to construct lexemes. So far we have seen that many words are constructed by the addition of bound morphemes either word-initially or word-finally. This process is known as **affixation** and is the most **productive** of the strategies used to form words. We will look at affixation in Section 3.4. Two further strategies which are also very productive are **compounding** and **conversion** and we will consider these in Sections 3.5 and 3.7. Section 3.8 will deal with the range of other strategies which are employed.

The term **word formation** is being used here as a useful blanket term. As we have already seen, some words are not really 'formed' in that they cannot be further divided into morphemes. Nevertheless, we may need to consider the origin or source of such words in order to provide a contrast with 'forming' processes such as affixation and compounding, and to provide an overview of the full range of strategies used in contemporary English to create open class words.

3.4   AFFIXATION

Affixation is the process by which bound morphemes (other than roots) are added to bases, either word-initially or word-finally, to form new words. A bound morpheme which is added in this way is an **affix**. An affix which occurs word-initially is more specifically termed a **prefix**, while one which is added word-finally is a **suffix**. In some languages, the word-formation process may employ an **infix** – a bound morpheme which is inserted within the word. This is not a strategy used in English word formation although speakers occasionally infix a taboo word into another word as in *hoo-bloody-ray*. This is clearly done for effect – the effect being achieved by the fact that English words are not normally interrupted in this way.

It is important to make a distinction between prefixes and suffixes because these two types of bound morphemes behave rather differently in forming words. One particular difference is that a prefix will not normally change the class of a word. So, for example, when the prefix *dis-* is added to the verb *agree*, the resulting word – *disagree* – is still a verb. A prefix, then, is normally **class-preserving**. By contrast, a suffix may be class-preserving (both *king* and *kingdom* are nouns) but is equally likely to be **class-changing**. For instance, the addition of the suffix *-ly* to the adjective *sad* results in an adverb *sadly*. A further difference between prefixes and suffixes is that there are many prefixes which can be added to at least two word classes whereas suffixes tend to be word-class specific. For example, the prefix *dis-* is found in nouns (*distaste, disservice*), verbs (*disagree, disappear*), adjectives (*dissimilar, disreputable*) and obviously the adverbs derived from these adjectives (*dissimilarly, disreputably*). By contrast, most suffixes occur with a specific class of words only. Furthermore, no morpheme which functions as a prefix can also function as a suffix. Table 3.1 shows some common prefixes of English while Table 3.2 shows some common suffixes.

Table 3.2 shows that the majority of suffixes are used to form either nouns or adjectives. There is a particularly large number of noun suffixes. By contrast, there are only a handful of verb and adverb suffixes. A general observation which we can make about both prefixes and suffixes is that some are far more productive than others. In other words, some affixes are used in the creation of words much more than others. The verb and adverb suffixes illustrate this. Of the four verb suffixes given in Table 3.2, *-ise/-ize* is used far more extensively to create new words than the other examples given. In recent years we have had *computerise, hospitalise, windowise* (meaning 'to find time for an

Table 3.1 Some common English prefixes

Prefix	Approximate meaning	Examples
anti-	against	antiseptic, anti-social
de-	reverse	destabilise, devaluation
dis-	reverse	disconnect, dismount
dis-	negative and opposite	disapprove, disloyal
in/im/il/ir-	opposite (and negative)	impatient, illogical
inter-	between	international, interplanetary
intra-	within, inside	intranet, intravenous
mega-	very large	megalith, megastore
mini-	small	minicab, minibar
mis-	incorrect, wrong	misinformation, mismatch
mono-	one	monosyllabic, monotone
neo-	new	neologism, neo-classical
non-	not	non-standard, non-entity
poly-	many	polygon, polymath
post-	after	postcolonial, postnatal
pre-	before	precaution, preparation
pro-	in favour of, for	pro-Europe, pro-life
pro-	forward	progress, proceed
re-	again	reconsider, revision
trans-	across	transfer, translate
un-	reverse	undo, unpick
un-	remove	uncover, unsaddle
un-	not	unhappy, unnecessary

appointment'), *anonymise* and many others. With regard to adverbs, *-ly* is a very common suffix as it occurs with many adjectives to form adverbs of manner – *happy/happily, quick/quickly* and so on. The other suffixes are less productive although it has become very common for speakers to coin adverbs with *-wise* as a more economical way of expressing *as far as x is concerned*: for example, *I'm feeling much better healthwise* or *Things haven't been going very well jobwise*.

Of the noun and adjective suffixes, again some are more productive than others. A suffix such as *-ment* occurs on many words but is rarely used now to form new words. Others, such as *-ee* and *-ism* are currently very productive. Table 3.2 includes established words (such as *government*) as well as more recent words (such as *ageism*) to illustrate this point. Some suffixes are themselves recently coined: *-oholic/aholic* is an example of this. It is clipped from *alcoholic* (interestingly taking *-ohol-* from the base of the word as well as *-ic*, the suffix) and has the meaning of 'addicted to' as in *shopaholic, chocoholic*. A similar example is *-athon*, clipped from *marathon* and now used to indicate other events which require endurance, such as *readathon* and *swimathon*.

There have often been objections to the suffixes *-ess* and *-ette* to denote female roles on the grounds that they imply women are in a disadvantageous

Table 3.2 Some common English suffixes

Noun suffixes		Adjective suffixes		Verb suffixes		Adverb suffixes	
-age	dotage	-able -ible	eligible	-ate	nominate	-fold	tenfold
-al	recital			-en	quicken	-free	scotfree
-ance -ence	permanence	-al -ial	practical	-ify	falsify	-ly	sadly
				-ise -ize	criticise	-wise	healthwise
-ancy -ency	tenancy	-ant -ent	diligent				
-ant -ent	defendant	-ar	regular				
		-ary	exemplary				
-ar/-er	registrar	-ate	delicate				
-ate	delegate	-ed	mannered				
-ation -tion	formation	-en	craven				
		-ful	truthful				
-ee	employee	-ic	economic				
-ery -ry	snobbery	-ing	swinging				
		-ish	childish				
-ess	actress	-ive	productive				
-ette	kitchenette	-less	feckless				
-ful	spoonful	-like	childlike				
-ing	dancing	-ly	friendly				
-ism	ageism	-ous	cavernous				
-ite	Blairite	-some	troublesome				
-ity	brutality	-y	picky				
-ive	collective						
-let	piglet						
-ling	fledgling						
-ment	government						
-ness	kindness						
-oholic -aholic	shopaholic						
-ship	leadership						
-some	twosome						
-athon	swimathon						

position in comparison with men. This is because the suffix for the female form (such as *actress, stewardess, usherette, ladette*) is an addition to a base, suggesting that the female form is an afterthought or is secondary to the male form. Also, there is an arguable imbalance between the male form being a free morpheme and the female form requiring a bound morpheme which is unable to stand alone and therefore suggestive of weakness. The suffix *-ette* is particularly objectionable to some users in that it is a **diminutive**, indicating a smaller version of something: a *kitchenette*, for instance, is a small kitchen. In recent years, these gender suffixes have to a great extent been replaced completely (*stewardess* has become *flight attendant*) or the male form has become generic, so both male and female performers are referred to as *actors*, for example.

Interestingly, *actress* is still used if a gender distinction needs to be made as with the Oscars for *Best Actor/Actress*.

It was noted above that most suffixes belong to one particular word class only. However, a handful of suffixes do occur on words of more than one class. If you look again at Table 3.2, for example, you will see that *-al* occurs in both nouns and adjectives, as do *-ate, -ful, -ing, -ive* and *-some*. You will also remember that while almost all prefixes are class-preserving, suffixes may be class-preserving or class-changing. So whereas *-ism*, for example, is added to a noun such as *age* to produce another noun, *ageism*, and is therefore class-preserving, a suffix such as *-ous* is added to the noun *cavern* to form the adjective *cavernous* and is therefore class-changing.

Another feature of affixes is that any one word may include more than one prefix and more than one suffix. However, prefixes and suffixes do not combine freely (for example, it would be impossible to have both *-ness* and *-ity* suffixing a word) and the order of occurrence of prefixes and suffixes is fixed, often due to the word class of the base. Here is a breakdown of possible and impossible combinations linked to the noun *disorganisation*:

dis -	organ -	is(e)	- ation
* dis -	organ		
	organ -	ise	
dis -	organ -	ise	
	organ -	is(e)	- ation
	* organ		- ation

You can see here that although the prefix *dis-* does occur with some nouns (we had the examples *distaste* and *disservice* above) there is a semantic restriction which prevents **disorgan*. This is because the prefix *dis-* is used to turn a positive meaning into a negative one. *Organ* has a more neutral meaning (when it refers to an institution used for a particular purpose) and this makes the addition of a prefix such as *dis-* inappropriate. With regard to the suffix *-ation*, we see that the combination **organation* is also impossible. Here, however, the restriction is a morphological, not a semantic one: this suffix only occurs on verbs and since *organ* is a noun, it is impossible to add *-ation* to it. These examples show us, then, that there can be both semantic and morphological restrictions on word formation.

Two suffixes which sometimes cause confusion are *-ed* and *-ing*. This is because both these forms also occur as grammatical endings (or **inflections**) on verbs. This is illustrated in:

The girl is walking to school
The girl has walked to school

However, both nouns and adjectives can be formed by the addition of the suffix *-ing* and adjectives can also be formed by the addition of *-ed*. When a new word is formed by adding *-ed* to a noun, the resulting word is always an adjective (as in *manner* and *mannered*). However, when *-ed* and *-ing* are added to verbs, a new noun or adjective may result, or an inflectional form of the verb may be produced. So, in *The girl enjoyed the dancing,* clearly *dancing* is a noun since it occurs after the definite article *the*. This form is sometimes referred to as a **deverbal noun** as it derives from a verb. In *The girl is walking to school,* the element *walking* is a verb since it occurs in a verb phrase after the primary auxiliary *is*. Similarly, in the following example the *-ed* form is a verb as it occurs in contrast to a present tense form in the first example and after a primary auxiliary in the second example:

> *The girl walk<u>ed</u> to school* (not *walk<u>s</u>*)
> *The girl has walk<u>ed</u> to school*

In the following examples, however, the *-ed* forms occur attributively (in other words, they precede the nouns they modify) and so in this context we are dealing with adjectives:

> *The confus<u>ed</u> girl had not reached school*   (compare *The lazy girl ...*)
> *The confus<u>ing</u> question had everyone foxed*   (compare *The tricky question ...*)

These adjectives can be referred to as **deverbal adjectives**, again to indicate that they derive from verbs. Some linguists prefer, however, to treat them and deverbal nouns as verb forms so you will sometimes find them referred to as verbs or more specifically as **participles**.

☐ **verb inflections** ⇨ 4.4

3.5 COMPOUNDING

If you compare the following two examples you will see that they each consist of three morphemes:

> *unfriendly*   *un + friend + ly*
> *child-friendly*   *child + friend + ly*

The difference between them is that whereas *unfriendly* consists of the root *friend* plus two affixes, *child-friendly* consists of the root *child* combined with the root *friend* suffixed by *-ly*. This construction, which consists of two roots and in fact two pre-existing words – *child* and *friendly* – is a **compound** or

compound word. In Chapter 2, we discussed what exactly a word might be. We observed that a word is not necessarily the same as a separate written element although the correlation between the two is a strong one. Compound words are often written as one element as in *lipstick* (a compound noun) or hyphenated as in *child-friendly* (a compound adjective) but they can be written as two separate elements such as *world power* or *Down's syndrome*. As we discussed in Chapter 2, there is a good argument for treating all compounds (whatever their written form) as one word or lexeme due to the virtual inseparability of the bases which form them. There is also the possibility of substituting compound words with alternative lexical items which are not compounds.

Compounding, like affixation, is a very productive way of forming words in English, and this process is particularly productive in relation to nouns and adjectives. Table 3.3 illustrates this.

Table 3.3 The formation of compound nouns and compound adjectives

compound nouns		
most productive combination	noun + noun	*bookcase*
		crash landing
		smokescreen
other possible structures	verb + noun	*pickpocket*
	adjective + noun	*mobile phone*
	noun + *and* + noun	*gin and tonic*
	noun + prepositional phrase	*mother-in-law*
compound adjectives		
most productive combinations	noun + adjective	*war-torn*
		world-weary
	verb + adverb/preposition	*throwaway*
other possible combinations	adjective + adjective	*ready-cooked*
	adjective + noun	*long-life*
	prepositional phrase	*in-house*
	adjective + infinitive	*ready-to-wear*

As you can also see from Table 3.3, compounding is typically the result of joining nouns, adjectives and verbs. Compound verbs are relatively rare and those which do exist are likely to be the result of **back-formation** or **conversion** (which we will cover in Section 3.7). However, there is a very large group of **multi-word verbs**, formed by the combination of the verb with an adverb or preposition, which behave differently from compound verbs. We will examine these in Section 3.6. Some examples of compound verbs are given in Table 3.4.

Table 3.4 Some compound verbs

Type	Examples	Formation
back-formation (a suffix is removed from an existing word)	*baby-sit* *fine-tune*	from the noun *baby-sitter* from the noun *fine-tuning*
conversion (change of word class but the form remains the same)	*cold-shoulder* *mastermind*	was a noun was a noun
other examples	*make do* *blackball*	verb + verb adjective + noun

A final matter we need to address before moving on from compounding is illustrated in the following examples:

> *psychology*   *technophobe*   *telegram*

At first glance, it doesn't seem particularly difficult to analyse these examples in terms of their morphemes. However, a problem exists in trying to decide which of the morphemes might be roots and which are affixes. In *technophobe* ('someone who is afraid of new technology'), for instance, is *techno-* a root to which the suffix *-phobe* has been added or is *-phobe* a root to which the prefix *techno-* has been added? It seems impossible to decide. If we argued that they were both roots, then we would be dealing with a compound word but the elements which make up compound words like *answerphone* (*answer* + *phone*) can stand alone, whereas neither *techno* (referring to technology in general, not to music) nor *phobe* are individual words. If, on the other hand, we explored the possibility of *techno-* and *-phobe* both being affixes we would have a further problem in that a prefix and a suffix alone cannot combine to form a word (for example, **disity* or **preness*). Also, these morphemes seem to have a more specific meaning than many affixes. The given examples, then, are neither **derived** words (those formed by adding affixes to a root) nor compound words but something in between. We call the morphemes which make up these in-between words **combining forms**.

3.6 MULTI-WORD VERBS

Whereas compound verbs are relatively rare (in contrast to compound nouns and compound adjectives), **multi-word verbs** (sometimes also known as

phrasal verbs) are very common in contemporary English. A multi-word verb is a combination of two or three elements:

> verb + preposition
> verb + adverb
> verb + adverb + preposition

One key feature of multi-word verbs is that their meaning is partly or wholly **idiomatic**. This means that the meaning cannot be fully deduced from the individual meanings of the elements which constitute the multi-word verb. For example, in *Fred ran up some heavy debts*, *ran* has nothing to do with fast physical movement and *up* has nothing to do with direction (although in the example *Fred ran up a steep hill* these are the meanings which would come into play). As a multi-word verb, *run up* has the equivalent meaning of *accumulate*. It is a feature of multi-word verbs that they can often be replaced by a single-word lexical verb.

One other feature of multi-word verbs, and a crucial way in which they differ from compound verbs, is that the adverb or preposition can sometimes be separated from the verb:

verb + preposition	*The doctor <u>relied</u> <u>on</u> her assistant*
	This is the assistant <u>on</u> whom the doctor <u>relied</u>
verb + adverb	*Sue <u>gave</u> <u>away</u> the secret*
	Sue <u>gave</u> the secret <u>away</u>
verb + adverb + preposition	*This is a matter I shall <u>take</u> <u>up</u> <u>with</u> my colleague*
	I shall <u>take</u> this matter <u>up</u> <u>with</u> my colleague

Multi-word combinations of the kind illustrated above are a highly productive way of forming verbs in English. Consider, for instance, how many combinations there are with *up*. Here are just a few examples:

multi-word verb	meaning	example
to listen up	*to pay attention*	*Now listen up!*
to put up	*to provide a bed*	*Can you put me up tonight?*
to take up	*to respond or discuss*	*Jane took up the subject at once*
	to begin learning	*Jane took up archery*
	to fill time	*The walk took up the whole day*
to talk up	*to praise*	*The manager talked up the firm*
to speak up	*to speak loudly*	*She spoke up amid the din*

3.7 CONVERSION AND BACK-FORMATION

Conversion is another productive method for creating new words by a change of word class without any alteration to the form of the word itself. For example, *access* is a noun in *The police gained access to the premises* but in recent years *access* has also come to be used as a verb as in *The programmer accessed the files on her PC*. Conversion is a particularly productive way of creating verbs from nouns and, to a slightly lesser extent, nouns from verbs. Here are some more examples:

> verbs from nouns
> *Julia Roberts <u>co-starred</u> with Hugh Grant in 'Notting Hill'*
> *The critic <u>rubbished</u> the actor's performance*
> *I've <u>programmed</u> your video to come on at eight*
> *Jeanne had to <u>elbow</u> her way through the crowd*

> nouns from verbs
> *The thief made a quick <u>lunge</u> at the handbag*
> *Keith took his old furniture to the <u>dump</u>*

However, it is not unusual for adjectives to be converted to nouns as in *There was no doubt she was his <u>equal</u>* or for adjectives to be converted to verbs as in *The athlete tried to <u>better</u> his previous performance*. Occasionally words of other classes may be the source for a conversion: *The opposition tried to out the president* uses the adverb *out* as a verb.

Of course, it is not always possible, when dealing with forms which belong to more than one word class and which have existed for a long time, to tell which word came first without checking in an etymological dictionary. Sometimes we can make an educated guess. For example, *bottle* the noun must have come before *bottle* the verb since the meaning of this verb is 'to put something in a bottle' – an impossibility if bottles do not exist! Conversion is a process which happens frequently in contemporary English and speakers will convert words fairly freely if needed.

Back-formation usually results in a change of word class, and in this respect it is like conversion. However, back-formation is the less productive of the two strategies. It involves the modification of a word, usually through the removal of a suffix (or suffix-like ending) but occasionally a prefix. Most typically, suffixes are removed from nouns to create new verbs:

noun	*television*	verb derived	*to televise*
noun	*emotion*	verb derived	*to emote*
noun	*reminiscence*	verb derived	*to reminisce*

If a prefix is removed, however, the word class will not change since prefixes are class-preserving:

adjective   *uncouth*   adjective derived   *couth*

3.8 OTHER WORD-FORMATION STRATEGIES

Affixation, compounding and conversion are the most productive of the word-formation strategies in English. However, there are a range of other strategies employed in modern English to form new words. Here is a brief survey of them.

An **acronym** is an economical way of expressing a phrase since the first letter (or letters), usually of each word in the phrase, is placed in sequence to form a new word. *Scuba,* for example, stands for *self-contained underwater breathing apparatus* and *AIDS* stands for *acquired immune deficiency syndrome.* Sometimes, when the initial letters do not form a new word, they are named individually as in *CID* (*Criminal Investigation Department*) or *BBC* (*British Broadcasting Corporation*). This type of acronym is known more specifically as an **initialism**. Sometimes a word can be a combination of an acronym and an initialism as in *CD-ROM,* where *CD* is an initialism (for *compact disk*) but *ROM* (*read only memory*) is an acronym.

Clipping involves reducing a longer word to one or two syllables, usually by removing some of the latter part, as in *cred* (from *credibility*), *mash* (from *mashed potato*) *combo* (from *combination*) and *mobile* (from *mobile phone*), but occasionally from the opening as in *phone* from *telephone.* Clippings tend to refer to everyday objects or ideas, something purists might regard as a kind of laziness in using the language, but it is perfectly natural to clip a word in frequent use. They can also suggest a kind of familiarity or popularity, such as *Glasto* for the Glastonbury Festival or *Wiggo* for the cyclist Bradley Wiggins (a reduction of sounds in the name rather than syllables). *Glasto, Wiggo* and *combo* also reflect the current trend of forming clippings with an additional *-o* sound. Clipping differs from back-formation in that it does not result in a word of a different word class.

A **blend** is a kind of compound although the base words are not joined in their entirety. Instead, part of one word is merged with part of another as in *brunch* (*breakfast* and *lunch*) and *smog* (*smoke* and *fog*). Sometimes it is possible to deduce the meaning of a blended word. However, some blends are not this transparent. For example, the computer term *bit* is a blend of *binary* and *digit.* Blends are most typically nouns although *ginormous* is an example of an adjective. Blends are also sometimes termed **portmanteau words**.

Eponymy is the use of a proper name to refer to an object or action. The resulting word is an **eponym**. Often, the object in question is an invention of the person after whom it is named. Speakers may be unaware that words such as *sandwich, wellington* and *diesel* are eponyms, although they may be more familiar with the source of examples such as *hoover* and *Mac*.

Every language contains a handful of words which are **onomatopoeic**. **Onomatopoeia** is when a noun or verb refers to a sound (such as *miaow* or *crash*) and supposedly imitates that sound. However, onomatopoeic words vary from language to language, which indicates that the imitation is only approximate. Onomatopoeic words are, though, the only words in any language where there is a strong correlation between the sound of a word and its meaning, although there may be a partial correlation in some words (such as the examples of *gruff, grumble* and *grumpy* discussed in Section 1.2).

A handful of words are formed by the process of **reduplication**, which involves the doubling of the first element of the word. Occasionally, this repetition will be identical (for example, *no-no* as in *That dress is a real no-no*) but more typically there will be a consonant or vowel variation in the second element as in *willy-nilly, helter-skelter* or *flip-flop*. Reduplicative words are often playful and are quite frequently used when speaking to very young children but speakers will sometimes use reduplication when being patronising or sarcastic.

Loanwords or **borrowings** are words which are adopted into English from another language. Of course, a very large proportion of English words have their origin in Latin, French, Norse and Greek – to such an extent that we are rarely conscious of these words as borrowings. In any case, most of these words have been **anglicised**. This means that they no longer take the form they would take in their language of origin but have been adapted to sound or look English. However, wholesale borrowing is relatively common. Some fairly recent borrowings include food words such as *sushi* from Japanese or *tortilla* from Spanish. Non-culinary examples include *anorak* (from Eskimo), *feng-shui* (from Japanese) and *glasnost* (from Russian).

3.9   MEANINGS AND MEANING RELATIONS

We will conclude our exploration of the English lexicon by taking a brief look at the meanings of the words in our language and the relationships between those meanings. In our discussion, you will notice that several of the technical terms we will use contain the bound morpheme *-onym*, which comes from the Greek word (*onyma*) for 'name'.

We saw in Chapter 2 that all English words belong to either an open class or a closed class. In discussing the meanings and the meaning relationships of words we will be concentrating on the open classes of words although some of the observations will also apply to some members of the closed classes. Also in Chapter 2, we briefly discussed the question of how large the English lexicon actually is. Although it is impossible, for the reasons we outlined, to be precise about the size of the lexicon, one thing we do know about English is that the lexicon is much larger than many other languages, probably larger than most other languages. The reason for this is an historical one. Various invasions and other social and historical changes have had a far-reaching impact on English which is why our language now consists of not only Germanic words descended from Old English (of the West Germanic family of languages) and from Old Norse (the North Germanic language of the Vikings), but also words from French, Latin, and Greek and from many other languages which have contributed just a handful of lexical items. Consequently, there are many words in our language which have very similar meanings but come from different sources. Here is an example:

Germanic *ask*   French *question*   Latin *interrogate*

In some contexts, these words could be used interchangeably:

> *The police <u>asked</u> the woman about the robbery*
> *The police <u>questioned</u> the woman about the robbery*
> *The police <u>interrogated</u> the woman about the robbery*

However, although *ask, question* and *interrogate* have very similar meanings in these three sentences, *interrogate* suggests a rather sterner style of questioning than *question* and certainly much sterner than *ask*. When words are deemed to have the same meaning, we say they are **synonyms,** or that they are **synonymous** with each other. However, we would probably be doubtful about saying that *ask, question* and *interrogate* were true synonyms, for the reason already given.

Let us consider another example of possible synonyms, this time the nouns *sight* and *vision*. Again, in certain contexts, they appear interchangeable:

> *The optician told Liz she had very good <u>sight</u>*
> *The optician told Liz she had very good <u>vision</u>*

Here, we might be tempted to think that *sight* and *vision* are synonyms. However, looking at the rest of the semantic territory which these two nouns cover we can see some problems with this:

> 1 *She looked quite a <u>sight</u> when I saw her yesterday*
> 2 *That was a <u>sight</u> for sore eyes*
> 3 *She was a <u>vision</u> of loveliness on her wedding day*

Example 1 above probably suggests to most speakers that something unpleasant has been seen whereas Example 2 suggests liking or approval. This illustrates that *sight* in the sense of 'something seen' can be used both positively and negatively. By contrast, *vision* as used in Example 3 has only a positive meaning and can even be used in the context of a religious or supernatural experience. These examples show, then, that *vision* and *sight*, which we at first considered to have identical meanings, have other aspects of meaning which prevent us from saying they are actually synonymous. This is true of almost all possible synonyms in the language. Logically, if two words really were identical in meaning, it is likely that one of them would fall from use (as has already happened with many words). Many linguists consider English, despite its very large lexicon, to have no true synonyms.

We have noticed in our discussion of the nouns *sight* and *vision* that each of these words has more than one meaning. We considered two possible meanings – 'ability to see' as well as 'something seen' – although both these words have further meanings. Many words function semantically in this way. In other words, they are **polysemous**. If you look up words such as *sight* and *vision* in a dictionary, you would find that the different meanings are separately numbered. However, we would not normally wish to argue that a noun such as *sight* should be treated as several distinct words or lexemes simply because it has several definitions. Another example might be the noun *mouse*, which we discussed in Section 2.1. The primary meaning of this word is in reference to a small rodent but a mouse can also be a timid female and, more recently, an item of IT equipment. Nevertheless, we would be unlikely to say that there are three separate words or lexemes all having the citation form <mouse>. This is because the meanings are clearly related to each other. Sometimes, however, two unrelated meanings may share the same citation form or word form and we would therefore wish to posit the existence of two separate lexemes to reflect this. An example of such a form is *rent*. There is a lexeme *rent* which means 'a payment for renting something' and there is a separate lexeme *rent* which means 'a rip or tear'. There is clearly no relationship between these two meanings (unlike the *mouse* meanings) and that is why we accept that we are dealing here with two separate lexemes. In fact, separate lexemes which share the same citation form often have differing etymologies, whereas the multiple meanings of single lexemes are often the result of metaphor (a person referred to as a mouse is timid like a mouse, and a computer mouse looks like a mouse). Words such as *rent* ('payment') and *rent* ('rip'), which are separate lexemes but take the same citation form, are **homonyms**. You may also come across **homophones** which are words that share neither meaning nor citation form but sound the same as in *site/cite/sight* or *pier/peer*.

To return to synonyms, another feature which often distinguishes words of very similar meaning (apart from the fact that they might not cover precisely the same semantic territory) is that, whereas one word might be used informally, another will be reserved for more formal usage. This is a matter of **register**, and the appropriate context in which to use a word is embedded in its meaning. Dictionaries often indicate that a word is **slang** (such as *shagged out* meaning 'very tired') or **informal** (such as *hog* in the sense of 'keep to oneself') or rather **formal** (such as *pleasantry,* meaning 'an amusing remark'). Of course, many, if not the majority of open class words can be used in all kinds of situations but even so there is a likelihood that we might prefer one word to another depending on context. For example, you may be more likely to use the first example below to a friend whereas you would choose the second example to talk to someone in authority at the school:

My younger sister bunked off school yesterday
My younger sister played truant from school yesterday

Speakers make subtle choices of this kind all the time. The fact that we rarely make linguistic blunders in our choice of words is evidence of the sophistication of our knowledge about not only the meanings but also the uses of the many items in our mental lexicon.

Another aspect of word meanings which has some relevance to what we have already discussed, both in terms of range of meanings and in terms of context and formality, is the contrast between **denotation** and **connotation**. A word's **denotative** meaning is normally the person, object, quality, idea, action or state to which a word refers. This is known as its **referent**. So the referent or denotative meaning of *pig* is a particular farm animal. This is also the meaning you would expect to find first and foremost in a dictionary. However, many words also have **connotative** meanings and these refer to the emotions or attitudes which a particular word may evoke. In this sense, *pig* can be a term of abuse either for a greedy person or a male who behaves badly or a police officer. These uses of *pig* all have negative connotations. Depending on the context in which a word is used, positive or negative connotations may come into play:

1 *We were finding it hard to see the path because <u>darkness</u> had fallen*
2 *Count Dracula was a lover of <u>darkness</u>*
3 *The prince was struck by the <u>darkness</u> of Cinderella's beautiful eyes*

In Example 1, *darkness* is used in a fairly neutral way to mean 'absence of light', whereas Example 2 brings into play the negative connotations of *darkness* through its association with evil. By contrast, the darkness of Cinderella's eyes in Example 3 is seen to be an attractive feature to the prince. Connotations, then, are often determined or brought out by context. Dictionaries will not always indicate all the connotations of a word but they will always indicate its denotation.

A further way of looking at the relationships between words relates to the fact that many words of the open classes seem to belong to sets. For example, *fruit* belongs in a set with *fish, meat, vegetable, grain, pulse* and so on. These nouns in turn belong in a blanket set of *food*. *Fruit*, however, as well as being a subcategory of *food*, can also be subdivided into types such as *apple* and *pear*. Sometimes it is helpful to represent these relationships in a **tree diagram** as shown in Figure 3.1. Here, *fruit* is the group to which *apple, pear* and so on belong. In this use, *fruit* is a **hypernym** – a name for an overarching category. Under the hypernym *fruit*, we see various kinds of fruit which all belong to that category. Each of these names is a **hyponym** or member of a category. (*Hyper-* incidentally means 'above' in Greek, while *hypo-* means 'below'). However, although *fruit* is a hypernym in relation to, say, *apple, fruit* is itself a hyponym of *food*. Identifying **hypernyms** and **hyponyms** can be a useful way of looking at how words are related in terms of more general or more specific meanings, and provide a way of organising words into sets. This does not mean, though, that all open class words will fit comfortably into this type of classification.

In contrast to the sets we can identify using hypernymic and hyponymic relations, many words fit comfortably into pairs. Typical examples include *black* and *white* (although these also belong in a set of hyponyms of *colour*), *happy* and *sad*, *dead* and *alive*. Pairs which express opposites are known as **antonyms**. These usually express extremes of something gradable. For instance, *white* is at one end of a shade spectrum and *black* is at the other. Similarly, *hot* is at one end of a heat spectrum and *cold* is at the other. Many words are thought of in pairs but are not strictly antonyms. One such example is *dead/alive*. If something is not black, that doesn't mean it is white. On the other hand, if something animate is not dead then it must be alive. So whereas *black* and *white* are strictly opposites and therefore antonyms, pairs such as *dead/alive* which are mutually exclusive are **complementary** to each other. Another type of pair is *lend/borrow*. Here, if one person is lending, another person must be borrowing.

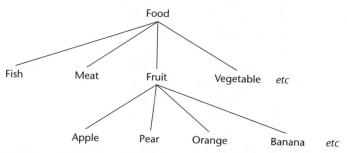

Figure 3.1 Some hypernymic and hyponymic relations

Learn and *teach* are similar pairs. These examples are said to be in a converse relationship.

Words sometimes denote their intended referent indirectly. A **metonym** has an association with the referent, such as the *Palace* (namely Buckingham Palace) referring to the British royal family. Similarly, a **meronym** is a part standing for the whole, such as *wheels* for a car or *head* in *headcount* for a person. Both **metonymy** and **meronymy** show language being used in a more figurative way, although both types are common in everyday usage, where figurative language is as likely to be found as in more formal or literary styles.

So far, we have looked at the meaning relationships of words with each other and of words in context. We will now briefly look at meaning relationships within derived words (those which are formed through affixation) and compound words. We have already considered some of the meanings which prefixes and suffixes attach to bases and how they indicate aspects such as reversal (*connect/disconnect*) or incorrectness (*information/misinformation*). A further point to note about affixes, however, is that their function will not always be the same. A salient example is the suffix *-ee*. In most cases, *-ee* indicates someone who is having something done to them: an *employee* is someone who is employed, a *detainee* is someone who is detained and so on. However, there are a good number of examples where this relationship doesn't hold:

1 y is an *employee*	x employed y
2 y is a *detainee*	x detained y
3 y is a *tutee*	x tutored y
4 y is an *absentee*	* x absented y
5 y is a *devotee*	* x devoted y
6 y is an *amputee*	* x amputated y

You can see here that whereas the x/y relationship is the same in Examples 1 to 3, this is not true of 4 to 6. Furthermore, although *absentee* and *devotee* are comparable (an *absent* person, a *devoted* person), *amputee* is different again. This variation in meaning relationships between morphemes is also found in compound words. Consider some of the examples from Table 3.3 of compound nouns formed by the joining of two nouns:

1 *bookcase*	a 'case' which is for books	x is for y
2 *crash landing*	a landing which is also a crash	x is also y
3 *smokescreen*	a screen which is made of smoke	x is made of y
4 *smokescreen*	a means of hiding one's intentions	?

The first three analyses show the relationship between the two bases of the compound word. However, although it is possible to express an x/y relationship between the bases, the relationship between x and y differs in each case. In addition, *smokescreen* has a metaphorical meaning (Example 4) and since this meaning is not transparent, it is hard to claim that there is a clear semantic relationship between *smoke* and *screen*.

Finally, we will consider a slightly different relationship which can exist between certain words as illustrated in the following examples:

rancid butter	* *rancid wine*
make a will	* *make a letter*
propose marriage	* *offer marriage*

The above examples show that some words typically occur together and that there are restrictions on these occurrences. For instance, we *make a will* but do not *make a letter;* we *write a letter* and may *write a will* but *make a will* sounds more natural. A typical or habitual combination of lexemes is known as a **collocation**. Collocations differ from compounds in that the combinations do not result in new lexemes. Nevertheless, our awareness of these typical combinations is further evidence of the sophistication of our lexical knowledge which was referred to above.

□ **meanings and word identification** ⇨ 2.1
□ **register** ⇨ 8.11
□ **loan words** ⇨ 12.4
□ **variation in synonyms** ⇨ 12.4
□ **variation in collocations** ⇨ 12.4

Lexical Frameworks: Exercises

Exercise 1: Lexemes

Identify the different lexemes in the following sentence (from *The Art of Travel* by Alain de Boton) and group them into word classes (according to their function in this sentence) using their dictionary citation form:

> *On disembarking at Amsterdam's Schiphol Airport, only a few steps inside the terminal, I am struck by a sign hanging from the ceiling that announces the ways to the arrivals hall, the exit and the transfer desks.*

Exercise 2: Homonymy and polysemy

In each of the following pairs of words, decide whether the two identical words are connected through homonymy or polysemy. The answer may be clear-cut or debatable.

	word	word class	definition
1a	*high*	adjective	'well above the ground'
1b	*high*	adjective	'having status or rank'
2a	*list*	verb	'to compile a written record of items'
2b	*list*	verb	'to lean to one side'
3a	*beam*	noun	'a long heavy piece of wood'
3b	*beam*	noun	'a ray of light'
4a	*skip*	verb	'to move lightly with little steps and jumps'
4b	*skip*	verb	'to pass over something or leave it out'
5a	*perch*	noun	'a place where a bird sits'
5b	*perch*	noun	'a type of fish'

Exercise 3: Word classes

Identify which word classes each of the following word-forms can belong to:

well
slow
blast
better

whatever
fast
if
round
rash
will

Exercise 4: Morphemes

Break the following complex words down into morphemes. You may need to use an etymological dictionary to help you:

percentage
percolate
periscope
permafrost
perdition
personal
Persian
pernicious
perky
perilous

Exercise 5: Latin roots

The following groups of words share the same Latin root. Identify the root, and work out the primary meaning of the root:

1. *reverse, converse, diverse, inverse, averse*
2. *transfer, conifer, referral, offer, preference*
3. *abduct, educate, deduce, seduce, induce*
4. *somnambulist, preamble, ambulance, perambulator*
5. *cursory, incur, occur, excursion, precursor, concurrent*

Exercise 6: Word formation strategies

The following neologisms have all been used in advertising, the media or social networking in recent years. Identify their word class, and the word formation strategies used to form them:

people-ready	(to describe businesses targeted in a software advertisement)
microbuffers	(in a toothpaste advertisement)
Rooneyesque	(to describe something done in the manner of Wayne Rooney, the footballer)
volcanicity	(a quality resulting from drinking a certain mineral water from volcanic rocks)
diplo language	(used by a television journalist reporting on diplomats discussing the Middle East crisis)
hairapy	(the treatment provided by a specific brand of shampoo)
retweet	(a forwarded tweet or the act of forwarding a tweet on Twitter)
tweetheart	(a romantic partner from a relationship developed on Twitter)
Merkozy	(a combined name for the German Chancellor Angela Merkel and the former French President Nicolas Sarkozy)
Arab Spring	(a series of uprisings starting in December 2010 in Arab nations in North Africa and the Middle East)

LEXICAL FRAMEWORKS: SUGGESTIONS FOR FURTHER READING

Language textbooks

Aitchison, Jean (2012) *Words in the Mind*, 4th edn (Oxford: Blackwell)
Explores how word meanings are acquired, stored and deployed, as well as looking at speakers' creativity in lexical use. The morphological make-up of words is also examined. A very accessible text, with lots of interesting illustrations and diagrams.

Bauer, Laurie (1983) *English Word-formation* (Cambridge: Cambridge University Press)
A standard text which gives a detailed profile of word-formation strategies, but which goes on to relate morphology to other levels of language and to explore theoretical issues.

Baugh, Albert C. and Thomas Cable (2012) *A History of the English Language*, 6th edn (London: Routledge)
A highly regarded history with a detailed focus on lexis, and including a survey of American English.

Hughes, Geoffrey (2000) *A History of English Words* (Oxford: Blackwell)
A fascinating and detailed study of the development of the English lexicon, ideal for readers interested in where words come from. It also gives a valuable outline of more recent changes.

Jeffries, Lesley (1998) *Meaning in English* (Basingstoke: Macmillan)
Chapters 3 and 4 of this textbook are particularly useful in exploring word meaning in terms of morphology, collocation and syntactic structure.

Katamba, Francis (2005) *English Words*, 2nd edn (London: Routledge)
Many aspects of lexis are dealt with in this book, including the English spelling system. There is an appealing range of examples to consider.

Minkova, Donka and Robert Stockwell (2009) *English Words: History and Structure*, 2nd edn (Cambridge: Cambridge University Press)
An historical approach to word formation is complemented by a consideration of semantic and phonological aspects of words. Packed with useful examples and word lists.

Reference books

Greenbaum, Sidney (1996) *The Oxford English Grammar* (Oxford: Oxford University Press)
A very detailed grammar, systematically arranged in small sections with a host of examples taken from the International Corpus of English. Sections 4, 8 and 9 provide information about word classes, word meanings, and word formation.

The Longman Dictionary of Contemporary English, 5th edn (2009) (Harlow: Pearson Longman)
An excellent dictionary primarily aimed at speakers learning English as a second language, but ideal for students wishing to explore English lexis in use.

The Oxford Dictionary of Synonyms and Antonyms, 2nd edn (2007) (Oxford: Oxford University Press)
Composed chiefly in the style of a thesaurus, this is a useful dictionary for exploring the extent of English vocabulary and meanings. It also contains some interesting word lists, for example of phobias and male/female animals.

Internet resources

blog.oxforddictionaries.com
The OxfordWords blog site run by Oxford University Press contains a wealth of articles on English vocabulary, ranging from word origins to new trends in language use. Topical subjects are also included.

www.bbc.co.uk/voices
A superb site (not updated since December 2011 but available for reference) which contains a fascinating survey of lexical variation in the British Isles.

www.collinsdictionary.com
A free online dictionary which also includes a thesaurus and various bilingual dictionaries. Pronunciation available with one click. Based on the vast Collins corpus of written and spoken language in use.

www.oed.com
The Oxford English Dictionary online is an invaluable resource, which is expanding all the time. It now includes an historical thesaurus, for instance.

Although full access to the dictionary requires a subscription, most university and public libraries provide access for their members.

www.worldwidewords.org

A fun and accessible site compiled by Michael Quinion, who wrote many of the entries for *The Oxford Dictionary of New Words*. The site explores the history of many words and phrases as well as current usage.

Part III
GRAMMATICAL FRAMEWORKS

FRAMEWORKS

4 Inflections

4.1 INFLECTIONS AS AN ASPECT OF GRAMMAR

Grammar is the set of rules of any given language that enable us to construct any sentence in that language which we recognise to be well-formed. In other words and to reiterate a point made in Section 1.1, the grammar of English would enable us to construct a correct sentence such as *once upon a time three ugly frogs turned into handsome princes* but would prevent us from forming a sentence such as **ugly three frog once turn into princes upon a time handsome*. From this example, you can see that the rules of grammar essentially deal with two aspects of language construction. On the one hand, they deal with the principles of stringing words together to form larger units of construction such as phrases, clauses and sentences. This aspect of grammar which is concerned with word order is called **syntax**. (Chapters 5, 6 and 7 are about syntax.) In addition to the **syntactic rules** in our grammatical knowledge, there is another set of rules which tell us how to adapt words according to the grammatical context in which they occur. For instance, in the well-formed sentence above you can see that, because there is more than one frog and therefore more than one prince, *frog* and *prince* are both in the **plural form** and this is indicated in writing by adding <-s> to the spelling. One of the things which we recognise to be wrong in the ill-formed sentence is that the noun *frog* is not in the plural form. Similarly, the well-formed sentence uses the form *turned* to indicate the past tense of the verb whereas the *-ed* ending of *turned* has been omitted in the ill-formed sentence. Again this strikes us as odd because we expect the past tense in the context of *once upon a time*. Endings such as the plural marking on *frog* and *prince* and the past tense ending on *turn* are known as **inflections**.

Grammar is subdivided into syntax and inflections. Because inflections are part of the internal structure of a word, they can also be classified as a branch of morphology. In Chapter 3 we looked closely at lexical morphology – the aspect which deals with the formation of new words or lexemes. In this chapter we will be looking at **inflectional morphology**. Figure 4.1 shows the relationship between grammar and morphology. The term 'grammar' is occasionally

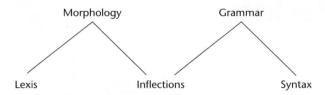

Figure 4.1 The relationship between morphology and grammar

misapplied. Sometimes speakers believe that 'their grammar isn't very good' or 'English doesn't have any grammar'. The truth is that all languages have grammar as it would be impossible to construct any well-formed sentences in any language without it. It is true to say though that the grammar of each language is different even though languages share grammatical similarities to some degree or another. Similarly, if a speaker genuinely wasn't very good at grammar then their sentences would be muddled as in the earlier example of *ugly three frog once turn into princes upon a time handsome.* No one with normal development actually speaks like this. In fact, phenomenally, all speakers of a language are subconsciously in possession of all the grammatical rules they need to know in order to speak that language naturally. Speakers of different dialects will have some variations of course but all dialects are governed by grammatical principles.

☐ **lexical morphology** ⇨ 3.1, 3.2, 3.3
☐ **grammatical variation** ⇨ 12.5, 12.6, 12.7

4.2   INFLECTIONS IN CONTEMPORARY ENGLISH

We saw above that inflections are a branch of grammar and that by inflections we mean endings which we add to a word to indicate aspects such as past tense or plural. One of the most important things about inflections is that they are not used to create a new word or lexeme. In Chapter 3 we looked at how suffixes such as *-ism* or *-ment* can be added to existing bases to form new words. So, for example, speakers have recently added *-ism* to *age* and so now we have both the noun *age* and the noun *ageism* in our lexicon. To the verb *manage* we have added *-ment* to give us both *manage* and *management*. When we add an inflection to a base, however, it does not create a new word. For example, no one would suggest that *mountain* and *mountains* in the following two sentences are separate lexical items:

> *The brave man climbed the dangerous mountain*
> *The brave man climbed three dangerous mountains*

In the second of these two examples, the inflection represented by <-*s*> has been added to *mountain* to indicate plurality. In Standard English it is obligatory to indicate when a noun is plural even though this might be inferred from the context since here there are *three* mountains. Inflections are used then to give us more grammatical information about words. They can be used to indicate singular or plural – what is sometimes known as **number** – and to indicate tense. They can also be used to indicate other features, as we shall see shortly. In Chapter 2 we considered how every word has some kind of abstract existence which can be realised in either speech or writing. This abstract form is a **lexeme**. When considering inflections, it can also be helpful to use the notion of a **stem**. A stem is what remains of a word when any inflections are removed from it. In other words, inflections are added to the stem of a word. So *frogs* is made up of the stem *frog* and the inflection -*s*, while *turned* is made up of the stem *turn* and the inflection -*ed*. (A stem is not quite the same as the root we discussed in Chapter 3 since the root can be less than the stem.)

If this book were about **Old English** (the English spoken from about AD 450 to about AD 1100) rather than contemporary English then the content of this chapter would be rather different and more extensive because English used to have far more inflections than it has now. The reason why English lost the majority of its inflections is not of relevance here but you might like to consider English in the light of any other languages you speak or are learning and compare the range of inflections in each language. If you are studying historical English then you will almost certainly come across some of the lost inflections.

In contemporary English there are only a handful of regular inflections in addition to quite a number of irregular ones. Inflections can be found on nouns and verbs, on some adjectives and adverbs, and – in a manner of speaking – on some pronouns. Inflections, then, occur on all open classes of words but only on pronouns as far as the closed classes are concerned.

> ☐ **lexemes** ⇨ 2.1
> ☐ **open and closed classes of words** ⇨ 2.3
> ☐ **suffixes** ⇨ 3.4

4.3 NOUN INFLECTIONS

Nouns can be inflected to show plurality and also to indicate possession. One interesting feature of common nouns, however, is that they do not all have a plural form. Consider the following examples:

An exciting <u>game</u> was taking place on the beach
Some exciting <u>games</u> were taking place on the beach

> *In schools, <u>hockey</u> takes place in the autumn term*
> *In schools, *<u>hockeys</u> take place in the autumn term*

The noun *hockey* does not have a plural form which is why **hockeys* sounds strange. There is quite a considerable number of nouns (both abstract – such as *misery, hatred* and *amazement* – and concrete – such as *hockey, music,* and *furniture*) which have no plural form. Because these nouns cannot be made plural and therefore their referents cannot be counted, they are known as **non-count nouns**. By contrast, nouns which have a plural form are **count nouns**. (Also there are one or two nouns which look plural because they end in <-s> but are in fact non-count nouns. These include *billiards, physics* and *politics*.)

There are also some nouns which don't fit comfortably into either of these categories. First, there are those which exist in the plural only. Examples of these include *trousers* and *scissors:*

> *The trousers are ready to wear*
> * *The trouser is in need of repair*
> *The scissors are blunt*
> * *The scissor is blunt*

A second group of nouns which are neither clearly count nor non-count nouns is the group of **aggregate nouns**. These are nouns which refer to entities made up of several parts. Some of these, like *trousers* and *scissors,* have no singular form, as with *goods* and *dregs* in the following examples:

> *The goods are ready for collection*
> * *The good is ready for collection*
> *The dregs in a bottle of wine taste unpleasant*
> * *The dreg in a bottle of wine tastes unpleasant.*

There are also some aggregate nouns which look singular but take a plural form of the verb:

> *The police have surrounded the building*
> * *The police has surrounded the building*
> *The cattle are lowing*
> * *The cattle is lowing*

Aggregate nouns such as these should not be confused with **collective nouns**. 'Collective' is a semantic term for nouns which refer to groups (usually of people or animals) but grammatically they are count nouns since they have both singular and plural forms. *Family* and *herd* are examples of collective nouns:

> *The family is (are) spending Christmas at home*
> *Three families are going on holiday together*
> *The herd is (are) grazing in the field by the river*
> *The herds are doing very well this year*

Both *family* and *herd* have plural forms. Interestingly, we sometimes use the plural form of the verb (*are*, in this case) with a singular collective noun as a concession to our notion that the noun refers to several units.

Some nouns have both a count form and a non-count one. This depends on the particular meaning of the noun which is being employed. *Wine* is a good example of this. When we talk of wine in the generic sense of a drink made from grapes then *wine* is a non-count noun:

> *Wine is an alcoholic drink made from grapes*
> * *Wines are alcoholic drinks made from grapes*

However, when we talk of different varieties of wine, then *wine* is a count noun: *Australian wines are as enjoyable as French ones.*

When they take the plural form, count nouns have either a regular or an irregular ending. Here are some examples of nouns which take the regular plural ending, sometimes known as the *-s* **plural**:

singular form	plural form
cake	*cakes*
bun	*buns*
gas	*gases*

All three examples here take a regular and predictable ending although this ending shows itself in different forms. In writing, some nouns add not <-s> word-finally but <-es>. This is driven by the fact that when they are pronounced in the plural, they actually add an extra syllable. It is impossible to say *gas-s*, so the noun becomes *gas-es* with two syllables rather than one. A vowel has been added to make the plural form pronounceable and distinct from the singular form. In speech we sometimes add the sound /s/ to make a noun plural (as in *cakes*) and sometimes /z/ (as in *buns*, which is pronounced 'bunz'). Whether we pronounce /s/ or /z/ depends on the consonant which precedes the inflectional ending, a process known as **assimilation**. In effect, though, these are all variant forms of the *-s* plural. (This form is actually a bound morpheme with different allomorphs.)

Table 4.1 Irregular plural forms

Irregular inflection type	Explanation	Singular / plural examples
zero inflection	the singular form is the same as the plural form	*sheep / sheep*
vowel mutation	the vowel within the word changes	*tooth / teeth* *mouse / mice* *man / men*
voicing of final consonant	a regular -s plural is added but also the last consonant in the stem is pronounced with a vibration of the vocal cords, changing the quality of the sound	*sheaf / sheaves* *hoof / hooves* *bath / baths*
irregular plural inflection	a handful of nouns retain an Old English inflectional form	*child / children* *ox / oxen* *brother / brethren*
foreign plurals	nouns which have come to English from other languages sometimes retain the regular plural form of their original language – although the regular plural form of English may also be used	Latin: *stimulus / stimuli* *antenna / antennae* *matrix / matrices* Greek: *phenomenon / phenomena* Hebrew: *cherub / cherubim* French: *gateau / gateaux*

There are a number of nouns which form plurals in other ways. Table 4.1 illustrates the range of irregular endings and gives some examples.

We now turn our attention to the **possessive form** of nouns. In English, possession can be denoted by an inflectional ending, and in written English this is most typically indicated by <-'s>. In the following example two nouns – the proper noun *Susan* and the common noun *dog* – have possessive inflections: *Susan's brother was preparing the dog's dinner.* Here, both *Susan* and *dog* take the possessive form. When we talk about the possessive form or possessive inflection, however, we are not always referring strictly to the ownership of one person or thing by another person or thing. For instance, in a phrase such as *a hard day's work* the day doesn't possess the work: instead, the implication is that the work lasted a day. We need to make a distinction therefore between the possessive inflection and a possessive meaning. Sometimes in English we use an *of*-construction rather than a possessive inflection, so we might talk about either *the journey's end* or *the end of the journey.* Sometimes, we wouldn't use the possessive inflection at all, so we might refer to *the window of the kitchen* or to *the kitchen window* but never to *the kitchen's window.*

Possessive inflections can be added to both singular and plural nouns. Above, the examples are all of singular nouns. Plural nouns can also take this form although in practice the possessive form is often not discernible because its spoken form is identical to the plural form. However, nouns with irregular plural endings can take overt possessive inflections as in for example *the children's playground* or *the teeth's whiteness.* In writing we indicate a plural which has a possessive quality by using an apostrophe: *the dogs' dinners.* It is also possible for the possessive inflection to apply to a word group rather than an individual noun. For instance, in

> *The teacher spoke to Chris and Jonathan's mother about their behaviour*

it is most likely the mother of <u>Chris and Jonathan</u> who was addressed (as opposed to someone called Chris as well as the mother of Jonathan), even though the inflection is attached to the noun *Jonathan.* (If the names were reversed, the inflection would of course be attached to *Chris.*) In effect, then, the inflection applies to the entire group *Chris and Jonathan*, rather than to *Jonathan* alone, a feature known as a **group possessive**.

Another term which is sometimes used when discussing noun inflections is **case**. This is a traditional grammatical term used particularly in languages where there is a fuller range of noun inflections than there is now in English. These inflections indicate aspects such as whether the noun is the subject of the sentence (the **nominative** case), the object of the sentence (the **accusative** case), or the possessor of something (the **genitive** case, hence **group genitive** as an alternative term for group possessive) to give just three examples. In modern English 'case' is a less appropriate term for talking about noun inflections. However, some linguists do refer to the possessive inflection in English as the genitive or genitive case. You might also come across the term **common case** which refers to any noun not in the possessive form, be it singular or plural.

☐ **nouns as a word class** ⇨ 2.4
☐ **morphemes** ⇨ 3.2
☐ **allomorphs** ⇨ 3.2
☐ **assimilation** ⇨ 10.6

4.4 VERB INFLECTIONS

We saw in Section 4.3 that there are two types of inflection that can be added to nouns: plural inflections and possessive inflections. Verbs are subject to a wider range of inflections although this range is still very limited in comparison with languages such as French and German. When we were looking at the plural forms of nouns we saw that there were both regular and irregular inflectional forms, and this is also true of verbs. We will begin with the regular forms.

The uninflected stem of the verb is known as the **base form** of the verb. This form is also referred to as the **infinitive** and we make a distinction between the **to-infinitive** (as in *to write*) and the **bare infinitive**, which does not contain the particle *to*. The base form of the verb may be varied by the addition of four regular inflections. These regular inflections are found only with lexical verbs. (The primary auxiliary verbs have irregular inflectional forms while the modal auxiliaries do not inflect at all and this of course sets them apart from lexical verbs.)

The first of these verb inflections is the *-s* inflection which marks the third person singular of the present tense as the following **paradigm** (or inflectional set) shows:

singular	first person	*I walk*
	second person	*you walk*
	third person	*he/she/it walk<u>s</u>*
plural	first person	*we walk*
	second person	*you walk*
	third person	*they walk*

If this **conjugation** (namely, this set of verb forms) were translated into French, for example, the verb would have a different inflectional ending for every person. In Standard English, however, the base form is used in the present tense for every person except the third person in the singular. (Like some of the irregular plural noun inflections, this is an historical hangover.) This inflection is used for all verbs, even those which have irregular forms elsewhere.

The relationship between the verb form and the subject which precedes it is one of **concord** (or **agreement**). In other words, the person and number of the subject controls the form the verb takes. In most lexical verbs in English, this is apparent only in the present tense, where the use of the third person singular requires the *-s* inflection. Otherwise the base form is used:

first person singular subject	*I like listening to Mozart*
third person singular subject	**<u>Miriam/she</u> like listening to Mozart*
	<u>Miriam/she</u> likes listening to Mozart

The second verb inflection found in English is again found on all verbs, whether or not they also have irregular inflectional forms. This is the inflection *-ing:* the base form of the verb plus the *-ing* inflection is known as the *-ing* **participle**. It occurs in various grammatical contexts which we will return to in later chapters but examples include:

> Fred was <u>walking</u> to the shops
> I am <u>hoping</u> to go to Australia soon
> <u>Following</u> in his father's footsteps was important to Bob
> He was sorry for <u>keeping</u> them <u>waiting</u>

The third regular verb inflection is the *-ed* inflection which is used to construct the past tense. Examples of regular verbs using this inflection include: *they walked, I gazed, she hoped* and *we admired*. The *-ed* inflection is sometimes realised in pronunciation as a /t/ and sometimes as a /d/ depending on the sound which precedes it.

The fourth regular verb inflection is the *-ed* **participle** inflection. It takes the same form as the regular past tense inflection but we make a distinction between these two inflections because their functions are different and also because irregular verbs may have different forms for the past tense and the *-ed* participle. Examples of the *-ed* participle might include

> They have <u>walked</u> three miles today
> Jane's painting was much <u>admired</u> by her friends
> <u>Considered</u> carefully, it wasn't a very good idea

To summarise then, regular lexical verbs have five forms. They either occur in the base form without any inflectional ending – and this is sometimes described as **zero inflection** – or they take one of four inflectional endings as Table 4.2 shows. As we observed earlier, all lexical verbs can take a regular *-ing* participle inflection. Similarly, all lexical verbs (with the exception of *be, have* and *do*) take the regular *-s* inflection to denote the third person singular in the present tense, even though the pronunciation of this inflection varies depending on the sound which precedes it. Either the regular *-ed* past tense inflection or the regular *-ed* participle ending, however, may occur in irregular verbs, although often both these inflections will be irregular. We will look next at how irregular verbs form the past tense and the *-ed* participle.

Let us begin by comparing an irregular verb, such as *take,* with the regular verb *walk* which we used above. Table 4.3 shows that the irregular verb *take* has a different form for the *-ed* participle from the form it has for the *-ed* past tense. Neither of these forms could have been predicted from the base form, hence the irregularity. Not all irregular verbs are irregular in the same way, however. *Take* has two irregular forms – one for the past tense and one for the *-ed* participle – but other combinations are possible, as Table 4.4 illustrates.

Table 4.2   Regular verb inflections

Form	Grammatical function	Example
-s	third person singular present tense	*she walks*
-ing	-ing participle	*she is walking*
-ed	simple past tense	*she walked*
-ed	-ed participle	*she has walked*

Table 4.3   A comparison of the inflections of *walk* and *take*

Base form	*walk*	*take*
-s	*walks*	*takes*
-ing participle	*walking*	*taking*
-ed past tense	*walked*	*took*
-ed participle	*walked*	*taken*

Table 4.4   Patterns of irregular verbs

Base form	-ed past tense		-ed participle
	regular	irregular	
show	*showed*		*shown*
make		*made*	*made*
lose		*lost*	*lost*
speak		*spoke*	*spoken*
swim		*swam*	*swum*
hurt		*hurt*	*hurt*

Irregular verbs, then, take various patterns. Some, like *show,* retain the regular past tense form but have an irregular -*ed* participle form. Others have either an irregular past tense which is identical to the irregular -*ed* participle form or an irregular past tense and a different -*ed* participle form. Some verbs have the base form for both. Some verbs change their vowel in their irregular forms (a feature known as **vowel mutation**) while others take an -*en* instead of an -*ed* inflection for the -*ed* participle.

In Section 2.10 we saw that English has three primary auxiliary verbs: *be, have,* and *do.* These are used to construct different aspects and voices in the verb phrase, although they can also occur as the lexical verb in a verb phrase. All three verbs are irregular but *be* is the most irregular verb in English. Table 4.5 compares the different forms of these three verbs. As you can see from the table, *be* is highly irregular in that it has three different present tense forms (all other verbs have only two) and two different past tense forms (all other verbs have

Table 4.5 The irregular primary verbs *be, have* and *do*

		be	*have*	*do*
base form		be	have	do
present tense				
singular	1st person	am	have	do
	2nd person	are	have	do
	3rd person	is	has	does
plural	1st/2nd/3rd person	are	have	do
past tense				
singular	1st person	was	had	did
	2nd person	were	had	did
	3rd person	was	had	did
plural	1st/2nd/3rd person	were	had	did
-ing participle		being	having	doing
-ed participle		been	had	done

only one) according to person. When looking at the various types of irregular verb in Table 4.4, you may have observed that despite the unpredictable forms of some verbs, a similarity between their different forms was still identifiable (particularly when you consider pronunciation in preference to spelling in the case of forms like *buy* and *bought*). However, with the highly irregular verb *be* (whose irregularity is the result of its historical origins in several different verbs) it is not possible to discern any family likeness between most of its forms: *be, are, am, is, was* and *were* appear fundamentally different and it would certainly not be accurate to claim that *am,* for example, is an inflectional form of *be*. When a particular form of a word, in this case a verb, is supplied by an unrelated form rather than by an inflectional ending, this is known as **suppletion.**

☐ **lexical verbs** ⇨ 2.5
☐ **auxiliary verbs** ⇨ 2.10
☐ **verb phrases** ⇨ 5.3

4.5   ADJECTIVE AND ADVERB INFLECTIONS

We saw in Chapter 2 that one of the qualities which both adjectives and adverbs share is their ability to be graded. What this means is that we can indicate to what extent a particular quality exists. For instance, we might say that a person is *tall,* or *extremely tall.* We might say someone ran *quickly* or that they ran *incredibly quickly.* Gradability, then, is a typical feature of adjectives and also of a lot of adverbs, particularly adverbs of manner. As well as grading adjectives and adverbs in this way, we can also use them to compare one person or thing with another. This is often done using the inflections *-er* and *-est* as the following examples show:

adjective *tall*		*Rosie is tall*
		Esther and Jenni are taller
		Laura is tallest
adverb *fast*		*Rosie ran fast*
		Esther and Jenni ran faster
		Laura ran fastest

The forms of adjectives and adverbs which have no inflectional endings are known as **absolute** forms. The *-er* inflection on an adjective or adverb gives the **comparative** form, and the *-est* inflection gives the **superlative** form.

Not all adjectives take the comparative and superlative inflections. If the word in question consists of three syllables or more, then it will probably construct the comparative by using the premodifying adverb *more* and the superlative by using the premodifying adverb *most*. Adverbs (as distinct from adjectives) which end in *-ly* all use *more* and *most*:

	absolute	comparative	superlative
adjectives	*tall*	*taller*	*tallest*
	beautiful	**beautifuller*	**beautifullest*
	beautiful	*more beautiful*	*most beautiful*
adverbs	*fast*	*faster*	*fastest*
	quickly	**quicklier*	**quickliest*
	quickly	*more quickly*	*most quickly*

We have seen in our discussion of the inflections of nouns and verbs that there are always some irregular forms. This is also true of adverbs and adjectives where suppletive forms often occur for the comparative and superlative. Table 4.6 shows the irregular forms of some key adjectives and adverbs.

Table 4.6 Irregular forms of adjectives and adverbs

Adjectives			Adverbs		
absolute	comparative	superlative	absolute	comparative	superlative
good	*better*	*best*	*well*	*better*	*best*
bad	*worse*	*worst*	*badly*	*worse*	*worst*
			much	*more*	*most*
			little	*less*	*least*

> ☐ **adjectives** ⇨ 2.6
> ☐ **adverbs** ⇨ 2.7

4.6 PRONOUN INFLECTIONS

So far, all the inflections we have identified and discussed have occurred on lexical words – namely, nouns, verbs, adjectives and adverbs. Inflections in the truest sense of the term do not occur on function words, but the discussion of inflections would be incomplete without mentioning the occurrence of suppletion in some personal pronouns. In Chapter 2 we saw how the personal pronouns take different forms which we refer to as subjective and objective forms. They are reproduced below:

		subjective	objective
singular	first person	*I*	*me*
	second person	*you*	*you*
	third person	*he*	*him*
		she	*her*
		it	*it*
plural	first person	*we*	*us*
	second person	*you*	*you*
	third person	*they*	*them*

The terms subjective and objective are derived from the position in which the pronouns typically appear: the subjective form normally appears in the subject position before the verb and the objective form normally occurs in the object position after the verb. So, the first person singular personal pronoun would normally be *I* before the verb and *me* after it:

> *I saw Pedro*
> *Pedro saw *I*
> *Pedro saw me*

However, in informal English we sometimes use the objective form in subject position, usually when it is joined with another noun or pronoun:

> *Me and Jane are great friends*
> *Jane and her went to Wimbledon together.*

We discussed in Section 4.3 the question of case in contemporary English and why it is not an especially appropriate term to use in relation to nouns. In Old English and in some other modern languages case can be applied to personal pronouns. In contemporary English it would be inappropriate to talk about subject and object cases for pronouns since the use of the different forms is not dictated strictly by position or function but partly by context and level of formality. It is more appropriate to refer to subjective and objective forms since these terms refer to typical rather than invariable occurrence.

Finally, in Section 2.8 we noted that there are several different types of pronouns, including demonstrative pronouns. Demonstrative pronouns might also be said to have inflected forms for the plural, although their irregularity is evident:

singular	plural
this	*these*
that	*those*

☐ **pronouns** ⇨ 2.8
☐ **contemporary English** ⇨ 4.2
☐ **case** ⇨ 4.3

5 Phrases

5.1 WHAT IS A PHRASE?

At the beginning of the previous chapter we established that grammar can be subdivided into two areas: **syntax** and **inflections**. Inflections are the grammatical endings which occur on open class words (and on some pronouns) and which give information about, for example, tense and number. An inflection is part of the internal structure of a word. Syntax, on the other hand, operates on a level higher than the word since it is concerned with the rules by which words are combined into larger units. It is possible to identify three larger units of construction, beginning with the smallest:

> phrases
> clauses
> sentences

This chapter and the following two chapters deal with these units of construction and therefore cover the range of syntactic rules which enable us to construct any well-formed sentence in the language. Chapter 8 shows you some of the strategies used to combine sentences into texts – what is known as **discourse**.

To illustrate what we mean by a phrase, take a look at the following example:

> *The black Labrador was chewing a juicy bone very noisily*

One way of looking at this sentence is to regard it as a linear sequence of words: *the* precedes *black, black* precedes *Labrador, Labrador* precedes *was* and so on. Although mental syntactic rules enable us to place words in an appropriate order the rules do not operate simply in this linear fashion. Initially, the rules operate on a phrase level, then on a clause level and then on a sentence level. So we need to approach our example not as a sequence of individual words but as a sequence of word groups or **phrases**. (Some grammars, incidentally, prefer the term 'group' to 'phrase'.)

In Chapter 1, we noted that if speakers are asked to divide the words in a sentence into groups, we can predict that they will all do it in the same way:

the black Labrador + was chewing + a juicy bone + very noisily

We would not expect anyone to group the words like this, for example:

the black + Labrador was + chewing a juicy + bone very noisily

The reason for this phenomenon is that we instinctively know that words are grouped into phrases and that these are the basic building blocks for larger syntactic constructions. Our instinctive ability to identify phrases is linked with an awareness of how clauses are structured. Confronted with an example such as:

was chewing a juicy bone very noisily

we recognise that information is missing about who was chewing. In other words, the **subject** slot is empty, and it can be filled by a phrase. Phrases are the building blocks of clauses because they fill clause slots in this way.

The example of *The black Labrador was chewing a juicy bone very noisily* consists of four phrases. If, having asked speakers to identify the phrases in this example, you asked them to select what they considered to be the key word in each phrase, there would be general agreement on this:

the black <u>Labrador</u>
was <u>chewing</u>
a juicy <u>bone</u>
very <u>noisily</u>

The key words have been underlined. These key words are known as **head words** or **heads**. They are the lexical items which are central to the phrase in the sense that some crucial information would be missing without the head word and the phrase would seem structurally incomplete. This is illustrated by the fact that the head words themselves, placed alone in sequence, normally result in a skeleton sentence which still makes a certain amount of sense and which captures the essence of the full example:

Labrador chewing bone noisily

In the four examples above, the head word occurs at the end of the phrase. This is often, but not always the case as we will see when we look at the full range of possibilities for structuring phrases.

There are five types of phrase:

noun phrase	abbreviated as NP
verb phrase	abbreviated as VP
adjective phrase	abbreviated as AdjP
adverb phrase	abbreviated as AdvP
prepositional phrase	abbreviated as PP

You will notice that each of the four open word classes (noun, verb, adjective and adverb) has an associated phrase type. Prepositions are the only closed class which has an associated phrase type, and prepositional phrases differ in kind from the other four types.

Normally, in order to identify a phrase type, you need to begin by identifying the head word. If the head word is a noun, then the phrase is a noun phrase; if it's a verb, then the phrase is a verb phrase and so on. However, this approach doesn't operate in quite the same way for a prepositional phrase, although a preposition will still be the head word.

Another important point to make about phrases is that, with the exception of prepositional phrases, they may actually consist of a single lexical item. They do not have to consist of at least two words. There are two main reasons why we should treat individual words as phrases. The first is that, given the basic principle that words group together to form phrases, we would not wish to have any words unaccounted for on that level of a clause's structure. This would not make for a very watertight or cohesive set of syntactic rules. Secondly, all phrases have the potential to be expanded: the head word may stand alone, or it may be **premodified** or **postmodified** by other elements. Consider this example:

Snakes appear dangerous

Here, it is impossible to divide the words into groups. What we have in fact are three single-word phrases. *Snakes* is a noun, so it is the head of a noun phrase, *appear* is a verb so it is the head of a verb phrase, *dangerous* is an adjective so it is the head of an adjective phrase. What this means is that the structure of this clause in phrasal terms is:

NP + VP + AdjP

It is possible to expand each of these phrases so that they become more than a single word:

NP	VP	AdjP
British grass snakes	*may appear*	*rather dangerous*

As mentioned above, a prepositional phrase differs from the other four types in that a preposition cannot stand alone as a phrase. This is linked to its status as a grammatical word rather than a lexical word.

In Section 1.5 we noted how linguists use different types of brackets to enclose various linguistic features or units. If you wish to mark off the phrases in a clause or sentence then you can use square brackets, so that the above example will look like this:

[*British grass snakes* $_{NP}$]   [*may appear* $_{VP}$]   [*rather dangerous* $_{AdjP}$]

You will also see that each bracket has been labelled to show what type of phrase it is. Bracketing isn't the only way of breaking down an example for analysis. Some linguists prefer to use tree diagrams and we will be looking at this method later in this chapter and in Chapter 7.

In the following sections, we will examine each phrase type in turn. We will be spending more time on noun phrases and verb phrases since they are typically more central and more complex than the other types. This is partly to do with their function in clause structures. All phrases – whatever their form – fulfil a function within a clause. This is something we will consider in Chapter 6.

5.2 NOUN PHRASES

A noun phrase may consist of a single lexical item. On the other hand, noun phrases have the capacity to be long and complex – more so than other phrase types. The following two examples illustrate this contrast:

NP	VP	AdjP
Doughnuts	*are*	*really fattening*
These large sugary <u>doughnuts</u> filled with jam and cream	*are*	*really fattening*

The second noun phrase is much longer, with additional elements occurring both before and after the head noun. Elsewhere in our discussions we have seen that the internal order of elements in a linguistic unit is fixed rather than random. For example, we noted in Section 3.4 that there is a restriction on the occurrence of affixes within the structure of a derived word. Similarly, noun phrases have an internal structure which dictates where additional elements occur in relation to the head noun. There are three possible positions for these elements. All four positions (the fourth being the head noun itself) are illustrated in the complex example given above and repeated below:

determiner	premodification	head noun	postmodification
these	*large sugary*	*doughnuts*	*filled with jam and cream*

Determiners are discussed in some detail in Section 2.9. They can be subdivided into three categories: predeterminers, central determiners and postdeterminers. Determiners are not obligatory but if they do occur they will be at the beginning of the noun phrase. Furthermore, determiners only occur in noun phrases.

There are a range of elements which can occur in a premodifying position. Most typically, premodifiers will be adjectives (including deverbal adjectives). It is possible to premodify a head noun with more than one adjective as in *large sugary doughnuts*. In theory there is no limit as to how many adjectives could premodify a head noun provided their meanings do not contradict each other, but in reality it is unlikely that there will be more than two or three at most, and in speech premodifiers are used far less than in writing:

It was a foolish, dangerous, expensive idea
? It was a foolish, dangerous, expensive, pointless, inopportune idea

When more than one adjective appears in the premodifying position, an ordering process may come into play. So if *a suitcase* was *blue, large* and *old*, speakers are likely to refer to it as *a large old blue suitcase,* placing the adjectives in the order of size, then age, then finally colour. Other combinations seem unnatural: **a blue old large suitcase, ?an old large blue suitcase, *a large blue old suitcase*. Gradable adjectives will occur before non-gradable ones, with the non-gradable adjectives often categorising rather than describing the noun. So woollen, which is non-gradable, would be preceded by *pretty*, which is gradable: *a pretty woollen dress* not **a woollen pretty dress.*

Nouns as well as adjectives can precede head nouns. The noun may be either a common or a proper noun. Here are some examples:

determiner	premodifying noun	head noun
a	*leather*	*suitcase*
several	*party*	*guests*
	printer	*cartridges*
the	*London*	*experience*
	Gucci	*fashion*

Additionally, nouns in the possessive form – again, both proper and common nouns – can also premodify head nouns:

	possessive noun	head noun
(the)	*children's*	*playground*
(a)	*composer's*	*music*
	plovers'	*eggs*
	London's	*churches*

One point to note here though is that the indefinite article which occurs in *a composer's music* belongs not to music but to *composer's*. We can demonstrate this by rewriting the phrase as an *of*-construction:

> *the music of a composer*
> * *a music of a composer*

Because music is a non-count noun (and has no plural form) it is impossible to precede it with an indefinite article. Whereas it is not possible to tell whether *the* in *the children's playground* belongs to *children's* or *playground,* in *a composer's music,* the *a* must belong to *composer* because it is syntactically impossible for it to belong to music.

So far we have looked at the premodification of head nouns by adjectives, by other nouns and by nouns in the possessive form. We have seen that, when more than one premodifying adjective occurs, there is likely to be a prescribed sequence for these adjectives. Further, when the head noun is premodified by more than one type of premodifier, again there is a given order in which these elements will occur. For example, suppose a head noun *music* were to be premodified by the adjective *difficult,* by the noun *piano* and by the possessive noun plus definite article *the composer's,* then the elements would take the following order:

> *the composer's   difficult   piano   music*

Any other combination would not seem natural. Premodifying nouns occur closer to the head noun than any adjectives because they typically categorise rather than qualify the head noun: in other words, *piano music* is a specific type of music but *difficult music* can be of any type. Possessive forms precede any premodifying adjectives and nouns.

Occasionally, elements other than adjectives or nouns may premodify a head noun. An adverb, for example, could occur in this position as in *the then headteacher,* and so could a short sentence such as *do as you please* in *their do-as-you-please attitude.* These are exceptions, though, and it is far more likely that any premodifying elements will be adjectives or nouns.

Finally, a word needs to be said about the premodification of premodifying elements. In the following noun phrase, the head noun *invitation* is premodified by the adjective *nice: a nice invitation*. It is possible to qualify the adjective *nice* with the adverb *rather* as in *a rather nice invitation*. It is clear that *rather* is attached to *nice* and not to *invitation* as it is not possible to remove *nice:* *a rather invitation*. This is not dissimilar to the observation we made earlier regarding *a composer's music* where we noted that *a* was attached not to the head noun *music* but to the premodifying possessive noun *composer's*. In addition, the fact that *nice* can be premodified in this way leads us to conclude that *nice* is itself a phrase (it can be expanded to *rather nice*) and that we are dealing here with a phrase within a phrase. We will return to this point later.

Let us now move on to the postmodification of head nouns. This is a more complex matter than the premodification of head nouns since there is again a range of items which can fulfil this function and, in addition, the postmodification has the potential to be more complex, as in this example where the head noun is underlined:

the <u>proposal</u> *for a new building which the committee put forward last week*

Here, the head noun *proposal* is postmodified by a prepositional phrase *for a new building* and by a **relative clause** *which the committee put forward last week*.

Head nouns can be postmodified by both phrases and clauses. It is very common for prepositional phrases to postmodify head nouns but adverb phrases occasionally occur **postnominally** (after the noun) when referring to time or place as in *the meeting yesterday* or *the trip abroad*. Only a handful of adjectives occur postnominally (reflecting the grammar of French, from which this structure derives historically) and in a limited range of contexts. Two examples are *apparent* in *heir apparent* and *elect* in *president elect*. The adjective *proper* also occurs after a noun when it is used emphatically as in *the meeting proper*.

A variety of clauses occur in postmodifying position. The clause may be a relative clause:

the proposal *which the committee put forward last week*

or a **that-clause**:

the belief *that God exists*

or a **comparative clause**:

Rachael gave a louder cry <u>than Miriam did</u>

or one of a range of **non-finite** clauses. These are all covered in detail in Section 6.13. Prepositional phrases and relative clauses are the most frequent types of postmodifers in noun phrases. Head nouns may be postmodified by more than one item although there are constraints on what may occur.

To conclude our discussion of noun phrase structure, a few further points need to be made about the head word of a noun phrase. We noted earlier that phrase type can be identified from the class of the head word. Normally, then, a noun is the head of a noun phrase. However, there are some exceptions to this. First, a pronoun can also be the head of a noun phrase. The pronoun may occur singly as a phrase or, like a head noun, it may be pre- or postmodified. Here are some examples:

NP	VP	
She	*has arrived*	personal pronoun only
Absolutely <u>anyone</u>	*may come*	pronoun + premodification
<u>Someone</u> who knows	*should be consulted*	pronoun + postmodification

Although pronouns can function as the head of a phrase in this way, there would be no real virtue in positing a pronoun phrase as a distinct phrase type. The reason for this is that the degree of overlap which would exist between noun phrases and pronoun phrases, in terms of both their internal structure and their typical function within a clause, would make for an uneconomical description of syntactic rules.

Cardinal numerals might also be the head of a noun phrase. They are classified in Section 2.8 as a subset of pronouns but with the qualification that they sometimes function more like nouns. Examples might include *the magnificent seven* or *the Guildford four*. Finally, some adjectives can occur **pronominally** (in the position of the noun). An example would be *innocent* in *The innocent were allowed to leave*. There is no likelihood here that *innocent* is a noun because, if it were, it would have a plural inflection since the verb *were* is plural. Adjectives are often used this way when the noun *people* might be understood:

the innocent	*were allowed to leave*
the innocent <u>people</u>	*were allowed to leave*
the charity workers were concerned about	*the homeless*
the charity workers were concerned about	*the homeless <u>people</u>*

However, adjectives can also be used pronominally to refer to a concept as in *She had a strong sense of the <u>divine</u>.*

This section has shown you something of the complexities of noun phrase structure. When a noun phrase is very long and complex you will need to take care to identify the head word correctly as the noun phrase may well contain more than one noun, as we have already seen. One way to identify the head word is to decide which word is most central to the meaning. Another method, when the noun phrase is in subject position (namely it is succeeded by a verb phrase) is to identify which element is controlling the verb phrase in terms of it being singular or plural:

NP	VP
The beautiful house admired by architects	*has burnt down*

In the noun phrase above, there are two nouns – *house* and *architects*. *House* is singular, whereas *architects* is plural. The first element of the verb phrase *has* is also singular. There is **concord** between a head noun in subject position and the following verb phrase so this shows that the head of the noun phrase is *house* rather than *architects*. We can double-check this by making *house* plural and *architects* singular:

NP	VP
The beautiful houses admired by the architect	*have burnt down*

Now *has* has become *have* in concord with the plural *houses*. This small test shows us then that *house* is the head word in this complex noun phrase.

☐ **determiners** ⇨ 2.9
☐ **noun inflections** ⇨ 4.3
☐ **phrases within phrases** ⇨ 5.6
☐ **clauses within phrases** ⇨ 6.13

5.3 VERB PHRASES

Noun phrases and verb phrases are the most central in the construction of clauses. One major contrast between noun phrases and verb phrases, however, is the much greater restriction on the number of elements which can occur in a verb phrase. Like noun phrases (and adjective and adverb phrases), verb phrases may consist merely of the head word. This single item will be a lexical as opposed to an auxiliary verb. Whereas a noun phrase has the potential to be extremely long, especially when it contains both pre- and postmodification, a verb phrase will be no longer than the following example:

NP	VP
Those naughty children	*might have been being told off*

A verb phrase of this kind, which has six elements, is rare. The first four elements – *might have been being* – are auxiliary verbs, while the lexical verb *told off* is a multi-word verb. Some speakers might question whether this example is natural, although it could occur in a sentence such as *I heard a lot of shouting so I thought those naughty children <u>might have been being told off</u> by their mother*.

A verb phrase, then, may be simple and consist of just a lexical verb (which may be a multi-word verb) or it may include one or more auxiliaries up to a maximum of four. Auxiliaries subdivide into primary auxiliaries and modal auxiliaries:

primary auxiliaries	*be, have, do*
modal auxiliaries	*can, could, shall, should, will, would, may, must, might*

The modal auxiliaries are used to add shades of meaning, such as obligation (*must*) or possibility (*might*) to the verb phrase. The primary auxiliaries *be* and *have* are used to construct different **aspects** and **voices**. The primary auxiliary *do* is used in question forms, in negative constructions, and for emphasis.

One of the features which verb phrases may possess is **tense**, and this is where we will begin our exploration of the many facets of verb phrases. We noted in Section 2.5 that all lexical verbs can exhibit a contrast of tense. There are only two tenses in English: the **past** and the **present**. The present tense is indicated either by the base form or by an -*s* inflection (in the third person singular), and the past tense is indicated by an -*ed* inflection on regular verbs or an equivalent form in irregular verbs. Sometimes speakers are under the misapprehension that the present tense only refers to the present time and that the past tense only refers to past time, but this is not necessarily the case. In an example such as *Wine appeals to many people* the verb *appeals* is in the present tense but the time reference is broader than the present moment since the sentence is stating a general truth. In *I said I would give him dinner when he arrived* the verb *arrived* is in the past tense, but in the context of the sentence it refers to a moment in the future. We need therefore to distinguish between the meaning of a sentence and the grammatical form of the verb phrase. Tense is a grammatical ending on a verb stem not a semantic reference to a particular time. In English, there exists only the past tense and the present tense in terms of inflectional endings. There is no future tense in English. If we want to make a future reference we need to use a structure such as *Fred <u>will</u> help* or *Fred <u>is going to</u> help*. Here are some examples of present and past tense contrasts in English in both regular and irregular verbs:

present tense	past tense
Jane <u>likes</u> music	*Jane <u>liked</u> music*

We <u>admire</u> her painting   *We <u>admired</u> her painting*
Phil <u>buys</u> a lot of wine   *Phil <u>bought</u> a lot of wine*
You <u>take</u> some liberties   *You <u>took</u> some liberties*

The above examples all contain simple verb phrases consisting of the lexical verb only. In each instance, the verb is marked for either present or past tense. When a verb or verb phrase is marked for tense it is **finite**. By contrast, when a verb is not marked for tense it is **non-finite**. If a finite verb phrase consists of a lexical verb only, then tense will, of necessity, be marked on that element. Otherwise, tense is marked on the first element of the verb phrase.

We will now consider the role and position of auxiliary verbs in verb phrases. Not only must auxiliary verbs (like *might* and *have*) precede lexical verbs but there is also a fixed order in which auxiliary verbs occur, with modal auxiliaries (like *might*) preceding primary ones (like *have*). So *Fred might have arrived by now* can be contrasted with the ill-formed example **Fred have might arrived by now*. We noted above that finite verb phrases are those which are marked for tense and that tense is always marked on the first element of the verb phrase. What this means is that if the verb phrase contains a modal auxiliary, then tense will be marked on the modal. Modals are unusual in that they do not have contrasting forms for tense in the way that lexical (and primary) verbs do. Nevertheless, if a modal is present, you need to assume it carries tense marking. The reason for this is that modal auxiliaries do not occur in non-finite verb phrases.

One important feature of verb phrases which consist of more than one element is that each auxiliary dictates the form which the following element takes. If there is a modal auxiliary present, the element which follows it will be in the base form. Consider the following examples:

	NP	VP	NP
1	*Jane*	*likes*	*music*
2	*Jane*	* *might likes*	*music*
3	*Jane*	* *might liked*	*music*
4	*Jane*	*might like*	*music*

Example 1 contains a verb phrase which consists of a finite lexical verb in the present tense – *likes*. Examples 2 and 3 illustrate how, when a modal is introduced, it is no longer necessary to mark the next element (in this case the lexical verb *like*) for tense. Example 4 shows how the element which follows the modal needs to take the base form if it is to be grammatical.

Although a verb phrase can only contain one modal auxiliary, it can contain up to three primary auxiliaries. The main purpose of primary auxiliaries is to indicate **aspect**. Aspect, like modality, gives us more information about the verb but from a rather different angle. Aspect indicates whether the action or state referred to by the lexical verb is in progress or is complete. This basic contrast is a contrast between the **progressive aspect** and the **perfect aspect**. These aspects are indicated using the primary auxiliaries *be* and *have*.

Aspects are combined with tense, resulting in two progressive combinations: the **present progressive** and the **past progressive**. Here are examples of them:

present progressive	*Sara is helping her sister*
	They are approaching the motorway
past progressive	*Sara was helping her sister*
	They were approaching the motorway

All four examples indicate that the actions in question (*helping* and *approaching*) were still in progress at the point referred to. You can see that there is a distinction between present and past progressive. Present and past are indicated on the first element in the verb phrase which, as we have already noted, is the element marked for tense in finite verb phrases. In order to construct the progressive aspect we use the primary auxiliary *be*. In the present progressive examples, the present tense is indicated by *is* and *are*. In the past progressive examples, the past tense is indicated by *was* and *were*. When *be* is used in this way, the following element will take the *-ing* inflection (in a similar way to the modal auxiliary triggering the base form). The resulting verb form in a lexical verb is known as the ***-ing* form** (or the ***-ing* participle**).

In contrast to the progressive aspect, we construct the perfect aspect using the primary auxiliary *have*. The perfect aspect denotes that the action or state referred to by the lexical verb is complete. However, in contrast to the simple past tense, the perfect aspect denotes that the completed action is still of current relevance. There are two perfect tense/aspect combinations: the **present perfect** and the **past perfect**:

present perfect	*Sara has helped her sister*
	They have approached the motorway
past perfect	*Sara had helped her sister*
	They had approached the motorway

Again, the first element in the verb phrase indicates present or past tense, so that the primary auxiliary takes the form *has* or *have* in the present perfect and the form *had* in the past perfect. The presence of the primary auxiliary *have* for the perfect aspect triggers the ***-ed* form** (or ***-ed* participle**) in the following element (or its equivalent if the verb is irregular). This is in contrast to the *-ing* form triggered by the primary auxiliary *be* for the progressive aspect.

Both the progressive aspect and the perfect aspect may occur with a modal auxiliary as the following examples show:

progressive aspect	progressive aspect + modal auxiliary
1a *Sara is helping her sister*	1b *Sara might be helping her sister*
perfect aspect	perfect aspect + modal auxiliary
2a *Sara has helped her sister*	2b *Sara might have helped her sister*

In Examples 1b and 2b the presence of the modal *might* triggers the base forms of *be* and *have*. Since tense is now marked on the modal auxiliary, the distinction between past and present aspect disappears. *Have,* however, as the primary auxiliary for the perfect aspect, continues to trigger the -*ed* form for the element which follows it – in this case the lexical verb – while *be* continues to trigger the -*ing* form.

It is also possible for the verb aspect to be both perfect and progressive, and again there is a contrast of past and present tense. This means that both a **present perfect progressive** and a **past perfect progressive** combination exist. The primary auxiliary *have* precedes the primary auxiliary *be* when this aspect is constructed:

present perfect progressive	*Debra has been skating*
	They have been dancing
past perfect progressive	*Debra had been skating*
	They had been dancing

We noted above that the primary auxiliary *have* triggers the -*ed* form in the following element. Here, the following element is the primary auxiliary *be* which is an irregular verb. The equivalent -*ed* form is *been*. In turn, the primary auxiliary *be* will trigger the -*ing* form as you can see in *dancing* and *skating*. Again, it is possible to include a modal auxiliary in these verb phrases, and again this modal auxiliary will have a knock-on effect on the form of the following element:

perfect progressive aspect no modal	perfect progressive aspect with modal
Debra has/had been skating	*Debra could have been skating*
They have/had been dancing	*They could have been dancing*

From the preceding discussion, then, we can see the range of tenses and aspects which it is possible to express in the verb phrase as well as the roles which auxiliary verbs play. In addition we can identify the relationship between the various elements of a verb phrase in terms of the form they take. This information is summarised in Table 5.1.

Table 5.1 Verb tenses and aspects

Verb phrase				
	Auxiliary verbs		Lexical verb (head)	
modal (eg *might*)	primary HAVE	primary BE		
	(marks for perfect aspect)	(marks for progressive aspect)		
triggers base form	triggers -*ed* form	triggers -*ing* form		
			ask	present tense
			asked	past tense
	have		*asked*	present tense, perfect aspect
	had		*asked*	past tense, perfect aspect
		am	*asking*	present tense, progressive aspect
		was	*asking*	past tense, progressive aspect
	have	*been*	*asking*	present tense, perfect progressive aspect
	had	*been*	*asking*	past tense, perfect progressive aspect
				with MODAL:
might	*have*		*asked*	perfect aspect
might		*be*	*asking*	progressive aspect
might	*have*	*been*	*asking*	perfect progressive aspect

So far we have seen a considerable amount which demonstrates the complex, multi-faceted nature of verb phrases. We have seen in earlier sections how verbs and verb phrases are marked to some extent for person and for singular or plural, and in this section we have seen how they can be marked for both tense and aspect. We now need to consider a further dimension and this is the feature of **voice**. Compare the following two examples:

NP	VP	
The singer	*was performing*	(*the song*)
The song	*was being performed*	(*by the singer*)

If you contrast the examples in terms of the relationship between the verb phrase and the noun phrase subject which precedes it, you will notice that in the first example the subject is actually doing the *performing* denoted by the verb. In other words, the singer is active in carrying out the performing. By contrast, the *song* of the second example is inactive and is, as it were, having the performing done to it. The contrast between these two examples is a contrast of voice. The verb phrase in the first example is **active** (or in the **active voice**) while the verb phrase in the second example is **passive** (or in the **passive voice**). This in turn means that the clauses in which they occur are also active or passive. We will look more closely at active and passive clauses in Chapter 6, but here we are simply concerned with the form of the verb phrase in these constructions.

There is a contrast then between the active verb phrase *was performing* and the passive verb phrase *was being performed*. The passive phrase contains an additional auxiliary, also from the primary verb *be*. In this example, the additional element is *being*. When a clause is made passive, certain changes take place within the clause. However, a change is also evident within the verb phrase. We have already seen that *be* is used as a primary auxiliary to indicate the progressive aspect. In addition, *be* is used to indicate the passive voice. The difference is that when *be* marks the progressive aspect it triggers the *-ing* form in the following element (as in *was performing*) but when it marks the passive voice it triggers the *-ed* form, hence *was being performed*. All the tenses and aspects which were summarised in Table 5.1 were in the active voice. Table 5.2 shows the same range of tenses and aspects but in the passive voice. You will also see that modal auxiliaries can occur in passive verb phrases.

At the beginning of this section we noted that the longest well-formed verb phrase in English could consist of up to four auxiliaries plus the lexical verb, and we had the example of *those naughty children <u>might have been being told off</u>*. We can see now that this verb phrase comprises the elements shown in Table 5.3. Although it is unlikely you will come across – or use yourself – many verb phrases which contain four auxiliary elements, it is important to know the manner in which a verb phrase can be extended, particularly as there is a clear contrast between strategies used for expanding noun phrases and those used for expanding verb phrases.

The final dimension of verb phrases which we need to consider is another contrast, this time in terms of **finite** and **non-finite** verb phrases. As we have already seen, a verb or verb phrase which is marked for tense is finite. The tense will be marked on the first element or only element of the verb phrase. All the following examples of verb phrases are finite:

	NP	VP
1	*John*	*tried*
2	*John*	*has tried*
3	*John*	*is trying*
4	*John*	*might have tried*

In the first example, the verb phrase consists solely of the lexical verb *tried*. As we can contrast *tried* which is past tense and *tries* which is present tense, this

Table 5.2 Verb tenses and aspects in the passive voice

Verb phrase					
Auxiliary verbs				Lexical verb (head)	
modal (eg *might*)	primary HAVE	primary BE	primary BE		
	(marks for perfect aspect)	(marks for progressive aspect)	(marks for passive voice)		
triggers base form	triggers *-ed* form	triggers *-ing* form	triggers *-ed* form		
			am	*asked*	present tense
			was	*asked*	past tense
	have		*been*	*asked*	present tense, perfect aspect
	had		*been*	*asked*	past tense, perfect aspect
		am	*being*	*asked*	present tense, progressive aspect
		was	*being*	*asked*	past tense, progressive aspect
	have	*been*	*being*	*asked*	present tense, perfect progressive aspect
	had	*been*	*being*	*asked*	past tense, perfect progressive aspect
					with MODAL:
might	*have*		*been*	*asked*	perfect aspect
might		*be*	*being*	*asked*	progressive aspect
might	*have*	*been*	*being*	*asked*	perfect progressive aspect

Table 5.3 Analysis of a complex VP *might have been being told off*

modal auxiliary	primary auxiliary HAVE (perfect aspect)	primary auxiliary BE (progressive aspect)	primary auxiliary BE (passive voice)	lexical verb TELL OFF
triggers base form	triggers *-ed* form	triggers *-ing* form	triggers *-ed* form	
might	*have*	*been*	*being*	*told off*

tells us the verb is marked for tense and the verb phrase is therefore finite. In Examples 2 and 3, as well as the head verb there is a primary auxiliary verb and any tense will be marked on this first element. Again, we can establish a contrast between *has* and *had* and between *is* and *was*, and this tells us that *has tried* and *is trying* are also finite verb phrases. In Example 4, the presence of the modal auxiliary *might* is evidence of tense marking so this last verb phrase is also finite. By contrast, here are some sentences which contain non-finite verb phrases:

> <u>To arrive</u> on time was their objective
> <u>To have arrived</u> on time was their objective

In the first example, the verb phrase consists of the base or infinitive form with the **infinitive particle** *to*. It is impossible to make a past/present contrast between *arrive* and *arrived* since we cannot say **to arrived*. (Tense marking is not possible on the infinitive particle, of course.) This shows us that *to arrive* is a non-finite verb phrase. The second example also has the verb in the infinitive form which here exhibits the perfect aspect. However, *have* must be in the base form not the present tense form since **to had arrived* is not possible. Non-finite verb phrases can also take the base form of the verb but without the *to* particle:

> *Susan has helped <u>wash up</u>*

In this example the finite verb phrase *has helped* is complemented by the non-finite verb phrase *wash up*. This is a multi-word verb in the base form: no contrast with *washed up* would be acceptable in this context.

Verb phrases which begin with *-ed* or *-ing* participles are also non-finite:

> 1 <u>*Summoned*</u> *to an urgent meeting, Philip left at once*
> 2 *Philip went out for a walk, <u>hoping</u> to see a rainbow*
> 3 <u>*Having been caught*</u> *asleep at work, Philip was fired*

Examples 1 and 2 contain the single-word verb phrases *summoned* and *hoping* which are non-finite. So too is Example 3 *having been caught* which contains two auxiliaries – *having* which indicates perfect aspect and *been* which indicates passive voice. The verb phrase is non-finite because the first element *having* is not marked for tense. You will notice, however, that Examples 1, 2 and 3 also contain finite verb phrases (*left, went out* and *was fired*). This is because non-finite verbs lack the grammatical completeness which a finite verb gives to a sentence. To summarise, non-finite verb phrases have no marking for tense. They will take one of the following forms:

> base or infinitive form of the verb with or without *to*
> -*ing* form as the first or only element
> -*ed* form as the first or only element

It is difficult to discuss verb phrases as being finite or non-finite without referring to their role in the structure of clauses and sentences but we will be dealing with this shortly.

In this section we have seen how verb phrases can carry a complex load of grammatical information regarding features such as tense, aspect, voice and finiteness. One final point needs to be made before we move on to look at the three remaining phrase types. We noted at the start of this chapter that phrases are identifiable groups of words (and even single-word phrases have the potential to be expanded into multi-word phrases). We have seen that the internal structure of phrases is rule-governed and this means that phrases cannot include elements other than those allowed by the phrase structure rules. What this essentially means is that a verb phrase will comprise a lexical verb plus any auxiliaries (or possibly the infinitive particle *to* if it is a non-finite verb phrase) but nothing else. However, there is an exception to this principle and that is when an adverb, which is a more mobile class of word, interrupts the verb phrase as in the third and fourth examples below:

1   *have been told off*
2   * *have mother been told off*
3   *have <u>certainly</u> been told off*
4   *have been <u>severely</u> told off*

Disjuncts such as *certainly* tend to occur after the first auxiliary whereas adverbs of manner are more likely to occur immediately before the lexical verb to modify its meaning: here the children have not just been told off but *severely* told off. Adverbs are not a central part of the verb phrase structure but it is important to be aware that they can appear in the positions shown.

□ **lexical verbs** ⇨ 2.5
□ **adverbs** ⇨ 2.7
□ **auxiliaries** ⇨ 2.10
□ **verb inflections** ⇨ 4.4
□ **active and passive clauses** ⇨ 6.9
□ **non-finite clauses** ⇨ 6.10
□ **variation in verb phrases** ⇨ 12.6

5.4   ADJECTIVE AND ADVERB PHRASES

In contrast to noun phrases and verb phrases, we will be able to deal with adjective phrases and adverb phrases fairly briefly. Adjective phrases and adverb phrases are not dissimilar in their range of possibilities for pre- and postmodification which is why we will deal with them in the same section. In accordance with the construction principles we have already noted for noun phrases and verb phrases, an adjective or adverb phrase may consist merely of the head word or it may be expanded into a longer phrase with pre- or post-modifying elements. To begin with, here are some examples of adjective and adverb phrases which contain only a head word:

NP	VP	AdjP
The hungry cat	*was feeling*	*aggressive*
My new shoes	*felt*	*uncomfortable*

NP	VP	AdvP
The hungry cat	*snarled*	*aggressively*

NP	VP	NP	AdvP
My new shoes	*pinched*	*me*	*uncomfortably*

In the above examples, the adjective and adverb phrases occur in the same position at the end of the sentence. This is not, however, a restriction on where they can occur: we will resume a discussion of the position the various phrases take when we move on to clause structure in Chapter 6.

We saw earlier that there exists the potential to expand noun phrases by adding quite a number of premodifying elements. Head words in adjective and adverb phrases are most typically premodified by a single adverb, normally an intensifier:

The hungry cat was feeling <u>extremely aggressive</u>
My new shoes felt <u>incredibly uncomfortable</u>
The hungry cat snarled <u>really aggressively</u>
My new shoes pinched me <u>so uncomfortably</u>

Very occasionally, a head adjective or head adverb is postmodified by an adverb such as *enough* or *indeed* but this is fairly unusual and often sounds quite formal. More typically, head adjectives and head adverbs will be post-modified by a prepositional phrase or by one of a range of clauses (as we shall see later). In this respect, they resemble noun phrases.

☐ **intensifiers** ⇨ 2.7
☐ **clauses as postmodifiers in adjective and adverb phrases** ⇨ 6.13

5.5 PREPOSITIONAL PHRASES

Prepositional phrases differ from the other four types of phrase in that a preposition cannot stand alone as the head word of a phrase. Although a preposition is still the head word in a prepositional phrase, it has to be accompanied by another element – or **prepositional complement** – if the phrase is to be complete. Most typically, the prepositional complement will be a noun phrase. Consider this example:

NP	VP	PP
Jackie	*was searching*	*in the cupboard*

Here, the prepositional phrase consists of the preposition *in* complemented by the noun phrase *the cupboard*. We could represent this structure in either of the following ways:

[*in the cupboard* PP]
[*in* [*the cupboard* NP] PP]

The second example shows the structure of the prepositional phrase in rather more detail. The noun phrase in the example above is a simple one in that it consists only of a determiner plus the head noun. However, there is no restriction on the relative simplicity or complexity of a noun phrase which complements a preposition in this way. Here are a few more examples of prepositional phrases, with the noun phrase underlined:

around <u>London</u>
under <u>a stone</u>
for <u>my closest friend</u>
to <u>the best friend ever</u>

In addition to being complemented by noun phrases, prepositional phrases can also consist of the preposition followed by an adverb (or adverb phrase): *by tomorrow, above here, until now* are just three examples. In common with nouns, adjectives and adverbs as heads, prepositions can also be complemented by different types of clauses, a feature we will look at closely in Chapter 6.

We now return to the matter of prepositional phrases being able to postmodify head nouns, head adjectives and occasionally head adverbs. We will begin by taking a head noun as an example.

NP	VP	NP	NP
Clive	*gave*	*Kate*	*a large bouquet*

As you can see, there are three noun phrases in the above example. Two of them consist simply of proper nouns, *Clive* and *Kate*. The third noun phrase consists of the head noun *bouquet* plus a determiner and a premodifying adjective *large*. Supposing we now wished to specify what kind of flowers were in the bouquet, we could add the prepositional phrase *of roses:*

NP	VP	NP	NP
Clive	*gave*	*Kate*	*a large bouquet of roses*

In the new example *bouquet* is both premodified by *large* and postmodified by *of roses*. The head noun is still *bouquet* as we can see if we make this noun phrase the subject of a sentence. It is *bouquet* which will govern whether the verb is singular or plural, not *roses:*

> A large <u>bouquet</u> of roses is very romantic
> * A large <u>bouquet</u> of roses are very romantic

However, not all prepositional phrases in a sentence will necessarily be part of an extended noun phrase. Look at this example:

> Heidi cycled fifty miles for charity

You may at first consider whether the correct analysis of this example is

> [*Heidi* NP] [*cycled* VP] [*fifty miles for charity* NP]

The difference, though, between *fifty miles for charity* and *a large bouquet of roses* is that *for charity* can occur in a different position in the sentence whereas *of roses* cannot:

> For charity Heidi cycled fifty miles
> Heidi, for charity, cycled fifty miles
> * Of roses Clive gave Kate a large bouquet
> * Clive gave Kate of roses a large bouquet

The fact that *of roses* cannot be removed from its position after *bouquet* indicates that it is an integral part of the noun phrase of which *bouquet* is the head. *For charity*, by contrast, is a separate phrase as shown by its mobility within the sentence. The correct phrasal analysis of this example is:

> [*Heidi* NP] [*cycled* VP] [*fifty miles* NP] [*for charity* PP]

We noted in Section 5.4 that prepositional phrases can also postmodify head words in adjective and adverb phrases. Here are some examples:

adjective phrase	*Peter felt <u>ready for a beer</u>*
	Maureen appeared <u>aware of the danger</u>
adverb phrase	*<u>Unhappily for Sara</u>, she fell off her bike*
	Brian didn't win the race, <u>surprisingly in my opinion</u>

The range of adjectives taking prepositional phrase complements is much greater than the range of adverbs doing so. The adverb structures, as in the examples above, normally give a viewpoint or opinion.

> ☐ **prepositions** ⇨ 2.11
> ☐ **clauses as postmodifying elements** ⇨ 6.13

5.6 EMBEDDING

We have seen in Sections 5.2, 5.4 and 5.5 that phrases are expanded by adding words of other classes – for example by premodifying an adjective with an adverb – or by adding other phrases – for example postmodifying a head noun with a prepositional phrase. The occurrence of one linguistic unit within another is sometimes referred to as **embedding**. When we say that one linguistic item is embedded within another, we are also implying that the embedded item is in some way subordinate to or dependent on the item in which it is embedded. If we took our earlier noun phrase *a nice invitation* as an example, we might describe the adjective (or indeed adjective phrase) *nice* as being embedded within the noun phrase as the adjective is less central than the head noun *invitation*. It might also be helpful to think of an adjective phrase being embedded within the noun phrase when we consider how the adjective *nice* could be modified by the intensifier *rather* to give *a rather nice invitation:*

[*a* [*rather nice* ~AdjP~] *invitation* ~NP~]

Here we can see the relationship between *rather* and *nice* (there is no direct relationship between *rather* and *invitation*) and their combined relationship with the head noun *invitation*.

The concept of embedding is particularly useful in that it allows us to see the potential for repeated patterns in syntactic structure. For example, a prepositional phrase which postmodifies the head of a noun phrase may contain a noun which is itself postmodified. Consider the complex noun phrase in the following example:

NP	VP	NP
Jane	*told*	*an amusing story about her friend with measles*

The complex noun phrase in this sentence can be analysed as follows:

[*an amusing <u>story</u>* [*about* [*her friend* [*with* [*measles* NP] PP] NP] PP] NP]

The head of the whole phrase is *story*. This head word is postmodified by the prepositional phrase *about her friend*. This prepositional phrase contains the noun phrase *her friend* and the head of this noun phrase, *friend*, is itself postmodified by the prepositional phrase *with measles*. There is no possibility that this last prepositional phrase modifies *story* rather than *friend* since **an amusing story with measles* would be distinctly odd. Instead, what we see is a kind of Russian doll effect with one phrase embedded within another and the resulting phrase in turn being embedded in a higher level phrase. The ability

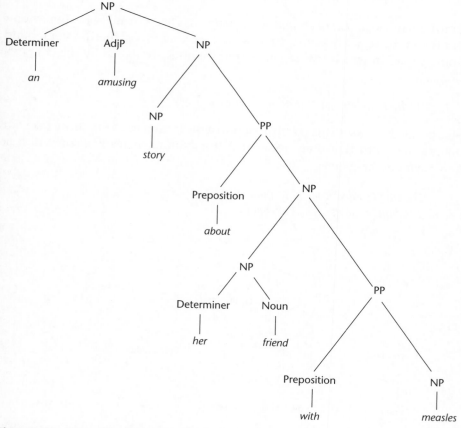

Figure 5.1   An example of phrasal recursion

of patterns to repeat themselves in this way is known as **recursion**. To show you the full pattern of recursion in what may be a slightly clearer fashion, this example is presented in a tree diagram in Figure 5.1.

5.7 COORDINATION AND APPOSITION OF PHRASES

Although we will look at the internal structure of clauses in the next chapter, we will consider briefly here the way phrases can be linked together in two specific ways within a clause or sentence. **Coordination** is the joining together of two linguistic units on an equal footing and most typically uses the conjunction *and* (although *but* and *or* are also found). Here is an example of noun phrase coordination:

PP	NP	VP	NP
For supper	*Lloyd*	*cooked*	*salmon fillets and new potatoes*

In this analysis *salmon fillets and new potatoes* has been treated as a single noun phrase but if we analyse it further we can see that it is actually a compound noun phrase in which two separate noun phrases are joined by the conjunction *and:*

[[*salmon fillets* NP] *and* [*new potatoes* NP] NP]

Figure 5.2 also shows this construction in a diagrammatic form. If we take our analysis a step further then we see that this example is really a conflation of two separate statements:

For supper Lloyd cooked salmon fillets
For supper Lloyd cooked new potatoes

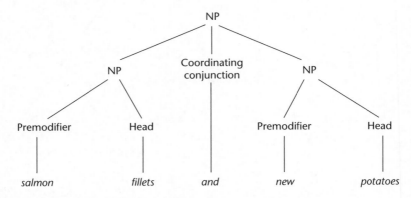

Figure 5.2 An example of a compound noun phrase

This shows how the coordination of phrases can be used as a very economical way of expressing meaning.

It is not just noun phrases which can be coordinated. Here are some examples of other phrases being joined in this way:

Daniel *bathed and changed* the baby	*VP coordination*
Helen was *tired but happy*	*AdjP coordination*
Rachael slept *soundly and peacefully*	*AdvP coordination*
Louise worked *with speed and with diligence*	*PP coordination*

We noted above that coordination involves the joining of elements on an equal basis. Not only are the elements in the above compounds equal in syntactic terms, they are the same in formal terms. What this means is that a noun phrase can only be coordinated with another noun phrase and so on. A combination of, say, an adjective phrase with an adverb phrase would be impossible: **Helen was tired but happily.*

Another way in which noun phrases co-occur is through **apposition**, as in the following example:

NP	VP	NP	NP	PP
Jo	*asked*	*her friend's sister*	*an English teacher*	*for some help*

In this sentence there are two adjacent noun phrases – *her friend's sister* and *an English teacher* – which actually refer to the same person. These are known as **noun phrases in apposition**. Apposition is another way of achieving economy in language: we can analyse the given example as a merging and reduction of something like *Jo asked her friend's sister for some help* and *Jo's friend's sister is an English teacher*. Economy is an aspect of language which we will consider further in the following chapters on sentences, clauses and discourse.

☐ **coordinating conjunctions** ⇨ 2.12

6 Clauses

6.1 WHAT IS A CLAUSE?

A **clause**, like a phrase, is a unit of syntactic construction. In Chapter 5, we saw how phrases are formed from words and that each phrase type has its own particular internal structure. As phrases are formed from words, so clauses are formed from phrases. This does not mean that a clause is a random group of phrases: a clause has a specific structure, as we shall see shortly. As a unit of construction, then, a clause is a larger unit than a phrase. The unit of construction larger than the clause is the sentence, which will consist of one or more clauses. We will look more closely at sentence structures and types in Chapter 7.

Although there are many different types of clause fulfilling a range of functions within sentences, it is possible to identify the features which typify a clause. We will therefore begin by looking at the most central clause types. Much of the rest of our discussion will then be about modifications to these basic types.

Most central to a clause is its **verb element**. We have already seen that verb phrases are multi-faceted in the way they provide information about tense, aspect, voice and so on. Typically, a clause contains a verb phrase which is **finite** (meaning it is marked for tense) and which is active rather than passive since this is the voice most frequently used by speakers. The verb phrase is normally preceded by a subject element and followed by any elements needed to make the clause grammatically complete. Consider the following example:

Catherine has gained ten GCSEs

This is an example of a typical clause. The verb *has gained* is both active and finite. The meaning of the verb is completed by the noun phrase *ten GCSEs*. The verb is preceded by the subject noun phrase *Catherine*. This structure is typical of clauses in that it is the structure we use to make a statement. This is known as a **declarative** structure.

At present, this clause only contains **obligatory** elements. What this means is that if we remove any of the phrases from the clause, it would be syntactically incomplete. It would be possible of course to add some optional items to this clause:

Fortunately, Catherine has gained ten GCSEs *this summer*

However, in our discussion we will mainly be concentrating on the obligatory elements in clauses as these will enable us to identify the basic clause structures of English. The features, then, which most typify a clause are that the verb phrase will be finite and in the active voice and the structure of the clause will be declarative.

6.2   THE FIVE CLAUSE ELEMENTS

Clauses are made up of a combination of clause elements. There are five clause elements, each one having a different function within the clause:

subject
verb
object
complement
adverbial

(These may be abbreviated as S, V, O, C, A.) We saw above that clauses typically contain a verb and a subject. They also contain any items needed to complete the meaning of the verb, most typically objects or complements. Sometimes verbs will require an obligatory adverbial but normally adverbials are optional elements in a clause.

The verb element is always realised by a verb phrase. The other elements are likely to be realised by phrases but it is possible that another clause can fulfil the role of a clause element. It is important to make a clear distinction between phrase types and clause elements. Consider the following example:

function	S	V	O
	The black Labrador	*has bitten*	*Mr Allington*
form	NP	VP	NP

If we analyse this clause in terms of phrase structure then we can see it consists of NP + VP + NP. In terms of clause elements, however, the structure is SVO. When we identify *the black Labrador* as a noun phrase, we are analysing its **form**. When we identify it as the subject of the clause, we are analysing its

function. You will notice there are two noun phrases in the clause: although *the black Labrador* and *Mr Allington* share the same form, they each have a different function within the clause. The next five sections will take you through the five clause elements, explaining their functions and looking at the positions in which they occur within a clause.

6.3 SUBJECT ELEMENT

The **subject** typically occurs before the verb element in what may be termed the **subject position**. Here are some examples:

subject	verb + other elements
1 *Helen*	*has been tidying her CD collection*
2 *These friends*	*are looking for a new house*
3 *It*	*is going to rain shortly*
4 *There*	*will be a storm tonight*

The subject element is very likely to be a noun phrase, such as *Helen* in Example 1 and *these friends* in Example 2. Occasionally, you will come across *it* or *there* in the subject position as in Examples 3 and 4. These are unusual subjects in that they refer to nothing in particular. When *it* or *there* are used in this way, the subject is termed a **dummy subject**. A clause can also occur in subject position. We will consider this in Section 6.12.

A key feature of the subject function is that the subject dictates whether the verb will be singular or plural, as far as such a distinction is possible. Sometimes, it may also be possible to make a distinction between first, second or third person. This distinction will come into play most obviously when the verb *be* is employed, either as a lexical verb or as a primary auxiliary:

subject	verb		
I	*am considering*	*a career move*	1st person
you	*are making*	*a terrible mistake*	2nd person
She / Helen	*is having*	*another baby*	3rd person

In many instances, however, there will be no specific marking for person or number on the verb because there are so few verbal inflections in English.

☐ **verb inflections** ⇨ 4.4
☐ **clauses as clause elements** ⇨ 6.12

6.4   VERB ELEMENT

Whereas the subject element can take the form of a noun phrase, or a dummy subject, or even another clause, the verb element has to be a verb phrase. The verb element is the most central part of the clause, and the lexical verb present in the verb phrase will also dictate what obligatory elements will follow the verb. Consider these two examples:

subject	verb
Paul	*fell*
* *Paul*	*broke*

Whereas the first example is complete as it stands, the second example *Paul broke* is incomplete. (What is missing is an object element after the verb.) This shows us that there is a close relationship between the lexical verb and the rest of the clause. In other words, the choice of lexical verb will dictate what element or elements, if any, should follow the verb element in order to make the clause grammatically complete. This is known as **verb complementation**. (The terms 'complement' and 'complementation' meaning the obligatory element(s) which follow verbs are distinct from 'complement' as a specific type of clause element.)

Due to the existence of this special bond between the verb and its following elements, a clause has traditionally been divided into two parts: the **subject** and the **predicate**. The predicate is the verb element plus any verb complementation. The subject is, if you like, the focus or topic of the sentence while the predicate is what we want to say about the subject. If we complete the example *Paul broke* by adding *his ankle* then the clause could be analysed like this:

subject	predicate
Paul	*broke his ankle*

Paul is our chosen topic or focus while *broke his ankle* is what we want to say about *Paul*. You may sometimes find the verb element of a clause referred to as a **predicator** which is indicative of its role within the predicate.

We have already looked in some detail in Section 5.3 at the complexities of verb phrases. We saw that they can be marked for modality, tense, aspect and voice as well as to some extent for number and person. As we have just seen, though, the verb element does not function in isolation but exerts a semantic and grammatical influence over other elements. Of all the elements in a clause, the verb element is the most important and the most obligatory.

☐ **verb phrases** ⇨ 5.3

6.5 OBJECT ELEMENT

The incomplete clause in the previous section (*Paul broke*) was completed by adding an **object**:

subject	verb	object
Paul	*broke*	*his ankle*

The object element contrasts with the subject element in that its position is after the verb element. Whereas all verbs can be preceded by a subject, only some verbs need to be followed by an object element. Verbs which require an object are **transitive verbs**. You can see from the example above that *break* is a transitive verb. If you contrast this with the earlier example, *Paul fell,* which is grammatically complete as it stands, then you can see that some verbs do not require an object or any other complementation. These are **intransitive verbs**.

Like the subject element, the object is most typically a noun phrase, as in the example *Paul broke his ankle*. However, the object can also be a clause - an aspect which we will consider in Section 6.12. There are many transitive verbs but there are also some verbs which are followed by two objects:

S	V	O	O
Jane	*gave*	*Phil*	*this book on wine*
Andrew	*bought*	*Kathy*	*a sports car*
Gill	*told*	*Imogen*	*a bedtime story*

Verbs which take two objects are **ditransitive**. Although there are two objects complementing each of these verbs, the two objects do not behave identically. The first object can be moved to the end of the clause if the noun phrase is converted to a prepositional phrase with *to* or *for*:

> *Jane gave this book on wine to Phil*
> *Andrew bought a sports car for Kathy*
> *Gill told a bedtime story to Imogen*

This shows that the first object is rather less central than the second one. The people in our examples – *Phil, Kathy* and *Imogen* – are really recipients of the actual item which was given, bought or told. For this reason, the first, less central type of object is sometimes referred to as an **indirect object** (O_i) while the second is the **direct object** (O_d). So a new example might be analysed as:

S	V	O_i	O_d
Judith	*promised*	*Matthew*	*a present*

Some verbs, such as *promise*, can be both ditransitive as in the above examples or **monotransitive**, taking just one object. For example, *Judith promised many things* would be a grammatically complete clause with one object. Similarly, some verbs can be used both transitively and intransitively – *read* and *write* are examples.

☐ **clauses as clause elements** ⇨ 6.12

6.6 COMPLEMENT ELEMENT

We have seen so far that some verbs require no complementation, and that some verbs (namely, transitive verbs) require an object. There is also a small group of verbs which are followed by a **complement** as opposed to an object element. Consider these examples:

S	V	O
The committee	*have made*	*a decision*

S	V	C
Sue	*was feeling*	*very sleepy*

There is a significant difference in function between *a decision* in the first example and *very sleepy* in the second. Whereas *a decision* has a referent which is distinct from the subject referent *the committee*, *very sleepy* refers to *Sue*, the subject of the clause. Another difference is that the first example can be rearranged to give the passive clause *a decision has been made by the committee* whereas **very sleepy was being felt by Sue* is not grammatically possible. So, just as an object is needed to provide completeness in a clause that contains a transitive verb, a complement is needed to give completeness when there is a **copula** or **copular verb** in the clause. Copular verbs make up just a small set of verbs and include: *be, feel* (in the sense used above), *seem, appear, become*. The verb *be* is the most central of all the copular verbs and you may sometimes come across it referred to simply as **the copula**.

In our previous example, the complement was an adjective phrase *very sleepy*. However, it is equally likely to be a noun phrase as in *Andrew became a QC*. Prepositional phrases can be complements when they follow a copular verb: they describe someone's mood, position or state as in *Phil was in a daze*. Further, complements do not necessarily refer to the subject of the sentence. A distinction can be made between a **subject complement** (C_S) and an **object complement** (C_O). (These are sometimes referred to as the **subject predicative** and **object predicative** respectively and you can use these terms if you wish to avoid confusion with the term 'complement'.) The subject complement gives us more information about the subject of the clause, and the object complement gives us more information about the object element. Here are some examples of both types of complement:

S	V	C_S	complement type
Armstrong	*became*	*the first man on the moon*	NP
The weather	*has turned*	*very nasty*	AdjP
No one	*was*	*in danger*	PP

S	V	O	C_O	complement type
The judges	*pronounced*	*Jackie*	*the winner*	NP
Chris	*made*	*Sara*	*really angry*	AdjP
Grace	*considered*	*herself*	*at an advantage*	PP

Verbs which take both an object and an object complement are **complex-transitive** verbs. Whereas the range of copular verbs which take a subject complement is limited, there is a wide range of verbs which take an object and an object complement. The relationship between the object and the object complement can be expressed using the copula *be*:

S	V	O	C_O	
The judges	*pronounced*	*Jackie*	*the winner*	(*Jackie was the winner*)
Chris	*made*	*Sara*	*really angry*	(*Sara was really angry*)
Grace	*considered*	*herself*	*at an advantage*	(*She was at an advantage*)

This relationship is fundamentally different from the relationship between an indirect and direct object:

Andrew bought Kathy a sports car   (**Kathy is a sports car*)

This provides a useful way of distinguishing between verb types when dealing with verbs that take two complements.

6.7 ADVERBIAL ELEMENT

The adverbial element is so-called because it functions like an adverb. This means that its position is less fixed than that of the other clause elements. Adverbials also have a wider range of functions in terms of meaning. An adverbial element is most likely to be an adverb phrase or a prepositional phrase, although a clause can also function as an adverbial. Here are some examples of adverbials in a variety of clause positions:

Julia speaks French <u>very fluently</u>	AdvP as adverbial
I would like <u>nevertheless</u> to go to America	AdvP as adverbial
Terry was digging up the weeds <u>in his garden</u>	PP as adverbial
<u>At a glance</u> she looked very poorly	PP as adverbial

The above examples show you how the adverbial element can occur in various positions. A further point to note about these particular adverbial examples, however, is that they are not obligatory. They could all be removed without any real loss of meaning and without causing grammatical incompleteness. This is another way in which adverbial elements differ from other clause elements. Only a small number of verbs require an adverbial for their complementation. For example, the verb *hare* (meaning 'to speed') is grammatically incomplete without an adverbial:

S	V	A
*Mick	*hared*	
Mick	*hared*	*along the road*

Other verbs may require an obligatory adverbial depending on which meaning is adopted. For instance, *lean* needs no complementation when it means 'not be upright' but requires an adverbial when it means 'be supported in a sloping position':

S	V	
The tower at Pisa	*leans*	

S	V	A
Mick's bike	*was leaning*	*against the garden wall*

Further examples include *last* in the sense of 'have a specific duration' and *live* in the sense of 'have a home somewhere':

S	V	A
The opera	*lasted*	*nearly three hours*
My friends	*live*	*in Monmouth*

The verb *put* requires both an object and an adverbial when it carries the meaning of placing something somewhere:

S	V	O	A
Terry	*put*	*the rubbish*	*in the dustbin*

This is a commonly used verb. You can see that it would be grammatically incomplete without the adverbial element.

Sometimes, it is hard to decide whether obligatory prepositional phrases are adverbial elements or object or subject complements. Compare the previous example with a seemingly similar sentence:

| Terry | put | *the rubbish* (O) | *in the dustbin* (A) |
| Terry | put | *the boat* (O) | *in danger* (C$_O$) |

In the first sentence, the prepositional phrase *in the dustbin* is classified as an adverbial as it has a clear locational meaning: locational and temporal meanings are characteristic of obligatory adverbials. By contrast, the prepositional phrase *in danger* is clearly not locational or temporal, but instead describes a feature of the object *the boat*. Furthermore, although it is possible to express the relationship between *the rubbish* and *in the dustbin* and between *the boat* and *in danger* using the copular *be*, only the relationship between the second pair of examples can be easily expressed using a fuller range of copular verbs:

The boat was in danger
The rubbish was in the dustbin

The boat seemed in danger
*The rubbish seemed in the dustbin

The boat sounded in danger
*The rubbish sounded in the dustbin

The boat looked in danger
*The rubbish looked in the dustbin

The classification of *in danger* as an object complement can therefore be further justified on the basis of its ability to combine with verbs that typically take subject complements.

There may, conversely, occasionally be an argument for treating the obligatory element following the copular *be* as an adverbial rather than a subject complement when it takes the form of a prepositional phrase. Compare *the boat was in danger*, where *in danger* is a subject complement describing the subject *the boat*, with *Mick's bike was against the garden wall*, where the locational meaning of *against the garden wall* would justify a classification of this prepositional phrase as an adverbial element, just as it is in *Mick's bike was leaning against the garden wall*.

☐ **meanings of adverbial elements** ⇨ 7.11

6.8   CLAUSE STRUCTURES

We have now looked at the functions of the five elements which make up clauses and we have also seen which different forms those elements can take. We can therefore summarise what we have covered in terms of the range of basic clause structures possible. The examples given below have already been used in the preceding five sections.

clause structure	example			
S V	*Paul*	*fell*		
S V O	*Paul*	*broke*	*his ankle*	
S V O_i O_d	*Andrew*	*bought*	*Kathy*	*a sports car*
S V C_s	*Sue*	*was feeling*	*very sleepy*	
S V O C_o	*Chris*	*made*	*Sara*	*really angry*
S V A	*Mick's bike*	*was leaning*	*against the garden wall*	
S V O A	*Terry*	*put*	*the rubbish*	*in the dustbin*

All the clause elements in these structures are obligatory. If any element were removed then the clause would be incomplete. Of course, the above examples do not represent the full range of clause structures possible. They represent a syntactic starting point: any clause can therefore be analysed in terms of these basic structures. Here is an example which contains more than the obligatory elements:

S	V	A	Vocative
The taxi	*is waiting*	*outside,*	*Louise*

The first three elements here conform to the SVA clause structure. However, the adverbial element is not obligatory: *the taxi is waiting* is syntactically complete but some additional information is given by the adverbial *outside*. Also in this example, you can see that the remark is being addressed to *Louise*. In speech in particular we often name the person or persons we are speaking to. This method of address is a **vocative**. The vocative is an optional not an obligatory element, and is more peripheral than the adverbial in that vocatives do not enter into clause structures as such.

   You will also notice that the basic structures given above all contain the subject followed by the verb as the minimum structural elements. Any verb complementation such as an object follows the verb element. For this reason English is sometimes referred to as an SVO language. This is in contrast to a language such as Japanese which has an SOV order or Welsh which is VSO. Interestingly, something like 75 per cent of the world's languages have an SVO clause structure in common with English.

6.9 ACTIVE AND PASSIVE CLAUSES

In Section 5.3 we saw how a verb phrase could be either active or passive and how this in turn will make the clause active or passive. Here are examples of both types:

active   *Everyone admired Gill's garden*
passive   *Gill's garden was admired by everyone*

In an active clause, the subject is normally the **agent**. What this means is that the subject is carrying out the action referred to by the lexical verb. The object on the other hand is the **affected** (or **patient**) – the person or thing to which the verb is being done, as it were. Agent and affected refer to semantic as opposed to grammatical roles. We instinctively know that, if the verb is active, the grammatical subject is likely to be an agent.

Only a transitive verb – like *admire* – can be made passive. (This includes transitive multi-word verbs such as *look after.*) The passive is often seen as a trans-formation from the active rather than as a primary structure in its own right. This is because the active voice is far more typical and natural to language than the passive voice. In order to convert an active clause such as *Everyone admired Gill's garden* to a passive one, the object of the active clause has to be moved into subject position. The verb phrase is then modified by using the auxiliary *be* so that *admired* becomes *was admired*. This transformation results in *Gill's garden was admired*. The presence in the verb phrase of the auxiliary *was* (followed by an *-ed* form) to mark the passive voice indicates that the grammatical subject is now the affected not the agent. Finally, there is an option with regard to the agent, *everyone*. This element can either be omitted since *Gill's garden was admired* is grammatically complete, or it can be added in a ***by*-phrase**: *Gill's garden was admired by everyone*. The by-phrase functions as an adverbial element in the passive clause:

S	V	A
Gill's garden	*was admired*	*by everyone*

Although only transitive verbs can become passive, not all transitive verbs can undergo this process. This is due to the semantic properties of the verbs in question. We had an example earlier of *Paul broke his ankle*. This clause could not be made passive – **Paul's ankle was broken by Paul* – because, despite being the subject of an active clause, *Paul* here has an affected role not an agent role. On the other hand we could passivise *Paul broke a glass bowl* because *Paul* is the agent of this clause: *A glass bowl was broken by Paul*.

Although passives come less naturally to us as speakers than active clauses, they are very useful in a variety of contexts. For instance, if you didn't know who the agent was then a passive would be a useful construction:

active   *? has murdered Mr Constable*
passive   *Mr Constable has been murdered*

Similarly, you may wish to avoid indicating who the agent is either because it isn't especially important or because you don't wish to ascribe responsibility:

active   *The headteacher has increased the homework for Year 11*
passive   *The homework for Year 11 has been increased*

The passive is also an appropriate construction for focusing on the affected since it brings this element to the front of the clause:

active   *the earth orbits the sun*
passive   *the sun is orbited by the earth*

Finally, the passive often sounds more formal than its active counterpart. As already mentioned, the active voice is more instinctive for speakers and used far more extensively than the passive, and young children take quite a while to assimilate the passive construction. This supports our earlier point that clauses are typically active, although the passive has a range of valuable functions in our language.

6.10   NON-FINITE CLAUSES

We noted above that not only are clauses typically active, they are also typically finite, meaning the verb element is marked for tense. However, verbs, as we saw in Section 5.3, may also be non-finite. If the verb element in any clause is not marked for tense then the clause itself will also be non-finite. When a clause is non-finite, then it does not sound grammatically complete on its own. Non-finite clauses therefore normally occur as part of a higher level clause which does contain a finite verb. In the following examples of sentences which contain a non-finite clause, the non-finite clause has been underlined and is labelled to show its clause elements:

to-infinitive
without subject   *The aim was <u>to explore (V) the area (O)</u>*
with subject   *The captain wanted <u>the crew (S) to explore (V) the area (O)</u>*

bare infinitive
without subject   *Phil helped <u>cook (V) the dinner (O)</u>*
with subject   *She made <u>Julian (S) wash up (V)</u>*

-ing participle

without subject   *Loving (V) wine (O) he moved to Bordeaux*

with subject   *Norman (S) loving (V) wine (0) they gave him some claret*

-ed participle

without subject   *Treated (V) kindly (A) the Labrador will be good*

with subject   *Business (S) finished (V) they all went home*

None of the underlined non-finite clauses could stand alone and still sound grammatically complete. They all occur instead with or within finite clauses. Another feature of non-finite clauses is that they may or may not have a subject element whereas finite clauses typically have a subject preceding the verb. When no subject element is present in the non-finite clause, the subject has to be inferred. For example, in *Loving wine he moved to Bordeaux* the subject of the verb *love* can be found in the subject of the finite clause *he*.

☐ **non-finite verb phrases** ⇨ 5.3
☐ **clauses as clause elements** ⇨ 6.12

6.11 MAIN AND SUBORDINATE CLAUSES

Within the structure of a sentence, a clause is either **main** or **subordinate**. Consider the following example:

> *When Ruth arrives, I might open a bottle of wine.*

You can see that this sentence contains two verb phrases: *arrives* and *might open*. The latter has a subject pronoun *I* and is complemented by the object *a bottle of wine*, making *I might open a bottle of wine* an SVO clause. The verb *arrive* is an intransitive verb so it has no complements but it does have a subject, namely *Ruth*. *Ruth arrives* is also a clause and its structure is SV. This clause, however, differs from the other one in that it is introduced by the subordinating conjunction *when*. If we separate these two clauses we will notice a crucial difference between them:

> **When Ruth arrives*
> *I might open a bottle of wine*

Whereas the second clause can stand alone and still be grammatically complete, this is not true of *When Ruth arrives*. This clause needs to be attached to a free-standing clause as part of a complete sentence. Any clause which has the potential to stand alone is a **main clause**. A clause which does not have this capacity is a **subordinate clause**. Because a subordinate clause depends on a main clause for grammatical completeness, it is sometimes referred to as a **dependent clause**. Similarly, a main clause is sometimes referred to as an **independent clause**.

We noted at the beginning of this chapter that a sentence will consist of one or more clauses. If a sentence consists of only one clause then that clause has to be a main clause or the sentence will be grammatically incomplete. A main clause always contains a finite verb and typically contains an overt subject. It may of course be active or passive. We will look more closely at sentences containing more than one clause in Chapter 7.

We saw in the previous section that our examples of non-finite clauses were grammatically incomplete when taken in isolation. This demonstrates that any clause which is non-finite is subordinate. So too is any clause which is introduced by a subordinating conjunction. Many clauses which begin with a *wh*-word are also subordinate. There are many different types of subordinate clause and these can be analysed both in terms of their forms and their functions. We will look at some of these aspects in the following sections and in the next chapter.

☐ *wh*-**words** ⇨ 2.13
☐ **main clauses as simple sentences** ⇨ 7.8
☐ **main clauses in compound sentences** ⇨ 7.9
☐ **main clauses in complex sentences** ⇨ 7.10
☐ **subordinate clauses** ⇨ 7.10

6.12   CLAUSES AS CLAUSE ELEMENTS

In Sections 6.3 to 6.7 we looked at the five clause elements and their functions, and we considered the phrase types which were likely to perform these roles. We noted that the verb element has to be a verb phrase but the other elements are less prescribed. For example, we saw that the subject complement could be a noun phrase (*Armstrong became <u>the first man on the moon</u>*), an adjective phrase (*The weather has turned <u>very nasty</u>*) or a prepositional phrase (*No one was <u>in danger</u>*). We will now move on to consider how clauses can fulfil the function of the subject, object, complement and adverbial elements. Any clause which functions as a clause element in this way will be a subordinate clause since it will be unable to stand alone.

We will begin by considering one of our earlier examples a little more closely, namely *The aim was to explore the area.* Here, there is a finite verb *was* and the subject of this verb is *the aim.* We know that *be* is a copular verb and therefore requires a complement to follow it. Here, though, the complement is not a noun phrase or adjective phrase but another clause *to explore the area.* We can represent this analysis as follows:

S	V	C
The aim	*was*	*to explore the area*

Alternatively, we can represent this example as a tree diagram as in Figure 6.1:

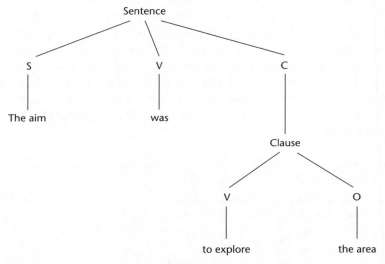

Figure 6.1   An example of an embedded clause functioning as a clause element

The tree diagram shows how the complement element of the finite clause is realised by a non-finite clause. Here we have another example of **embedding**, since the non-finite clause is embedded within the finite one. You will also notice that the label at the top of the tree diagram is 'sentence' not 'clause'. This is because we are dealing here with more than one clause. When a clause occurs in a position where we most typically expect to find a noun phrase then the clause is a **nominal clause**. A nominal clause may occur as subject, object or complement (as we have just seen). Here are examples of nominal clauses in subject and object positions:

S	V	C	
Algebra	*is*	*difficult*	NP as subject
To study algebra	*is*	*difficult*	non-finite clause as subject

S	V	O	
Tim	*wants*	*a foreign holiday*	NP as object
Tim	*wants*	*to start a theatre company*	non-finite clause as object

We will now take a closer look at the example: *Treated kindly, the Labrador will be good*. Here, we have a complete finite clause *the Labrador will be good,* which has an adverbial element *treated kindly* added at the beginning. We saw in Section 6.7 that the adverbial element is likely to be an adverb phrase or a prepositional phrase but could also be a clause. Here it is a non-finite clause. A clause which functions as an adverbial is termed an **adverbial clause**. The following examples show an adverb phrase, a prepositional phrase and a clause functioning as the adverbial element:

A	S	V	C	
Probably	*the Labrador*	*will be*	*good*	AdvP as adverbial
In all likelihood	*the Labrador*	*will be*	*good*	PP as adverbial
Treated kindly	*the Labrador*	*will be*	*good*	clause as adverbial

We saw in Figure 6.1 that a clause may be embedded in another clause when it performs the function of a clause element such as the complement in *The aim was to explore the area*. In this example, the non-finite clause *to explore the area* is an obligatory element since the sentence would be incomplete without it. This is in contrast to the role of the non-finite clause *treated kindly* since here the function of the non-finite clause is as an optional adverbial element. Figure 6.2 gives a diagrammatic representation of the full example *Treated kindly, the Labrador will be good*.

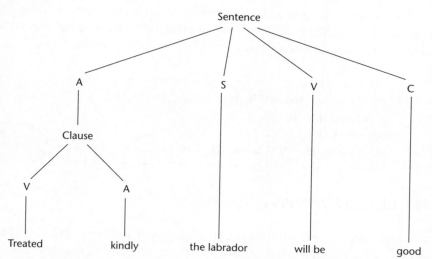

Figure 6.2 An example of a clause functioning as an adverbial element

It isn't just non-finite clauses which function as clause elements. Compare the non-finite examples already given with finite clauses introduced by a subordinating conjunction:

clause as subject

	S		V	C
non-finite	*To study algebra*		*is*	*difficult*
finite	*That algebra is difficult*		*is*	*a well-known fact*

clause as object

	S	V	O
non-finite	*Tim*	*wants*	*to start a theatre company*
finite	*Tim*	*wonders*	*whether he can start a theatre company*

clause as complement

	S	V	C
non-finite	*The aim*	*was*	*to explore the area*
finite	*The aim*	*was*	*that they should explore the area*

clause as adverbial

	A	S	V	C
non-finite	*Treated kindly*	*the Labrador*	*will be*	*good*
finite	*If he is treated kindly*	*the Labrador*	*will be*	*good*

We can see then that clause elements can take the form of either phrases or clauses, and that clauses which perform clause element functions can be either finite or non-finite. This should give you some idea of how complex syntactic structure can be. It is therefore an extraordinary phenomenon that we are able to operate our mental set of syntactic rules without having to think about it and that we are all able to construct sentences of considerable complexity without error.

- ☐ **phrases embedded within phrases** ⇨ 5.6
- ☐ **nominal relative clauses** ⇨ 6.14
- ☐ **subordinate clauses** ⇨ 7.10
- ☐ **meanings of adverbial elements** ⇨ 7.11

6.13 CLAUSES WITHIN PHRASES

In Chapter 5 we saw how nouns (or pronouns) and adjectives could be post-modified by, for example, prepositional phrases and how prepositional phrases could take noun phrases and adverb phrases as the prepositional complement.

We are returning to phrase structure in this section to see how head nouns and head adjectives can be postmodified by a range of clause types and how prepositional phrases can take clauses as their complements. We will begin with nouns and adjectives. Here is the full range of clauses which appear as postmodifiers in these phrase types:

noun phrases	**adjective phrases**
non-finite *to*-infinitive clause	non-finite *to*-infinitive clause
non-finite *-ing* clause	non-finite *-ing* clause
non-finite *-ed* clause	
that-clause	*that*-clause
relative clause	
	wh-clause
comparative clause	comparative clause

There is only a partial overlap between the sets of clauses which each phrase type allows for postmodification. We will look at each type in turn, beginning with the non-finite clauses. The head nouns and head adjectives have been underlined:

	noun phrase	adjective phrase
to-infinitive clause	a <u>place</u> to stay	<u>happy</u> to help
	a <u>place</u> for people to stay	<u>happy</u> for you to help
non-finite *-ing* clause	the <u>storm</u> brewing at sea	<u>busy</u> getting ready
non-finite *-ed* clause	the <u>storm</u> weathered at sea	

The *to*-infinitive clauses can appear with or without an overt subject. As we have seen before, if there is no subject present before the verb then the subject and consequently the agent has to be inferred from the context. So if, for example, the noun phrase *a place to stay* occurred in the context of *I am looking for a place to stay* then the inferred meaning is *I am looking for a place <u>for me</u> to stay*. When a subject is present in the non-finite clause then the clause is introduced by the subordinating conjunction *for*.

Both nouns and adjectives can be postmodified by ***that*-clauses**. These are subordinate clauses introduced by the subordinating conjunction *that*. The verb in the clause will be finite. Here are some examples. Again, the head noun or adjective has been underlined:

noun phrase	adjective phrase
1 the <u>belief</u> that God exists	4 <u>glad</u> that you're feeling better

2 *a faint <u>hope</u> that he will phone*   5 *<u>afraid</u> that she'll see a ghost*
3 *the <u>view</u> that plants have feelings*   6 *<u>anxious</u> that he be caught*

One feature of these clauses is that speakers will often omit *that,* usually because this is less formal: *I'm glad Ø you're feeling better.* This isn't always possible, however: **the view plants have feelings* (rather than *the view that plants have feelings*) seems awkward.

If you look at Example 6 in the previous paragraph you will see that the verb element is unusual: *be caught* rather than *is caught.* This use of the infinitive form of the *be* auxiliary as opposed to the third person singular present tense is sometimes used when the adjective expresses a wish or hope. This use is known as the **subjunctive mood** and it contrasts with all the other verbs we have looked at which are **indicative**. The subjunctive is rarely used in English and it is becoming rarer. You are now more likely to hear speakers say *anxious that he is caught* than *anxious that he be caught.*

We now move on to **relative clauses**, which only postmodify nouns and pronouns. We have already seen that some syntactic structures are particularly economical. This is certainly true of relative clauses. Consider these two sentences:

> *That man bought his shirt in C&A*
> *I saw that man*

We can conflate these two sentences by using a relative clause. There are two options and the relative clause in each has been underlined:

> *That man <u>who/whom I saw</u> bought his shirt in C&A*
> *I saw that man <u>who bought his shirt in C&A</u>*

In each case, the relative clause postmodifies the head word *man.* The relative clause is so-called because it is normally introduced by a **relative pronoun** which has the function of referring us back ('relating' us, if you like) to a preceding noun. The noun to which the relative pronoun refers – in these examples *man* – is the **antecedent**. As well as being introduced by a relative pronoun, the relative clause can be introduced by a handful of other items. Here is the full range:

relative pronouns	*which*	*(that)*	*the colour which I selected*
	who	*(that)*	*the man who shops at* C&A
	whom	*(that)*	*the man whom I saw*

relative determiner	*which*		*(he became) president which position suited him very well*
	whose		*the man whose wallet I found*
relative adverbs	*when*	*(that)*	*the moment when they knew*
	where	*(that)*	*the place where they met*
	why	*(that)*	*the reason why it happened*

The relative pronoun *whom* is used when the antecedent would be the object of the verb in the relative clause. *Whom* is becoming archaic, however, and speakers tend to use *who*. All three *wh-* relative pronouns and all three relative adverbs can be replaced by *that*, again usually to provide a more informal tone: *the colour that I selected* is less formal than *the colour which I selected*. The relative pronoun *that* is distinct from the subordinating conjunction *that* at the start of *that*-clauses. If the clause is a relative clause you will probably be able to replace *that* with *who, whom* or *which*:

> the man that shops at C&A
> the man who shops at C&A
> the belief that God exists
> *the belief who/whom/which God exists

Sometimes it is possible to omit the relative pronoun at the start of the relative clause:

> the man who/whom/that I saw
> the man Ø I saw
> the colour which/that I selected
> the colour Ø I selected

This is because the relative pronoun will be understood from the context. Where no relative pronoun occurs in a relative clause, we say that the clause has a **zero relative pronoun**.

Finally, relative clauses can be introduced by a preposition and relative pronoun. This can be seen in a sentence such as *Scope is the charity <u>for which</u> I did a sponsored walk* (Example 1 below). Alternatively, the preposition can be placed at the end of the relative clause as Example 2 shows:

> 1 *Scope is the charity <u>for</u> which I did a sponsored walk*
> 2 *Scope is the charity which I did a sponsored walk <u>for</u>*

The structure of Example 1 is more formal than that of Example 2.

Let us return briefly to the postmodifying *-ing* and *-ed* clauses we considered at the start of this section. Here again are the two noun phrase examples, this time incorporated into a sentence:

> *The lifeguards discussed <u>the storm brewing at sea</u>*
> *The sailors described <u>the storm weathered at sea</u>*

Some linguists interpret the postmodification in these noun phrases as a reduction of a fuller clause:

> *the storm <u>which was</u> brewing at sea*
> *the storm <u>which was</u> weathered at sea*

These forms are now relative clauses, the first one containing a verb in the progressive aspect and the second containing a verb in the passive voice. Because the postmodifying non-finite *-ing* and *-ed* clauses have this capacity to be expanded into full relative clauses, they are sometimes referred to as **reduced relative clauses**.

We will now return to adjectives to see how they can be postmodified by *wh*-clauses. *Wh*-clauses are introduced by a *wh*-word. Here is a selection of examples with the adjectives underlined:

1 <u>*uncertain*</u> *what he is doing*
2 <u>*happy*</u> *where they were living*
3 <u>*doubtful*</u> *what to do*
4 <u>*confident*</u> *which way to go*

As you can see from these examples, the *wh*-clause can be either finite (Examples 1 and 2) or non-finite (Examples 3 and 4).

The final type of clause which can occur in both adjective and noun phrases is a **comparative clause**. Since comparative clauses can also postmodify adverbs we will consider noun, adjective and adverb phrases together here. There are two types of comparative clause. The first type actually expresses comparison and uses *than* as a subordinator as illustrated below:

noun phrase
Victoria did <u>less homework than she intended</u>
Vanessa has got <u>a better suntan than I have</u>

adjective phrase
The patient felt <u>healthier than the doctor had expected</u>
Louise is <u>more talented than her friends are</u>

adverb phrase
Bill drove the car <u>more carefully than his wife did</u>
Andrew revised for his exams <u>much less thoroughly than he had intended</u>

The head word in each of these phrases is followed by a *than*-clause. All these clauses contain a finite verb. In noun phrases, as in adverb phrases, the head word will be premodified by *more* or *less* or, in a noun phrase, the head noun may be premodified by an adjective in the comparative form as in *a better suntan*. In adjective phrases, the adjective will either take the inflectional comparative form as in *healthier* or again will be premodified by *more* or *less*.

The second type of comparative clause expresses equivalence:

noun phrase
Victoria did not write <u>as good an essay as she had hoped</u>
The aid worker helped <u>as many as she could</u>

adjective phrase
Bill's reactions were not <u>as quick as Vanessa's were</u>

adverb phrase
At the interview Martin performed <u>as impressively as anyone performed</u>

The comparative constructions here involve the correlative subordinators *as … as*. The first *as* precedes the head word and the second *as* introduces the postmodifying clause. Noun phrases which take comparative clauses do so in a different way from adjective and adverb phrases. One possibility is that the first *as* will be attached to an adjective which premodifies the head noun: *as good an essay as she had hoped*. This process affects the order of elements in the noun phrase since the adjective is moved into a position in front of the determiner. The second possibility is that the head word in the noun phrase will be a pronoun: *as many as she could*.

To complete this section, we will briefly look at clauses as prepositional complements. These will be either *wh*-clauses or *-ing* clauses as you can see in the following examples where both the preposition and its complement have been underlined:

1 *This is an event <u>for whoever wants to get involved</u>*
2 *They discussed the problem <u>of how they would raise some money</u>*
3 *<u>In trying to help,</u> she actually made matters worse*
4 *Why don't you go out for a walk <u>instead of watching the television</u>*
5 *It was really a question <u>of finding the right person for the job</u>*

Examples 1 and 2 show prepositional phrases where the prepositional comple-ment is a *wh*-clause. Here, the prepositional phrases are embedded in noun phrases postmodifying the nouns *event* and *problem*. In Examples 3 and 4, the preposition is complemented by an *-ing* participle clause. The prepositional phrase here is not embedded in a noun phrase but functions as an adverbial element to the main clause. In Example 5, the complement is again an *-ing* clause but here the prepositional phrase is postmodifying the noun *question*.

☐ **wh-words** ⇨ 2.13
☐ **noun phrases** ⇨ 5.2
☐ **adjective phrases** ⇨ 5.4
☐ **prepositional phrases** ⇨ 5.5
☐ **non-finite clause** ⇨ 6.10

6.14 NOMINAL RELATIVE CLAUSES

A **nominal relative clause**, as the name suggests, shares features of both nominal clauses and relative clauses. All nominal relative clauses begin with a *wh*-word. Here are some examples which were originally given in Chapter 2:

> *Where to go was quite a problem*
> *Who to ask was quite a problem*
> *Which option to select was quite a problem*

The feature these clauses share with other nominal clauses is that they occur where a noun phrase might occur. In the above examples they are all in subject position although it is equally possible for them to occur as objects or complements:

> *He asked what had happened*   object
> *The impersonator became whoever they wanted him to be*   complement

These clauses resemble relative clauses insofar as they begin with a *wh*-word but, in contrast to relative clauses, the antecedent is implied rather than overt. So the nominal relative clause *what had happened* could be reformulated as a noun phrase with the head noun postmodified by a full relative clause: *the event which had happened*. Similarly, *whoever they wanted him to be* could be expanded into *the characters which they wanted him to be*.

☐ **wh-words** ⇨ 2.13
☐ **nominal clauses** ⇨ 6.12
☐ **relative clauses** ⇨ 6.13

6.15 NEGATIVE CLAUSES

So far virtually all our examples have been in the **affirmative**. This means that the proposition expressed by a sentence is taken to be true. If we wish to deny the truth of a statement, then we need to make it grammatically **negative**. This is normally done using the negative particle *not*:

affirmative	negative
1a *Ravin is a good manager*	1b *Ravin is not a good manager*
2a *Emma might come home*	2b *Emma might not come home*
3a *Emma might have come home*	3b *Emma might not have come home*
4a *Louise liked the film*	4b *Louise did not like the film*

The verb phrases in the examples have been underlined. You can see that the negative particle is added to the verb phrase. There are rules which govern where the negative particle is positioned. If the lexical verb is *be* and the verb phrase contains only the lexical verb then the negative particle will occur after the verb. You can see this in Examples la and lb. Examples 2a, 2b and 3a, 3b show that when the verb phrase contains auxiliaries, the negative particle is added after the first auxiliary. In Examples 4a and 4b you can see that a single-word verb phrase requires the primary auxiliary *do* to be added to the verb phrase so that the negative particle can be positioned after this auxiliary. When *do* is used in this way it is referred to as an **operator**.

Very often when we make a verb phrase negative, we form a **contraction**. This is when a word is shortened in the process of being joined to a preceding word. Thus *is not* becomes *isn't, did not* becomes *didn't* and so on. Contractions are used a great deal in speech since they sound less formal than uncontracted forms.

Clauses and sentences can also include negative items other than the negative particle, although they do not negate the truth of a clause or sentence in the way 'not' does. Here are some examples:

He told me never to do it again	(adverb)
It really is no use	(determiner)
She said nothing about a trip to America	(pronoun)
Nobody came to answer the door	(pronoun)

The position of *never* in the first example is crucial to the meaning of the sentence. There is a contrast in meaning between *He told me never to do it again* and *He never told me to do it again*. This is because a negative element does not affect any preceding phrases or clauses, but only those which follow it.

☐ **auxiliary verbs** ⇨ 2.10

6.16 VERBLESS CLAUSES

So far, we have considered finite clauses as most typical of clause type and structure and non-finite clauses as a less central type. To complete the picture we need to consider clauses which do not contain a verb element at all – **verbless clauses**. Here are some examples:

> *Although unhappy with the decision, Debra agreed to help*
> *Paul would like some champagne and caviar, if available*

The verbless clauses in the above examples are underlined. The reason these examples could be considered clauses is because they both begin with a subordinating conjunction, which normally introduces a full subordinate clause. Further, both these examples have the potential to be expanded into full clauses:

scj	S	V	C
although	Ø	Ø	*unhappy with the decision*
although	*she*	*was*	*unhappy with the decision*
if	Ø	Ø	*available*
if	*they*	*are*	*available*

It is possible then to analyse these examples as verbless clauses functioning as adverbial elements of the main clauses in which they occur. Here are some further examples of verbless clauses:

> *Without any money, Sara couldn't go on holiday*
> *Angry at her sister, Sara stomped out of the room*

It is a little more difficult to argue that these are clauses, however. *Without any money* is a prepositional phrase while *angry at her sister* is an adjective phrase. Both examples are functioning as adverbial elements to the main clauses. If we were to treat these examples as verbless clauses it would have to be on the basis that they could be expanded into full clauses either by adding a non-finite verb element or by adding a subordinating conjunction, a subject element and a verb element:

V	C			
being	*without any money*			*Sara couldn't go on holiday*

scj	S	V	C	
since	*she*	*was*	*without any money*	*Sara couldn't go on holiday*

V	C	
feeling	*angry at her sister*	*Sara stomped out of the room*

scj	S	V	C	
because	*she*	*was*	*angry at her sister*	*Sara stomped out of the room*

The adverbial elements in the examples are now subordinate clauses rather than phrases. It may seem something of a contradiction in terms to have a verbless clause since a verb element is a prerequisite of a clause. On the other hand, this approach allows for a more comprehensive analysis in terms of clause structures. You need to decide for yourself which approach to take. The argument for treating those examples which begin with a subordinating conjunction as a verbless clause is perhaps stronger than the argument for treating phrases functioning as adverbial elements in this way.

Of course, in speech in particular we often omit clause elements because we rely a lot on context for interpretation of meaning. For example, if someone goes into a pub and says *pint of bitter* to the bar attendant then this will be interpreted as *I would like a pint of bitter*. The other clause elements are unnecessary. These kinds of fragments are sometimes termed **minor sentences**.

7 Sentences

7.1 WHAT IS A SENTENCE?

A sentence is the largest unit of syntactic structure. In the previous chapter we looked at the structure of clauses. A sentence must consist of at least one clause but it may consist of several. If a sentence contains just one clause then that clause needs to be a main clause for the sentence to be grammatically complete. If the sentence consists of more than one clause, then for the same reason there will need to be at least one main clause.

It is important to emphasise here that when we talk about sentences we are talking about structural principles rather than written conventions. When we write we indicate sentence divisions by beginning a sentence with a capital letter and concluding it with a full stop. However, a writer may punctuate in a way which doesn't entirely correspond with grammatical sentence boundaries. For example, suppose a writer had written this:

I agreed to go with them. Although I wasn't really happy with the idea.

A teacher may well correct this punctuation on the grounds that the second sentence cannot stand alone and should therefore be connected to the first sentence. The writer, on the other hand, might argue that they had deliberately separated off the second written sentence because they wanted to make it seem like an afterthought. They may also have wanted their writing to be informal. In other words, a writer may adapt punctuation conventions to suit their own purposes. Consider the following example from a novel by Susan Hill:

It will be all right, I shan't have to stay here, even now.

In terms of written conventions we are dealing here with one sentence. The writer is trying to give the impression of a character's flow of panicky thoughts which is presumably why the sentence has been punctuated in this way. Grammatically, however, there are two sentences here:

S	V	C
It	*will be*	*all right*

S	V		A	A
I	*shan't have to stay*		*here*	*even now*

As you can see, there are two main clauses and since there is no conjunction joining them together we should treat them as two distinct sentences grammatically. These examples show you how grammatical sentences may not equate with written punctuated sentences. That is why you should think of a sentence primarily in terms of grammatical rules, not as something you see written on the page.

Another consideration is that when we speak we do not speak in neat grammatical sentences. Sometimes speakers leave what they are saying unfinished. Sometimes they make a false start and have to restructure what they are saying. Equally, they might lose the thread of what they are saying so that the end of the 'sentence' doesn't fully correspond with the start. Often speakers join the units of their speech together with items like *and, but* and *so*, which can make it difficult to decide where sentences might begin or end. This is another reason why we should think of a sentence as part of our mental set of syntactic rules. Neither spoken nor written language will necessarily divide neatly into sentences. Nevertheless, when we speak or write we are still using the implicit notion of the sentence to guide the way we structure our language. If we had no mental sense of clauses and sentences, we would have no awareness of grammatical incompleteness and yet all speakers have the ability to judge whether a given string of words is grammatically complete or incomplete.

In this chapter we will be looking at sentences from several angles. We will begin by looking at structural variations to clauses which give rise to different types of sentence and at how structural variations can change the focus of a sentence. We will then go on to look at how clauses join together to form sentences larger than one clause. Finally we will look more closely at the adverbial element in a clause or sentence since this element has a much wider range of functions than the other four clause elements.

- ☐ **conjunctions** ⇨ 2.12
- ☐ **clause structures** ⇨ 6.8

7.2 SENTENCE TYPES

We saw in Chapter 6 that a declarative clause consists of a subject and predicate (where the predicate is the verb element plus any verb complementation) and is the most typical clause structure. It therefore follows that this is also the most representative type of sentence structure. We will now move on to look at the other possibilities for sentence structure and we will be looking at them in terms of variations on the declarative structure. There are four **sentence types**:

type	typical use	example
declarative	**statement**	*You're wearing a new dress*
interrogative	**question**	*Are you wearing a new dress?*
imperative	**directive**	*Buy yourself a new dress*
exclamative	**exclamation**	*What a lovely new dress you're wearing*

Here again we are dealing with the distinction between form and function. The labels in the left-hand column indicate the syntactic form the sentence will take while those in the second column indicate the functions that these forms normally perform. Significantly, though, these forms and functions do not always correlate. Consider this sentence, which takes the declarative form:

> *That coffee's very hot*

If this were uttered by a speaker who had just put the palm of their hand against a coffee pot to test the temperature, then the sentence could reasonably be interpreted as a statement. If, however, they said it having gulped down a mouthful of the coffee and burnt themselves then it is probably functioning as an exclamation. If it were spoken urgently to a child about to touch the coffee pot then it could be functioning as a command, telling the child not to touch. These examples show us that in various contexts the function of a particular type of sentence may vary. Sometimes, the selection of sentence type is linked to appropriateness of use. A parent might tell their noisy child *Be quiet*, which is an imperative form, but they might use an interrogative form *Would you mind turning down your radio?* to noisy neighbours since it sounds more polite even though a command or request is implicit in the utterance.

It is very important to maintain a clear distinction between the form and the function of sentence types. In the next four sections we will examine the four types and look at the syntactic rules which underlie their construction.

7.3 DECLARATIVE SENTENCES

We looked in some detail at declarative structures in Chapter 6 where we saw that they typically have an overt subject, a verb element and any necessary verb complementation. The declarative sentence may also contain one or more adverbial elements. Here is an example:

S	V	O	A	A
Philip	*will visit*	*his dentist*	*in Streatham*	*today*

The obligatory elements here are the subject, verb and object, while the adverbial elements are optional extras which provide additional information. The SVO structure tells us that this clause is declarative.

We noticed above that a declarative sentence is normally used to make a statement. This statement may of course have a more specific purpose. For instance, the statement *I'd like you to come shopping with me* could express an invitation as well as stating a fact about the speaker. There are some verbs which have a very precise purpose in that the actual uttering of those verbs performs the function to which they refer. For example

> I *promise* that I won't tell anyone your secret
> I *swear* I will tell the truth
> I *name* this ship Titanic
> I now *pronounce* you husband and wife

By uttering these verbs the speaker actually performs the act of promising, swearing, naming or pronouncing. That is why these verbs are referred to as **performative** verbs. However, they are only performative when used by the speaker in the first person, in the simple present tense and in a declarative context. *Will you swear to tell the truth?* is a question, not an actual commitment.

Declarative sentences are by far the most common structures we use in language and may be regarded as typifying the order of elements in English. However, many of the sentences we utter will be variations on this basic order as we shall see in the following sections.

☐ **declarative structure in clauses** ⇨ 6.1

7.4   INTERROGATIVE SENTENCES

Interrogative sentences are normally used to ask a question. Here are some examples:

1 *Are you very rich?*
2 *Does he speak Russian?*

3 *Could they have reached the summit?*
4 *What is the capital of Peru?*
5 *What did the thief take?*
6 *When will we finish this job?*

The first three questions differ in kind from the other three in the type of answers they elicit. The straightforward answer to the questions in Examples 1, 2 and 3 would be *yes* or *no* (although of course in reality speakers often give fuller answers than this). Questions which expect the answer *yes* or *no* are **yes-no** questions. These contrast with Examples 4, 5 and 6 where more specific information is required even if that only involves one word. You will notice that these three examples all begin with a *wh*-word. Questions of this kind which require a specific response are **wh-questions**.

Questions normally require an interrogative structure. Most characteristic of interrogative structure as a departure from declarative structure is a change of position between the subject and the verb:

declarative			interrogative		
S	V	C	V	S	C
You	*are*	*very rich*	*Are*	*you*	*very rich?*

In this example, the subject *you* and the verb *are* have changed positions. This is the simple signal that the sentence has become interrogative. However, this simple exchange only takes place with the verb *be*. Consider this example:

declarative			interrogative			
S	V	O	V_{op}	S	V	O
He	*speaks*	*Russian*	*Does*	*he*	*speak*	*Russian?*

We observed a similar process to this when we were looking at negative clauses in Section 6.15. If we follow the same principle we used for *You are very rich* to make *He speaks Russian* an interrogative then our outcome would be **Speaks he Russian?* Instead of merely inverting the subject and verb we need to use the primary auxiliary *do* as the **operator**. It is the operator which changes places with the subject while the rest of the verb phrase retains its position after the subject. If the verb phrase already contains an operator, in other words if there is already an auxiliary in the verb phrase, then there is no need to add the auxiliary *do*. If the verb phrase contains more than one auxiliary, then it is the first auxiliary which is the operator. (You may also remember that this is the auxiliary which carries tense.) In our third *yes-no* example, then, there is no need of the auxiliary *do*:

declarative

S	V	O
They	*could have reached*	*the summit*

interrogative

V_{op}	S	V	O
Could	*they*	*have reached*	*the summit?*

Here, the first auxiliary in the declarative verb phrase *could* is the operator and changes places with the subject. The process by which declarative structures are made interrogative is known as **subject-operator inversion**. Remember though that the operator rule does not apply when the lexical verb *be* constitutes a single word verb phrase where **subject-verb inversion** is sufficient.

The formation of *wh*-questions also usually requires subject-operator inversion but two additional processes are involved, namely the substitution of one sentence element with a *wh*-word and, often, the bringing of this element to the front:

declarative			interrogative			
S	V	O	$O_{Wh\text{-}}$	V_{op}	S	V
The thief	*took*	*my wallet*	*What*	*did*	*the thief*	*take?*

In this example, three processes have taken place to form the question. The object element about which the question is being asked, namely *my wallet,* has been replaced by a *wh*-pronoun and then brought to the front of the sentence. In addition, subject-operator inversion has taken place. In this case, the primary auxiliary *do* has been added to fulfil the operator function. A similar process has taken place in the following example, but this time the question word replaces an adverbial element:

declarative				interrogative				
S	V	O	A	$A_{Wh\text{-}}$	V_{op}	S	V	O
We	*'ll finish*	*this job*	*today*	*When*	*will*	*we*	*finish*	*this job?*

You can also see from this example that the verb phrase contained an auxiliary so it was unnecessary to supply an operator. We saw that in *yes-no* questions we do not need to add an operator for the lexical verb *be*. The same is true of *wh*-questions. Also, when the subject of a sentence, whatever the lexical verb, is substituted with a *wh*-word, no inversion takes place:

declarative			interrogative		
S	V	C	S$_{Wh-}$	V	C
Lima	*is*	*the capital of Peru*	*What*	*is*	*the capital of Peru?*
S	V	O	S$_{Wh-}$	V	O
Pippa	*married*	*Mick*	*Who*	*married*	*Mick?*

In the examples we have looked at so far the *wh*-word, which is normally either a *wh*-pronoun or *wh*-adverb, replaces a complete clause element. However, the *wh*-word may replace just part of a phrase:

declarative			interrogative			
S	V	O	O$_{Wh-}$	V$_{op}$	S	V
Lloyd	*is wearing*	*his pink shirt*	*Which shirt*	*is*	*Lloyd*	*wearing?*

In this example the *wh*-determiner *which* replaces only part of the NP *his pink shirt*. However, the *wh*-element of the sentence is still brought to the front as in constructions where the *wh*-word replaces an entire element.

There is one other method of asking questions. This is through the use of a **tag question**. A **question tag** is added to a declarative sentence to produce a rather different type of interrogative structure. Here are some examples:

declarative	question tag
He said he'd be here by six,	*didn't he?*
The cat <u>has</u> had its supper,	*hasn't it?*
They <u>couldn't</u> come to the party tonight,	*could they?*
Tracy <u>hasn't</u> been to your flat,	*has she?*

The tag is formed from an auxiliary verb and a pronoun. The auxiliary verb is the operator from the verb element in the main clause of the declarative sentence. Where no operator is present in the declarative, as in the first example, *do* is used in the tag (unless the lexical verb is *be*). The pronoun refers back to the subject of the declarative sentence. You will also notice that when the declarative sentence is positive the tag is negative and vice versa. Normally, a negative tag expects the answer *yes* while a positive one antici-pates *no* as a response.

> ☐ *wh*-pronouns ⇨ 2.8, 2.13
> ☐ *wh*-determiners ⇨ 2.9, 2.13

7.5   IMPERATIVE SENTENCES

An imperative sentence is normally used to direct someone to do something, as you can see from the following examples:

Shut the door at once
Have a good day
Please stop making that noise
Do be quiet

The meaning of the imperative may be quite strong or forceful as in *Shut the door at once* or it may be more gentle and positive as in *Have a good day*. The third example above is introduced by the **politeness marker** *please* which softens the abruptness of *stop making that noise*.

In an imperative sentence the subject element is normally omitted and the lexical verb is in the base form:

A	S	V	O
	Ø	*Shut*	*the door*
	Ø	*Have*	*a good day*
Please	Ø	*stop*	*making that noise*

The verbs in declarative and interrogative sentences will correspond to their subject in terms of first, second or third person. Because the imperative doesn't normally have an overt subject, the question of person is less relevant. However, imperatives are assumed to be in the second person. If the subject were present it would take the form of the second person pronoun *you*: *You have a good day! You be good!* Very occasionally, the imperative is in the third person in which case it has an overt subject:

S	V	O
Nobody	*drink*	*my gin and tonic*
Latecomers	*see*	*me*

Auxiliaries do not normally occur in imperatives although the auxiliary *do* can be used to soften the imperative as in *Do be quiet*. In addition, *do* is used to make the imperative negative as this auxiliary must precede the negative particle *not*: we could contrast *Stop talking* with *Don't stop talking* therefore.

☐ **1st, 2nd and 3rd person** ⇨ 2.8

7.6 EXCLAMATIVE SENTENCES

Exclamative sentences resemble interrogative sentences in so far as a *wh*-word is used in their construction and the *wh*-element is fronted. Here are some examples:

> *What a lovely day it is*
> *What nonsense you talk*
> *How quickly you did that*
> *How they gossip*

Exclamatives only use the *wh*-words *how* and *what* so in this respect they are dissimilar to interrogatives which use a much wider range of *wh*-words. The other major difference is that there is no subject-operator inversion. The *wh*-word is attached to one of the sentence elements and that element is then brought to the front of the sentence. The rest of the sentence structure remains unchanged:

declarative	exclamative	fronted element
It is a lovely day	*What a lovely day it is*	complement
You talk nonsense	*What nonsense you talk*	object
You did that quickly	*How quickly you did that*	adverbial
They gossip (a lot)	*How they gossip*	adverbial

In the last example above *how* is not attached to another element but fills the place of an assumed adverbial such as *a lot* or *a great deal*.

Sometimes you will find that exclamatives consist of simply the *wh*-element and the rest of the sentence is omitted or understood:

full exclamative	reduced exclamative
What a lovely day it is	*What a lovely day*
What nonsense you talk	*What nonsense*
How amazing that is	*How amazing*

Exclamatives are rarely used for anything other than to express exclamations. In this they differ from the other sentence types which have more flexibility of function as we have already seen.

7.7 OTHER STRUCTURAL VARIATIONS

We will look now at some other ways in which sentence structure can vary. In these instances, however, the structural variation does not result in a new sentence type or in a change of voice from active to passive, but in the placing of greater focus on one part of the sentence or in the better balancing of the sentence's structure. The variations we will be looking at may involve the change in position of a clause element or the removal of an item from its normal position within a phrase.

We will begin by looking at **extraposition**. As the name suggests, this involves moving a linguistic item (normally a subordinate clause) out of its normal clause position and placing it later in the clause or sentence, usually after the other obligatory elements. Here is a typical example:

SVC structure

S	V	C
That Jane is very thoughtful	*is*	*common knowledge*

structure after extraposition

dummy S	V	C	extraposed S
It	*is*	*common knowledge*	*that Jane is very thoughtful*

The first example above shows the regular declarative SVC structure of the sentence. The subject of the sentence is a subordinate *that*-clause *That Jane is very thoughtful*. This is quite a problematic structure despite conforming to the SVC pattern. Most typically, subjects are noun phrases rather than clauses. Subordinate clauses are often easier to process when they follow the main verb of the sentence rather than precede it. Further, the complexity of the subject element causes quite a high information load at a point where the main verb, which has a pivotal function in a sentence, has not yet been introduced. These are all reasons why we should extrapose the subject. In the reorganised sentence above the subject has been moved to a position after the complement. However, this leaves the subject position empty and so it is filled with the dummy subject *it*. Because the dummy subject is signalling the removal of the actual subject to a later position in the sentence, it is referred to as **anticipatory *it***.

Extraposed subjects are always clauses but they need not necessarily be finite *that*-clauses. Here is an example with a non-finite *-ing* clause as the subject:

SVC structure

S	V	C
Keeping bees	*can be*	*rather tricky*

structure after extraposition

dummy S	V	C	extraposed S
It	*can be*	*rather tricky*	*keeping bees*

It needn't be the subject of a clause which is extraposed. Here is an example of the object of a complex-transitive verb being extraposed:

SVOC structure

S	V	O	C_o
*The teacher	*made*	*that coursework was due in*	*clear*

structure after extraposition

S	V	dummy O	C_o	extraposed O
The teacher	*made*	*it*	*clear*	*that coursework was due in*

In this example, it is so natural for speakers to extrapose the object that the SVOC structure is grammatically unacceptable. This is due to the high information load in the object element preceding the far simpler complement element. The other advantage of the extraposed structure is that the most important part of the information in the sentence, namely *that coursework was due in,* is postponed until the end of the sentence where it will receive greater attention.

Another type of extraposition is when a relative clause is removed from the noun phrase in which it occurs:

A *book which reveals new information about the religious beliefs of William Shakespeare* (S) *was published* (V) *today* (A)

The subject noun phrase here contains a very long relative clause which post-modifies the head noun *book*. This results in the part of the sentence preceding the main verb being uncomfortably longer than the adverbial which closes it. Without the adverbial, the sentence would seem even more awkward. In order to redress this problem, the relative clause can be removed from the noun phrase and positioned at the end of the sentence, even after the non-obligatory adverbial:

S	V	A	extraposed relative clause
A book	*was published*	*today*	*which reveals...*

Immediately, the sentence seems more balanced. In addition, attention is now focused on the most important information in the sentence, which is contained in the relative clause and concerns Shakespeare's religious beliefs.

Another structure which, like some of the examples of extraposition, makes use of *it* as a dummy subject is the **cleft sentence**. The purpose of this structure is again to place more focus on a particular piece of information within the sentence. Consider this example:

S	V	O	A
Terry	*plays*	*jazz piano*	*for fun*

Here, we may wish to place emphasis on *Terry* to distinguish him from, say, *Clive*. We can do this by rearranging the sentence as follows:

dummy S	V(*be*)	C (focus + relative clause)
It	*is*	*<u>Terry</u> who plays jazz piano for fun*

The rearranged sentence is introduced by a dummy subject, followed by the verb *be*, then the focus of the sentence, *Terry*, and finally the rest of the information in the sentence placed in a relative clause. If we wanted to place the emphasis on *jazz piano*, this is equally possible:

dummy S	V(*be*)	C (focus + relative clause)
It	*is*	*<u>jazz piano</u> that Terry plays for fun*

We could even if we wish place the focus on *for fun* (as a contrast perhaps to *for a living*) and contain the rest of the information in a *that*-clause:

dummy S	V(*be*)	C (focus + *that*-clause)
It	*is*	*<u>for fun</u> that Terry plays jazz piano*

As you can see, a cleft sentence provides a versatile structure for drawing attention to the information given by a variety of sentence elements.

We saw in Section 6.3 that *there* can function as a dummy subject as well as *it*. *There* is used as a dummy subject in conjunction with the verb *be*. Consider this example as a possible response to being asked what was in the wine rack:

> **Six bottles of white wine and four of red are*

Here the respondent is using the verb *be* to state the existence of something, namely six bottles of white wine and four bottles of red wine. The reason this answer is grammatically unacceptable, however, is that the verb *be* is a copular verb and needs to be followed by a complement. (Only very rarely can this verb be used without a complement: *I think therefore I am* is an example.)

A possible way to make the answer grammatically complete might be to add *in the wine rack:*

	S			V	C	A
	? Six bottles of white wine and four of red			*are*	*Ø*	*in the wine rack*

An alternative, and more natural response (partly because the inclusion of *in the wine rack* seems rather redundant) is to move the subject noun phrase into complement position and insert the dummy subject *there* into the subject slot:

dummy S	V	C
There	*are*	*six bottles of white wine and four of red*

The sentence is now grammatically complete and sounds completely natural as a response to the question (not, of course, that sentences of this structure are only used as answers to questions). The noun phrase which was formerly the subject has moved into the complement position although interestingly it still possesses two key features of a grammatical subject. First, it provides the information on which the main verb is predicated. Second, it still controls whether the verb is singular or plural as these examples demonstrate:

dummy S	V	C
There	*has been*	*an accident*
There	*have been*	*two accidents*

This SVC structure, then, is unusual in this respect. When *there* is used as a dummy subject in this way to state the existence of whatever is referred to by the noun phrase in complement position, it is known as **existential** *there*.

The existential *there* construction may be used to change the focus of a sentence as well as to achieve the kind of grammatical completeness which we have just been considering. A sentence containing a lexical verb other than *be* could be rearranged in this way:

S	V	A
A raven	*is flying*	*towards us*

dummy S	V	C
There	*'s*	*a raven flying towards us*

The rearranged structure has the property of giving more emphasis to the subject of the original sentence, *a raven*. You will notice how the rest of the information is placed as a non-finite postmodifying clause to *raven*. A full relative clause might also occur:

S	V	O
Only three students	*have gained*	*A grades*

dummy S	V	C
There	*are*	*only three students who have gained A grades*

In these two examples, the SVO sentence is perfectly natural grammatically. However, the rearranged sentence gives even greater emphasis to *only three students*.

So far, we have seen that many sentences are restructured in order to achieve greater emphasis on one of their elements. The part of the sentence whose content is of most importance is the **focus**. We normally expect this to come at the end of a sentence – what is known as **end-focus** – and we have seen already how extraposed and cleft structures enable large units of important information to be moved to this position or at least away from initial position. However, it is possible to change the focus of a sentence without the addition of the dummy subjects *there* and *it*. One way to do this in speech is to place greater stress on one element. In writing this is sometimes achieved by underlining as you can see if you compare the following two examples:

Philip had <u>*three fillings*</u> at the dentist's
<u>*Philip*</u> had three fillings at the dentist's

The underlining in the first example implies that the writer hadn't expected Philip to have any treatment at all, while the underlining in the second sentence suggests there was some confusion as to who had the fillings. An alternative method of indicating the focus of a sentence is to move an element out of its normal position:

O	S	V	A
Three fillings	*Philip*	*had*	*at the dentist's*

Here the object element has been moved to the front of the sentence and this unusual position enables the speaker to focus on *three fillings* and thus imply surprise at the subject's need to have dental treatment. The process of moving an element to the beginning of a sentence in this way is known as **fronting**.

In contrast to fronting, **end-shift** may be employed to move a subject to the end of the sentence:

Keith hates kidney beans and chick peas
Hates kidney beans and chick peas does Keith

The rearranged sentence above has the advantage of giving prominence both to the verb element *hates,* emphasising the strength of feeling, and to the subject *Keith,* drawing attention to who exactly is doing the hating. You will notice that the auxiliary *does* is added at the end (as if from *Keith does hate...*) although it is sometimes possible simply to remove the subject to the end:

Showed themselves to be an absolute dead loss <u>the Conservative government</u>

Sometimes, a sentence may be inverted through both fronting and end-shift:

C	V	S
Of most concern	*has been*	*the cause of the disease*

Here, there are several reasons why we instinctively know that an exchange of subject and complement positions has taken place as opposed to this being an SVC structure. First, we would judge *The cause of the disease has been of most concern* to be the most natural arrangement for the example. Further, the complement here is a prepositional phrase and it is unlikely that this form would fulfil the subject function. *The cause of the disease* is typical of a subject element in that it is a noun phrase but it also governs whether the verb is singular or plural as the following example shows:

C	V	S
Of most concern	*<u>have</u> been*	*the <u>causes</u> of the disease*

There are many possible variations on basic clause and sentence structure. While some variations are used so that sentences perform different functions such as asking a question or issuing a command, others are used, as we have seen in this section, to change the emphasis of a sentence or to make it more manageable or balanced.

☐ **subject element** ⇨ 6.3
☐ **dummy subject** ⇨ 6.3
☐ **object element** ⇨ 6.5
☐ **complement element** ⇨ 6.6
☐ **subordinate clauses** ⇨ 6.11

7.8 SIMPLE SENTENCES

At the beginning of this chapter we noted that a sentence may consist of just one clause. Such a sentence is a **simple sentence**. The clause in a simple sentence has to be a main clause. In other words, it has to contain a finite verb and must be grammatically complete as it stands. If for instance the clause were introduced by the subordinating conjunction *because,* then it would not be a simple sentence but the subordinate part of a larger sentence. Neither of the following could be termed simple sentences even though they only contain one clause:

S	V	O
Lloyd	*overcoming*	*his fear of spiders*

scj	S	V	O
Because	*Lloyd*	*overcame*	*his fear of spiders*

Both examples contain only one clause which has an SVO structure. The first example however is not a main clause because the verb is non-finite. The second example is not a main clause as the presence of the subordinating conjunction *because* prevents it from being grammatically complete. The first example could be converted into a main clause by adding a tensed auxiliary to the verb phrase – *Lloyd is overcoming his fear of spiders* – while the second would be an independent clause if *because* were removed to give *Lloyd overcame his fear of spiders*. Both of these examples are now simple sentences.

When we talk about a sentence being a simple sentence we are referring to its grammatical structure not to the information load it contains. The following example is a simple sentence despite its length and relative complexity:

S
The venerable precentor of Gloucester Cathedral whom I met last summer

V	O
has been organising	*a musical tour of antipodean churches*

This is a long sentence and it is complex in that it contains some quite specialised vocabulary and the subject noun phrase in particular contains a lot of modification. Grammatically, however, this sentence is simple, its structure being SVO.

By contrast, the shortest declarative sentence possible could consist of only two words:

S	V
Someone	*coughed*

Here, the subject takes the form of a noun phrase which consists of just the pronoun *someone*. The verb phrase is in the simple past tense and so it contains no auxiliary verbs. Because the verb *cough* is intransitive, the sentence is complete without the need for any verb complementation. Of course, it is possible to expand any simple sentence by adding adverbials. Provided these adverbials are not themselves clauses, then the sentence remains a simple one:

A	S	V	A	A
Suddenly	*someone*	*coughed*	*loudly*	*in the next room*

The adverbials which have been added here take the form of two adverbs (*suddenly* and *loudly*) and one prepositional phrase (*in the next room*).

A simple sentence need not be declarative. Imperative, interrogative and exclamative sentences are simple as long as they contain a main clause only:

Fetch my newspaper	imperative
Where's my newspaper	interrogative
What a useless newspaper this is	exclamative

It is important to make a clear distinction between sentence type and sentence structure. Sentence type will be either declarative, imperative, interrogative or exclamative. The structure of a sentence will be simple, compound or complex. We have also looked at function (statement, question, directive or exclamation) as a further aspect of sentences.

So far we have seen that simple sentences contain one verb element and that this occurs within a main clause. Consider the following example which contains two verb elements:

S	V	O
I	<u>*know*</u>	*a man who has an irrational fear of spiders*

This sentence is an SVO main clause which has *know* as its verb. The object element of the clause is a noun phrase which has *man* as its head. You will see though that *man* is postmodified by the relative clause *who has an irrational fear of spiders*. Since the sentence contains this subordinate clause, it might not seem like a simple sentence. However, compare it with this sentence:

S	V	O
The man	*knows*	*that his fear of spiders is irrational*

Here, the object element is not a phrase but a subordinate *that*-clause:

scj	S	V	C
that	*his fear of spiders*	*is*	*irrational*

If we remove this subordinate clause then the sentence will be incomplete:

S	V	O
The man	*knows*	*Ø*

This incompleteness results from the fact that the object element was realised by a clause. If we remove the subordinate relative clause from *I know a man who has an irrational fear of spiders* then a complete grammatical sentence remains:

S	V	O
I	*know*	*a man*

This is because the subordinate clause was only part of the object noun phrase and therefore had a rather different function in the sentence from the subordinate clause which constituted the entire object element. When a sentence which contains only one main clause has a subordinate clause as part of one of its elements and that subordinate clause can therefore be removed without loss of grammatical completeness, then that sentence is still a simple sentence. So we treat *I know a man who has an irrational fear of spiders* as a simple sentence. If, on the other hand, a subordinate clause (finite or non-finite) makes up an entire element in a clause and grammatical incompleteness will result if it is removed, then the sentence is not simple but **complex**. We will deal with complex sentences in Section 7.10.

☐ **relative clauses** ⇨ 6.13

7.9 COMPOUND SENTENCES

There are two ways of incorporating more than one clause into a sentence (apart from embedding one of them in a phrase). One option is to link two or more clauses on an equal basis so neither clause is dependent on the other. The alternative is to place clauses in an unequal relationship so that one is grammatically dependent on the other. The latter method produces a **complex sentence**, the former a **compound sentence**. The process of forming a compound sentence by joining two or more clauses on an equal grammatical footing is known as **coordination**.

We saw in Chapter 5 that the words in a sentence are grouped together first and foremost into phrases and that every word is part of a phrase even if that phrase only contains one word. There is, however, an exception to the principle that all words are grouped into phrases and this exception concerns conjunctions, particularly when they are used to join clauses. The conjunctions which we use to join clauses on an equal basis and thus form compound sentences are **coordinating conjunctions. Coordinator** is an alternative term for a coordinating conjunction.

There are three central coordinators. These are *and, but* and *or.* Here is an example of two main clauses joined with *and* to form a compound sentence:

S	V	O	ccj	S	V	O
I	*read*	*a book*	*and*	*she*	*watched*	*a film*

This compound sentence consists of two main SVO clauses. In this example, it would be possible to reverse the sequence of the clauses:

S	V	O	ccj	S	V	O
She	*watched*	*a film*	*and*	*I*	*read*	*a book*

The coordinating conjunction must remain between the two clauses, however. This is in contrast to a subordinating conjunction such as *while* which can occur at the beginning of the sentence:

> *She watched a film and I read a book*
> * *And I read a book she watched a film*
> *She watched a film <u>while</u> I read a book*
> *<u>While</u> I read a book she watched a film*

The reason it is impossible to place a coordinating conjunction anywhere other than between the two clauses which it joins is that the conjunction is a linking element joining the clauses on an equal grammatical basis. A subordinating conjunction by contrast introduces a clause and makes it subordinate to the main clause in a sentence. Because it is attached to a specific clause in this way rather than linking two clauses, if the clause moves its position, then the subordinating conjunction will move with it.

There is a restriction on the order of the main clauses which *and* joins if the clauses refer to events which occurred in a particular sequence:

> *The attendant opened the front door and I entered the hotel*
> * *I entered the hotel and the attendant opened the front door*

The restriction evident in the second example above is a semantic one and not a grammatical one.

A compound sentence contains at least two main clauses but more are possible. The coordinators *and* and *or* can be used to join three or more main clauses:

> *Jo can come to your house or you can go to hers or you can meet at the pub*
> *The phone rang and the doorbell went and the dog was barking all at once*

By contrast, *but* can only join two main clauses. This is not due to any grammatical property possessed by this conjunction, but to its semantic function of expressing contrast or the opposite of what is expected:

> *William likes Baba the Elephant but Benedict prefers The Teletubbies*
> *The task was difficult but they enjoyed themselves*

There is then a greater restriction on *but* in its capacity to link clauses than there is on the conjunctions *and* and *or*.

The coordinator *or* is sometimes accompanied by *either* at the beginning of the first clause in a compound sentence. This gives emphasis to the alternatives expressed:

> <u>*Either*</u> *Gregory will cook the supper or Clare will fetch a takeaway*

The pair *either/or* are **correlative**. You will see above that *either* occurs at the beginning of the first clause in the compound. In Section 5.7 we saw that coordinators can join phrases as well as clauses. *Either/or* can join both phrases and clauses, as can their negative counterparts *neither/nor*. However, when *neither/nor* coordinate clauses, the clause structure changes:

> *Julia decided to take either the bus or the train*
> *Julia liked neither her job nor the commuting*
> * *Neither Julia liked her job nor she liked the commuting*
> *Neither <u>did</u> Julia like her job nor <u>did</u> she like commuting*

The correlative pair *both/and* has the capacity to join phrases but not clauses:

> *Both Terry and Julia washed up*
> * *Both Terry washed the dishes and Julia dried them*

It is important to distinguish between coordination of clauses and coordination of phrases since this enables us to explain why not all the sentences above are grammatically possible.

The less central coordinator *nor,* which we have just seen operating as a correlative, is the negative counterpart of *or.* This coordinator replaces *or* when the first clause in a compound sentence is negative, and again it requires a different clause structure with an operator preceding the subject:

> *The pizza hadn't been delivered nor had the restaurant phoned*

Like *or, nor* can coordinate more than two clauses. It can also coordinate phrases as well as clauses.

The other less central coordinator is *for.* In many respects this behaves like one of the central coordinators. We can compare it to *and* in terms of the position in which it occurs, for example:

> *We were feeling cold and it was snowing*
> *We were feeling cold for it was snowing*
> **And it was snowing we were feeling cold*
> **For it was snowing we were feeling cold*

However, *for* differs from the other coordinators in that it is restricted to the linking of main clauses. It is like *but* in that it can only link two main clauses. However, it cannot link phrases nor can it link two subordinate clauses on an equal basis, a property which the other coordinators possess.

In a compound sentence we very often repeat in the second clause some of the information given in the first:

> 1a *Terry cut the grass and <u>Terry</u> weeded the flower beds*
> 2a *Terry painted the ceiling and Julia <u>painted</u> the walls*

In Example 1a the subject *Terry* occurs in both clauses while in Example 2a the verb *painted* occurs in both clauses. Sometimes we reiterate information for the purpose of emphasis, but often there is no need to repeat an item just given. Therefore we simply omit the item which would have been repeated because it will still be understood by our audience. This omission of retrievable information is known as **ellipsis**. Ellipsis can be indicated by using the Ø symbol. Here are Examples 1a and 2a reformulated using ellipsis:

> 1b *Terry cut the grass and Ø weeded the flower beds*
> 2b *Terry painted the ceiling and Julia Ø the walls*

Ellipsis is a feature very commonly found in compound sentences and is another example of the economy we practise in language. Similar omission, however, is not possible when one clause is subordinate to another:

1c   *Since Terry cut the grass, he also weeded the flower beds*
1d **Since Terry cut the grass, Ø also weeded the flower beds*
2c   *Terry painted the ceiling while Julia painted the walls*
2d **Terry painted the ceiling while Julia Ø the walls*

This is a significant constraint on ellipsis and indicates one of the important differences between clauses joined through coordination and those joined in an unequal relationship through subordination.

> ☐ **conjunctions** ⇨ 2.12
> ☐ **coordination of phrases** ⇨ 5.7
> ☐ **ellipsis** ⇨ 8.7

7.10   COMPLEX SENTENCES

A **complex sentence** contains at least two clauses. However, in contrast to a compound sentence where the clauses are equal grammatically, one of the clauses will be subordinate and will constitute an entire element of the main clause. We saw in Section 6.11 that a range of clause types can be subordinate and we will look more fully at this range shortly. For the sake of completeness in this section we will also be reiterating some of the points made in Section 6.12 and we will be looking again at how subordinate clauses function as clause elements.

The verb element of a clause has to be a verb phrase so it is impossible for an entire clause to fulfil this function. However, a clause can function as any of the other clause elements. First, we will consider how clauses can act as the subject, object or complement element in a higher level clause. For the time being, we will use examples of *that*-clauses rather than other types of subordinate clauses:

clause as subject

S	V	C
That Brian has the flu	*is*	*obvious to everyone*

clause as object

S	V	O
Guy	*knows*	*that Brian has the flu*

clause as complement

S	V	C
The problem	*is*	*that Brian has the flu*

In all three examples above, one of the clause elements is a subordinate clause. This means that all these examples are complex sentences. When a subordinate clause acts as an obligatory clause element in this way, the subordinate clause is **embedded** in the main clause. Figure 7.1 gives a diagrammatic illustration of the relationship of the embedded subordinate clause to the main or **superordinate** clause.

Sometimes, however, the function of a subordinate clause is less central than this. This is when the subordinate clause functions as a non-obligatory adverbial element of the superordinate main clause.

A	S	V	O	A
When Brian recovers from the flu	*he*	*will ride*	*his bike*	*again*

There are two adverbials in this complex sentence. The adverbial at the end of the sentence is the adverb *again*. The adverbial element at the start of the sentence however is a subordinate clause and it is the presence of this clause in the sentence which makes it a complex one.

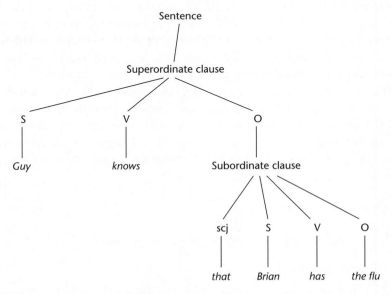

Figure 7.1 The relationship between superordinate and subordinate clauses

We will now look more fully at the range of possibilities for the form which a subordinate clause can take. We will select just one of the clause elements – the object element – for our range of examples. First, the subordinate clause may be non-finite:

bare infinitive

		S	V	O
without subject	1	*Fenella*	*dared*	*jump in the deep end*
with subject	2	*Alissa*	*watched*	*Jane wash up*

to-infinitive

		S	V	O
without subject	3	*Phil*	*wants*	*to start a music company*
with subject	4	*Jane*	*wants*	*Phil to start a music company*

-ing participle clause

		S	V	O
without subject	5	*Emma*	*likes*	*driving her new car*
with subject	6	*Tajal*	*saw*	*Emma driving her new car*

-ed participle clause

		S	V	O
with subject	7	*Bill*	*saw*	*Chris beaten to a pulp*

An almost complete range of non-finite clauses, both with and without overt subjects, can fulfil the object function of a superordinate clause (and of course the range of non-finite clauses can function as subject, complement and adverbial elements too).

The subordinate clause which functions as a clause element can also be a finite clause. Here is an example of a finite *that*-clause functioning as the object element:

S	V	O
Jo	*knew*	*that her new job offered excellent prospects*

If we analyse the subordinate clause in this example, you will see that it is declarative in structure:

scj	S	V	O
that	*her new job*	*offered*	*excellent prospects*

We could compare this finite clause to any of the non-finite subordinate clauses given previously, such as this one from Example 6:

S	V	O
Emma	*driving*	*her new car*

Even the subordinate clauses from Examples 1, 3 and 5 above which lack an overt subject can be analysed as having a declarative structure particularly since the subject can be understood by retrieving it from the main clause. If we take Example 3, *Phil wants to start a music company*, it is clear that the understood subject of *to start* is *Phil*:

S	V	O
(Phil)	*to start*	*a music company*

This non-finite clause is declarative in structure since it has an implied subject followed by the verb and the object which complements the verb *start*.

So far, all our examples of subordinate clauses have been declarative, whether they have contained finite or non-finite verb elements. However, subordinate clauses can also be interrogative or exclamative. A finite declarative clause, when functioning as a subject or object or possibly a complement element, will be a *that*-clause. If the subordinate clause is finite but interrogative then the subordinators will be either *if* or *whether* when the interrogative is a *yes-no* question:

S	V	O	
Clare	*wondered*	*whether Gregory was back*	*(Is Gregory back?)*
Simon	*asked*	*if he could use the phone*	*(Can I use the phone?)*

If the interrogative, however, is a *wh*-question, then it will begin with a *wh*-word (pronoun, adverb or determiner):

S	V	O	
Clare	*asked*	*who had phoned*	(*wh*-pronoun)
Clare	*wondered*	*where Gregory had gone*	(*wh*-adverb)
Clare	*inquired*	*what time it was*	(*wh*-determiner)

We saw in Section 7.4 that in *wh*-interrogatives, the *wh*-word is brought to the front of the clause and there is subject-operator inversion unless the *wh*-word is the subject of the sentence. In subordinate interrogative clauses this subject-operator inversion does not take place:

interrogative main clause

A_{Wh-}	V_{op}	S	V
Where	has	Gregory	gone?

interrogative subordinate clause

	A_{Wh-}	S	V
(Clare wondered)	where	Gregory	had gone

One of the signals of subordination here, in addition to the fact that the subordinate clause is functioning as the object of the main clause, is that the subject-operator inversion normally found in interrogatives does not occur. Non-finite clauses can also be subordinate *wh*-interrogatives but only when the non-finite verb is a *to*-infinitive:

S	V	O
Terry and Julia	have decided	where to go for their holiday
Terry and Julia	did not know	whether to go to America

The first subordinate interrogative above – *where to go for their holiday* – is a *wh*-interrogative while the second example – *whether to go to America* – is a *yes-no* interrogative. Neither of these non-finite clauses contains an overt subject and the subject of the infinitive has to be inferred from the main clause.

Subordinate clauses can be exclamative as well as declarative or interrogative. However, the range of clause types is far more limited here as the subordinate exclamatives only begin with *how* or *what* in the same way as a main clause exclamative. There is no word order variation:

main clause
What a nuisance homework can be

exclamative as embedded subordinate clause
Viren knows what a nuisance homework can be

main clause
How disappointing that film was

exclamative as embedded subordinate clause
Jon told Gill how disappointing that film was

Subordinate exclamative clauses are considerably more restricted in their range than interrogative and declarative clauses.

Complex sentences, then, contain a subordinate clause which functions as an element of the superordinate or main clause. When a subordinate clause occurs where a noun phrase would more typically occur (usually as the subject or object of the main clause), then the subordinate clause is a **nominal clause** and is embedded in the main clause. Sometimes, however, a subordinate clause is linked to the main clause in a more peripheral way. This is when the subordinate clause functions as the optional adverbial element of the main clause. It is these **adverbial clauses** which we will look at in the next section.

In this section and the preceding two sections, we have seen that sentences are essentially simple, compound or complex. Very often, however, a sentence will not fit neatly into one of these categories. Consider this example:

Sara wanted a new bike and Heidi wanted one too if she could afford it

Here, the main clauses *Sara wanted a new bike* and *Heidi wanted one too* are coordinated with the conjunction *and*. However, the second main clause also has a subordinate clause *if she could afford it*. This combination of two coordinated main clauses and one subordinate clause means the sentence is **compound-complex**. Similarly, a complex sentence may contain two subordinate clauses which are coordinated:

Heidi wanted a new bike if she could afford it and if she saw one she liked

The main clause here is *Heidi wanted a new bike*. The sentence contains an adverbial element *if she could afford it and if she saw one she liked* which consists of two subordinate clauses coordinated with *and*. Other combinations of main and subordinate clauses are possible. This wider range of options for sentence construction in no way detracts, however, from the salience of the three-way division between simple, compound and complex sentences.

☐ **subordinate clauses** ⇨ 6.11
☐ **clauses as clause elements** ⇨ 6.12
☐ **variation in sentence structure** ⇨ 12.7

7.11   ADVERBIAL CLAUSES

We saw in Section 6.7 that the adverbial element in a clause may be an adverb phrase or a prepositional phrase. These repeated examples illustrate this:

> *Julia speaks French <u>very fluently</u>*   AdvP
> *Terry was digging up the weeds <u>in his garden</u>*   PP

In addition, the adverbial element of a clause may be another clause, although this clause will be subordinate. In the following example, the subordinate clause which functions as the adverbial element is introduced by the subordinating conjunction *since:*

> A   S   V   O
> *Since it was very cold   Terry   lit   a fire*

We noted in Section 2.7 that adverbs as a word class can be subdivided into adjuncts, disjuncts and subjuncts according to their function. Similarly, adverbial elements – which of course function like adverbs whatever form they take – can also function as adjuncts, disjuncts or subjuncts. The same is true for adverbial clauses, although these largely function as adjuncts or disjuncts.

Adjuncts usually express manner, time, place or degree. Here are some examples of adverbials expressing the first three of these:

adverbial of manner
He walked <u>awkwardly</u>   AdvP
He walked <u>with a limp</u>   PP
He walked <u>as if he had hurt his foot</u>   subordinate clause

adverbial of place
He sat <u>here</u>   AdvP
He sat <u>in the garden</u>   PP
He sat <u>where he could</u>   subordinate clause

adverbial of time
He arrived <u>yesterday</u>   AdvP
He arrived <u>in the morning</u> PP
He arrived <u>after I left</u>   subordinate clause

Adverbs function as disjuncts when they comment on what is said or the way that something is said. Adverbials can also function in this way:

1	*Frankly, I don't think this is a good idea*	AdvP
2	*In all honesty, I don't think this is a good idea*	PP
3	*If I'm honest, I don't think this is a good idea*	subordinate clause
4	*Surprisingly, the party was a success*	AdvP
5	*In spite of the band, the party was a success*	PP
6	*Although the band was dire, the party was a success*	subordinate clause

In Examples 1 to 3 the adverbial element provides a comment on the way something is said, while in Examples 4 to 6 it comments on the content of the main clause.

Adverbials which function disjunctively often express condition, concession, reason, purpose or result. **Conditional clauses** often begin with the subordinating conjunction *if*, although other subordinating conjunctions such as *provided, supposing, unless* and *as long as* can also introduce them, as can some *wh*-words:

> *If you want, we can go and see the new James Bond movie*
> *Provided you're free, we can go and see the new James Bond movie*
> *Whenever you're free, we can go and see the new James Bond movie*

Concessive clauses, which express an unexpected qualification to the content of the main clause, normally begin with *although, though* or *while*:

> *Although you're angry, I'm going to do this anyway*
> *While I appreciate you're angry, I'm going to do this anyway*

Reason clauses are typically introduced by *as, because, for* and *since*:

> *I'm going to bed because I don't feel well*
> *I'm going to bed for that is the only way I can get rid of this flu*

Adverbial clauses can also be **purpose clauses** or **result clauses**:

So that he could see better, the boy stood on the box	purpose
The boy stood on the box so then he could see better	result

The subordinating conjunctions which normally introduce purpose clauses are *in order that, in order to, so, so as to* and *so that,* while *so* and *so that* can also introduce result clauses.

☐ **adverbs** ⇨ 2.7
☐ **subordinating conjunctions** ⇨ 2.12
☐ **adverb phrases** ⇨ 5.4
☐ **prepositional phrases** ⇨ 5.5
☐ **adverbial elements** ⇨ 6.7
☐ **subordinate clauses** ⇨ 6.11

Grammatical Frameworks: Exercises

Exercise 1: Noun plurals

1. The table below contains nouns which have irregular plurals. Complete the table (the first example has been done for you) by identifying the irregular plural, the type of irregular plural, and whether the noun can also take the regular plural inflection. Where there is the possibility of using a regular plural form as well as the irregular one, what is likely to influence the user's choice?

Singular noun	Irregular plural	Type of plural	Can regular plural be used?
cactus	cacti	regular Latin plural	yes – cactuses
corona			
bacterium			
goose			
criterion			
syllabus			
curriculum			
stigma			
louse			
appendix			
kibbutz			

2. The following extract is from a book by Trinny Woodall and Susannah Constantine giving women guidance on fashion. Identify the plural nouns and comment on the forms they take. Identify and comment on any unusual word forms in this passage.

> ### TROUSERS
> *Our least favourite trouser has pleats at the waist and tapered legs which end at the ankle. And it's usually black too. Get rid of it, or them, immediately. And bin any jeans which are stone washed, drainpipe, studded or way too tight. You've probably got several pairs you no longer wear taking up valuable space in your wardrobe.*

Exercise 2: Irregular verb forms

Irregular verbs can be subdivided into various categories.

1. Work out the *-ed* past tense form and the *-ed* participle form of the following bases: *blow, cut, go, hit, keep, send, sew, shut, swell, take, teach*
2. Group the verbs according to their patterns of irregularity. Explain your groupings.

Exercise 3: Phrase structures

In speech, phrases, especially noun phrases, are typically less complex than they are in formal writing. The following passage is an extract of speech from a conversation between two teenagers discussing the television series *Lost* in which the noun phrases, adjective phrases and prepositional phrases have been underlined.

1. Identify the type of each phrase.
2. Identify any pre- or postmodification in the phrase
3. Comment on the level of complexity of these phrases in this spoken extract

A	when's <u>that</u> coming back on
B	<u>that</u> should be back on soon
A	yeah <u>I</u> think (.)
B	<u>it</u>'s great but <u>it</u> pisses <u>you</u> off
A	<u>it</u>'s after (.)
B	I mean <u>you</u> sort of get into <u>the story</u>
A	yeah
B	for <u>it</u> to be continued <u>next week</u>
A	right (.) but then <u>you</u> can watch <u>it</u> <u>on E4</u>
B	I mean <u>it</u> was <u>good</u> (.) <u>very cleverly written</u> again but (.)
A	yeah <u>I</u> agree <u>nothing</u> has really developed <u>since the first series</u>
B	<u>nothing</u> really and to be <u>honest</u> when <u>it</u> comes on <u>I</u> don't think <u>I</u> even want to watch <u>it</u>
A	<u>I</u> enjoyed <u>the last episode</u> when <u>they</u> were <u>on the raft</u> and <u>they</u> came and <u>they</u> took <u>the boy</u>
B	yeah (.) right (.) and there's like <u>four episodes of them trying to get into that hatch thing</u>

Exercise 4: Verb tenses and aspects

Change the verb phrase in the following sentence into the tense and/or aspect specified.

The students <u>protest</u> about funding in education

1. present tense, progressive aspect
2. past tense, perfect aspect
3. progressive aspect with modal *could*
4. past tense, perfect progressive aspect
5. simple past tense

Exercise 5: Verb complementation

For each of the following verbs, decide if they are intransitive and/or what obligatory complementation they take according to their different meanings. For example, *argue* can be intransitive (*The children argued*) or it can take an object (*The lawyer argued the case*).

1. *arrive*
2. *believe*
3. *cook*
4. *grow*
5. *hand*
6. *make*
7. *shove*
8. *swear*
9. *telephone*
10. *weep*

Exercise 6: Active and passive clauses

Transform the following active clauses into their passive counterparts, maintaining the agent in the new version:

1. *The police were chasing the thief down the road*
2. *Jo made Sara and Mick this beautiful wedding cake*
3. *William has tidied the house ready for their return*
4. *Amy and Rebecca tell me you like cycling*
5. *The elephants have been entertaining visitors here for many years now*

Exercise 7: Clause structures

Identify the clause structure of the following examples, and label the elements using S, V, O, C, A. Are there any instances of embedding?

1. *Bradley Wiggins has won the most prestigious race in cycling*
2. *Are you feeling better today*
3. *I think they've arrived by now*
4. *The pyramids of Egypt are much bigger than I imagined*
5. *The woman who lives next door showed me her new computer*

Exercise 8: Sentence types and structures

For each of the following examples, identify the sentence type (declarative etc.) and structure (simple etc.):

1. *What a fantastic holiday we've had*
2. *If you insist on waiting, then you must be patient and wait in silence*
3. *Go upstairs and fetch my coat*
4. *When you get back, would you like some spaghetti bolognese*
5. *That horror film is the scariest I've ever seen*
6. *Listen*
7. *How happy she was after winning the lottery*
8. *That book was long but interesting*
9. *Did he make his decision or are we still waiting for it*
10. *Is your mother keen on cricket or football*

Grammatical Frameworks: Suggestions For Further Reading

Language textbooks

Bloor, Thomas and Meriel Bloor (2004) *The Functional Analysis of English*, 2nd edn (London: Hodder Arnold)
A grammar text which introduces the functional approach to grammar associated with Michael Halliday. Useful for readers wanting to explore a different model of grammar.

Croft, William and D. Alan Cruse (2004) *Cognitive Linguistics* (Cambridge: Cambridge University Press)
An introduction to an important field of linguistics which explores how the brain processes language, based on the premise that there is no specific mental language facility.

Downing, Angela and Philip Locke (2006) *English Grammar: A University Course*, 2nd edn (London: Routledge)
A detailed coursebook organised into 60 modules, with lots of texts and exercises. Takes a functional approach, so there is a strong emphasis on context.

Halliday, M. A. K. and Christian Matthiessen (2004) *An Introduction to Functional Grammar*, 3rd edn (London: Hodder Arnold)
Challenging but comprehensive coverage of functional grammar for textual analysis.

Jeffries, Lesley (2006) *Discovering Language* (Basingstoke: Palgrave Macmillan)
A very useful text for reinforcing what is covered here, and for showing further how tree diagrams can be used. It also contains chapters on the other levels of language, as well as semantics.

Poole, Geoff (2011) *Syntactic Theory*, 2nd edn (Basingstoke: Palgrave Macmillan)
For readers who want to move beyond descriptive grammar to understand the theoretical approach developed by Noam Chomsky.

Tallerman, Maggie (2005) *Understanding Syntax*, 2nd edn (London: Hodder Arnold)

This will be of interest to readers wishing to learn more about the grammar of human languages in general. It has a wealth of examples, and some challenging exercises.

Reference books

Aarts, Bas (2011) *Oxford Modern English Grammar* (Oxford: Oxford University Press)
Moving from the basics to the complexities of English, this new Oxford grammar has the additional benefit of covering both British and American English.

Biber, Douglas, Geoffrey Leech and Susan Conrad (2002) *The Longman Student Grammar of Spoken and Written English* (Harlow: Longman)
Another valuable grammar for further exploration of the differences between speech and writing, and which includes information on frequency of use. There is also an accompanying workbook available.

Carter, Ronald and Michael McCarthy (2006) *The Cambridge Grammar of English* (Cambridge: Cambridge University Press)
A recent reference grammar which covers both speech and writing using illustrations from a corpus of real life examples. A CD ROM which contains audio recordings supports this publication.

Greenbaum, Sidney (1996) *The Oxford English Grammar* (Oxford: Oxford University Press)
A very detailed grammar, systematically arranged in small sections with a host of examples taken from the International Corpus of English.

Greenbaum, Sidney and Gerald Nelson (2009) *An Introduction to English Grammar*, 3rd edn (Harlow: Pearson Education)
A useful title in that it covers both the theory and the application of grammar, the latter including problems of usage. Punctuation and spelling are also covered.

Huddleston, Rodney and Geoffrey K Pullum (2005) *A Student's Introduction to English Grammar* (Cambridge: Cambridge University Press)
Point-by-point explanations are accompanied by lots of examples and exercises.

Internet resource

www.ucl.ac.uk/internet-grammar
University College London's Internet Grammar of English is an easy-to-use online grammar course for undergraduates and contains a very full glossary. The IGE is now also available as an app for Apple and android devices.

Part IV

DISCOURSE FRAMEWORKS

8 Beyond Sentences

8.1 DISCOURSE

In Part III we looked in considerable detail at syntactic structures: we saw how to construct increasingly larger units, moving from phrases to clauses and then from clauses to sentences. The structure of a sentence is the point at which grammar traditionally stops. This is because it is possible to delimit what a sentence might be, but virtually impossible to delimit anything larger than a sentence, with sentences being used to build all kinds of larger units ranging from short messages to epic novels. Further, it is possible for users of a language to be able to make intuitive judgements about whether sentences are well-formed in grammatical terms, but how to make similar judgements about stretches of sentences is less apparent, especially when considering conversational structures. There would, however, be an incompleteness about our study of the frameworks of English if we did not pay attention to the way in which we join sentences together to achieve our communicative ends. After all, the very reason for human beings acquiring lexical and syntactic knowledge is so that we can use language in a range of situations and for a range of purposes in order to communicate with one another. Here, then, we will be studying **discourse**. Discourse is any sequence of sentences which makes up a complete unit or **text** (although in principle a text could consist of just one sentence, for example in a proverb such as *Too many cooks spoil the broth*). Sometimes the term discourse is used specifically to refer to conversation, but here we are using it in the more general sense of a linguistic unit, be it spoken or written, larger than a sentence. However, discourse is far more than just the largest unit of linguistic construction. It is the means by which we put our implicit knowledge of lexical, grammatical and other frameworks to use in our daily encounters and actions. It is, if you like, language let loose upon the world.

We have already explored a considerable number of aspects which make a linguistic unit complete and grammatical. This sense of completeness goes beyond the level of a sentence and is something we can identify in groups of sentences. Consider the following extract:

Anything said in a normal way bounced off me. One of the most impressive ruins in England, this former royal castle was besieged by parliamentary forces in 1646. Twoflower was a tourist, the first ever seen on the discworld. It was darkening slowly outside. In another minute Tod and Terry found themselves in the street just in time to catch a tram for Nelson's Pillar. His comments prompted speculation that the Clinton administration was not concerned about the dollar's weakness. I'm going to be sharing a flat with three others. Joe Hogan makes sciobs, traditional baskets for straining and serving potatoes. In Victorian times, it was the home of the local blacksmith and today it forms a comfortable base for exploring this delightful corner of Devon. Put the lower-section battens in place under the top-section battens and measure down from the top to the bottom edge of the lower batten.

You won't have read more than a couple of lines before you realised that there was something rather strange about this 'text'. It consists of ten sentences but it is quite clear that these sentences do not follow in a sequence nor do they together add up to a coherent and complete passage. The explanation for this is that each sentence was selected at random from a range of different texts and the new 'text' created is therefore entirely artificial. The randomness of the selection of the sentences is evident to a reader and, in addition, most speakers of English would have little difficulty in suggesting the source of each individual sentence in the extract. The final sentence, for example, was taken from a DIY manual, while the penultimate sentence comes from a catalogue of properties for self-catering holidays. The very fact that a reader would be able to identify this extract as a 'non-text' shows that we do possess a clear sense of what a coherent text or group of sentences is like. The phenomenon of sentences belonging together is known as **textuality**. In this chapter we will be exploring exactly what it is that gives a text textuality. In general terms, this is brought about by **cohesion**. Cohesion is a blanket term for a range of linguistic signals and strategies which enable us to know that sentences belong together and in a particular sequence. In Sections 8.4 to 8.10 we will be studying a variety of cohesive devices.

8.2 TEXT AND CONTEXT

When we move from looking at the internal structures of the language to examine the nature of discourse, a new and important dimension comes into play, namely the importance of the **context** in which speech or writing occurs. Discourse exists not in a void but in real-life situations in which its primary role is to bring about some kind of communication between speaker or writer and addressee. At this point, it becomes possible – and appropriate – to explore how aspects such as the relationship between those involved in the communicative act and the purpose of the communication have an influence on the choices the language users make. Linguists have often observed that the full meaning conveyed in discourse is not necessarily the apparent or literal meaning conveyed merely by the words which are spoken or written in single sentences or utterances. Consider, for example, this brief conversational exchange:

Key

(.)		micropause
(1.0)		pause measured in seconds
//	*//*	overlapping speech
=		latching on

A: *I don't like cucumber (1.0)*
B: *it's so good for you though (.) it's good // for your skin //*
A: *// I know I eat // it (.) I just don't*
      really like it (.) I don't like tomatoes either =
B: *= I don't put tomatoes in*
A: *I know (1.0) can I have pork pie in it as well (.) please*

Taken out of context, the first three turns in this exchange could occur in a general discussion between two people about food fads. Only in the last two turns does it become apparent that B is preparing some food for A. In fact, B is A's mother, and is preparing her a packed lunch. Once we are aware of this as the context for the conversation, A's first turn takes on a new dimension of meaning. Rather than simply stating her dislike for cucumber, A, who is watching her mother make the packed lunch, is implying that she doesn't really want it in her meal. Effectively, she is saying *I don't like cucumber so don't put it in my lunch*. By implying rather than stating this message she maintains a degree of politeness towards her parent. Her later comment about tomatoes conveys a similar implied message: *I don't like tomatoes so don't put them in either.* A's mother is obviously able to infer this meaning as she retorts with *I don't put tomatoes in.* A replies that she knows this, possibly to retract any hint of accusing her mother about the tomatoes. When A comes, at the end of the extract, to relaying a message about what she would like in her lunch box – *can I have pork pie in it as well* – she is far more direct and uses an interrogative structure rather than the declaratives she used previously. The politeness marker *please* which is added after a brief pause is an indication of the need to be appreciative of what her mother is doing for her.

We can see then that the speakers in the extract convey far more than they literally say, and that **implication** and **inference** are part of this process. Clues to meaning are given through grammatical choices as well as other aspects of the discourse, and the context in which the talk is taking place is also of relevance, as is the relationship between the participants. A significant body of work has been done on how the context of discourse influences both the linguistic features that users adopt and the way in which they infer meaning from what is said or written. (**Pragmatics** is the branch of linguistics which deals with the interpretation of meaning which is not explicit.) Even an outline exploration of these **functional** approaches is well beyond the scope of this book, although we will touch on context again in Section 8.11. Instead, our examination of discourse will concentrate on **formal** aspects of text, identifying the strategies which speakers and writers use to construct texts, whatever their context of use.

☐ **sentence types and functions** ⇨ *7.2*

8.3 SPOKEN AND WRITTEN DISCOURSE

In this chapter, we will be looking at both spoken and written language, and this will include some consideration (in Section 8.12) of electronically mediated language (which can sometimes seem hard to classify as belonging categorically to one or the other mode). Although spoken texts are typically spontaneous and therefore less polished than written texts, the basic principles of construction are the same when we consider texts in either **mode** which have been produced by a single speaker or writer. (**Interactional** spoken discourse, which consists of at least two speakers, will be considered in Sections 8.7 to 8.10.) Here is an example of a spoken text. It is a transcription of a young woman telling her brother about an incident that happened to her at her place of work, a clothes shop:

Key

(.)	micropause
(1.0)	pause measured in seconds
bold text	shows emphasis
<u>underlining</u>	shows the speaker is whispering
<u>on</u>	held syllable
whe.	unfinished word
huuuhhh	sound used to express fear
(laughter)	shows laughter by the speaker

last week (.) <u>on</u> late night (.) Thursday erm (.) one of the part-timers Steve (1.0)
he came over to me he went (.) Ellie come here (.) so I went back to the changing
room (.) and er <u>he said look at that</u> look at that (.) so I put my head round the
door (.) and there was <u>a</u> and the curtain was closed and there was a leg sticking
5   *out and a hand sticking out underneath the thing (.) and he went <u>someone's</u>*
*<u>collapsed in the changing room</u> (1.0) I was (.) <u>so</u> **scared** (.) I was like **huuuhh***
*(.) looked at him like that and he was like **huuuhh** (.) what do we **do** what do*
*we **do** he was like come and have a look and I couldn't look because I was so*
scared (.) the leg and an arm (.) sticking out under <u>the</u> curtain (1.0) and (.) then
10 *he we. he said I'll (.) he said come a. w. w. what are we gonna do and I just*
stood outside going (.) looking for like the supervisor going whe. (.) thinking (.)
you know just going w. w. w. what am I gonna do (.) and then (.) and then he
came out with another one of the girls who worked there (.) and she was behind
the curtain (.) pretending she had collapsed (laughter)

A characteristic of this spoken anecdote, and something which occurs naturally in spontaneous speech is **non-fluency**. Because her speech is unplanned, there are several occasions when the speaker stumbles slightly over what she is saying. For example, in line 4, she makes a **false start** – *there was <u>a</u> and the curtain was closed* – when she abandons her first structure *there was <u>a</u>* (the held word suggesting she is uncertain how to continue with this structure) and replaces it with *and the curtain was closed*. In lines 10 and 12 the speaker has to make several attempts to articulate a word: *w. w. what are we gonna do* and *w. w. w. what am I gonna do*. This is known as **recycling**. At line 12, the speaker repeats herself unnecessarily: *and then (.) and then*. This is an example of **non-fluent repetition**. **Non-fluency features** such as these occur throughout spontaneous speech but their existence does not mean that spontaneous speech lacks cohesion as we shall see in the following sections.

If we look beyond the non-fluency features in this example, we can see that the speaker essentially employs the clause structures that we examined in Chapters 6 and 7. For example, a string such as *so I went back to the changing room* is clearly analysable as a subject (S) and verb (V) clause, with the addition of three adverbial (A) elements:

A	S	V	A	A
So	*I*	*went*	*back*	*to the changing room*

Having said this, there are differences between the choices which speakers make in spontaneous and informal speech and those which writers make in more polished, formal texts. For instance, spontaneous speech often contains more colloquial lexis such as *went* or *was like* meaning 'said' and also less specific lexis such as referring to the curtain as *the thing* in line 5. Grammatical differences also occur: for example, in lines 1–2 when the speaker is introducing the anecdote, she says *one of the part-timers Steve (1.0) he came over to me*. This structure begins by specifying one of the sentence elements, in this case the subject (*one of the part-timers Steve*), and following it with a full clause containing reference to that element (*he*). This is a **topic-comment structure**:

topic	**comment**
one of the part-timers Steve	*he came over to me*

This strategy is common in spontaneous speech, especially in a spoken anecdote of this kind, but is rarely found in writing. Other features typical of spontaneous speech include a high frequency of ***and* coordination** to join clauses (*I put my head round the door (.) and there was a and the curtain was closed and there was a leg sticking out and a hand sticking out underneath the thing (.) and he went...*) and a low frequency of **passive** constructions, there being none in this particular extract.

> ☐ **clause elements and structures** ⇨ 6.2–6.8
> ☐ **passive constructions** ⇨ 6.9

8.4 LEXICAL COHESION

Cohesion can operate on both a lexical level and a grammatical level and we will begin by considering how words and the meanings of words can give a text cohesion. The lack of lexical cohesion was one of the indicators that the extract given in Section 8.1 was not an integrated whole. Consider the key lexical words from the first three sentences:

1 *said normal way bounced*
2 *impressive ruins England former royal castle besieged parliamentary forces*
3 *Twoflower tourist first ever seen discworld*

Not only is there no repetition of any word but, more significantly, there are no lexical words in Sentence 1 which have a close connection with any of those in the other two sentences, and the same can be said for Sentences 2 and 3. In a cohesive text, we would expect there to be lexical links between sentences. Compare this extract which is the opening section of a news item on a university website:

Gene involved in sperm-to-egg binding is key to fertility in mammals (1 May 2012)

Experts from Durham University have identified a new gene that could help the development of fertility treatments in humans in the future.

Scientists from Durham University, UK, and Osaka University, Japan, looking at fertility in mice, have discovered for the first time that the gene, which makes a protein called PDILT, enables sperm to bind to an egg, a process essential to fertilisation.

The team found that when the gene was 'switched off' in male mice, less than three per cent of females' eggs were fertilised compared to more than 80 per cent in mice when the gene was left switched on.

It is the first time that a gene of this type has been linked to fertility.

A reader would be in no doubt here that this text is a cohesive one. The lexis is one of the main indicators that these sentences belong together. For one thing, several lexical words are repeated: the noun *gene* occurs six times in this short extract, while the noun *fertility* occurs three times by itself, as well as in the compound noun *fertility treatment*. The theme of fertility is also reinforced through the associated noun *fertilisation* and the verb *were fertilised*. The headline phrase *sperm-to-egg binding* is repeated in a re-worked form in *enables sperm to bind to an egg*, and the phrase *the first time*, which occurs twice, reinforces the idea that this is an article about *a new gene*. Together, the lexemes relating to the **semantic field** of reproduction in mammals establish the central topic of the article. The focus on *mammals* in the title is developed through other items within the same lexical set, namely *humans* and *mice*, which are hyponyms of 'mammal'. The article is about a scientific discovery, and the researchers are referred to with three synonyms: *experts*, *scientists* and *the team*. The work of the scientists is referred to through a series of verbs – *have identified, looking at, found, has been linked* – while the antonyms *'switched off'* and *switched on* are used to help explain how the discovery was made.

If we now return to the example of spontaneous speech from Section 8.3, we can identify the lexical cohesion in this piece of discourse too. Here is the text again:

last week (.) on late night (.) Thursday erm (.) one of the part-timers Steve (1.0) he came over to me he went (.) Ellie come here (.) so I went back to the changing room (.) and er he said look at that look at that (.) so I put my head round the door (.) and there was a and the curtain was closed and there was a leg sticking

> *out and a hand sticking out underneath the thing (.) and he went <u>someone's</u>*
> <u>*collapsed in the changing room*</u> *(1.0) I was (.) <u>**so**</u> **scared** (.) I was like **huuuhh***
> *(.) looked at him like that and he was like **huuuhh** (.) what do we **do** what do*
> *we **do** he was like come and have a look and I couldn't look because I was so*
> *scared (.) the leg and an arm (.) sticking out under <u>the</u> curtain (1.0) and (.) then*
> *he we. he said I'll (.) he said come a. w. w. what are we gonna do and I just*
> *stood outside going (.) looking for like the supervisor going whe. (.) thinking (.)*
> *you know just going w. w. w. what am I gonna do (.) and then (.) and then he*
> *came out with another one of the girls who worked there (.) and she was behind*
> *the curtain (.) pretending she had collapsed (laughter)*

There is again a great deal of lexical cohesion in this passage. For example, the *changing room* is mentioned twice to draw attention to the scene of the joke, and the *curtain* which is so crucial is mentioned three times. Considerable attention is drawn to the limbs (through repetition of *leg* and through the use of *hand* and then *arm*) and to the fact they are *sticking out*. Although this is an unprepared speech, the speaker brings drama to her story by frequent use of lexical items which focus on the need to investigate what has happened in the changing room:

> *Ellie come here*
> *I went back*
> *look at that* (x 2)
> *come and have a look*
> *I couldn't look*

Another theme which the speaker uses, often implicitly, to give the text cohesion is that of fear, and this is introduced about halfway through the anecdote:

> *I was so scared* (x 2)
> *huuuhh* (x 2)
> *what do we do* (x 2)
> *what are we gonna do*
> *what am I gonna do*
> *I just stood outside*

You can see then that in a cohesive text there are many lexical signals which establish the unity of the text and, as it were, reassure the reader or listener that what they are receiving is a deliberate sequence of sentences. The particular extracts we have just considered are quite dense in the number of lexical and semantic connections that exist but any text will contain comparable connections. Lexical cohesion, then, can be established either through the repetition of lexical items or through the meaning relationships of lexical items within particular semantic fields or lexical sets.

☐ **lexical words** ⇨ 2.3
☐ **antonyms & other meaning relations** ⇨ 3.9

8.5   REPETITION

Repetition is an important strategy for achieving cohesion in a text. The repeated item may be a single lexical word, a word group, a clause, a particular structure or even a sound. In the previous section we saw how, in the university website article, the repetition of certain lexical words such as the nouns *gene* and *fertility* not only played a part in developing the subject matter of the news report, but also gave a sense that we were reading a cohesive text. Similarly, we saw repetition in the spoken extract, for example of the nouns *changing room* and *curtain*. It is important to make a distinction between repetition of lexical words and repetition of grammatical words. This is because we need to repeat grammatical words all the time due to their particular syntactic function. The choice of a lexical item, by contrast, is more topic-specific and has a deliberateness about it which the selection of grammatical words does not typically have. Most of the time we barely notice the repetition of grammatical words. In this paragraph alone, the definite article *the* has been used 15 times so far and the coordinating conjunction *and* has been used 5 times.

Phrases or parts of phrases may also be repeated. In the university website article the *gene* referred to in the headline is inevitably referred to several times throughout the article. Here are the references to it in the first four sentences:

... *a new gene* ...	Sentence 1
... *the gene*	Sentence 2
... *the gene* ... (twice)	Sentence 3
... *a gene of this type* ...	Sentence 4

The first mention of the gene provides more specific detail about it, namely its newness, but thereafter a simple noun phrase is sufficient to refer to the topic of the article. You will also see that in Sentence 1 it is *a new gene*. Once its identity has been established, however, it is referred to as *the gene*, although interestingly the indefinite article is reintroduced in Sentence 4 with the notion of a particular kind of gene: *a gene of this type*.

Repetition of single words or word groups is a common strategy for giving a text cohesion. Less common, because more obviously deliberate, is the repetition of larger units of construction. Very often, when this occurs, it will be within a persuasive, rhetorical or literary context. Consider this extract about gravity from *Wonders of the Universe* by Brian Cox and Andrew Cohen, a book published in 2011 to accompany a television series:

> *Gravity holds the water in our oceans and hugs the atmosphere close to the planet. It's the reason why the rain falls and the rivers flow; it powers the ocean currents and drives the world's weather; it's why volcanoes erupt and earthquakes tear the land apart. Yet gravity also plays a role on an even grander stage. Across the Universe, from the smallest speck of dust to the most massive star, gravity is the great sculptor that created order out of chaos.*

Clearly, there is lexical cohesion in this extract, but the repeated structures also add to its cohesive quality. The first four sentences (using syntax not punctuation to determine the sentence boundaries) show structural repetition, or **parallelism**, through the use of coordinated clauses:

	gravity	*holds...*	*and*	*(gravity)*	*hugs...*
It's the reason why	*the rain*	*falls*	*and*	*the rivers*	*flow*
	it (gravity)	*powers...*	*and*	*(gravity)*	*drives*
It's why	*volcanoes*	*erupt*	*and*	*earthquakes*	*tear...*

The structural similarity is enhanced by the use of the same coordinator throughout, as well as by the fact that the verbs are all in the present tense. There is additional patterning through the alternating subjects of *gravity* in the first and third sentences and other elements (*rain, rivers, volcanoes, earthquakes*) in the second and fourth. Looking at the four sentences in their entirety, there is also alternation of sentence types: the first and third are compound sentences, while the second and fourth are complex, with the *wh*-adverb *why* introducing a relative clause and a nominal relative clause respectively. In the next two sentences, *gravity* is retained as the grammatical subject, and therefore as a cohesive device, but a new structural pattern is introduced:

Yet	*gravity*	*also plays a role on an even grander stage.*
Across the Universe		
from the smallest speck of dust		
to the most massive star		
	gravity	*is the great sculptor that created order out of chaos.*

These are both simple sentences, although they differ in length. Unlike the preceding sentences, the subject is preceded by an adverbial element, first with the simple adverb *yet*, and then by the longer combination of prepositional phrases which build up to the most important idea of gravity as *the great sculptor* of the universe.

Finally, we will look briefly at phonological repetition. Just as clausal repetition and parallelism give a text a sense of being more consciously crafted, phonological effects achieved through repetition probably do this to an even greater extent. Consider this chapter opening from the novel *Waterland* by Graham Swift:

> *The Great Ouse. Ouse. Say it. Ouse. Slowly. How else can you say it? A sound which exudes slowness. A sound which suggests the slow, sluggish, forever oozing thing it is. A sound which invokes quiet flux, minimum tempo; cool, impassive, unmoved motion. A sound which will calm even the hot blood racing in your veins. Ouse, Ouse, Oooooouse ...*

In this extract, Swift is describing a river in East Anglia. He uses the repeated /uː/ sound, which occurs not only in the name of the river but also in *exudes, oozing* and *unmoved*, in order to suggest the heavy motion of the river. This is possibly the most noticeable example of repetition in this extract but you can see that Swift also uses lexical repetition as well as extensive parallelism through the structure of the noun phrase *a sound* ... where the head word *sound* is postmodified by a relative clause introduced by *which*. This level of crafting and repetition would be highly unexpected in everyday speech or even in informative language such as a newspaper report, but it is a common feature of more polished and literary discourse.

8.6 REFERENCE

We saw in the previous section that repetition is often used when there is a need to make frequent reference to a particular item or in order to achieve a particular effect. Sometimes when frequent reference is required, however, repetition can seem unnecessary and clumsy. This is particularly the case when an item is repeated not long after it has first been mentioned. Here is the opening of an article about ancient Egypt from the April 2006 edition of the BBC *Focus* magazine:

> *When the first European travellers visited Egypt at the beginning of the 19th century, they were amazed at the antiquities they discovered along the river Nile. One site was particularly intriguing. In a desolate valley on the west bank of the river at Luxor, the site of the ancient city of Thebes, they found rock-cut*
> 5   *tombs, decorated with strange scenes of people and animal-headed gods along with a form of picture-writing – hieroglyphs.*

Some of these tombs had been open for centuries, for the walls bore inscriptions left by ancient Greek and Roman visitors. They were, however, empty and only shattered fragments of burial equipment were found.

In the first paragraph, the underlined items – *the first European travellers* and the three instances of the pronoun *they* – are **co-referential**. In other words, they all refer to the same **referent**, namely the travellers from Europe. To write *the first European travellers* in all four positions would be needlessly repetitive so the pronoun *they* is used to avoid this. When an element refers to a previous element in this way it is an **anaphor**, and its reference is **anaphoric**. The item to which the anaphor refers us back is its **antecedent**. Antecedents may be single words or phrases, or they may be whole sentences or strings of sentences. Anaphors occur frequently in discourse. They act as a cohesive device as they establish links across sentences (although an anaphor and its antecedent may occur within the same sentence, as you can see in the first sentence of the article). Anaphors are often pronouns, but determiners and adverbs can be anaphors too. For example, in line 7, the determiner *these* in *these tombs* refers back to the *rock-cut tombs* of the previous sentence.

Less common but nevertheless of importance in cohesion is **cataphor** or **cataphoric** reference. Cataphors refer forward and, like anaphors, can be pronouns, determiners or adverbs. The second sentence of the above extract contains a cataphor: *One site was particularly intriguing.* Here, the determiner *one* is cataphoric as it signals that this site will be the topic of subsequent sentences. In fact, anaphors and cataphors can refer to anything from a single word to any number of sentences. The advantage of using a cataphor is that it sets up an expectation of information to come and alerts the audience to pay attention to what follows.

Although the process of retrieving the referent of an anaphor or cataphor is normally straightforward, there are both structural and semantic restrictions on the scope of the reference. Look again at the second paragraph of the extract, which consists of two sentences:

Some of these tombs had been open for centuries, for the walls bore inscriptions left by ancient Greek and Roman visitors. They were, however, empty and only shattered fragments of burial equipment were found.

In this paragraph, the reader needs to identify the antecedent of *they* in the previous sentence. This pronoun cannot refer to *the first European travellers* since it no longer has proximity to this noun phrase, and other possible antecedents have now been introduced. Looking at the preceding sentence, the most likely antecedents are the subject of the main clause *Some of these tombs*, the subject of the subordinate clause *the walls*, or the last plural noun phrase to be introduced *ancient Greek and Roman visitors*. Identifying antecedents is sometimes a matter of looking at meaning rather than grammatical position. We are told that *they* were *empty*, indicating that the *tombs* must be the antecedent, since neither *walls* nor *visitors* can be *empty* in this context.

Anaphors and cataphors are devices for making **endophoric reference**. This is the process by which one item in a text refers to another item within the same text and both items share the same referent. Anaphors and cataphors can make reference both within sentences and across sentence boundaries. They are most typically pronouns but they can also be determiners or adverbs. By contrast with endophoric reference, a reference may be **exophoric** and refer to something related to the situation or context in which the discourse occurs rather than something within the discourse itself. The first page of the article about ancient Egypt from which the above extract was taken featured a photograph of an excavated tomb with the caption:

Is this the tomb of Queen Nefertiti?

Here, the pronoun *this* refers not to anything about to be mentioned in the text of the article but to the photograph which the caption accompanies. The pronoun *this* is therefore used contextually rather than textually here. This is an example of exophoric reference.

Exophoric references, because they are context-bound, are normally **deictic**. **Deixis** refers to the way certain words indicate time, location or person within the context of utterance. In the example *Is this the tomb of Queen Nefertiti?* the use of *this* implies that the tomb in question is the one in the photograph close to the caption. If, by contrast, a speaker visiting Egypt said to the guide *Is <u>that</u> the tomb of Queen Nefertiti?* as they approached an excavation site then the inference is that the speaker is still some distance away from it.

Deictic words often operate in contrasting pairs. Here are some more examples:

indicating time	indicating location	indicating person
now/then	*here/there*	*I/you*
today/yesterday	*this/that*	*I/we*
today/tomorrow	*these/those*	*he/they*

- ☐ **adverbs** ⇨ 2.7
- ☐ **pronouns** ⇨ 2.8
- ☐ **determiners** ⇨ 2.9

8.7 ELLIPSIS

Ellipsis was introduced in Section 7.9 with the examples:

> *Terry cut the grass and Ø weeded the flower beds*
> *Terry painted the ceiling and Julia Ø the walls*

Ellipsis is essentially the omission from a clause or sentence of an element which can nevertheless be inferred, usually because it is recovered from elsewhere in the text. We are able to identify that something is understood because we are aware of a syntactic gap in a structure. In the first of the above examples, we are aware that the subject of the second clause *weeded the flower beds* is missing and we are able to find this missing information by referring to the subject of the first clause, namely *Terry*. In the second example, it is the verb element *painted* which is missing, and we again refer to the preceding clause to find the missing element. We saw in Chapter 6 that English syntax is based on a typical clause structure of subject and verb plus any verb complementation. Often it is our implicit knowledge of what a complete clause should be which enables us to identify that an element (or elements) has been ellipted. The reason why ellipsis occurs in syntactic structures has already been touched on: essentially, we use language in an efficient and economic way and do not favour repetition unless it is for emphasis or for clarification. Some repetition can be avoided by using anaphors: ellipsis is basically another method of avoiding repetition.

The examples given at the start of the previous paragraph showed ellipsis operating within compound sentences. It is also possible for ellipsis to operate across sentence boundaries and speech turns. It is therefore another important cohesive device in discourse, especially spoken discourse. Consider this conversational extract where Francine is talking about a local nightclub:

> Francine: *I went to The Works on Friday*
> James: *did you (.) who with*
> Francine: *Jo and some friends*

Francine's first turn is grammatically complete, as is appropriate for the introduction of a new topic in the conversation:

S	V	A	A
I	*went*	*to The Works*	*on Friday*

However, James's reply, if considered in isolation, is clearly grammatically incomplete:

wh-word	operator	S	V	A	A	
	did	*you*	Ø	Ø	Ø	
who	Ø	Ø	Ø	Ø	Ø	*with*

Despite this incompleteness, the meaning is perfectly clear because it can be retrieved from Francine's turn:

> *did you go to The Works on Friday*
> *who did you go to The Works on Friday with*

In the first part of his reply (*did you*), James ellipts the verb and adverbial elements from Francine's preceding clause as there is no need to repeat them. In the next part of his reply (*who with*), he also ellipts the operator and the subject element he had supplied previously. In her reply to James's question, Francine also uses ellipsis:

S	V	A	A	A
Ø	Ø	Ø	Ø	*with Jo and some friends*

Here, Francine ellipts all the clause elements of her original statement and simply adds the additional information James required. There is no likelihood, however, that James and Francine would misunderstand each other despite the extensive use of ellipsis in their responses. Conversation would seem very laboured and long-winded if we did not use it wherever possible.

In the previous section, we identified the difference between endophoric and exophoric reference. Endophoric reference occurs within the text and therefore, whether it is achieved through anaphor or cataphor, is a textual cohesive device. By contrast, an exophoric reference refers to the context or situation in which discourse occurs. Ellipsis is normally endophoric but can be exophoric. For example, a sign by an escalator saying *Keep to the right* would clearly mean *Keep to the right of the escalator,* while someone buying tickets at a cinema box office might simply say to the cashier *three adults please* meaning *I'd like tickets for three adults please.*

☐ **clause structures** ⇨ 6.8
☐ **operators** ⇨ 7.4

8.8 COHESION IN INTERACTIONAL DISCOURSE

Spoken interactional discourse differs from most other types of written or spoken discourse in that it is constructed by two or more speakers. Nevertheless, cohesive devices of the kind we have examined in Sections 8.4 to 8.7 are still employed to unify the text and help to establish a sense of shared meaning and understanding. Consider the following extract which involves four teenage boys – Ben, Chris, Jamie and Zak – talking about a fish tank which they are looking at. The tank belongs to Chris.

Key
(.)		micropause
(4.0)		pause measured in seconds
//	*//*	overlapping speech
=		latching on

1	Zak:	*we have to clean the tank*
2	Chris:	*clean // the tank //*
3	Ben:	*// yeah that's // the // down side //*
4	Chris:	*// yeah I know //*
5	Zak:	*// trust me when // you have to (.) er (.) clean the tank it's so boring =*
6	Ben:	*= yeah I can // never be bothered //*
7	Jamie:	*// least it's not a big // tank*
8	Zak:	*Chris (.) can I get a submarine for it*
9	Chris:	*no*
10	Jamie:	*you should have um got two sharks*
11	Chris:	*I shouldn't have got two // sharks //*
12	Jamie:	*// what // they expensive*
13	Ben:	*when they get bigger aren't they gonna eat all the other fish*
14	Chris:	*nah (.) they won't eat the other fish*
15	Ben:	*not much of a shark is it*
16	Zak:	*yeah I know (.) you could start hugging it // and that //*
17	Jamie:	*// looks nice // though*
18	Ben:	*that's about as big as a goldfish (4.0) what they called*
19	Jamie:	*call it Phil*
20	Chris:	*might do*
21	Jamie:	*call it Paul*
22	Chris:	*maybe*

We saw in Section 8.4 that lexical cohesion is a salient feature of texts that have a single author. Here, the existence of lexical cohesion (through a set such as *fish, shark, goldfish*) shows the participants' commitment to their chosen topic, as well as their mutual willingness to construct the conversation cohesively. There is also a semantic field of unwanted obligation in the opening section when the sub-topic of cleaning the tank is introduced:

turn 1	we <u>have to</u> clean the tank
turn 3	yeah that's the <u>down side</u>
turn 4	yeah I know (that's the <u>down side</u>)
turn 5	when you <u>have to</u> clean the tank it's <u>so boring</u>
turn 6	yeah <u>I can never be bothered</u>
turn 7	<u>least</u> it's <u>not a big tank</u>

Another cohesive feature of this extract is the way the boys constantly repeat each other, sometimes verbatim (such as *clean the tank* in turns 1 and 2) and sometimes partially (such as *aren't they gonna eat all the other fish / they won't eat the other fish* in turns 13 and 14). Endophoric reference occurs across turns: for example, the pronoun *it* in turn 8 is an anaphoric reference to the tank, and the pronoun *they* in turns 12, 13 and 14 is an anaphoric reference to *two sharks*. Ellipsis occurs frequently, for example in turn 4 where *that's the down side* is implied in Chris's utterance as it can be retrieved from the previous turn. However, ellipsis also occurs in other turns where the ellipted item can be deduced from different contexts. For example:

turn 7	*(at) least it's not a big tank*	full lexical item deduced from lexical context
turn 17	*(it) looks nice though*	subject deduced from grammatical context
turn 20	*(I) might do*	subject deduced from grammatical and interactional context

The ellipsis adds to the informality of this conversation, but also illustrates the way in which speakers both construct meaning and acknowledge it.

8.9 STRUCTURE IN INTERACTIONAL DISCOURSE

As we have seen in the previous section, speakers contribute to the cohesion of a conversation in a variety of ways. In addition, interactional discourse is characterised by the fact that the participants take turns, and the orderly construction and organisation of these turns is part of the way in which they collaborate to construct **dyadic** (consisting of two speakers) or **multi-party** (consisting of three or more speakers) discourse. Here is an extract of conversation which took place between two sixth form students:

Key

(.)	micropause
?	unit functioning as a question

1	A:	*what are you up to?*
2	B:	*tidying (.) tidying the house*
3	A:	*how are you today?*
4	B:	*okay (.) you?*
5	A:	*not bad (.) not bad (.) what have you been doing?*
6	B:	*tidying and doing my (.) erm psychology work*
7	A:	*oh cool (.) do you wanna do anything later?*
8	B:	*no I need to tidy the house*
9	A:	*oh okay*

The whole of this extract consists of paired turns such as

turn 1	*what are you up to?*
turn 2	*tidying (.) tidying the house*

or three-part turns such as

turn 7	*(.) do you wanna do anything later?*
turn 8	*no I need to tidy the house*
turn 9	*oh okay*

which are the building blocks of conversation. Not only do these structures allow interactional discourse to proceed in an orderly fashion, they allow the participants to work together in constructing and developing the meaning of the discourse. Two-turn units such as turns 1 and 2, and

turn 3	*how are you today?*
turn 4	*okay*

are **adjacency pairs**, two-part building blocks which consist of an initiating utterance or **first pair part**, followed by a relevant response, or **second pair part**. Adjacency pairs allow the orderly construction of interactional discourse, but also allow speakers to signal to each other that they are mutually understood. The two parts of an adjacency pair consist of related turns which typically occur in a necessary sequence such as question and answer, invitation and acceptance, complaint and apology.

Also identifiable in the above extract are three-part structures consisting of an adjacency pair and then a **follow-up** turn by the first speaker. For example:

turn 5	first pair part	A:	*what have you been doing?*
turn 6	second pair part	B:	*tidying and doing my (.) erm psychology work*
turn 7	follow-up	A:	*oh cool*

At any one point in a conversation, a speaker has a choice of responding to a previous utterance or initiating a new one of their own. Sometimes, in one turn, a speaker will do both. In the above example, for instance, speaker A offers a follow-up comment *oh cool* before initiating a new structure with *do you wanna do anything later?*.

Participants in a conversation are adept at managing these structural units, and adjacency pairs are rarely left incomplete. Even in an apparently chaotic piece of multi-party talk such as this extract from a conversation in a café between Dan, Rob, Alex and Craig, adjacency pairs can be identified.

Key

(.)	micropause
(1.0)	pause measured in seconds
// //	overlapping speech
(laughs)	indicates laughter by the speaker

1	Craig	*not here (.) sit in the non-smoking area (.) by that bloke*
		(they sit down at a table)
2	Dan	*pass a couple of menus then Craig (.) behind you mate*
3	Rob	*have you spoken to Bill about tonight (.) // what's happening //*
4	Alex	*// he ain't coming // (.) said he can't afford to*
5	Craig	*yeah he's had to fork loads out for his car // what you having //*
6	Rob	*// is it fixed yet //*
7	Dan	*umm (1.0) I reckon (.) I'll have a hot ch. // no a cuppa tea and //*
8	Alex	*// yeah they gave him // a courtesy car for a week but I think he's got his // back now //*
9	Dan	*// slice o' // carrot cake*
10	Rob	*mate carrot cake's freaking horrible*
11	Craig	*// (laughs) //*
12	Dan	*// it's well nice //*
13	Rob	*a panini I'm starving*
14	Craig	*good choice*

Despite the apparent chaos of this conversation caused by the extent to which the speakers overlap and the fact that two topics (what to eat, and their friend Bill) are being discussed simultaneously, clear structural units can be identified. We can see this if we first extract the turns which relate to Bill, a topic which is introduced at turn 3:

Rob	(turn 3)	*have you spoken to Bill about tonight (.) what's happening*
Alex	(turn 4)	*he ain't coming (.) said he can't afford to*
Craig	(turn 5)	*yeah he's had to fork loads out for his car*
Rob	(turn 6)	*is it fixed yet*
Alex	(turn 8)	*yeah they gave him a courtesy car for a week but I think he's got his back now*

The discussion about Bill is far more orderly than may at first appear. Essentially it consists of two question and answer adjacency pairs between Rob and Alex. At turn 5, Craig provides a follow-up comment to Alex's answer in turn 4. While the exchange about Bill involves mainly Rob and Alex, Dan's turns are all concerned with the topic of what to eat. Craig participates in both topics, as we can see in turn 5 when he comments on Bill and then asks a question *what you having* which Dan answers in his next turn. Alex's answer to Rob's question about whether Bill's car is fixed comes two turns later after Dan has replied to Craig's question. Despite there being four speakers and two topics in this conversation, it is nevertheless orderly, with no adjacency pair remaining incomplete for long.

Later in the café, the assistant comes over to see if they are ready to order, and this exchange takes place between her and Craig:

1 Craig	*(.) err hi yeah a BLT sandwich please*
2 Assistant	*on white or brown*
3 Craig	*umm (1.0) white please thanks*
4 Assistant	*anything else*
5 Craig	*no that's it thanks (.) thank you*

In turn 1, Craig requests a sandwich, thus producing the first part of an adjacency pair. The assistant does not, however, complete the pair. Instead, she initiates a new pair with the question *on white or brown*. Only when Craig has answered this does she offer an implied acceptance of his request with *anything else*. (This also functions as the first part of the final adjacency pair in turns 4 and 5.) In other words, the structure of this exchange is as follows:

first pair part – pair 1	*(.) err hi yeah a BLT sandwich please*
first pair part – pair 2	*on white or brown*

second pair part – pair 2   *umm (1.0) white please thanks*
implied second pair part – pair 1 ⎫   *anything else*
first pair part – pair 3   ⎬
second pair part – pair 3   ⎭   *no that's it thanks (.) thank you*

The first adjacency pair cannot be completed until the information provided by the second pair is obtained, which is why pair 2 has been **embedded** in pair 1. The embedding of one pair within another is a common structural device in interaction known as an **insertion sequence**.

8.10   DISCOURSE MARKERS

A further strategy for structuring, organising and managing text is the use of **discourse markers**. These are lexical items which perform the functions of indicating the relationship of one section of text to another, and of signalling the sections and boundaries of a text. They can also signal the speaker or writer's position in relation to the text, or indicate the position they would like the addressee to adopt. Discourse markers are drawn from a range of word classes, and their functions as discourse markers are not necessarily the same as their functions or meanings at sentence level. The discourse markers which typically occur in writing (or in a prepared monologue of some kind) are different from those employed by speakers in interactional spoken discourse. Because of their role in acting as textual signposts, discourse markers can be described as having a **metalinguistic** function. In other words, they are linguistic items which draw attention to and indicate the way language is being used textually.

Table 8.1 gives some examples of discourse markers. There are a range of adverbs and adverbials which can act as discourse markers, and just a sample of them is offered here. Some conjunctions are also frequently used as discourse markers, typically occurring at the start of an utterance or sentence

Table 8.1   Examples of discourse markers

Type	Examples
adverbs / adverbials	*however, moreover, nevertheless, therefore, thus, yet* *first(ly), second(ly)* etc *consequently, finally, in conclusion, next, then* *actually, in fact, in other words, of course*
conjunctions	*and, because, but, or*
interjections	*anyway, oh, okay, right, so, well*
monitoring devices	*I mean, mind you, you know, you see*

rather than between clauses. Other discourse markers are harder to categorise in terms of word class, even though at a sentence level most of them are readily analysable. Here they have been classed as either **interjections** (since they function outside the main clause structure) or labelled as **monitoring devices** (as they involve some regulation of the speaker's or addressee's position towards the text).

Here are two examples of discourse markers in use. The first is a telephone voicemail message:

1 *oh dear we're not having much luck are we (.) it's Clive (.) erm (.) returning*
2 *your your your various calls and yes it would be great to organise a meal (.)*
3 *and erm (.) well give us a try at some point (.) things are a bit quieter now that*
4 *the university has stopped so (.) erm (.) and the diary has suddenly gone (.)*
5 *rather quiet so (.) it would be very nice to meet up (.) soon (.) okay (.) bye now*

In this brief message, a range of discourse markers (underlined) are used by the speaker. (In order to appreciate what discourse markers add to the text, try leaving them out. The essential meaning is still conveyed but the text seems peremptory and less coherent.) As well as initiating the message, the use of *oh dear* at the beginning signals the speaker's disappointment at having to leave a message rather than speak to the recipient directly. The conjunction *and* is a frequently used discourse marker in speech and can have a range of functions. In line 2, it signals a shift to a topic related to the *various calls* the recipient has made. In line 4, it has an additive function, offering a further reason why the speaker is available to meet up. In line 3, the speaker seems to use *and* as a continuer, but then abandons it in favour of *well*, which here has the function of moving the discourse on to indicate what should happen next. It also marks a shift from declarative to imperative mode and softens the force of the directive to the recipient. The interjection *so* in lines 4 and 5 is used differently from the other markers discussed so far as it indicates the end of an information unit, especially as it is followed by, rather than following, a pause. In line 5, *okay* is a pre-closing signal indicating that the message is about to end, and *bye* is accompanied by *now*, which fully closes down the message given that the recipient is not available to say goodbye back.

The second example is of a written text, and is taken from a guide to the football teams for the 2006 World Cup by the commentator John Motson. (The names of the players selected for the England team appeared in bold in the original article.) The discourse markers have again been underlined:

Once again England have been struck by the curse of the metatarsal, and you can understand Sven-Goran Eriksson's determination to include **Wayne Rooney***, without whom <u>you have to say</u> their chances of winning the tournament are weakened by at least 40 per cent.*

5   *Sven has picked a squad that certainly gives him options in terms of formation. The inclusion of Theo Walcott has been the big talking point. I've seen him for Southampton and he is lightning fast, but I don't think Sven's picked him with a view to starting him. He's a player you can throw on with 20 minutes to go and he'll frighten the opposition with his pace.*

10   *Choosing Walcott over Jermain Defoe was one of only two really tricky decisions Sven had to make, the other being* **Aaron Lennon** *instead of Shaun Wright-Phillips. Lennon is another who can come on and inject genuine pace on the right. <u>Other than that</u> I don't think there are any real surprises in the squad.*

15   *Once* **Sol Campbell** *and* **Ashley Cole** *proved their fitness they were bound to be in. I think Sven's right to include* **Stewart Downing** *because he needs a truly left-sided player, especially as it gives him the option to deploy Joe Cole elsewhere. Cole could play off the main striker if Rooney isn't fit, as could* **Steven Gerrard***. <u>So</u> it's anyone's guess who'll line up*

20   *in attack, but <u>what you can say</u> is they'll need Rooney to come in at some point if they're going to win the World Cup.*

<u>Nevertheless,</u> by the time they meet Sweden in the third game, both countries should have beaten Paraguay and Trinidad & Tobago and might be playing to avoid Germany in the next round.

Immediately, you can see that the incidence of discourse markers is less frequent than in the spontaneous spoken text. This is partly because writing allows other ways of marking text boundaries, such as the use of paragraphs or bullet points. You can also see that the discourse markers used here are different from those used in the spoken example. In lines 3 and 20, the metalinguistic clauses *you have to say* and *what you can say* act as discourse markers as they strengthen the writer's observations about the importance of Wayne Rooney to the team. *Other than that* in line 13 and *So* in line 19 signal that the topics discussed in these two paragraphs are almost finished. (*So* is used here very differently from its counterpart in the spoken example.) The adverb *nevertheless* at the start of the last paragraph is more associated with written language due to its formality. Here it indicates a move to the final point the writer wishes to make, as well as a qualification of the point which precedes it.

You can see, then, that discourse markers are a heterogenous group of linguistic items which perform a wide range of textual functions. They essentially operate outside normal clause and sentence structure, providing instead orientation points relating to the text in which they occur.

> ☐ **adverbs** ⇨ 2.7
> ☐ **conjunctions** ⇨ 2.12
> ☐ **variation in discourse markers** ⇨ 12.8

8.11 REGISTER

So far we have seen how textuality is established in discourse through the use of various structural devices, and how discourse markers can be used to guide a reader or listener through a piece of discourse. Lingustic features like these are cohesive strategies used in all kinds of discourse. In other words, you are just as likely to find them in a short story as you are in a business letter or a voicemail message. What makes a piece of discourse distinct, however, is its **register**: the configuration of its textual features and meanings as determined by a range of contextual factors. These factors include the use and subject matter of a text (its **field**), whether it is transmitted through speech or writing (**mode**), and the relationship between its participants (**tenor**). In varying ways, these factors will also affect the degree of formality in the text. Compare these two examples, both of them relating to the 2011 road cycling world championships and describing the final moments of the men's road race, which was won by the British cyclist Mark Cavendish. The first example is from a live television commentary, while the second is from a detailed race report on the British Cycling website:

Example 1: live commentary

Key	
CB	Chris Boardman (commentator)
HP	Hugh Porter (commentator)
(.)	micropause
(.h)	micropause with an intake of breath
// //	overlapping speech
happ.	unfinished word

CB   *well Cavendish er now probably in about twelfth position but he had some space to move up didn't take it (.) clearly happy with the position he's not going for a traditional chain er traditional train he's gonna let Stannard try to lead him into this corner // we've got //*

HP   *// what happ. // sorry Chris what happened there Stannard is leading Geraint Thomas out who looked back anxiously to see where Cav was (.) and Cav's not on the wheel (.) so now he's got a lot of work to do here*

CB   *well Geraint Thomas is there he's looking back to see if he can find Mark Cavendish he's dropping back a little bit (.h) he's got a few seconds to sort this out but not more than twenty seconds*

HP   *you're right so Cavendish now (.) we're gonna focus on him and see whether he can actually get through it's all about timing your effort (.) Australia at the front (.) are beginning to lead this one out (.) here we go the full commitment (.) it's all about timing your effort to perfection here (.) there's Geraint Thomas on the far left (.) he nearly collided with the barriers (.) Australia now really beginning to flex their muscles at the front (.) saw a shot of Geraint Thomas as well (.) and also Mark Cavendish can Cavendish find a way through (.) it looks as though he's hemmed in at the moment (.) but remember (.) he has the explosive finishing power (.) the line's getting nearer (.) and nearer (.) where's the Manx Express (.) can he come through (.) here he comes (.) the Manx Express (.) Mark Cavendish on the left of our screen (.) he's gonna be the world champion (.) look for the salute he's the world champion (.) Mark Cavendish has won the world title (.) for Great Britain and we've waited since 1965 (.h) when Tommy Simpson won in San Sebastian (.h) the silver medal going to Matt Goss of Australia (.) and André Greipel of Germany (.) getting the bronze he timed it to absolute perfection*

Example 2: online report

from **'Cavendish is World Road Champion'** by Eddie Allen

...2km to go and the German and Australian teams began to come to the fore, threatening to swamp the Brits. The GB train had suddenly diminished to Thomas and Stannard, Stannard forced his way through on the barriers with Thomas and Cavendish on his wheel. However, going into the final few hundred yards Cavendish appeared to be boxed, having dropped back from Thomas's wheel. Thomas looked back and slowed up, re-establishing contact with Cavendish. But the Manxman had slotted onto Lars Boom's wheel, playing a waiting game, before coming through on the Dutchman's right, momentarily slotting onto Matt Goss's wheel before jumping clear.

Goss followed and came close but Cavendish's timing and positioning was perfect. Arms raised, Cavendish took the world title after a dominant, courageous performance from the entire GB team. Behind, Greipel and Cancellara battled for third in a photo finish, the massive German given bronze after the photo was examined.

In terms of field, the shared subject matter of the two examples is evidenced by the high incidence of proper nouns referring to the cyclists and to the countries they represent as well as by the lexis that relates to cycling and racing. However, the grammatical features differ significantly. Since Example 1 is a real-time commentary, there is a predominance of present tense and aspect, namely the simple present (*Geraint Thomas is there, here he comes*), the present progressive, (*he's looking back, the line's getting nearer*) and the present perfect (*has won*). By contrast, Example 2 uses the simple past tense (*began, forced, appeared ...*) and past perfect (*had suddenly diminished, had slotted onto*) to report on events, although the heading uses the present tense *is*, as is conventional for news reports. The speed at which the live commentary must proceed, especially in the closing stages of the race, means that there is a certain amount of ellipsis (*Ø didn't take it, Australia now Ø really beginning*), a feature which is largely absent from the Example 2 report as a whole, but interestingly can be found at the start of this extract (*Ø 2km to go*), perhaps indicating that the writer was trying to capture something of the excitement and pace of the live event. The speed and nature of the live commentary also appears to have affected sentence length and structure, particularly towards the end of the race where there is a high incidence of simple sentences in contrast to the more complex structures of the report (*But the Manxman ... jumping clear*) where hindsight gives the writer the opportunity to make syntactic connections between the various moves in the race.

The texts are in different modes. Example 1 exhibits some of the typical features of spontaneous speech, such as self-correction (*traditional chain er traditional train*) and overlapping speech, but is generally very fluent, as is expected from professional commentators. Although not marked on the transcription, tempo also varies, with a marked increase in speed as the race draws to a close. Because the commentary is the combined effort of two commentators, there is also evidence of turn-taking and interactional markers such as *sorry Chris* and *you're right*. The report from which Example 2 is taken follows a prescribed format, and the webpage itself includes typical interactive features of an online publication, with a 'share' option and various links being available at the start of the report as well as a slideshow of photographs.

Tenor concerns the relationship between the writer or speaker and their audience: in other words, the existing or preferred relationship between the participants in the discourse. The two examples use different strategies to establish this relationship. In the live commentary, which is more obviously interactive in that both commentator and television viewer are watching the events as they unfold, this is done through the use of the inclusive (or so we can assume) first person plural pronoun (*we're gonna focus, the left of our screen, we've waited*) and also through interactive sentence types, both interrogatives (*can he come through*) and imperatives (*look for the salute*). The commentators also make some informal lexical choices (*to sort this out, he's hemmed in*) and Hugh Porter refers to Cavendish by two of his nicknames, *Cav* and the *Manx Express*. By contrast, although Example 2 has a similar audience to Example 1 (namely, road cycling fans), it follows the more formal conventions of written news reports by adopting the third person and using only declarative sentences. In addition, the lexis seems in places to be more formal (*a dominant, courageous performance*) and is twice used in conjunction with the passive voice: *Cavendish appeared to be boxed* (compare the live commentary's *it looks as though he's hemmed in*, although *is hemmed in* is also passive) and *after the photo was examined*. However, and probably more significantly, both extracts employ various strategies to enhance the excitement for the viewer or reader about the way the race moved towards its conclusion. For example, the commentator Hugh Porter uses a contrastive negative (*where Cav was ... Cav's not on the wheel*), an informal discourse marker followed by a noun phrase which evaluates the situation (*here we go the full commitment*) and lexical repetition (*the line's getting nearer (.) and nearer*) to convey the tension. In the online report, where the outcome is already known, Eddie Allen employs lexical items which connote aggression (*threatening to swamp, forced his way through*) as well as the metaphor *playing a waiting game*, which is only resolved, as it were, three subordinate clauses later with *before jumping clear*.

Finally, the concept of **genre** can be helpful when looking at different types of discourse. A genre is a particular type of speaking or writing identifiable by its form and its specific features. Language users are aware of the conventions for a huge variety of different genres, although some are more clearly defined than others. Many genres can be divided into distinctive sub-genres, so the cycling commentary considered above will differ in significant ways from a commentary on a sport such as tennis which doesn't involve racing. Experience teaches us what to expect from different types of discourse and the patterns to use for them. When we go up to the counter in a shop, for example, we expect the sales assistant to begin with a question such as *Can I help you?* Equally, we are aware of any failure to follow conventions of genre. Comedians often make use of this awareness for comic effect. There might be humour in describing a surgical operation in the style of a sports commentary, for instance.

When we create a text, then, we not only use lexical and grammatical devices to link the sentences of that text together, but we also adopt the appropriate register for that particular text. Unity in discourse is ultimately achieved therefore through the working together of cohesive devices on both a textual and a contextual level.

8.12 ELECTRONICALLY MEDIATED DISCOURSE

Although the binary division of spoken or written is often a helpful way to approach the study of discourse, there is no clear-cut distinction between the characteristics of the two modes, with examples from one often exhibiting some of the properties more typical of the other. The advent of electronically mediated communication (which started with the telephone and radio and is now of course widely internet-based) has resulted in many new types of text coming into existence, some of them very similar to existing spoken and written genres, some of them more distinctive. In previous sections we have considered four examples transmitted with the use of electronic technology, two of which (the voicemail message and the television sports commentary) are clearly in the spoken mode and two (the news item on the Durham University website and the race report on the British Cycling website) in the written mode, appearing in a very similar form online as they would in print. In this section, we will look at an example from the social networking site Twitter, where the discourse, although obviously 'written' (that is, typed), often exhibits structural features drawn from interactional spoken language.

Twitter describes itself as 'a real-time information network'. This description highlights the fact that messages (or tweets) appear instantly, making it possible for a user to receive information as soon as it is submitted. Twitter also refers to itself as a site where users can follow 'conversations', have 'access to … voices' and 'listen in' to the exchanges. This certainly suggests it is possible to conduct a kind of conversation on Twitter: although there will be delays between the turns, in theory these could be relatively brief – generally the amount of time it takes to compose the short message. In practice, exchanges are probably more likely to have longer gaps between them. The following is an example of a 'conversation' between two university friends which took place over three days:

tweet	time/date	sender	message
1	12.37am Saturday 12 May	HC	*96 cupcakes baked, iced and ready to parrtttyyy.*
2	11.15am Sunday 13 May	RS	*@HC got any spares? I'm in need, sorry haven't rung yet- prepping for eng exam on tues and am in a very bad place- free on tues eve?*
3	3.50pm Sunday 13 May	HC	*@RS yeah was just REALLY hungry. :) not weally. Was my aunties birfday party xx*
4	10.09am Monday 14 May	RS	*@HC aw lucky auntie- happy bday to her! Can't wait to get baking again soon...and catch up witchu! Will call 2moz eve if ur free...*
5	3.46pm Monday 14 May	HC	*@RS am v. much into baking these days :) fun times. Tomo eve sounds good babe xx*

In terms of the topics of the tweets, the sequence seems fairly cohesive, particularly with reference to the baking and the birthday party. Structurally, it has a lot of similarity with a regular face-to-face conversation as a topic-based analysis reveals:

tweet	message	topic
1	*96 cupcakes baked, iced and ready to parrtttyyy.*	baking
2	*got any spares? I'm in need,*	baking
	sorry haven't rung yet- prepping for eng exam on tues and am in a very bad place-	reason for not ringing
	free on tues eve?	fixing a time to chat
3	*yeah was just REALLY hungry. :)*	baking
	not weally. Was my aunties birfday party xx	reason for baking
4	*aw lucky auntie- happy bday to her!*	reason for baking
	Can't wait to get baking again soon...	baking
	and catch up witchu! Will call 2moz eve if ur free...	fixing a time to chat
5	*am v. much into baking these days :) fun times.*	baking
	Tomo eve sounds good babe xx	fixing a time to chat

Despite the delay between turns, the topic of baking is maintained through all 5 tweets. There is a clear adjacency pair related to the reason for the baking in tweets 3 and 4: *Was my aunties birfday party / aw lucky auntie- happy bday to her!*. In tweet 4 RS initiates an adjacency pair in order to fix a time for the two friends to chat, and HC responds to this in tweet 5. However, a previous attempt by RS in tweet 2 to initiate topics received no response in tweet 3, hence RS's second attempt in tweet 4 to try to organise a time to talk on the phone, the topic of the reason for not ringing having been abandoned. In general, then, although the exchange of tweets relies on the structures of face-to-face interaction, it is arguable that the time lapse has caused a small break-down in the structural flow of the exchanges.

Posting a tweet is not necessarily about starting a conversation. The first tweet in the above sequence could easily have functioned as a one-off post about HC's activities. Many tweets receive no response whatsoever. On the other hand, especially when a tweeter has many followers, it is possible to receive a large number of replies to a single tweet. This, then, is where the use of Twitter for social interaction varies considerably from regular conversation: first, a tweeter will not necessarily expect a response to what might be termed their initiating utterance; second, they might receive several replies (often within a short space of time), as if in an unregulated conversation between a large number of people, far more than might participate in a face-to-face inter-action. The original tweeter then has to decide whether and how to respond to these replies. Unlike typical face-to-face conversation, there is no obligation to take another turn or to include all participants. Clearly, while all electroni-cally mediated texts owe something to their non-electronic predecessors, one of the points of interest is the extent to which structure and cohesion might be influenced by the electronic medium, particularly in terms of the remoteness of participants and the different conventions which are established due to the specific nature of the text and the way it is generated.

Discourse Frameworks: Exercises

Exercise 1: Cohesive devices

In this extract, Daniel is telling Kate about a television programme. Identify the cohesive devices in their conversation.

Key

(.)	micropause
(2.0)	pause measured in seconds
// //	overlapping speech
=	latching on
(laughs)	indicates laughter by the speaker

1	Daniel	*the basic story is his brother's on death row*
2	Kate	*yeah =*
3	Daniel	*= for a crime he didn't commit (2.0) so he's trying to get his brother out*
4	Kate	*so they escape together*
5	Daniel	*so he's trying to get his brother out together*
6	Kate	*okay =*
7	Daniel	*= umm but of course he's done every plan of the prison on his body and the tattoos mean nothing to anybody but him*
8	Kate	*so how did he do that if he's in prison (.) did he have needles and ink*
9	Daniel	*no he done it beforehand (.) before he went into prison (.) planned everything (1.0) and had all the tattoos done =*
10	Kate	*= so did he know the layout of the prison and stuff*
11	Daniel	*yeah he had all the blueprints*
12	Kate	*that's clever*
13	Daniel	*all the blueprints yeah it's a really clever =*
14	Kate	*= so he got himself into prison*
15	Daniel	*yeah*
16	Kate	*just to get himself // and his brother out //*
17	Daniel	*// and his brother out // yeah*
18	Kate	*is this a true life story*
19	Daniel	*no no no it's just (.)*
20	Kate	*(laughs) I thought it was true*
21	Daniel	*no it's just a programme that's on once a week*

Exercise 2: Structure in spontaneous conversation

This is an extract from an argument between two teenage sisters. Despite the fact this a competitive, confrontational exchange, what conversational structures can be identified? Is the argument essentially orderly?

Key

(.)	micropause
(2.0)	pause measured in seconds
// //	overlapping speech
=	latching on
<u>*my*</u>	indicates emphasis
some.	unfinished word
(indecipherable)	indecipherable speech

1	Charlotte	*you always use <u>my</u> hairbrush*
2	Annabel	*no I // don't //*
3	Charlotte	*// yeah // you do you always use mine*
4	Annabel	*yeah but Charlotte that was before when I couldn't // find my //*
5	Charlotte	*// yeah but //*
		then I always let you use it <u>yes</u> I do =
6	Annabel	*= yeah but Charlotte that's*
		because I <u>ask</u> (2.0) I always ask if I want I want to borrow
		// some. //
7	Charlotte	*// exactly // and I always let you so (.)*
8	Annabel	(indecipherable)
9	Charlotte	(indecipherable)
10	Annabel	*I would Charlotte I'd happily let you* (indecipherable) *my hair*
		bands if you'd just ask me rather than going through my things
		and saying (.) oh she's not using that I'll take that and then just
		leave it // (indecipherable) *//*
11	Charlotte	*// whatever // I don't care (.) Annabel you actually mistake*
		me for someone that actually cares
12	Annabel	*yeah well exactly maybe you should start caring 'cos*
		// you don't like //
13	Charlotte	*// but I don't //*
14	Annabel	*you wouldn't like it if I take (.) <u>mess</u> up all your things and took*
		all your things so maybe you wouldn't // m. //
15	Charlotte	*//* (indecipherable) *//*

16	Annabel	*yeah but Charlotte you really could if I just went and took all*
17	Charlotte	*your stuff when you really needed it (.) you'd be a bit // like //*
		// when d'you //
		ever do that
18	Annabel	*exactly I'm not saying that but (.) when you go* (indecipherable)
		you could quite happily go and buy yourself a packet of new hair
		bands <u>99p</u> (indecipherable) *but you just can't be <u>bothered</u> to*
19	Charlotte	*oh* (indecipherable)
20	Annabel	*oh for god's sake it's useless* [starts to cry] *you're so horrible I*
		hate you
21	Charlotte	*I hate you too*

DISCOURSE FRAMEWORKS: SUGGESTIONS FOR FURTHER READING

Blakemore, Diane (1992) *Understanding Utterances: Introduction to Pragmatics* (Oxford: Blackwell)
Using relevance theory as the underpinning approach, this textbook covers a wide range of contextual and stylistic aspects of pragmatics.

Brown, Gillian and George Yule (1983) *Discourse Analysis* (Cambridge: Cambridge University Press)
A standard textbook which deals with both spoken and written discourse. It provides detailed analyses of how texts are constructed and pays a lot of attention to context and interpretation.

Cameron, Deborah (2001) *Working With Spoken Discourse* (London: Sage)
An excellent and highly readable survey of different approaches to studying spoken discourse with helpful guidance on carrying out personal research.

Carter, Ronald (2004) *Language and Creativity* (London: Routledge)
An intriguing study of the richness and creativity of everyday conversation, with examples drawn from the huge Cambridge and Nottingham Corpus of Discourse in English (CANCODE).

Chapman, Siobhan (2006) *Thinking About Language* (Basingstoke: Palgrave Macmillan)
A fascinating discussion of the questions to be asked about language which will interest readers wishing to develop their ideas on language as a phenomenon.

Crystal, David (2006) *Language and the Internet*, 2nd edn (Cambridge: Cambridge University Press)
A thought-provoking exploration of the ways in which the Internet has influenced our language use, with detailed analysis of a range of Internet genres.

Fairclough, Norman (2003) *Analysing Discourse* (London: Routledge)
Written primarily to teach the methodology to social scientists, this is useful for any readers who wish to learn more about analysing written and spoken language from a social perspective.

Georgakopoulou, Alexandra and Dionysis Goutsos (2004) *Discourse Analysis*, 2nd edn (Edinburgh: Edinburgh University Press)
An introduction to the theory and methodology of analysing discourse, which takes the approach of dividing discourse into narrative and non-narrative.

Graddol, David, Jenny Cheshire and Joan Swann (1994) *Describing Language*, 2nd edn (Milton Keynes: Open University Press)
Contains useful chapters on face-to-face interaction and the analysis of spoken and written discourse, as well as covering other aspects of language.

Halliday, M. A. K. and R. Hasan (1976) *Cohesion In English* (London: Longman)
A standard and authoritative text on the subject of cohesion.

Levinson, S (1983) *Pragmatics* (Cambridge: Cambridge University Press)
A well established text on the theories of how we interpret and identify implied meaning.

Schiffrin, Deborah (1993) *Approaches to Discourse* (Oxford: Blackwell)
This comprehensive text begins with a useful overview and some important definitions, and goes on to compare six key approaches.

Tannen, Deborah (2005) *Conversational Style*, 2nd edn (Oxford: Oxford University Press)
A practical and theoretical exploration of talk among friends.

Tannen, Deborah (ed.) (1993) *Framing in Discourse* (Oxford: Oxford University Press)
Drawing on a wide range of uses and contexts, this book shows how speakers use metalinguistic signals to construct and understand spoken discourse.

Internet resources

www.bl.uk
The British Library website provides an opportunity to view a remarkable range of historical texts, and there is a 'turning the pages' facility for some texts. Excellent learning resources are available in the 'language and literature' section.

www.natcorp.ox.ac.uk
The site of the British National Corpus which describes itself as 'a 100 million word collection of samples of written and spoken language from a wide range

of sources'. The corpus consists of contemporary texts and is ideal for looking at specific lexical items in a range of contexts. More complex analysis can be undertaken using Xaira software. This requires a subscription but a trial period is available. However, the corpus can also be accessed through a Brigham Young University website at http://corpus.byu.edu/bnc/.

www.collinslanguage.com/content-solutions/wordbanks
Collins WordBanks Online provides access to the corpus which is used to resource Collins dictionaries, and includes 'The Bank of English' which was set up in conjunction with Birmingham University. A subscription is required, but a one-month trial is available free of charge.

Part V
PHONOLOGICAL FRAMEWORKS

9 Phonetics and Phonemes

9.1 PHONETICS AND PHONOLOGY

Phonetics is the study of the sounds of speech – how we produce speech, how we perceive speech, and what characterises each particular sound. There are several branches of phonetics but we will only be dealing here with **articulatory phonetics**. This is the area of phonetics which deals with the actual production of speech sounds. When we talk about speech sounds we are referring to the individual sounds which make up words. A simple word like *bat,* for example, is made up of three distinct sounds. We will be concerned here with discovering what precisely we do in physiological terms in order to produce individual sounds such as these and many others.

Closely related to phonetics is **phonology**. Whereas phonetics deals with the physical production and perception of speech, phonology is more concerned with sound systems and patterns. Although phonetics is distinct from phonology, for the sake of simplicity phonetics is included here as an aspect of the **phonological frameworks** which are dealt with in this penultimate part of the book. Clearly, both phonetics and phonology, which relate to sounds and sound systems, are in contrast to the other frameworks we have covered which are concerned with lexical, grammatical and discourse structure. In this chapter, we will begin by looking at speech production (a branch of phonetics), but in conjunction with this we will also move beyond the realm of phonetics proper in order to identify the system of speech sounds – or **phonemes** – which characterise English. In the following chapter we will look at the way in which these speech sounds combine to form syllables and words. Then in Chapter 11 we will conclude our exploration of the phonological frameworks of English by looking at features such as stress and intonation which affect syllables, words and strings of words.

One important point to make before we begin to consider speech sounds and their production concerns the primacy of speech. Because most of us have never struggled with speech in the way we may have struggled with reading and writing, it is easy to take spoken language for granted and to rate it as less valuable than the written language. Speech is important not only because it provides us with a versatile and instant means of communication but also because human language materialises first and foremost as speech. This is why no study of the frameworks of English would be complete without a specific study of phonology.

9.2 A REPRESENTATIVE ACCENT

In Chapter 1 we discussed the desirability of having one particular variety of English to refer to when looking at lexical and grammatical frameworks. The variety selected was **Standard British English**. This was chosen because it has common currency: even if people do not speak Standard English, they will almost certainly write it sometimes and they will be very familiar with it as a national dialect used, for example, in newspapers, in business and legal documents, and in much public broadcasting.

Standard English is a **dialect**: in other words, it is a variety characterised by certain lexical and grammatical features. All speakers of English have a dialect, be it Standard English or some other variety. Similarly, all speakers have an **accent**. Accent is the term we use to refer to characteristics of pronunciation. Often, we can identify where someone comes from by their accent. Through television and film, and through our everyday experiences, most British speakers are familiar with the accents of Belfast, Glasgow, Edinburgh, Cardiff, Liverpool and Newcastle to name just a few of the regional accents of the United Kingdom. (And most of us are also adept at recognising accents from Australia, America, Asia and so on.) Selecting a representative accent for our study of the phonology of English is not an entirely straightforward matter. We cannot simply select the accent used by speakers of Standard English since they do not all speak the same accent. Linguists have traditionally selected an accent known as **Received Pronunciation** (often abbreviated as **RP**) to represent British English and this, therefore, is the accent we will use here, although other British and global accents will be discussed in Chapter 12. The Queen speaks RP but hers is a variety associated with the aristocracy and with older speakers which is known as **conservative RP**. In this book, what is meant by RP will be the **mainstream** variety of the accent. You can hear this spoken by many national newsreaders and by well known media or public figures such as Joanna Lumley, Stephen Fry and Jeremy Paxman.

There is an irony about selecting RP to study in that relatively few people in Britain (3–5 per cent is the usual estimate) have an RP accent. However, it is perceived as representative of English in that it is the accent taught to many foreigners and it is the pronunciation given in dictionaries (sometimes alongside General American). Although it has the disadvantage of sometimes being associated with social privilege, it also has the advantage of not being associated with any specific geographical region.

9.3   PHONEMES

In this chapter, then, we are looking at the way sounds are produced and at the range of sounds which occur in English as represented by Received Pronunciation. We have already seen that words are the chief building blocks of language, although it is possible to analyse words in terms of the smaller units of meaning (or morphemes) which comprise them. On a phonetic level, we can analyse words in terms of distinct, individual sounds. To repeat our earlier example, in the word *bat* you can distinguish three separate sounds. We can test the theory that there are three distinct sounds in *bat* by seeing if each sound can be substituted with another and whether a different word is the result of this substitution. The first sound of *bat* could be replaced to form *rat,* the second to form *bet,* the third to form *bad.* (Of course, the first element of *rat* could be substituted with /br/ to give *brat,* but the fact that /br/ can be divided into /b/ and /r/ means it is not a minimal or smallest possible unit of sound.) Each of these words – *bat, rat, bet* and *bad* - must, then, be made up of three distinct sounds. If a single sound substitution enables us to make a distinction between two different words (as in *bat* and *rat*), this is proof that the two sounds involved are each meaningful sounds in the language.

Sometimes, a particular sound can be pronounced in different ways depending on the position or context in which it occurs. For instance, compare the way you pronounce /l/ at the start of *loop* with /l/ at the end of *pool.* In RP, word-initial /l/ is different from word-final /l/ in that the latter involves far more spreading of the back of the tongue against the roof of the mouth. The word-initial /l/ is known as **clear *l*** while the word-final /l/ is **dark *l*.** Despite this difference of pronunciation, however, we are unlikely to claim that these two sounds are distinct sounds in the way that /b/ and /p/ are. On the contrary, they represent different surface realisations of the same underlying sound. Similarly, some Scots speakers might pronounce *rat* with a slightly rolled /r/ at the beginning, whereas an RP speaker is unlikely to roll the /r/. This does not mean that the Scots speaker is uttering a different word from the RP speaker, merely pronouncing the same word in a slightly different way. We can conclude therefore that there is a difference between the underlying 'model' sounds which make up words and the surface realisation of these sounds by various speakers. These underlying sounds are **phonemes**. Phoneme is an abstract concept in the way that lexeme is also abstract, as we saw in Chapter 2. The surface forms of the phonemes, which vary depending on the position of a sound or on the speaker's accent, are **allophones**. Clear *l* and dark *l* are allophones of the phoneme /l/ just as the various pronunciations of the sound at the beginning of *rat* are allophones of the phoneme /r/. The study and identification of allophones is largely beyond the scope of this chapter since we are primarily concerned with discovering how we produce sounds and with identifying the set of phonemes which underpin the sound system of the language. We will continue to use the term phoneme on occasions but in many instances the terms **sound** or **speech sound** will be sufficient for our purposes.

Using the method of contrasting pairs of words (such as *bat/rat, bat/bet, bat/bad*) we can work out how many distinct sounds or phonemes a language possesses. The complete set of phonemes in a language or in a particular accent of a language is known as a **phoneme inventory**. If you collected together all the phonemes which occur in every language of the world you would discover that the phonemes of English make up only a proportion of all the possible sounds which occur in human speech. Some languages have fewer phonemes than English, others more. The number of sounds in a language may or may not be significant. What is certainly of interest though is the actual selection of sounds. Language is not a haphazard phenomenon and this awareness should prompt us, when we have collected together the phonemes of RP, to see what patterns we can find in the selection and to see how the sounds are related.

□ **morphemes** ⇨ 3.2

9.4 THE INTERNATIONAL PHONETIC ALPHABET

One of the problems of writing down speech sounds, or making a **transcription,** is indicating them clearly to the reader. It is fairly easy to show that *bat* contains three speech sounds because it is easy to grasp the relationship between each of the three letters of the written word and the sounds they represent. However, the letters <b,a,t> (remember that angled brackets < > are used in linguistics to identify letters) do not always stand for the sounds they represent when *bat* is pronounced. For example, <a> represents different sounds in *harp, pace* and *asleep* and <t> represents different sounds in *nation, hatch* and *theme*, while <b> doesn't represent any sound at all in *dumb.*

This problem of there not always being the same correspondence between letters and sounds led a group of linguists concerned with the teaching of foreign languages (and who formed themselves into the **International Phonetic Association**) to devise a special alphabet in which one symbol always represented the same sound and in which there was a symbol for every possible sound a language learner might need. This special alphabet is known as the **International Phonetic Alphabet** (**IPA** for short) and it is an indispensable tool for the study of phonetics and phonology as it makes the task of identifying and referring to sounds much easier. In phonetics, it is the sound of a word which is of importance and not its written form: *dumb,* for example, only has three phonemes /d, ʌ, m/ even though it has four letters. We write phonetic symbols in slant brackets / / in order to distinguish sounds from letters. Essentially, the symbols in slant brackets represent the under-lying phonemes but do not give any detailed information about how these phonemes are realised, such as whether or not a /r/ sound is rolled. This type of transcription is known as a **broad** transcription. It is possible to use additional symbols and special markings called **diacritics** in a transcription in order to identify allophones. An allophonic or **narrow** transcription of speech is placed within square [ ] brackets.

One word of warning: despite the principle outlined above of one symbol to one speech sound in the IPA, it is not impossible that you will come across some variations in the course of your studies. This is largely because American linguists use a slightly different set of symbols from British linguists. The symbols used in this book are in common use, however, so you need have no worries about them being recognised should you use them yourself.

☐ **list of IPA symbols** ➪ pp. 330–31
☐ **diacritics** ➪ p. 331

9.5 THE VOCAL TRACT

Before looking at the English phoneme system and the consonants and vowels it contains, we need to take a brief look at the **vocal tract** where the sounds are produced. The vocal tract begins at the **voice box** or **larynx** and ends at the **lips**. The larynx is essentially a casing of cartilage rings at the top of the

trachea. The front of the larynx protrudes slightly below the chin and jaw (especially in men) and so you can probably feel it. In the larynx are two small but extremely important muscles, stretching from front to back, which can open and close. These are the **vocal cords** (although you may occasionally find them referred to as the **vocal folds**). The space between them is known as the **glottis**.

The section of the vocal tract between the larynx and the **uvula** (the piece of flesh which hangs down at the back of the mouth) is known as the **pharynx**. Above the pharynx, the vocal tract branches into the **nasal cavity** and the **oral cavity**. For the majority of sounds in English, the **soft palate** (or **velum**) is raised, blocking off the nasal cavity. However, there are three nasal consonants in English for which the soft palate is lowered (as in Figure 9.1), allowing air to pass through the nasal cavity.

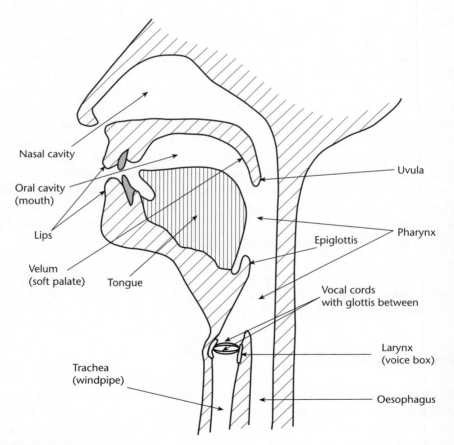

Figure 9.1 The vocal tract

Our interest in the production of the sounds of English is centred on the larynx and everything above it. However, the **lungs** are crucial to the production of sound. English phonemes are made by the air passing from the lungs, up the trachea, then through the larynx and the rest of the vocal tract. This flow of air is known as an **airstream**. If the airstream flows out from the lungs it is an **egressive pulmonic airstream**. All sounds in English are made by using an egressive pulmonic airstream. (Some languages make use of an **ingressive pulmonic airstream**, which involves air being drawn into the lungs as the sound is made.) It is the action of the vocal folds at the top of the larynx and the shape of the mouth that determine which sound is produced.

9.6   THE CONSONANTS OF ENGLISH

Many people traditionally distinguish between **consonants** and **vowels** in terms of the letters of the alphabet: <a, e, i, o, u> and sometimes <y> are the vowels and the rest are consonants. Again, you need to forget about letters and spellings and think about sounds or phonemes. In phonetics, a consonant involves some kind of narrow, partial or complete **closure** (or **stricture**) in the vocal tract – usually in the mouth. This closure is brought about by different parts of the mouth making some kind of contact with each other. By contrast, a vowel sound involves no closure or contact of this kind and the airstream flows unobstructed out of the mouth. Try saying aloud once more the separate sounds of *bat* and you will discover that only the middle sound is a vowel. (The first sound involves the lips closing together, and the third sound requires the tongue to come into contact with the ridge which runs behind the upper teeth, while the middle sound has the tongue lying fairly flat in the mouth, with no obstruction being caused to the airstream.)

The English of Received Pronunciation is based on a system of 24 consonants. (There is very little variation for other accents.) The IPA symbols for the consonants are given in Table 9.1 in something resembling alphabetical order to make it easier for you to learn them. Many of the IPA symbols are the same as the letters from the Roman alphabet which you would probably associate with that sound anyway. Some of the other symbols are drawn from the Greek alphabet (/θ/) or from Anglo-Saxon orthography (/ʒ, ð/). Two symbols (/ŋ, ʃ/) are modifications of Roman letters. The handwritten form <ɡ> rather than the printed <g> is used for the sound at the beginning of *get*.

Although it is helpful to see the IPA symbols for the first time in something approximating to alphabetical order, this strategy does little to

Table 9.1 RP consonants

/b/	bead
/d/	deed
/dʒ/	jet
/f/	feed
/g/	get
/h/	heed
/j/	yet
/k/	keep
/l/	let
/m/	met
/n/	net
/ŋ/	ring
/p/	pet
/r/	reed
/s/	seed
/ʃ/	shape
/t/	tape
/tʃ/	cheat
/θ/	thin
/ð/	then
/v/	vet
/w/	win
/ʒ/	measure
/z/	zone

illuminate the patterns which underlie the consonant system of English. There are ways of looking at the above consonants which tell us much more about their relationship to each other. So far, we have no way of describing what differentiates one consonant from another, although we have seen how exchanging phonemes results in different words being produced. By looking at specific characteristics of the individual consonant sounds, we will be able to perceive their relationship to each other and also understand how they are produced in the vocal tract. We classify consonants according to three aspects:

> place of articulation
> manner of articulation
> presence or absence of voice

If you take a closer look at the mouth as depicted in Figure 9.2, it is possible to identify various **places of articulation**. A place of articulation is the part of the vocal tract where the complete or partial closure necessary for a consonant sound is made. The places of articulation used in the consonant phoneme

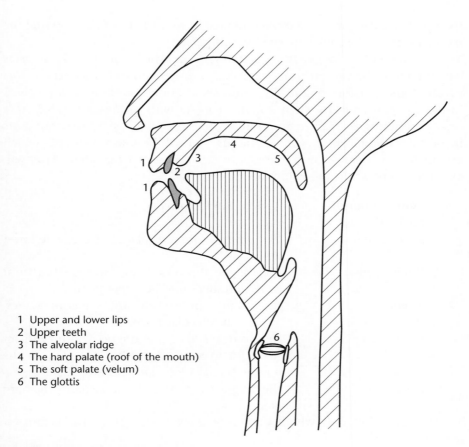

1 Upper and lower lips
2 Upper teeth
3 The alveolar ridge
4 The hard palate (roof of the mouth)
5 The soft palate (velum)
6 The glottis

Figure 9.2   Places of articulation

system of RP are the **lips**, the **upper teeth**, the hard ridge behind the upper row of teeth known as **the alveolar ridge**, the roof of the mouth or **hard palate**, the **soft palate** at the back of the mouth (also known as the **velum**), and the **glottis**.

The parts of the mouth involved in making speech sounds are called **articulators**. Three parts of the mouth cannot move: the upper teeth, the alveolar ridge and the hard palate. These are therefore known as **passive articulators**. The other parts can move and are the **active articulators**. The **tongue** is a very important active articulator as it is often brought into contact with another part of the mouth in order to make a closure. It is useful to distinguish the different parts of the tongue, namely the **tip**, the **blade**, the **front** and the **back**, and also the **sides**. The blade is the tapered front part of the tongue with the tip at its extremity. When the tongue is at rest, the front lies opposite the hard palate and the back opposite the soft palate.

Although the tongue is such an important articulator, the special terms which refer to the various places of articulation refer to the other articulators involved and not the tongue. For example, although the tongue is involved in the articulation of /t/ when it makes contact with the alveolar ridge, /t/ is described simply as an alveolar sound. If you go through the list of consonants in Table 9.1 and make the various sounds, you will be able to work out which articulators are involved and thus identify the places of articulation. They will all fall into one of the following categories:

Type of sound	Articulators involved
bilabial	the lips
labio-dental	the upper front teeth placed against the lower lip
(inter-) dental	the tongue (tip and sides) between the front teeth and touching the upper teeth
alveolar	the tongue (tip or blade, and sometimes sides) against the alveolar ridge
palato-alveolar	the tip or blade of the tongue making contact with the alveolar ridge, while the front of the tongue is raised towards the hard palate
palatal	the tongue (front and/or sides) against the hard palate
velar	the back of the tongue against the velum (or soft palate)
glottal	the vocal cords

You will find that some sounds are very easy to classify, while others may be a little trickier. Table 9.2 shows where the sounds are made.

Table 9.2 Places of articulation for RP consonants

Bilabial	Labio-dental	Dental	Alveolar	Palato-alveolar	Palatal	Velar	Glottal
/b/	/f/	/θ/	/d/	/dʒ/	/j/	/g/	/h/
/m/	/v/	/ð/	/l/	/ʃ/		/k/	
/p/			/n/	/tʃ/		/ŋ/	
/w/			/r/	/ʒ/			
			/s/				
			/t/				
			/z/				

Another means of classification needs to be introduced if further relationships between the consonants are to be seen. This involves looking at the **manner of articulation**. Consider the four bilabial phonemes identified in Table 9.2. They are all made at the same place of articulation (namely the lips) but it is impossible that they are all made in the same manner or we would not be able to distinguish between them. Identifying the manner of articulation allows us to classify sounds according to what happens to the airstream as it passes through the vocal tract. We can distinguish five types of sound in terms of manner of articulation. A sound may be a **plosive**, a **nasal**, a **fricative**, an **affricate** or an **approximant**.

An example of a plosive sound is /b/ at the start of *bead*. As /b/ is a bilabial sound, the lips are the articulators involved in its production and the lips are also therefore the place of articulation. The lips are closed as air passes from the lungs and up the trachea into the mouth (where the soft palate is raised, shutting off the nasal cavity). When the air reaches the mouth, because the lips are closed there is a build-up of air pressure behind them. When the lips open, the pressure is suddenly released and this causes a small explosion or plosive sound to result.

In the production of /m/ (as in *met*), which is a nasal sound in terms of the manner of articulation but also a bilabial sound as far as place of articulation is concerned, the lips are closed as for /b/. However, in contrast to plosive sounds, the soft palate is lowered so that released air can also pass through the nasal cavity. As with a plosive sound, pressure builds up in the mouth but the pressure is lower as some of the air can escape through the nasal cavity. When the air is released by opening the lips there is a small burst or explosion of air as with a plosive sound but it is less prominent due to the lower air pressure in the mouth before the air is released. The sound also has a different quality because there is resonance in the nasal cavity as the air escapes. If you hold your hand close to your face and then utter /b/ and /m/ alternately, you will feel the difference in the strength of the explosion. For /m/ you will also feel some air escaping through your nostrils. Because both plosives and nasals involve a complete closure or stopping off of the vocal tract at one of the places of articulation before the release of air, these two types of sounds are collectively known as **stops**.

An example of a fricative sound is /s/ (as in *seed*). As with plosives, the nasal cavity is blocked off through the raising of the velum. This consonant is an alveolar sound, so the blade of the tongue is touching the alveolar ridge. However, in contrast to plosive and nasal sounds, the closure isn't so tight that no air at all can escape. The air passes through but there is friction because of the proximity of the tongue to the alveolar ridge. This gives the sound its turbulent or fricative quality. Fricatives also contrast with plosives and nasals in that they can be extended as long as you have breath to articulate them. Stop consonants, on the other hand, are momentary.

An affricate sound is a combination of a plosive and a fricative. An example is /ʧ/ (as in _cheat_). This sound begins as a plosive /t/ with the airstream blocked by the tongue being positioned against the alveolar ridge. The air which has built up in the mouth is released more gently than in a plosive consonant: as a result the closure is partially maintained, and this causes a brief fricative sound – in this case /ʃ/ – to follow. Affricates are fairly rare consonants in all languages. There are only two in English: /ʧ/, which we have just discussed, and /ʤ/ (as in _jet_) which is a combination of /d/ followed by /ʒ/.

The four approximant sounds in RP – /w, l, r, j/ – are slightly problematic consonants. Some phoneticians call them **semi-consonants**, and others call them **semi-vowels**, which gives an indication as to why they are problematic. When approximant sounds are produced, the restrictions to the air passage are less than those for the preceding four types since closure in the vocal tract is never total, nor is friction ever produced at the place of articulation. This makes approximants more like vowels. However, a good argument for treating them as consonants relates to their positions in words, since they appear where consonants rather than vowels normally occur: compare _back_ and _tack_ to _whack, lack, rack_ and _yak_. Also, there is some contact between articulators in the production of the approximants – although the obstruction to the airstream is only partial.

The consonant /l/ is sometimes referred to as a **lateral** (meaning 'at the side') or **lateral approximant** to distinguish it from /r/, which is a **central approximant**. It is lateral because the blade of the tongue touches the alveolar ridge above the front teeth and the air escapes at the sides of the mouth; /r/ is central because the sides of the tongue are very close to or touching the alveolar ridge above the back teeth and the air escapes down the middle of the mouth. You can contrast the tongue positions for /l/ and /r/ by sucking in instead of uttering these sounds. For /l/ you will feel the sides of your tongue tingle as the air is sucked over them while for /r/ you will feel this sensation on the blade of your tongue. The term **liquid** (or **liquid approximant**) refers to the two approximants /l/ and /r/.

The consonant /w/ is produced by a partial closure of the lips (and is therefore a bilabial approximant), but the back of the tongue is raised towards the soft palate so we describe /w/ as having a secondary velar articulation. Finally, /j/ is a palatal approximant since the sides (and to some extent the front) of the tongue are raised towards the hard palate (try contrasting /j/ and /r/) and the air, as with /w/ and /r/, escapes down the centre of the mouth.

If you now work through the rest of the consonants (/p, f, v, θ, ð, d, n, t, z, ʃ, ʒ, g, k, ŋ, h/) you should be able to identify their manner of articulation.

It is then possible to combine the features of place and manner of articulation in a table to show how the consonants of English are classified. This is shown in Table 9.3 which reveals that in many instances there are still two phonemes which fulfil a particular description. For example /s/ and /z/ are both alveolar fricatives. A further feature must be identified which will enable us to distinguish between these two phonemes, and this feature is **voicing**. The presence or absence of voice when a phoneme is produced is caused by the state of the vocal cords in the larynx. If the folds are open when the air passes through the larynx then the airstream flows freely and the phoneme is voiceless. On the other hand, if the vocal cords are almost closed then the air causes them to vibrate as it passes through and the sound is voiced. You can test this by putting your finger on your larynx and saying the sounds /s/ and /z/ alternately. You will be able to feel your larynx vibrate when you make the /z/ sound.

In English, a distinction between a voiceless phoneme and its voiced counterpart is only found in plosives, fricatives and affricates. For all the pairs of consonants in Table 9.3 (excluding /l/ and /r/ which are both voiced), one is voiced and the other voiceless. The fricative /h/ (sometimes also referred to as an **aspirate**) is unlike the other consonants in being produced at the glottis, not in the mouth. It is voiceless because to produce it the vocal cords need to be more open than for voiced consonants but not fully open as when breathing out normally and silently. (The friction for /h/ is partly produced at the glottis, but there is likely to be some friction in the rest of the vocal tract too.) In English, all three nasal phonemes and all the approximants are voiced. In Table 9.3, the voiceless plosive, fricative and affricate phonemes appear on the upper line, the voiced ones on the lower.

Table 9.3   Consonants of RP showing place and manner of articulation

	Bilabial	Labio-dental	Dental	Alveolar	Palato-alveolar	Palatal	Velar	Glottal
Plosive	/p/			/t/			/k/	
	/b/			/d/			/g/	
Fricative		/f/	/θ/	/s/	/ʃ/			/h/
		/v/	/ð/	/z/	/ʒ/			
Affricate					/tʃ/			
					/dʒ/			
Nasal	/m/			/n/			/ŋ/	
Approximant	/w/			lateral /l/		/j/	(/w/)	
				central /r/				

Now that the 24 consonants have been arranged on a grid, you have all the information you need to refer to each one individually. Of course, you can refer to them by phonetic symbol, but you may find that for some reason you will need to give a more specific definition. When describing a consonant in full, begin by stating whether or not it is voiced (if there is a contrast), then state the place of articulation and finally the manner. So /g/ is a voiced velar plosive and /m/ is a bilabial nasal.

The advantage of having arranged the consonants in a grid as shown in Table 9.3 is that we can observe the entire consonant system of RP in terms of the distribution of these speech sounds. One interesting feature is that more phonemes are articulated at the alveolar ridge than at any other point, but the lips are also frequently used. This fact leads us to infer that these places of articulation are particularly important in human language generally. A considerable amount of work has been done examining the phonemes of other languages. In many ways, English turns out to be fairly typical, both in the number of phonemes it possesses and in the way they are distributed. Most of the consonants which occur in English are frequently found in other languages. Some of the less common consonants which occur in English are the affricates /ʧ/ and /ʤ/ and the fricatives /ʒ, θ, ð/ (and it is worth noting that children are often slower to master these consonants than most of the others). English is quite unusual in having nine fricatives, and in having more fricatives than plosives. The study of phoneme universals has also revealed that languages do not normally have nasals unless they have plosives at the same place of articulation, and this is of course true of English.

☐ **consonant variation in other accents** ⇨ 12.9

9.7 THE VOWELS OF ENGLISH

All consonants are produced by a specific kind of closure in the mouth. This closure is either total (for plosives, nasals and affricates), almost total so that the airstream causes friction at the place of articulation (affricates again and fricatives), or partial and not close enough to cause friction (approximants). By contrast, no such closures are used for vowels, which rely instead on the shape of the lips and the position of the tongue in the mouth, without the tongue coming into contact with the other articulators as it does for consonants. With this knowledge, it is possible to draw up a descending scale of closure and articulator contact as shown in Table 9.4. Vowels might be viewed as being at one end of a **continuum** of closure (or **narrowing**) and as being

Table 9.4 Degrees of consonant and vowel closure

Is the sound dependent on contact between articulators?	Type of contact between articulators	Consonant or vowel?
yes	total closure	consonant (plosive, nasal, affricate)
yes	almost total closure (+ resulting friction)	consonant (affricate, fricative)
yes	partial closure of the mouth (no friction)	consonant (approximant)
no	none necessary	vowel

distinct from consonants in that they are not dependent for their production on contact between the articulators. To get a clearer idea of how this narrowing continuum works, consider the following set of sounds:

/t/   total closure, with the tip/blade (and sides) of the tongue against the alveolar ridge

/s/   almost total closure, with the tip/blade (and sides) of the tongue against the alveolar ridge but not so tightly as for /t/ since friction is produced

/l/   partial closure, with the tip/blade of the tongue against the front of the alveolar ridge (and the front of the tongue raised towards the hard palate) but no contact between the tongue and the ridge at the sides of the mouth

/i/   (the vowel sound in *keen*) – no contact between the tongue and other articulators but the blade/front of the tongue is moved towards the alveolar ridge (and the hard palate)

These four sounds all involve the same part of the mouth, utilising the tip, blade or front of the tongue and the alveolar ridge. If you say them in a sequence you should be able to distinguish between the four types of closure and the way in which the vowel narrowing differs from the other three types. For /i/, the front section of the tongue is very close to touching the alveolar ridge or the hard palate. However, no contact is made between the front of the tongue and the alveolar ridge, nor are the articulators close enough for any friction to be caused. The airstream has a free passage through the mouth. (You may feel the sides of the back of the tongue touching the back upper teeth. The tongue is a large muscle and will often inadvertently touch other parts of the mouth without this being essential to the production of a particular sound.) Not all vowels rely on the same amount of narrowing in the mouth as the vowel /i/, so the vowels themselves may also be said to be on a narrowing continuum. Table 9.5 lists the vowels of RP in 'alphabetical' order in terms of the phonetic symbols which represent them. This is again for the purposes of introducing these sounds. However, the vowels have already been divided into two types – **monophthongs** and **diphthongs**. (The <ph> in these terms is pronounced /f/.) A monophthong is a pure vowel. In other words, when the vowel is spoken in isolation, the position of the mouth remains unchanged. By contrast, a diphthong is a **glide** from one vowel position towards another. As you pronounce a diphthong you will feel the shape of your mouth alter slightly.

There are 20 vowels in RP. As with the IPA symbols for consonants, some vowel symbols resemble or are letters of the Roman alphabet, while others look a little less familiar. Diphthongs are represented by two symbols, the first being the vowel with which the glide begins and the second being the vowel towards which the glide moves. In writing, the symbols /ɑ/ and /a/ are simply different shapes for the same letter, but in the IPA they represent two distinct sounds, as do /ɜ/ and /ɛ/ (the same shape but facing different directions), and /i/ and /ɪ/ (the latter is written as a capital <I> but should be the same size as the other symbols). The symbol /ə/ is an upside down <e>, /ɒ/ an upside down <a> and /ʌ/ an upside down <v>. In RP, /a/ and /ɛ/ only occur in diphthongs.

The fact that diphthongs are each represented by two symbols may be misleading as it suggests that a diphthong is not one phoneme but two. The diphthongs are, however, treated as distinct phonemes because they are not simply sequences of one vowel followed by another, but single elements of a slightly more complex nature than monophthongs in that the tongue glides from one position to another. For example, the diphthong represented by /eɪ/ is not the phoneme /e/ followed by the phoneme /ɪ/. To pronounce /e/ and /ɪ/ as a sequence of two monophthong vowels would yield two separate syllables, while the diphthong /eɪ/ is a single syllable. Further, the initial part of a diphthong

Table 9.5 The vowels of RP

monophthongs	/æ/	b<u>a</u>t	diphthongs	/aɪ/	b<u>uy</u>
	/ɑ/	b<u>ar</u>d		/aʊ/	b<u>ough</u>
	/e/	b<u>e</u>t		/eɪ/	b<u>ay</u>
	/ɜ/	b<u>ir</u>d		/ɛə/	b<u>ear</u>
	/ə/	<u>a</u>bout		/əʊ/	b<u>eau</u>
	/i/	b<u>ea</u>d		/ɪə/	b<u>eer</u>
	/ɪ/	b<u>i</u>t		/ɔɪ/	b<u>oy</u>
	/ɒ/	b<u>o</u>mb		/ʊə/	t<u>our</u>
	/ɔ/	b<u>oar</u>d			
	/u/	f<u>oo</u>d			
	/ʊ/	b<u>oo</u>k			
	/ʌ/	b<u>u</u>t			

is always more prominent than the latter part, suggesting some relationship between these two positions. Finally, all the diphthongs share a characteristic of some of the monophthong vowels, that feature being **length**.

We need now to move away from simply listing the vowels of RP and find a systematic way of classifying them just as we did for the consonants. You will recall that consonants were classified according to place of articulation, manner of articulation and the presence or absence of voice. These three aspects enabled us to formulate Table 9.3 which showed a full classification of the 24 consonant phonemes of RP. They also enabled us to give each consonant its own specific description. We saw just now how vowels are distinct from other sounds in that they do not rely on contact between articulators or on the same degree of closure in the mouth. Also, a contrast between voiced and voiceless vowels is impossible because all vowels are voiced. However, the classification by place and manner of articulation which we used for consonants has some bearing on how we can classify vowels systematically. A slightly different method must be found for classifying the vowels, although for the sake of economy and unity it is undesirable to make our classification too different. Something else which needs to be borne in mind when classifying vowels is that, because of the nature of their production, there must inevitably be a degree of approximation in mapping them.

Manner of articulation cannot be applied in the same way to vowels as to consonants since there are no contrasts between plosive, nasal, fricative, affricate and approximant sounds. However, we can make a contrast of **length**. Although this is quite difficult to measure and it is possible also to prolong vowels at will, it is true to say that in RP some vowels are regularly or typically given greater duration than others. Therefore we can use length to make an initial division of the monophthong vowels. (Diphthongs need not concern us here since they possess the feature of length by being glides.)

A concrete way of demonstrating that some vowels are longer than others can be provided by looking at some simple **monosyllabic** words (words of one syllable). A contrast can be made between monosyllabic words which end in a consonant and those which end in a vowel. Table 9.6 contrasts examples of words with the **closed** structure CVC (consonant-vowel-consonant) with those of an **open** CV (consonant-vowel) structure, where the vowel is not followed by a final, closing consonant. The table shows that only five of the twelve monophthongs appear in RP in an open CV structure. This is linked to the fact that they have the feature of length. Length is indicated by a modified colon : after the vowel in question (although a regular colon : is sometimes used). From now on the five long monophthong vowels of RP will normally be written with a length mark to distinguish them from the short vowels. It was mentioned above that diphthongs, because they involve a glide from one vowel to another, have the feature of length. It is not surprising therefore that,

Table 9.6 The occurrence of monophthongs in CVC and CV words

Monophthong	CVC word	Phonetic transcription	CV word	Phonetic transcription
/æ/	b<u>a</u>t	/bæt/	–	–
/ɑ/	b<u>ar</u>d	/bɑːd/	bar	/bɑː/
/e/	b<u>e</u>t	/bet/	–	–
/ɜ/	b<u>ir</u>d	/bɜːd/	burr	/bɜː/
/ə/*	–	–	–	–
/i/	b<u>ea</u>d	/biːd/	bee	/biː/
/ɪ/	b<u>i</u>t	/bɪt/	–	–
/ɒ/	b<u>o</u>mb	/bɒm/	–	–
/ɔ/	b<u>oar</u>d	/bɔːd/	bore	/bɔː/
/u/	f<u>oo</u>d	/fuːd/	boo	/buː/
/ʊ/	b<u>oo</u>k	/bʊk/	–	–
/ʌ/	b<u>u</u>t	/bʌt/	–	–

*/ə/ can appear without a following consonant, but normally not in a monosyllabic word. The occurrence of /ə/ is discussed in Sections 10.3, 11.2 and 11.3.

like the long monophthong vowels, they appear in open CV structures (for example, *bear* /bɛə/ and *boy* /bɔɪ/, and all the other examples in Table 9.5).

So far, then, we have seen that all vowels are voiced. They cannot be distinguished in terms of manner of articulation in the same way as consonants, but we can make a contrast between short and long vowels. Short vowels are always monophthongs while long vowels may be monophthongs or diphthongs. We can now consider whether the concept of place of articulation has any bearing on how we might classify vowels, although we clearly cannot refer to the role of articulators in the same way we did for consonants. (It is worth mentioning here that in English the soft palate is normally raised for vowels, so that air escapes through the oral cavity only. This feature is usually taken for granted when describing RP vowels.)

For consonants, we have seen how the contrast between, say, a bilabial sound and an alveolar one involves a difference in the shape of the mouth at the moment of articulation because of the different articulators involved. Similarly with vowels, the mouth does not retain the same shape. You can tell this if you contrast /ɪ/ with /ɑː/ or /e/ with /uː/, for example. As you contrast these phonemes, you should be able to feel your tongue moving into different positions and your lips changing shape. It is these changes which give the vowels their distinctive qualities. These two aspects of vowel articulation – tongue position and lip shape – can be used to complete the classification of vowels.

The tongue position for monophthong vowels is usually plotted by a dot on a grid that relates to the shape of the mouth. The idea of a grid was introduced by the phonetician Daniel Jones (1881–1967). The shape in which it is usually drawn now is very similar to his original design. To understand the grid, you need first to imagine its lines being plotted in the mouth as shown in Figure 9.3, which shows a cross-section of the head. The grid has been super-imposed on the mouth in such a way that each corner of the grid indicates the points, front and back, where the tongue will be at its highest or lowest, particularly when the mouth is opened quite wide. In Figure 9.3, however, the mouth is only slightly open and the tongue is in a neutral position. If you now look at Figure 9.4 which shows the grid in greater detail, you will see that various labels have been added. The labels at the top – **front**, **central** and **back** – refer to the front, central (the back of the front and the front of the back) and back areas of the tongue. You will remember that the front of the tongue lies opposite the hard palate, while the back of the tongue lies opposite the soft palate. For a front vowel, the front of the tongue will be raised towards the alveolar ridge and the hard palate; for a back vowel, the back of the tongue will be raised towards the soft palate. For central vowels, the tongue tends to be flatter than for front or back vowels. The labels at the side of the grid denote the height of the tongue and therefore the amount of space between

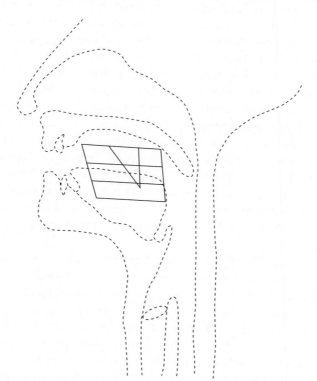

Figure 9.3 The vowel grid superimposed on the mouth

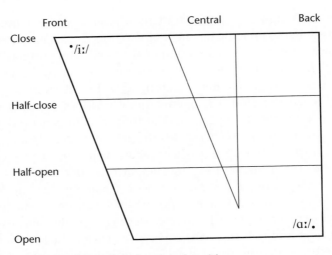

Figure 9.4   The vowel grid with /iː/ and /ɑː/ positions

the tongue and the hard and soft palates when the vowel is produced. A **close vowel** will have a relatively small cavity between the tongue and the palate, while an **open vowel** will have a relatively large one, especially since the jaw is slightly lowered for open vowels. There are two intermediate measures of tongue height – **half-close** and **half-open**. So to produce the vowel /iː/, the tongue is pushed slightly forward and up towards the alveolar ridge and the hard palate (similar to the position it takes to articulate /t/, as we saw earlier). By contrast, the /ɑː/ sound requires the tongue to be low. This is why doctors ask you to 'say ah' when they examine your throat: it forces you to lower your tongue. The two vowels /iː/ and /ɑː/ have been marked on Figure 9.4 using a dot. The dot is placed on the grid to show the highest point the tongue reaches in the production of any particular vowel. The dot also indicates which part of the tongue is raised highest. The vowel /iː/, then, is a close front vowel while /ɑː/ is an open back vowel. Figure 9.5 shows the contrasting tongue positions of these two vowels.

The shape of the lips was also mentioned above as a feature which contributed to the distinctive quality of each vowel. Try once more contrasting the sounds /iː/ and /ɑː/: you will notice your lips are far more spread for /iː/ than for /ɑː/. Now try positioning your tongue for /iː/ but rounding your lips: you will find that the vowel you produce is distinct from /iː/ (and of course has its own IPA symbol - /y/). When classifying vowels, the shape of the lips is usually given less attention than the height of the tongue and the part of the tongue that is raised, but we will return to this in a moment.

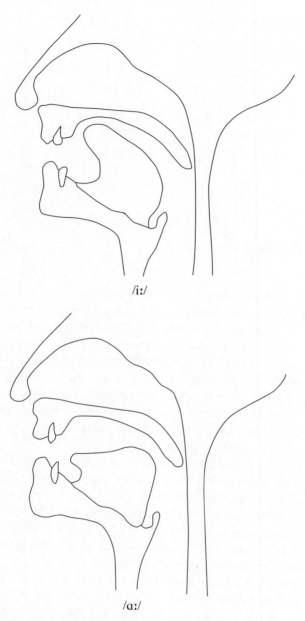

/iː/

/ɑː/

Figure 9.5   Tongue positions for the vowels /iː/ and /ɑː/

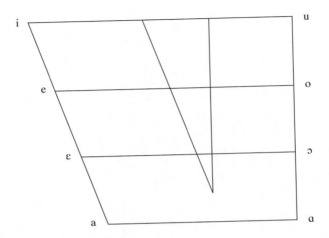

Figure 9.6 The eight cardinal vowels

You will probably have noticed that the vowels /iː/ and /ɑː/ appear very near two extremes of the vowel grid. This means they are very useful as points of reference. Daniel Jones identified eight reference points around the grid, working out which vowels would be produced if the tongue fell from high to low at the front or back of the mouth in equal measures. These reference vowels are known as **cardinal vowels** and are shown in Figure 9.6. When cardinal vowels are written they are often preceded by *C* as an indication that the phonetic symbol represents a cardinal vowel, which is a positional reference point, rather than a phoneme, which is part of the set of speech sounds of a given language. Another point to notice about the eight cardinal vowels is that they do not all have a counterpart in English or in RP. For instance, the English vowel /e/ is positioned between the cardinal vowels *C*/e/ and *C*/ɛ/, with *C*/e/ being closer to the vowel in the French word for 'tea', *thé*. Similarly /a/ does not have an RP equivalent although it is close to the vowel sound in *bat*. The cardinal vowel /o/ is found in French in the pronunciation of, for example, *beau* meaning 'beautiful'. The /iː/ and /ɑː/ of RP are not normally plotted at the extremes which the cardinal vowels represent.

If you utter the vowel sounds from the following words in the sequence below, then you are essentially moving your tongue through the range of positions on the cardinal vowel grid, starting with *C*/i/, then working down the left side of the grid and back up to *C*/u/. When you listen to the eight cardinal vowels you may find it difficult to hear some of the differences between them, especially between the half-open and half-close sounds *C*/ɛ/ and *C*/e/, and *C*/ɔ/ and *C*/o/. If you practise producing these vowels, you should find the distinctions will become clearer:

C /i/   as in RP b*ea*d
C /e/   as in French *thé*
C /ɛ/   close to RP b*e*d, (RP /e/ is somewhere between C/e/ and C/ɛ/)
C /a/   close to RP b*a*t (which is slightly less open than C/a/)
C /ɑ/   as in RP b*ar*d
C /ɔ/   as in RP b*oar*d
C /o/   as in French b*eau*
C /u/   as in RP f*oo*d

When you work through this sequence, you will also notice the way the shape of your lips changes as you go. For /i/ (point 1), the lips are spread; they are still spread for /a/ but less so than for /i/; when you reach /u/ (point 8) you will find your lips have become very rounded. So these cardinal vowels move from spread to rounded lips. This aspect of the cardinal vowels is often assumed rather than mentioned explicitly, but it is important to remember that lip shape is a factor in producing these vowels. The eight cardinal vowels examined here are the eight **primary cardinal vowels**. If you start again at 1 with lips rounded – reversing the process – you will produce the eight **secondary cardinal vowels**. However, the secondary set is not of relevance here since the English vowels relate most closely to the lip shapes of the primary set.

Now we have a fuller frame of reference for plotting vowels, we can position the RP monophthongs on the grid. Figure 9.7 shows the eight (primary) cardinal vowels labelled on the outside of the grid, with the 12 monophthong

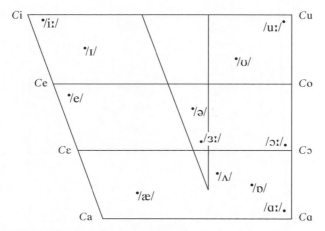

Figure 9.7 Cardinal vowels and RP monophthongs

phonemes of RP labelled within the grid. As mentioned above, not all the primary cardinal vowels have a counterpart in RP. This is not especially significant, bearing in mind that the cardinal vowels are only points of reference. What is interesting is that the vowels are fairly evenly distributed between the front and the back of the mouth. It would be rather surprising if they were nearly all at the front or nearly all at the back. Also, many phonologists consider it significant that most of the monophthongs can be grouped into pairs which are phonetically similar, with one short and one long vowel in each pairing. Five such pairings can be identified in RP: /ɪ/ and /iː/, /æ/ and /ɑː/, /ɒ/ and /ɔː/, /ʊ/ and /uː/, /ə/ and /ɜː/.

The 'neutral' sound /ə/ which occurs more or less in the middle of the grid is of particular interest. It is so common in English that it has a special name – **schwa**. To articulate schwa you have your mouth in what is likely to be its most natural position. Keep your tongue in what might be called its resting position, open your lips slightly (neither spreading them nor rounding them), and add voice: /ə/ is the sound you will probably produce, or something quite close to it. One of the reasons why schwa is so common in English is because vowels in unstressed syllables normally revert to it. More will be said about this in Chapter 11.

The grid (Figure 9.7) used for plotting pure (monophthong) vowels can also be used to plot the eight diphthongs of RP, using an arrow to indicate the direction of the glide in terms of tongue height and which part of the tongue is highest. This is shown in Figure 9.8. You will notice from Figure 9.8

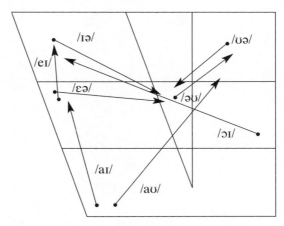

Figure 9.8 Tongue height and direction in RP diphthongs

Table 9.7   RP diphthongs

closing diphthongs	gliding to /ɪ/	/eɪ/
		/aɪ/
		/ɔɪ/
	gliding to /ʊ/	/əʊ/
		/aʊ/
centring diphthongs	gliding to /ə/	/ɪə/
		/ɛə/
		/ʊə/

that three diphthongs move towards /ɪ/, and another two towards /ʊ/. In all five instances, the finishing vowel position is more close (that is, there is less distance between the highest part of the tongue and the hard or soft palate) than the starting position. These five diphthongs are often therefore referred to as **closing diphthongs**. The other three diphthongs move towards /ə/ as the finishing position and, since /ə/ is a central vowel, these diphthongs are often referred to as **centring diphthongs**. Table 9.7 summarises these findings.

We have now completed our survey of the twenty vowels of RP. As with consonants, it is acceptable to refer to the vowels simply by their phonetic symbols. However, you may want to distinguish between length and type so you might, for instance, refer to the short monophthong /æ/, the long monophthong /ɑː/ or the diphthong /aɪ/. If you want to give more detail about how the vowels are articulated you should do so in terms of the vowel grid. Begin by indicating the tongue height and then refer to the part of the tongue raised: so /e/ is a half-open front vowel, /ɜː/ is a half-open central vowel and /uː/ is a close back vowel. (Schwa is termed a mid-central vowel.) You may also wish to add information about whether the lips are rounded or unrounded. So /uː/ is a rounded vowel or, more fully, a close back rounded vowel.

Diphthongs can be described as closing or centring. The closing diphthongs can be divided between those for which the tongue movement is towards the front of the mouth (towards /ɪ/) and those for which the movement is towards the back of the mouth (towards /ʊ/). If you need to be more specific than this, you will need to make reference to the vowel which occurs at the starting point of the glide and the vowel which the glide moves towards.

☐ **schwa in unstressed syllables** ⇨ 11.2
☐ **vowel variation in other accents** ⇨ 12.10

9.8 PHONETIC TRANSCRIPTIONS

It is very likely in the course of your language studies that you will need to transcribe speech. In order to study someone's vocabulary, there is no point in transcribing what they say phonetically (that is, using phonetic symbols). On the other hand, to make a study of their accent, or to study the speech of a young child to see how many of the phonemes of English they have mastered, you will need to use the phonetic alphabet to make some or all of your transcription.

A few tips about transcribing speech might therefore be valuable here. Since it is almost impossible to transcribe speech in real time, the normal practice is to make the transcription from a recording. Until you become very quick and confident, it is probably best to begin by transcribing in ordinary English spelling, and then go back over a few words at a time, converting the words to the IPA. It's not a good idea to do this from memory: you will need to listen to that section of the recording again. One reason for this is that the speaker's accent may be different from yours and you may imagine them saying a word as you would say it. Another reason is that speakers aren't always consistent in their pronunciation and you may well need to identify any variations in their speech. It is also important to remember that, although when we write we leave spaces between words and sometimes between letters, when we speak we run sounds and words together. The result of this **connected speech** is that many speech sounds change their character slightly or are even lost altogether because they are influenced by the sound which precedes or succeeds them. For example, the words *next* and *day* spoken in isolation are pronounced [nekst] and [deɪ], but when spoken together the /t/ at the end of *next* is often lost because the following sound (the /d/ of *day*) is similar in every feature except voicing. The utterance that results will probably be [neks deɪ]. The same is true of *prime minister*, which is often pronounced not as [praɪm mɪnɪstə] but as [praɪmɪnɪstə] because the first word ends with the same phoneme that begins the second word.

When transcribing in phonetic symbols, it is usual to leave gaps between words as you would in speech. However, if you feel a speaker is almost treating two words as one (as some people seem to treat *prime minister*) you could do so too. IPA transcription does not employ punctuation nor is there a distinction between capital and lower case letters. Brackets are only needed at the beginning and end of your transcription.

You may find when transcribing English that you can hear a new sound for which you do not know the symbol. Some of the additional symbols you may need are given with the list of phonetic symbols at the back of this book, along with a list of diacritics (the marks which enable us to give additional information about the pronunciation of phonemes). If you still need a new symbol you can look it up in either of the two reference books recommended at the end of Part V. Alternatively, there is no reason why, for the purposes of your transcription, you couldn't invent a symbol – but remember to identify it in a key.

☐ **connected speech** ⇨ 10.6
☐ **additional symbols and diacritics** ⇨ pp. 331–32

10 Segmental Phonology

10.1 WHAT IS SEGMENTAL PHONOLOGY?

In Chapter 9, we were concerned with phonetics – with the way in which the consonants and vowels of English (as represented by RP) are produced and how they can be classified. We touched briefly on some of the interesting features which emerged from the classification. In this chapter, we move on to look more closely at the **phonology** of English. Whereas phonetics is chiefly concerned with the production of individual speech sounds, phonology is concerned with the phoneme systems of languages and with the individual sounds – or **segments** – when they are no longer in isolation but grouped together in syllables and words. Phonology is often divided into two broad areas – **segmental phonology** and **suprasegmental phonology**. Suprasegmental phonology deals with aspects of speech such as pitch and intonation which colour speech at the syllable level and beyond. We will cover suprasegmental phonology in Chapter 11. Segmental phonology deals with the distribution of the phonemes, how they vary in different environments, and how phonemes group together to form syllables and words.

We have already seen how we can classify the sounds of a language as a set of distinct segments which we have termed phonemes. We have also touched on the fact that the realisation of a phoneme may vary from accent to accent or from speaker to speaker (an example was given of the /r/ at the beginning of *rat* sometimes being rolled). Phonologists consider that the phoneme is an abstract concept. In other words, a phoneme is an idealised or stylised version of the sound in question and isn't 'real'. Phonologists therefore make a contrast between phonemes, which make up the sound system of a language on an abstract level, and allophones, which are the sounds speakers actually produce.

To summarise, we have already touched on two aspects of segmental phonology in Chapter 9: namely, the phoneme system which underpins the RP accent of English and the fact that phonemes have varying surface realisations which are termed allophones. In this chapter, we will move away from considering speech sounds in isolation and look instead at how speech sounds operate in combinations with each other.

□ **phonemes and allophones** ⇨ 9.3

10.2 THE DISTRIBUTION OF CONSONANTS

In Chapter 9 we formulated a table which showed the 24 consonants of RP in terms of place and manner of articulation, and also voicing. For easy reference, this table is repeated here as Table 10.1. We discovered that RP has 6 plosives, 2 affricates, 9 fricatives, 3 nasals and 4 approximants. This distribution shares several features with other languages of the world, which enables us to conclude that the consonant phoneme inventory of English is not especially remarkable, except perhaps in its abundance of fricatives.

So far, then, we have mainly examined these phonemes in isolation. We now need to move on to see how they combine to form syllables and words. The distribution of its phonemes, along with any allophonic variation, are two phonological features which give English its own particular flavour. What is said here about English phonemes is not necessarily true of other languages, although there are bound to be some features in common. If you speak or are studying any other languages, you will probably find it interesting to make some comparisons.

We will begin our study of the distribution of consonants in syllables and words by looking at the positions in which they occur. First, we will examine **monosyllabic** and **disyllabic** words (disyllabic words have two syllables) to see which consonants occur singly in the positions we identify.

Table 10.1 Consonants of RP showing place and manner of articulation

	Bilabial	Labio-dental	Dental	Alveolar	Palato-alveolar	Palatal	Velar	Glottal
Plosive	/p/			/t/			/k/	
	/b/			/d/			/g/	
Fricative		/f/	/θ/	/s/	/ʃ/			/h/
		/v/	/ð/	/z/	/ʒ/			
Affricate					/tʃ/			
					/ʤ/			
Nasal	/m/			/n/			/ŋ/	
Approximant	/w/			lateral /l/		/j/	(/w/)	
				central /r/				

To keep things simple, then, the monosyllabic words will have the structure CVC (where C stands for consonant and V stands for vowel), and the disyllabic words will be CVCV(C). (We will consider groups of consonants or **consonant clusters** later in this chapter.) The words used as examples will be transcribed into the phonetic alphabet in order to focus on their pronunciation. There are three positions in which the consonants can occur: **word-initial** (at the beginning of a word), **word-final** (at the end of a word) and **word-medial** (between vowels in a word of two syllables or more, and therefore at the boundary of two syllables). Table 10.2 lists the possible positions of the 24 consonants.

Table 10.2 The distribution of consonants in RP

Consonant	Word-initial		Word-final		Word-medial	
Plosives						
/p/	pet	/p̱et/	cup	/cʌp̱/	taper	/teɪpə/
/b/	bead	/ḇiːd/	dab	/dæḇ/	baby	/beɪbiː/
/t/	tape	/ṯeɪp/	bat	/bæṯ/	matter	/mætə/
/d/	deed	/ḏiːd/	bad	/bæḏ/	raider	/reɪdə/
/k/	keep	/ḵiːp/	back	/bæḵ/	backer	/bæḵə/
/g/	get	/g̱et/	bag	/bæg̱/	nugget	/nʌgɪt/
Affricates						
/ʧ/	cheat	/ʧ̱iːt/	teach	/tiːʧ̱/	teacher	/tiːʧə/
/ʤ/	jet	/ʤ̱et/	hedge	/heʤ̱/	lodger	/lɒʤə/
Fricatives						
/f/	feed	/f̱iːd/	doff	/dɒf̱/	tuffet	/tʌfɪt/
/v/	vet	/v̱et/	save	/seɪv̱/	cover	/kʌv̱ə/
/θ/	thin	/θ̱ɪn/	bath	/bɑːθ̱/	python	/paɪθən/
/ð/	then	/ð̱en/	lithe	/laɪð̱/	mother	/mʌð̱ə/
/s/	seed	/s̱iːd/	mass	/mæs̱/	NASA	/næsə/
/z/	zone	/ẕəʊn/	maze	/meɪẕ/	razor	/reɪzə/
/ʃ/	shape	/ʃ̱eɪp/	rush	/rʌʃ̱/	rasher	/ræʃ̱ə/
/ʒ/	(genre)	(/ʒɒnrə/)	(beige)	(/beɪʒ/)	measure	/meʒə/
/h/	heed	/ẖiːd/	–	–	ahead	/əẖed/
Nasals						
/m/	met	/m̱et/	bomb	/bɒm̱/	timer	/taɪmə/
/n/	net	/ṉet/	learn	/lɜːṉ/	tiny	/taɪniː/
/ŋ/	–	–	wrong	/rɒŋ/	singer	/sɪŋə/
Approximants						
/w/	win	/w̱ɪn/	–	–	toward	/təw̱ɔd/
/r/	reed	/ṟiːd/	–	–	carer	/kɛərə/
/l/	let	/ḻet/	hill	/hɪḻ/	pillar	/pɪlə/
/j/	yet	/j̱et/	–	–	–	–

As you can see from Table 10.2, most of the consonants occur in all three positions specified. The six plosives, the two affricates and most of the fricatives have full distribution in English. Of the other fricatives, /ʒ/ is something of an oddity, appearing at a later stage in the development of the language than the other fricatives. Word-initially, /ʒ/ only occurs in a handful of French loan words such as *genre* and *gigolo* (although it is hard to say how many speakers consider them to be 'foreign') and we also use it in French phrases such as *je ne sais quoi, joie de vivre* and *le mot juste*. The words in which /ʒ/ appears word-finally are also of fairly recent French origin and many speakers pronounce these words with [ʤ] rather than [ʒ] to give [beɪʤ] *beige* and [gærɪʤ] *garage*, for example. (Some speakers also replace the [ʒ] at the start of *gigolo* with [ʤ].) The word-medial /ʒ/ developed historically in sequences where /z/ was followed by /j/ or /ɪ/. Generally, /ʒ/ is fairly rare. However, it is probably sufficiently established in Modern English for speakers to feel comfortable with it, despite its rarity and the frequently occurring word-final variant [ʤ].

The consonant /h/ presents a slightly different picture. /h/ is common at the beginning of words, although rarer word-medially. However, it never occurs in English at the end of a word. Although in Old English /h/ occurred in word-final position (as in *neah*, meaning *near*), its place and manner of articulation have perhaps influenced the way it is used in Modern English. Because /h/ is articulated at the glottis, the mouth is able simultaneously to be shaped ready for the following vowel. The fricative /h/ has therefore come to be a period of aspiration or audible breath preceding the start of a vowel. Since no vowel follows the final /h/ in an isolated word, /h/ has become redundant in this position.

Phonologists often claim that the two affricate phonemes of English – /ʧ/ and /ʤ/ – are redundant members of the phoneme inventory. The manner of articulation for affricates – a plosive followed by a short fricative sound – suggests we might make our inventory more streamlined if we dropped the affricates altogether and treated /ʧ/ and /ʤ/ instead as a plosive + fricative sequence. (The phonetic symbols themselves suggest they are sequences rather than distinct phonemes, although they are sometimes represented by /č/ and /ǰ/ rather than /ʧ/ and /ʤ/.) There are good arguments both for the single phoneme analysis and for the two-phoneme sequence analysis, but since the argument cannot easily be resolved (if at all) and since many of the other textbooks you are likely to use will treat these sequences as separate phonemes, we will retain the two affricates here as separate phonemes of the inventory.

Of the nasals, /m/ and /n/ appear in all three positions but /ŋ/ does not appear at the beginning of words. The reason for this is also historical. Old English had no /ŋ/ phoneme, but when /n/ preceded the velar plosives /k/ or /g/ speakers gave it a velar as opposed to an alveolar articulation, creating the allophone [ŋ] for /n/. Later, southern English lost /g/ from the word-final cluster [ŋg] and /ŋ/ became a separate phoneme. The fact that /ŋ/ is derived originally from a cluster of two consonants which itself never occurred word-initially explains why /ŋ/ is never found in that position.

The approximants are the phonemes with the most limited distribution in single consonant occurrences, although they are very productive in clusters. This is perhaps not surprising given their ambivalent position somewhere between the other consonants and the vowels. All four approximants occur word-initially. In RP, only /l/ occurs word-finally, although in many other accents so does /r/. (Most Americans will say *bar* [bɑr] and *her* [hɜr], for example. Accents where /r/ appears in positions where it would not be realised in RP are known as **rhotic** accents.) Both /l/ and /r/ appear frequently word-medially. The bilabial approximant /w/ appears word-medially but is fairly rare, while /j/ does not appear word-medially in English. In fact /j/ appears to be a rather marginal consonant of English, being the only palatal consonant. Of the four approximants, the alveolars /l/ and /r/ seem the most productive as single consonants.

Clearly, the distribution of the consonants is not quite as cut and dried as we might like it to be. The grey areas may prompt us to ask questions about the phoneme inventory but they do not invalidate the process of classifying the phonemes. Too many patterns are visible for the distribution to be a matter of coincidence. The grey areas not only make us question our classification constructively but also help us to focus on aspects such as regional variations, and (although this is not within the scope of this book) the way the language has changed over the centuries and is still changing. In addition, although all languages operate within identifiable frameworks, it would be naïve to expect any language to evolve into some preconceived idea of 'perfection'.

Phonemes are realised in speech by allophones. Phonemes are subconsciously given certain allophonic variants by speakers either because of the influence of adjacent phonemes in neighbouring words or because of the position of the phoneme in a word. We will consider the influence adjacent phonemes have on each other later in this chapter. For the purpose of illustration, we will refer here to two key instances in RP where an allophone is linked to consonant position.

The first instance is one which we have already discussed in Chapter 9 and concerns the approximant /l/. We saw how word-initial /l/ differs from word-final /l/, a distinction between what are known as **clear** *l* and **dark** *l*. (Dark *l* is represented by the symbol [ɫ].) *Dark l* also occurs before another consonant in words such as *shelf* [ʃeɫf], *field* [fiːɫd], *pulse* [pʌɫs], and *film* [fɪɫm]. Another example of allophonic variation which is a key feature of RP is the aspiration of word-initial /p, t, k/. This means that the articulation of these voiceless plosives when they occur at the beginning of a word (but not in a cluster) is followed by a short period of glottal friction (as for /h/) before the following vowel begins. This is in contrast to a word-final voiceless plosive which is not followed by aspiration. Aspirated sounds can be indicated by a superscript ^{h}: [p^h, t^h, k^h]. In a narrow transcription, then, words like *cup* and *tart* will be written as [k^{h}ʌp] and [t^{h}ɑːt] respectively.

> ☐ **RP consonant** ⇨ 9.6
> ☐ **connected speech** ⇨ 10.6
> ☐ **rhotic accents** ⇨ 12.10

10.3   THE DISTRIBUTION OF VOWELS

RP has seven short vowels, five long monophthong vowels and eight diphthongs, which are also long vowels. The two vowel grids – one showing the monophthongs, the other showing the diphthongs – are repeated here as Figure 10.1. In Section 10.2 we looked at the distribution of RP consonants to see which ones have full distribution (that is, word-initially, word-medially and word-finally) and which ones have some limitation on their occurrence. It is valuable to do the same with vowels. You can see this in Table 10.3. Here, the vowels are shown both in **closed syllables**, which means they are preceded and followed by a consonant (CVC) or simply followed by a consonant (VC), and in **open syllables** (CV) where no consonant follows. Only monosyllabic words are shown.

We have already seen that in RP the short vowels do not occur in open CV syllables: this enabled us to distinguish them from the other vowels. There are two further gaps in the table for short monophthongs. The first is /ʊ/ not occurring in VC monosyllables. In fact, no words begin with /ʊ/ in RP. This vowel does, however, occur in this position in other accents to give, for example, [ʊp] *up*, [ʊðə] *other*, and [ʊndə] *under*. In RP, all these words have /ʌ/ initially. This phoneme is a later addition to English (from about the 17th century) which has not been introduced into all accents. In RP, however, /ʌ/ has replaced /ʊ/ word-initially as well as in other positions.

The other gap here relates to **schwa**. It is difficult to discuss schwa without discussing stress (which we do in Chapter 11) since schwa only occurs in unstressed syllables. This accounts for the absence of schwa in monosyllabic words which, in isolation, are cited with the full, stressed value given to their

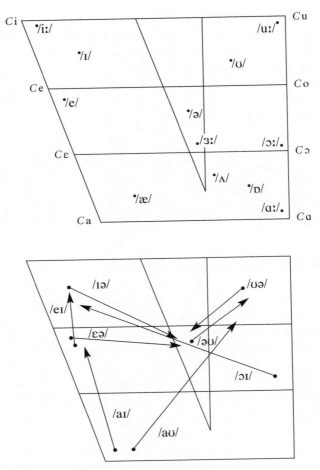

Figure 10.1 RP monophthongs and RP diphthongs

vowels. (This also raises the question of whether schwa is a true phoneme of English or simply an allophonic variant of other vowel phonemes. This is not an issue we will pursue here, however.)

Of the long vowels and diphthongs, the only gaps relate to the centring diphthongs in VC structures. /ɪə/ and /ɛə/ occur alone in RP in *ear* and *air*, while in **rhotic** accents (those in which /r/ occurs in positions where it has been lost in RP) they occur in a VC structure as [ɪər] and [ɛər]. RP also has *aired* /ɛəd/, which is derived from *air* plus an -*ed* verb inflection. This evidence suggests that all the long vowels and diphthongs are used very productively in English, with the possible exception of /ʊə/. It is difficult to find examples of /ʊə/ in monosyllables (although it is easier when /ʊə/ is preceded by /j/ as in /pjʊə/

Table 10.3   The distribution of vowels in RP

vowel	CVC		VC		CV	
Short monophthongs						
/ɪ/	bit	/bɪt/	it	/ɪt/	–	–
/e/	bet	/bet/	egg	/eg/	–	–
/æ/	bat	/bæt/	at	/æt/	–	–
/ɒ/	bomb	/bɒm/	of	/ɒv/	–	–
/ʊ/	book	/bʊk/	–	–	–	–
/ʌ/	but	/bʌt/	up	/ʌp/	–	–
/ə/	–	–	–	–	–	–
Long monophthongs						
/iː/	bead	/biːd/	eave	/iːv/	bee	/biː/
/ɑː/	bard	/bɑːd/	art	/ɑːt/	bar	/bɑː/
/ɔː/	board	/bɔːd/	ought	/ɔːt/	bore	/bɔː/
/uː/	food	/fuːd/	ooze	/uːz/	boo	/buː/
/ɜː/	bird	/bɜːd/	irk	/ɜːk/	burr	/bɜː/
Closing diphthongs						
/eɪ/	bait	/beɪt/	age	/eɪdʒ/	bay	/beɪ/
/aɪ/	bite	/baɪt/	ice	/aɪs/	buy	/baɪ/
/ɔɪ/	void	/vɔɪd/	oil	/ɔɪl/	boy	/bɔɪ/
/əʊ/	bode	/bəʊd/	ode	/əʊd/	beau	/bəʊ/
/aʊ/	fowl	/faʊl/	out	/aʊt/	bough	/baʊ/
Centring dipthongs						
/ɪə/	beard	/bɪəd/	(ear)	(/ɪə/)	beer	/bɪə/
/ɛə/	laird	/lɛəd/	(air)	(/ɛə/)	bear	/bɛə/
/ʊə/	gourd	/gʊəd/	–	–	tour	/tʊə/

pure and /kjʊə/ *cure*). Interestingly, words with /ʊə/ often have variable pronunciation such as [pɔː] or [pɔə] rather than [pʊə] for *poor*. In 1947, the phonetician D. B. Fry made a study of how frequently each of the various phonemes of RP occurred. The diphthong /ʊə/ was found to account for only 0.06 per cent of all phoneme occurrences, and was at the bottom of the frequency scale. There is some support for the view that this particular phoneme might be lost from RP in the future.

One allophonic feature of vowels which you may find it useful to know about is **nasalisation**. This occurs when the velum has been lowered during the articulation of the vowel and air passing through the nasal cavity gives the vowel a slightly different quality from usual. The diacritic ~ indicates that a vowel has been nasalised. Nasalised vowels usually precede nasal consonants. They don't occur frequently in English but speakers occasionally use them in words of French origin like *restaurant* [restərõn(t)].

☐ **RP vowels** ⇨ 9.7
☐ **schwa in unstressed syllables** ⇨ 11.2

10.4   SYLLABLE STRUCTURE

So far, we have examined the phonemes of English either in isolation or in terms of the positions in which consonants and vowels occur. We now move on to study **phonotactics**, which is the way phonemes group together in English to form syllables. Syllables vary in the way they are constructed but they nevertheless conform to a set pattern and we shall be concerned in this section with discovering what that pattern or **syllable template** is.

Central to the structure of a syllable is a vowel. A long monophthong may be a monosyllabic word on its own (*are* /ɑː/, for example) as may a diphthong (for example, *ear* /ɪə/). By contrast, a single consonant cannot constitute a word. In a monosyllabic word, the vowel may be preceded and succeeded by a consonant or consonants. If, on the other hand, a consonant is preceded and succeeded by a vowel, as in *other* /ʌðə/, a disyllabic word results. This suggests that there is a direct relationship between the number of vowels and the number of syllables in a word. If we work on the premise of one vowel to one syllable, having already established that a vowel can occur on its own or with consonants either side, we can start with a preliminary syllable template of consonant – vowel – consonant. In the following diagram, +/– indicates that there may or may not be a consonant in this position. Also, there may be more than one consonant.

+/– consonant(s)	vowel	+/– consonant(s)

Table 10.3 showed that most of the vowels can begin syllables in English as can most consonants. What we now need to discover is which consonant groups can occur at the beginning of a syllable. For the time being, we will continue to concentrate as far as possible on monosyllabic words so that word and syllable structure coincide, and we will move on to words of more than one syllable when we have established the full syllable template.

If you work your way through a random selection of words, you will quickly discover that the maximum number of consonants which can begin a syllable in English is three. Examples of this include *spread* /spred/, *squirm* /skwɜːm/ and *scrape* /skreɪp/. However, there are restrictions on which consonants can form a cluster of this kind. You won't be able to find any words beginning with, say, /gdn/ or /θph/.

We saw in Section 10.2 that all the consonants except /ŋ/ can begin a word in English. They represent a central group known as **initial consonants**. Any consonants which can precede them are **pre-initial consonants** and those which can follow are **post-initial consonants**. This means we are looking at a word-initial structure of

monosyllabic word / syllable				
+/– consonant(s)			vowel	+/– consonant(s)
pre-initial consonant	initial consonant	post-initial consonant	V	C

We can deduce which two-consonant sequences can begin an English word by trying out the various combinations. Table 10.4 shows the consonants which occur in pre-initial and in post-initial position. What emerges is that

Table 10.4   Word-initial two-consonant clusters

Pre-initial consonant /s/	Initial consonant	Post-initial consonant /w/	Post-initial consonant /l/	Post-initial consonant /r/	Post-initial consonant /j/
spin	/p/		play	pray	puny
	/b/		bleed	breed	beauty
stick	/t/	twin		train	tune
	/d/	dwell		drain	dune
skin	/k/	queen	clean	creep	cute
	/g/	(Gwent)	glean	grin	
	/ʧ/				
	/ʤ/				
sphinx	/f/		flip	frail	few
	/v/				view
	/θ/	thwart		threat	thurible
	/ð/				
	/s/	swim	slip		pseudonym
	/z/				(Zeus)
	/ʃ/	(schwa)		shred	
	/ʒ/				
	/h/				hue
small	/m/				muse
snail	/n/				news
	(/ŋ/)				
swim	/w/				
slip	/l/				(lewd)
	/r/				
pseudonym	/j/				

the options are systematically limited. The pre-initial consonant can only be /s/ and it can only be followed by nine other consonants: the voiceless plosives /p, t, k/, the voiceless labio-dental fricative /f/, a nasal (but not /ŋ/, which doesn't occur word-initially) or an approximant (but not /r/). It is significant that the plosives and the fricative which can follow /s/ are all, like /s/, voiceless.

The post-initial consonants are all approximants. A number of initial + post-initial combinations appear, but the gaps are worth noting. The six plosives combine very productively with the approximants although not all combinations are possible. The affricates do not occur in consonant clusters at all, while the combinations of fricative + approximant and nasal + approximant are fairly limited. Sometimes, combinations seem possible because proper names exist which have them word-initially, such as /gw/ in *Gwent* and /zj/ in *Zeus*. It is difficult to decide whether they should be included as representative or not. *Schwa* is an example of /ʃw-/ but the only other examples of this combination are proper names, so /ʃw-/ is probably not representative of a typical English consonant cluster.

Moving on to three-consonant clusters, we find that they are related to the combinations possible for two-consonant clusters. For example, /spr-/ (as in *spring*) is only possible as an English cluster because the initial consonant /p/ can be preceded by /s/ and followed by /r/ in two-consonant clusters. In Table 10.5, the shaded areas indicate that the combination in question will not occur. The unshaded areas show which combinations can, in theory, occur, and contain examples of those which actually do. It is difficult to say precisely why possible combinations such as /stw-/ and /slj-/ fail to occur. It could be that they are **accidental gaps**, meaning that it would seem perfectly natural to a native speaker to have a word beginning with this combination but there happens not to be one, or there may be some other reason relating, perhaps, to the rarity of part of the combination such as /sf-/ or /lj-/.

Table 10.5 Word-initial three-consonant clusters

Pre-initial + initial consonant /s/ + C	Post-initial consonant /w/	Post-initial consonant /l/	Post-initial consonant /r/	Post-initial consonant /j/
/sp/		splash	spray	spew
/st/	–		string	stew
/sk/	squeak	sclerosis	scream	skewer
/sf/		–	–	–
/sm/				–
/sn/				–
/sw/				
/sl/				–
/sj/				

Although it is not a matter which we will pursue here, phonologists have given a considerable amount of attention to which vowels can follow word-initial consonants and consonant clusters, and which ones can precede word-final consonants and consonant clusters. Some consonants and consonant clusters combine with many of the vowels while others have far fewer partners: /j/, for instance, in clusters such as /fj-/, /stj-/ and so on, almost always occurs before /uː/.

Word-finally, the consonant picture is rather different and certainly less simple than for word-initial clusters. Whereas word-initial clusters have up to three consonants, word-final clusters have a maximum of four consonants. We have already seen that all the consonants occur alone word-finally with the exception of /h, w, j/. The approximant /r/ does not occur word-finally in RP although it does in rhotic accents. The large group of singly occurring consonants can be said to fill the **final consonant** position. Consonants which precede them are **pre-final**, and those which follow are **post-final**. This means we have a template for final consonants similar to the one established for initial consonants, with the addition of a second post-final slot for those words which end in a four-consonant cluster or in certain three-consonant clusters:

monosyllabic word / syllable							
+/– consonant(s)			vowel	+/– **consonant(s)**			
pre-initial consonant	initial consonant	post-initial consonant	V	**pre-final consonant**	**final consonant**	**post-final consonant**	**(post-final consonant)**

Table 10.6 shows which pre-final consonants can combine with the final consonants.

In pre-final position, the consonant will be a nasal, the voiceless alveolar fricative /s/, or the lateral approximant /l/. (The approximant /r/ also occurs in rhotic accents.) If we compare these final combinations with the pre-initial + initial consonant combinations, we discover an interesting contrast: only /s/ occurs in the pre-initial consonant position whereas the pre-final consonant position has not only /s/ but also four other consonants – /m, n, ŋ, l/ – as options. The final + post-final combination also has several possibilities, as Table 10.7 shows.

You will notice that a number of the examples in Tables 10.6 and 10.7 are marked with an asterisk. This is to show that they are the result of adding an **inflection** to an existing word. This may be the plural ending for nouns which is articulated as /-s/ or /-z/ depending on whether the final consonant of the noun is voiceless or voiced. So *toff* /tɒf/ adds /-s/ while *bag* /bæg/ adds /-z/. Alternatively, the inflection may be a verb ending as in *hushed* or *raised*. Again, whether the final consonant is voiceless or voiced is relevant to the final consonant of the verb in its **base** form: *hush* /hʌʃ/ will add /-t/, while

Table 10.6 Word-final two-consonant clusters (pre-final C + final C combinations)

Pre-final consonant /m/	Pre-final consonant /n/	Pre-final consonant /ŋ/	Pre-final consonant /l/	Pre-final consonant /s/	Final consonant
bump	–	–	help	wasp	/p/
–	–	–	bulb	–	/b/
–	tent	–	kilt	haste	/t/
slammed*	hand	hanged*	bold	–	/d/
–	–	chunk	hulk	whisk	/k/
–	–	–	–	–	/g/
–	hunch	–	filch	–	/ʧ/
–	sponge	–	bulge	–	/ʤ/
bumf	–	–	elf	–	/f/
–	–	–	shelve	–	/v/
warmth	tenth	–	health	–	/θ/
–	–	–	–	–	/ð/
–	tense	–	else	–	/s/
Thames	cleanse	wings*	falls*	–	/z/
–	–	–	Welsh	–	/ʃ/
–	–	–	–	–	/ʒ/
–	–	–	–	–	(/h/)
–	–	–	film	–	/m/
–	–	–	kiln	–	/n/
–	–	–	–	–	/ŋ/
–	–	–	–	–	(/w/)
–	–	–	–	–	/l/
–	–	–	–	–	(/r/)
–	–	–	–	–	(/j/)

raise /reɪz/ will add /-d/. (/s/ and /z/ can also be verb inflections as in *speaks* or *listens*.) Some consonant clusters only exist word-finally because they occur as the result of an inflection being added to a noun or verb.

You can see the correlation between voiced and voiceless consonants in clusters throughout Table 10.7, not just in the asterisked words, but in examples such as *lapse* and *tuft*. If you examine Tables 10.6 and 10.7 together, however, you will find that some consonants – particularly the nasals /m/ and /n/ and the approximant /l/ – are able to combine with both voiced and voiceless consonants.

We now move on to consider word-final three-consonant clusters. Table 10.8 lists the pre-final + final combinations and gives examples showing which of the five post-final consonants can follow them. (You will remember from examining the word-initial clusters that a three-consonant cluster only occurs if its first two elements and its last two elements occur separately as two-consonant clusters. The same principle applies to word-final combinations.) Again, the shaded areas indicate impossible

Table 10.7   Word-final two-consonant clusters (final C + post-final C combinations)

Final consonant	Post-final consonant /s/	Post-final consonant /z/	Post-final consonant /t/	Post-final consonant /d/	Post-final consonant /θ/
/p/	lapse	–	opt	–	depth
/b/	–	sobs*	–	sobbed*	–
/t/	blitz	–	–	–	eighth
/d/	–	adze	–	–	–
/k/	axe	–	act	–	–
/g/	–	bags*	–	bagged*	–
/tʃ/	–	–	thatched*	–	–
/dʒ/	–	–	–	hedged*	–
/f/	toffs*	–	tuft	–	fifth
/v/	–	loves*	–	loved*	–
/θ/	meths	–	bathed*	–	–
/ð/	–	lathes*	–	writhed*	–
/s/	–	–	haste	–	–
/z/	–	–	–	raised*	–
/ʃ/	–	–	hushed*	–	–
/ʒ/	–	–	–	garaged*	–
(/h/)	–	–	–	–	–
/m/	–	Thames	–	slammed*	–
/n/	tense	cleanse	tent	hand	tenth
/ŋ/	–	wings*	–	hanged*	–
(/w/)	–	–	–	–	–
/l/	else	falls*	kilt	bold	health
(/r/)	–	–	–	–	–
(/j/)	–	–	–	–	–

combinations. Interestingly, the majority of the examples here are the result of adding the kind of noun or verb inflections discussed above. Only a handful of the examples end in three-consonant clusters in their own right, as it were. These are words such as *glimpse* /glɪmps/ and *twelfth* /twelfθ/ (although the latter is often reduced to [twelθ]).

Table 10.9 gives examples of final + post-final clusters which can be followed by a further post-final consonant. Almost all of these are, again, the result of adding inflections. The only exceptions are *next* /nekst/, *thousandth* /θaʊzəntθ/ and *sixth* /sɪksθ/. *Sixth* is unusual in that although there are instances of /-ks/ word-finally (as in *axe* /æks/) there are no instances of /-sθ/. If /-ksθ/ is not to be seen as an impossible combination (which it clearly isn't) the only solution is to treat /-sθ/ as an accidental gap. You may like to consider which of the gaps in Tables 10.6 and 10.7 are accidental, and which are truly impossible combinations given the restrictions on some voiced and voiceless consonants combining.

Table 10.8 Word-final three-consonant clusters (pre-final C + final C + post-final C combinations)

Pre-final + final consonant	Post-final consonant /s/	Post-final consonant /z/	Post-final consonant /t/	Post-final consonant /d/	Post-final consonant /θ/
/mp/	glimpse		prompt		–
/md/		–			
/mf/	nymphs*		galumphed*		–
/mθ/	–		–		
/mz/				–	
/nt/	tents*				thousandth
/nd/		hands*			
/ntʃ/			pinched*		
/ndʒ/				sponged*	
/nθ/	tenths*		–		
/ns/			tensed*		
/nz/				cleansed*	
/ŋd/		–			
/ŋk/	minx		defunct		
/ŋθ/	lengths*		–		
/ŋz/				–	
/lp/	helps*		sculpt		–
/lb/		bulbs*		–	
/lt/	kilts*				–
/ld/		holds*			
/lk/	hulks*		milked*		
/ltʃ/			filched*		
/ldʒ/				bulged*	
/lf/	gulfs*		engulfed*		twelfth
/lv/		shelves*		shelved*	
/lθ/	healths*		–		
/ls/			pulsed*		
/lz/				–	
/lʃ/			welshed*		
/lm/		films*		filmed*	
/ln/	–	kilns*	–	–	–
/sp/	wasps*		gasped*		–
/st/	masts*				–
/sk/	whisks*		whisked*		

Table 10.9   Word-final three-consonant clusters (final C + post-final C + post-final C combinations)

Final + post-final consonant	Post-final consonant /s/	Post-final consonant /z/	Post-final consonant /t/	Post-final consonant /d/	Post-final consonant /θ/
/ps/			lapsed*		
/pt/	opts*				–
/pθ/	depths*		–		
/bz/				–	
/bd/		–			
/ts/			blitzed*		
/tθ/	eighths*		–		
/dz/				–	
/ks/			next		sixth
/kt/	acts*				–
/gz/				–	
/gd/		–			
/tʃt/	–				–
/dʒd/		–			
/fs/			–		
/ft/	tufts*				–
/fθ/	fifths*		–		
/vz/				–	
/vd/		–			
/θs/			–		
/θt/	–				–
/ðz/				–	
/ðd/		–			
/st/	*masts**				–
/zd/		–			
/ʃt/	–				–
/ʒd/		–			
/mz/				–	
/md/		–			
/ns/			*tensed**		
/nz/				*cleansed**	
/nt/	*tents**				*thousandth*
/nd/		*hands**			
/nθ/	*tenths**		–		
/ŋz/				–	
/ŋd/		–			
/ŋθ/	*lengths**		–		
/ls/			*pulsed**		
/lz/				–	
/lt/	*kilts**				–
/ld/		*holds**			
/lθ/	*healths**		–		

You may also have noticed that several of the examples in Tables 10.8 and 10.9 are printed in italics. This is because they occur in both tables. This highlights the fact that, for some combinations, two analyses are possible. The /-nts/ ending of *tents*, for example, could be treated as:

pre-final consonant	final consonant	post-final consonant
n	t	s

or as

final consonant	post-final consonant	post-final consonant
n	t	s

Given that *tents* is the plural of *tent*, it is probably preferable to accept the former analysis as this gives /t/ as the final consonant of the word in its uninflected form. (If you look back to Tables 10.6 and 10.7, a similar situation exists with word-final two-consonant clusters, such as in *bold* and *tense*, where the first phoneme is a potential pre-final consonant and the second a potential post-final one.)

There are words in English which end in four-syllable clusters, but such clusters are rare. The words in which they occur are all either nouns which end in a three-consonant cluster and which have been given the plural inflection /-s/, or verbs which have a /-s/ inflection in the third person singular of the present tense (for example, (*s/he*) *sculpts*). In other words, there are no four-consonant final clusters in uninflected words in English.

10.5 THE SYLLABLE TEMPLATE

Now we have discovered which consonant clusters occur at the beginnings and ends of monosyllabic words in English, we have almost completed our syllable template. It is important to remember that consonants are an optional element of syllables while vowels are obligatory. We can therefore offer the following as a syllable template:

syllable							
+/– consonant(s)			vowel	+/– consonant(s)			
pre-initial consonant	initial consonant	post-initial consonant	V	pre-final consonant	final consonant	post-final consonant	(post-final consonant)

At the moment, we are presupposing that the three main slots of the template are, so to speak, equal and are a linear ordering of the phonemes which make up any particular syllable or monosyllabic word. However, this is something we need to reconsider as a special link can be found between the vowel and the consonants which succeed it. There is, after all, the phenomenon of rhyme. In rhyming pairs such as *sad* and *glad, straight* and *hate,* it is the vowel plus any following consonants which provide the rhyme – the constant element – while the word-initial consonant or consonants change. In addition, many phonologists have noted a link between the length of the vowel and the consonants which follow it. We have already seen how short monophthongs have to be followed in RP by one or more consonants, whereas almost all vowels (excepting only /ʊ/ and /ʊə/) can occur without a preceding consonant. These two aspects are sufficient here to indicate the special relationship between a vowel and any succeeding consonants, and lead to the following as a more appropriate syllable template:

syllable							
onset (*optional*)			rhyme				
			peak	coda (*optional*)			
consonant(s)			vowel	consonant(s)			
pre-initial consonant	initial consonant	post-initial consonant	V	pre-final consonant	final consonant	post-final consonant	(post-final consonant)

Here, the syllable template has been slightly restructured and some new labels have been introduced. The syllable has been divided into an **onset** – the opening consonant(s), if present – and a **rhyme**, which is the obligatory vowel followed by any final consonant. The vowel is termed the **peak** of the syllable because it is the 'centre' of the syllable where the **sonority** or volume of the voice is at its greatest. Any consonants which conclude a syllable are known as the **coda**. This analysis of the syllable is preferable to our original version in showing the special link between the peak and the coda, and we will use it from now on.

So far, our study has concentrated as far as possible on monosyllabic words since they automatically provide examples of possible syllables in English. We can now go on to consider how we might interpret the strings of consonants we find between syllable peaks in words of two syllables or more. Some of the clusters which occur word-finally will not occur word-medially because they are the result of adding inflectional endings. However, many combinations do occur word-medially and we must decide how to allocate the consonants in question to either the preceding or succeeding syllable.

In an example such as *toaster,* we find that the consonant cluster which occurs between its two syllables – /st/ – is acceptable both as a syllable onset (as in *stir*), and as a syllable coda (as in *toast*). So the onset/coda test alone cannot provide us with an answer to our question of which syllable /st/ belongs to. In matters of **syllabification** – the way in which a word is divided into syllables – we have to be guided by pronunciation. If you asked someone to pronounce the word *toaster* with a pause between the two syllables, the likelihood is that they would say /təʊ-/ and /-stə/ rather than /təʊst-/ and /-ə/. In fact, provided the cluster in question is an acceptable syllable onset group, the natural tendency in languages generally, not just English, is to treat a cluster which occurs between syllables as the onset of the next syllable rather than the coda of the preceding one. What is interesting is that the process of syllabification (which is phonological) may be at odds with the morphological make-up of a word. So although the noun *toaster* is formed, as far as its meaning is concerned, from the base *toast* and the -*er* suffix to denote 'something that toasts', we don't syllabify it as *toast* + *er*.

Of course, sometimes the morphemes in a word will correlate with its syllable structure. In an example such as *blackbird,* a compound noun, we can easily identify the free morphemes – *black* and *bird* – as also being the two syllables of the word. There is no problem therefore in analysing the /kb/ sequence which occurs between the vowels of *blackbird:* the /k/ is the coda of the first syllable while the /b/ is the onset of the second:

syllable 1				syllable 2		
onset		rhyme		onset	rhyme	
		peak	coda		peak	coda
initial consonant	post-initial consonant	vowel	final consonant	initial consonant	vowel	final consonant
b	l	æ	k	b	ɜː	d

In other examples, impossible strings occur word-medially and the syllabification of a word is not linked to its construction as it is in *blackbird.* An example of this is *magnet.* The consonant cluster /gn/ is an impossible onset and also an impossible coda. Instinct and 'broken' pronunciation in fact tell us that the syllabification of *magnet* is /mæg/ + /net/, the problem of the impossible cluster being solved by the assigning of /g/ to the first syllable, and /n/ to the second, resulting in two well-formed syllables.

In Chapter 9, we examined closely the vowel inventory of RP, dividing the vowels into monophthongs and diphthongs. Sometimes, a closing diphthong is followed by a glide towards schwa. This combination is known as a **triphthong.** Speakers will differ as to whether a triphthong results in one syllable or two. In a word such as *sour* /saʊə/, for example, or *fire* /faɪə/ the number of syllables a listener perceives will probably be influenced by the amount of prominence given to the middle element of the triphthong. In other examples, particularly those made up of a basic stem with an inflectional or derivational ending (such as <-er>), there will probably be general agreement that there are two syllables. This is true of words such as *slower* /sləʊə/ and *buyer* /baɪə/. These words have neither a coda for the first syllable nor an onset to the second (indicated in the chart by the symbol Ø):

syllable 1				syllable 2		
onset		rhyme		onset	rhyme	
		peak	coda		peak	coda
initial consonant	post-initial consonant	vowel	final consonant	initial consonant	vowel	final consonant
s	l	əʊ	Ø	Ø	ə	
b		aɪ	Ø	Ø	ə	

Finally, we need to consider **syllabic consonants**. We have worked on the assumption that a vowel is an obligatory element in a syllable. However, there is one exception to this principle which is found in words of two syllables or more. This is when a nasal (/m/ or /n/) or an approximant (/l/ and sometimes /r/) functions as the peak of the syllable. This occurs when the vowel in the syllable, because it isn't stressed, becomes so reduced that it effectively disappears, leaving the coda to function alone as the peak. So a word like *button* may be pronounced [bʌ] + [tɒn] in broken pronunciation while in natural speech it will be pronounced [bʌtən] (with the /ɒ/ of the second syllable being reduced to a schwa as it isn't stressed) or even [bʌtn̩]. (The diacritic ˌ is placed below the consonant in order to indicate that it is syllabic.) Syllabic consonants are fairly common in all accents of English but there are restrictions on when they can occur.

10.6   CONNECTED SPEECH

Throughout most of this chapter, we have been working towards an under-standing of how consonants and vowels group together phonologically to form syllables and words. We have seen how phonemes are given allophonic variants either as the result of their position in a word (/l/ may be clear or dark, for example) or because they are affected by adjoining phonemes (vowels, for instance, may become nasalised when adjoining nasal consonants). Also, we have to bear in mind that the articulation of phonemes varies depending on the accent of the speaker.

At the end of Chapter 9, we touched on how phonemes vary when in contact with adjacent phonemes from other words. These variations are the result of **connected speech**. When we write, we leave gaps between words so it is easy for the reader to process the text. When we speak, it is unnecessary to leave pauses between words much of the time and it would sound unnatural if we did. Given that segments affect each other within individual words, it is hardly surprising that this influence also operates across word boundaries.

When connected speech was first discussed in Section 9.8, we looked at the examples of *next day* and *prime minister,* and noticed how the /t/ at the end of *next* was lost before *day* and how the /m/ at the end of *prime* was lost before the /m/ at the start of *minister.* The term for this loss of a speech segment is **elision**. Elision is particularly likely to occur when clusters of consonants form or when identical segments occur in a sequence, and this happens frequently in connected speech. Syllabic consonants are also the result of elision. We saw above how a vowel sometimes becomes so reduced (as in *button*) as to disappear altogether, the syllable peak being filled by the succeeding consonant to give [bʌtn̩] rather than [bʌtən].

In some circumstances segments may be lost, but it is also common for segments to appear or be added at word boundaries. This phenomenon is known as **liaison**. In English, the segment which usually appears is /r/. RP, you will remember, is a non-rhotic accent, so words which end in /r/ in some accents will not do so in RP. For example, a speaker of a rhotic accent will pronounce *four* as [fɔr] whereas an RP speaker will pronounce it [fɔ:]. However, when *four* is followed by a word which begins with a vowel, the /r/ is likely to be pronounced in RP. So, like a speaker of a rhotic accent, an RP speaker may well pronounce *four apes* as [fɔr eɪps], with the /r/ emerging at the end of *four.* This occurrence of /r/ is known as **linking r**.

Because the presence of a linking *r* is so common in English, speakers frequently add /r/ in constructions where /r/ does not appear in rhotic accents but where the phonological environment is similar to that for linking *r*. In other words, the /r/ appears at the end of a word which in isolation ends with a vowel but which in connected speech precedes a vowel. For instance, *America* has no /r/ at the end, even in rhotic accents, but if *America* is placed before a word beginning with a vowel, such as *and* in *America and Canada,* the /r/ emerges to give [əmerɪkər ænd kænədə]. (However, because of the way syllabification works, listeners probably perceive the /r/ as the onset of *and* rather than the coda of the last syllable of *America.*) This type of /r/ is known as **intrusive r**.

We have seen how, in connected speech, segments can both disappear and appear. In other circumstances, they will become more like the segments which precede or follow them. This phenomenon is known as **assimilation**. There are three types of assimilation. The first type is **anticipatory assimilation** and it is quite common. In a phrase such as *ten pin bowling,* the /n/ at the end of *ten* is often pronounced [m] in anticipation of the fact that the following word, *pin,* begins with the bilabial phoneme /p/. In other words, the alveolar nasal becomes bilabial like /p/. This could also happen to the /n/ at the end of *pin* as this too precedes a bilabial phoneme (/b/). In connected speech, then, *ten pin bowling* will probably be pronounced [tem pɪm bəʊlɪŋ]. Much rarer is the type of assimilation known as **perseverative assimilation**. This is when a feature of one segment 'perseveres' and is found in the following segment. The two elements of the compound *ashtray* in isolation will probably be pronounced [æʃ] and [treɪ]. But in connected speech or simply in the utterance of *ashtray* by itself, it is likely a speaker will say [æʃʧreɪ]. Here, the fricative quality of the /ʃ/ at the end of *ash* has been carried over to the /t/ at the beginning of *tray,* causing it to surface as [ʧ]. Finally, there is **coalescent assimilation** or simply **coalescence**. This is when two segments merge into one. For example, in connected speech, *haven't you* is likely to be pronounced [hævənʧuː] with the /t/ at the end of *haven't* and the /j/ at the start of *you* being merged to give [ʧ].

☐ **phonetic transcriptions** ⇨ 9.8

11 Suprasegmental Phonology

11.1 WHAT IS SUPRASEGMENTAL PHONOLOGY?

In Chapter 9 we explored the phoneme inventory of English (as far as RP is concerned) and looked at how the consonants and vowels of RP are articulated. In Chapter 10 we considered the way these phonemes combine to form syllables and words and what happens to adjacent phonemes in connected speech. In other words, Chapter 10 covered **segmental phonology**. In this chapter, we will be going beyond the individual speech sounds of English and the patterns in which they occur in order to look at other aspects of speech which affect the way that syllables, words and strings of words are uttered. These aspects are known as **prosodic features** and include, most importantly, **stress, pitch** and **intonation**. Less central prosodic features are **voice quality, volume** and **tempo**. The study of these aspects is **suprasegmental phonology** although you will often encounter this area of phonology being referred to simply as **prosodics**.

11.2 WORD STRESS

We have already explored in some detail how syllables are constructed and we have seen that words may be **monosyllabic** (consisting of just one syllable), **disyllabic** (two syllables) or **polysyllabic** (three or more syllables). In this chapter, we will also be using the term **trisyllabic** to refer specifically to words of three syllables. We will begin this section by considering some disyllabic words. In the following examples a dot (·) has been used to indicate the syllable boundary:

a·muse	pa·per
be·tween	ba·by
ex·change	ear·nest
to·wards	peo·ple

If you utter these words you will notice that one syllable is given more prominence than the other. In fact, the words in the left-hand column give greater prominence to the second syllable while those in the right-hand column give greater prominence to the first syllable. The prominent syllables in these words are referred to as **stressed syllables**. By contrast, the other syllables are **unstressed**. Stressed syllables can be indicated by placing a vertical superscript line in front of them:

a|*muse*	|*paper*
be|*tween*	|*baby*
ex|*change*	|*earnest*
to|*wards*	|*people*

Speech in English, as in many other languages, is made up of both stressed and unstressed syllables. A non-native speaker who is learning English will sound distinctly unnatural, however accurate their grammar and however proficient their choice of lexis, if they do not get **word stress** correct.

Stress, then, is the means by which we give one syllable greater prominence than another. There are various ways in which this prominence is achieved. First, a stressed syllable may be uttered more loudly than an unstressed one. The difference in volume is rarely very marked but the increase in muscular energy which is involved when you make a syllable louder is significant. You will become aware of this if you try a simple experiment. Speak aloud the words in the two columns above and at the same time tap your hand on the desk whenever you utter a stressed syllable. This should prove very easy, the reason being that the muscular effort involved in hand-tapping corresponds with the muscular effort involved in increasing volume. If you now try the reverse – tapping your hand whenever you utter an unstressed syllable – you will find this activity much trickier and may even find yourself giving the unstressed syllables an unnatural amount of prominence. For an example of how volume can indicate the stressed syllable of a word, consider the difference between the noun \|*diplomat* and the adjective *diplo*\|*matic*. In both these words, the first three syllables are identical in terms of their CV structure. However, *diplomat* is stressed on the first syllable while *diplomatic* is stressed on the third syllable. There is no change to the way the phonemes are realised here so the change of stress must be the result of the volume given to the relevant syllable.

We saw in the previous chapter that a syllable has a vowel as its peak. A syllable may have prominence if it contains a long vowel. This is often in contrast to the vowels in unstressed syllables which are not always given their full value (a point we will return to shortly). Sometimes, though, we may lengthen a vowel in order to achieve contrastive stress. For example, look at the following exchange:

> A: *Did you say that someone who carries the incense in church is a thurible?*
> B: *No, a thuri<u>fer</u>*

When B replies to A here, they change the normal stress pattern of the word *thurifer* in order to highlight the difference between the two rather similar words *thurible* and *thurifer.* The latter is normally uttered with the stress on the first syllable but in B's reply to A the final syllable of *thurifer* is given prominence by lengthening the vowel. The final syllable is [-fɜː] rather than [-fə] and this lengthening gives it prominence for the purpose of clarification.

The third feature which may give prominence to a syllable is that there will be a marked change of pitch on that syllable. Pitch can be better understood by comparing speech to music, where one note differs from another by being higher or lower in pitch. Variations in pitch are caused by a change in the frequency of the vibration of the vocal cords and this occurs in speech as well as in singing. In fact, speakers constantly vary their pitch, albeit not very markedly most of the time. However, a syllable may be stressed by raising or lowering the pitch at which it is spoken by a greater degree than is normally the case. We will look more closely at pitch changes in Section 11.4.

Finally, a syllable will achieve prominence if it is in contrast to a syllable where the vowel has been reduced in value. This can be illustrated by returning to our earlier examples, which have been reordered below:

1	a'muse	2	to'wards	3	'paper	4	'people
5	be'tween	6	ex'change	7	'earnest	8	'baby

The unstressed syllables in the first four examples (*a'muse, to'wards, 'paper* and *'people*) contain the neutral vowel which we call schwa: /ə/. This vowel, however, represents a reduction in vowel value. We know this because when we say a word slowly or extra clearly we replace the schwa with a different vowel: for example, the syllable at the start of *a'muse* would be realised by the diphthong [eɪ] rather than by [ə]. *'People* is an interesting example: in an exaggerated pronunciation the second syllable would be realised as [ʊ] to give [piːpʊl] but normally the vowel in the second syllable is reduced to schwa or the vowel disappears altogether and the /l/ becomes a consonantal syllable. The natural pronunciation then is [piːpəl] or [piːpl̩]. In Examples 5, 6 and 7 (*be'tween, ex'change* and *'earnest*), the vowel [ɪ] in the unstressed syllables may again be regarded as a reduction of an underlying vowel. In *ex'change,* the initial syllable would be pronounced [eks-] rather then [ɪks-] if the vowel were given its full value, while the second syllable in *'earnest* would be [-nest] rather than [-nɪst]. In *beˈtween,* the underlying vowel in the unstressed syllable is /iː/. This is also the full value for the vowel at the end of ˈ*baby* but in this example the vowel in the unstressed syllable simply becomes reduced in length. So an exaggerated pronunciation of *baby* would be [beɪbiː] while the natural pronunciation is [beɪbi].

So far we have considered word stress in disyllabic words. When we utter monosyllabic words in isolation, we give the full value to the vowel which they contain. This is true for both lexical words and grammatical words. However, when monosyllabic grammatical words occur in connected speech, the value of their vowels is often reduced so that in context these monosyllabic words become unstressed. The preposition *from,* for example, in isolation would be pronounced [frɒm]. By contrast, in a string such as *the holiday from hell,* the vowel in *from* would be reduced to a schwa to give [frəm].

Many lexical words are polysyllabic and we need to consider their stress patterns. In many words of three syllables, one syllable is stressed and the other two are unstressed. Here are some examples:

ˈ*difficult*	*toˈmato*
ˈ*editor*	*ecˈcentric*
ˈ*pineapple*	*naˈrrator*

The stress falls either on the first syllable (as shown in the first column) or on the second syllable (as shown in the second column). In some words of three syllables, the stress will fall on the final syllable but when this occurs it is normal to give a little more prominence to the first syllable. Consider the way you would pronounce the following:

disbelief
counteract
contradict
auctioneer

Each of the above words is stressed on the third syllable. However, when you utter these words you will also give some prominence to the first syllable. This first syllable is not, then, unstressed like the second syllable but nor does it have the same degree of prominence as the final syllable. This degree of prominence somewhere between a stressed syllable and an unstressed one is referred to as **secondary stress**. The degree of stress given to the final syllable in the above examples may, by contrast, be termed **primary stress**. Secondary stress is also indicated by a vertical line in front of the relevant syllable but the line is a subscript rather than a superscript one:

ˌdisbeˈlief
ˌcounterˈact
ˌcontraˈdict
ˌauctioˈneer

The tendency is for words of three syllables to have simply a primary stress on the first or second syllable. If there is primary stress on the third syllable then it is likely that the first syllable will be given a secondary degree of stress. It is not impossible, however, for primary stress to occur on a first or second syllable and for secondary stress to occur on an adjoining syllable. This is particularly likely in compound words since the stress patterns from the two words which form the compound are retained to some extent. Here are some examples of both bisyllabic and trisyllabic compound words:

ˈblackˌsmith	ˌfreeˈwheel	ˈhamˌburger	ˌmarshˈmallow
ˈdiveˌbomb	ˌmidˈair	ˈdareˌdevil	ˌstrong-ˈminded

In these examples, *blacksmith* and *divebomb* are contrasted with *freewheel* and *midair* in that the first two have a primary stress on the first syllable and a secondary stress on the second syllable while the second two show the opposite pattern. You may wonder how you can be certain that these compound words contain a primary stress and a secondary stress as opposed to a primary stress and an unstressed syllable. If you put the compound words in a slightly fuller context you will be able to determine the different degrees of stress. For instance, if you contrast *I met a* ˈblackˌsmith with *I met a* ˈtiger, there is a clear difference between the value of *a* (which is unstressed in this context) and the value of *smith* whereas *a* and the *-ger* of *tiger* are comparable in both being unstressed.

The trisyllabic compounds *hamburger* and *daredevil* contrast with *marshmallow* and *strong-minded*. In the first pair the primary stress falls on the first syllable and the secondary stress falls on the second syllable, while the pattern is reversed for the second pair. Further examples show other possible patterns for compound words of three syllables. In the noun ˈmake-beˌlieve, for example, the primary stress is on the first syllable while the secondary stress is on the third syllable. In the adjective ˌsecond-ˈhand the primary stress is on the third syllable while the secondary stress is on the first syllable. In general then it is more typical for compound words to contain both primary and secondary stress but it is not impossible that simple or derived words will contain both.

We will now look briefly at words of four syllables. It is possible for four-syllable words to contain only one stressed syllable:

re$^|$sponsible
re$^|$suscitate
e$^|$cology
de$^|$livery

Most typically, the stress will fall on the second syllable of a four-syllable word. However, the following – less common – examples have stress on the first syllable:

$^|$*delicacy*
$^|$*culinary*
$^|$*automobile*

More typically, a word of four syllables will contain both a primary and a secondary stress. Here are just three examples:

$^|$*funda*$_|$*mental*
$_|$*sui*$^|$*cidal*
$_|$*visi*$^|$*tation*

The typical pattern is for syllables of primary or secondary stress to alternate with unstressed syllables. It is worth remembering here that we are only dealing with words uttered in isolation and that stress patterns change slightly in the context of connected speech.

So far, we have looked at word stress in terms of the position in which stressed and unstressed syllables may occur. We have not really considered what it is that governs where the stress occurs. This is a complex matter (too extensive for coverage here) and exceptions will always be found to any rules which are established. In very general terms, as well as the number of syllables in a word, the type of vowel (short or long) at the syllable peak and whether a syllable is open or closed can be significant factors, as can the presence of a consonant cluster as the syllable coda. In addition, whether a word is morphologically simple or complex will also affect the stress pattern.

Interestingly, there are some words in English where speakers disagree about the position of the primary stress. A salient example of this is the noun *controversy*. Some speakers give this noun a primary stress only, with this falling on the second syllable (*con$^|$troversy*), while other speakers give the word a primary and a secondary stress ($^|$*contro*$_|$*versy*). Other examples of words with more than one stress pattern include *kilometre, inventory* and *metamorphosis*.

Word class can also affect the likely stress pattern of a word. Consider, for instance, the noun ᵎrecord and the verb reᵎcord. These two examples of *record* are **homographs:** this means that they are represented in the same way in writing but differ in terms of meaning and pronunciation. However, the noun is given primary stress on the first syllable while the verb is given primary stress on the second syllable. This results in the vowels in the first syllables of these words having very different values, and a variation in length of the vowels in the second syllables:

| noun | ᵎ*record* | [rekɔd] or [rekʊd] |
| verb | reᵎ*cord* | [rɪkɔːd] |

Examples of this kind where word class is distinguished by the position of primary stress are nearly always noun/verb pairs. Further, the examples are all derived words consisting of a prefix plus a base. Other examples include *extract* and *contract*. There are probably about fifty such homographs in total.

- ☐ **derived words (affixation)** ⇨ 3.4
- ☐ **compound words** ⇨ 3.5
- ☐ **vowels, including schwa** ⇨ 9.7
- ☐ **syllable structure** ⇨ 10.4
- ☐ **syllabic consonants** ⇨ 10.5
- ☐ **pitch variations** ⇨ 11.4

11.3 RHYTHM

Rhythm refers to the pattern of stressed and unstressed syllables in speech. We often associate rhythm with a degree of regularity in this pattern in contrast to **arhythmic** speech where the pattern is irregular. The latter is likely to occur when we are nervous or hesitant in our speech. In general, though, our speech tends to be fairly rhythmic. What is of particular significance is the way we adjust the rhythm of our speech in order to make it more regular. Consider the following two noun phrases:

a cup of tea
a piece of cake

In these examples, the stressed syllables would be the monosyllabic nouns *cup*, *tea*, *piece* and *cake* while the grammatical words, *a* and *of*; would be unstressed and would be pronounced [ə] and [əv] respectively. The alternation between stressed and unstressed syllables in these examples results in a regular rhythm. If, however, we join these two phrases with the conjunction *and,* the regularity of the rhythm is slightly disrupted:

> a ˈcup of ˈtea and a ˈpiece of ˈcake

Here the regularity is broken by the fact that two unstressed syllables now occur between *tea* and *piece.* Of course, in normal spontaneous speech it is highly unlikely that there will be a consistent alternation between stressed and unstressed syllables. What speakers of English normally do to compensate for the irregularity in occurrence of stressed and unstressed syllables is to space the stressed syllables at approximately equal intervals. This adds something like a regular beat to the utterance. Here the example is shown again with dots over the stressed syllables. These dots also represent beats occurring at regular intervals:

> •   •   •   •
>
> a cup of tea and a piece of cake

Often, two or three unstressed syllables occur between stressed ones:

> • (1) • (2) • (2) •   (3) • •   (2) • (1)
>
> Nick and Hilary went to St Petersburg to see Laurence and Catherine

In the above example, the numbers in brackets indicate the number of unstressed syllables occurring between the stressed ones. As already mentioned, the likelihood is that speakers will space the stressed syllables at fairly regular intervals irrespective of the number of unstressed syllables which occur between them. Languages which use this strategy as a means of constructing rhythm are known as **stress-timed** languages (as opposed to **syllable-timed** languages such as French where all syllables have approximately equal duration). English is fundamentally a stress-timed language although there are some varieties of global English (such as Indian English) which have a rather different rhythmic pattern.

We saw in Section 11.2 that all words spoken in isolation contain at least one stressed syllable. We have just seen that in connected speech grammatical words such as *a* and *of* in *a cup of tea* will be unstressed. There are quite a number of monosyllabic grammatical words, *a* and *of* amongst them, which will be unstressed in some circumstances but stressed in others. These words are said to have both **strong** (namely stressed) and **weak** (unstressed) forms. They include the following:

pronouns	*she/her, he/him, we/us, you, them*
determiners	*the, a/an, some, her, his, your*
modal auxiliaries	*can, could, shall, should, must*
primary auxiliaries	*am/are/was/were, do/does, have/has/had*
prepositions	*as, at, for, from, of than, to*
conjunctions	*and, but, that, than*

In addition to the above, the primary auxiliaries *am, are, was* and *were* can also occur in both weak or strong forms when functioning as lexical verbs. There are various reasons why a weak or strong form may be selected. The position of a word in a sentence may affect the form it takes:

letter came <u>from</u> Milton Keynes	[frəm]
She didn't know where the letter had come <u>from</u>	[frɒm]

In the first of these two examples, *from* is unstressed and the vowel it contains is a schwa. In the second example, where *from* occurs at the end of the sentence, this preposition is realised in its strong form and the vowel is given its full value. Another reason to adopt the strong form of a word might be for the sake of **contrastive stress:**

You know Susan and Bill? Did you see <u>them</u> in the pub last night?	[ðəm]
No, I didn't see <u>them</u> but I did see Mick and Pippa	[ðem]

In the first example, no particular stress is needed on *them*. In the second example, however, stress is placed on this pronoun which refers to *Susan and Bill* in order to set up a contrast with *Mick and Pippa*. Another reason for adopting the strong rather than the weak form of a grammatical word would be simply to give it emphasis, not necessarily in contrast to another word or phrase as we have just seen:

You <u>shall</u> go to the ball, Cinderella	[ʃəl]

expresses a degree of confidence that Cinderella will go to the ball but

You <u>shall</u> go to the ball, Cinderella	[ʃæl]

is far more confident and assertive, an attitude which is conveyed by using the strong form of the modal auxiliary *shall*.

The choice between the strong and weak forms of the words we have just considered can of course have an effect on the rhythm of the sentence in question. Conversely, the rhythm of a sentence may have an effect on the stress patterns within individual words. We saw in the previous section, for example, that some polysyllabic words contain both a primary and a secondary stress. However, in connected speech, the normal distinction between primary and secondary stress may disappear. Earlier we had the example of ₁sui'cidal where in isolation the first syllable carries secondary stress and the third syllable carries primary stress. In the following context, however, this pattern has undergone a change:

The student made a 'sui₁cidal a'ttempt *to climb to the roof of the college*

It is likely here that the third syllable of *suicidal* will have no more stress than the first syllable, and possibly even less. This reflects a trend for a primary stress in one word to shift or be less prominent when the next stress which follows it, albeit in a different word, is also a primary stress. This can also be observed with compound words. In our earlier example of ₁second-'hand, we saw that the primary stress occurs on *hand*. In this sentence, however, the primary stress moves to the start of *second:*

Phil gave Jane some 'second-₁hand 'furniture

The occurrence of the primary stress at the start of *furniture* causes the primary stress in *second-hand* to shift to the initial syllable. We have already seen that stressed and unstressed syllables tend to alternate in speech or that stressed syllables will occur at roughly equal intervals. The above examples show a tendency among speakers to alternate primary and secondary stresses too. The inclination to alternate strong and weak syllables is sufficiently strong at times to move the primary stress not to a syllable of secondary stress but to a previously unstressed syllable. This can be seen in a compound such as *compact disk*. In isolation, the adjective *com'pact* is stressed on the second syllable but in *compact disk,* the stress in *compact* moves to the first syllable: 'compact 'disk.

- ☐ **lexical and grammatical words** ⇨ 2.3
- ☐ **syllable-timed varieties of English** ⇨ 12.11

11.4 INTONATION AND TONE GROUPS

We noted in Section 11.2 that syllables are sometimes given prominence by a marked change of pitch and that pitch varies according to the frequency of the vibrations of our vocal cords. **Intonation** is the way in which pitch rises and falls in speech. Pitch may change markedly (for example from a high pitch to a low pitch) on one syllable or it may change across several syllables. For the time being, we will concentrate on changes in pitch on single syllables. The term which we normally give to such pitch contours is a **tone**. Noticeable changes in pitch typically occur on stressed syllables although they might occur on unstressed syllables for the purpose of contrast or emphasis.

Consider the following sentence:

Heather has won a gold medal for swimming

We will focus on the adjective *gold* in this sentence and consider some of the different tones with which it could be said. Whatever tone is adopted, we can be certain that *gold* would be one of the stressed syllables in the example given its status as a monosyllabic lexical word. First of all, if the speaker did not wish to draw any particular attention to this word, then the likelihood is that it would be said without any noticeable change in pitch. In other words, *gold* would be uttered on a **level tone**. We can indicate that a syllable has a level tone by preceding it with a horizontal line: _*gold*.

However, if the speaker wished to draw more attention to *gold* then they could utter it with a **falling tone**. This means that the pitch of *gold* would move from high to low. At the start of the tone, the pitch will probably be the same or perhaps a little higher than the pitch used previously (ˌ*gold*) but if the speaker wanted to be even more emphatic then they might well start the tone on a noticeably higher pitch (ˈ*gold*). A falling tone is usually used to express certainty or finality. A slightly more exaggerated falling tone with a greater change in pitch will still express certainty and finality but with rather more emphasis.

In contrast to a falling tone, *gold* could be uttered with a **rising tone**. Again, the rise could be relatively gentle (ˌ*gold*) or more marked (ˈ*gold*) depending on the degree of attention the speaker wanted to draw to the word in question. A rising tone, in contrast to a falling tone, tends to suggest surprise or incompleteness. So if *gold* were uttered on a rising tone in the above example, it would probably have the effect of either turning it into a question or making the statement sound incomplete.

1 *Heather has won a* ˈ*gold medal for swimming?* (*Could you confirm this?*)
2 *Heather has won a* ˌ*gold medal for swimming and a* ˌ*silver for diving*

In Example 1 the rising tone on *gold* begins on a higher pitch and this turns the statement into a question. In the second example, the less marked rise on *gold* suggests the statement is incomplete. This is confirmed when the second part of the utterance – *and a ˎsilver for diving* – is added. You may notice that there is a falling tone on *silver* which suggests that the information is now almost complete.

Level, rising and falling tones are **simple tones**. They may be contrasted with **complex tones**. There are two main possibilities for complex tones: these are the **fall-rise tone**, which is used fairly commonly, and the **rise-fall** tone, which is more unusual. A fall-rise tone is often used to suggest qualified assertion or an element of doubt:

> *A ˇgold medal?*   (*Are you sure it was gold?*)

A rise-fall tone can be used to express a pleasant surprise or it can express an ironic attitude towards what is said:

> *A ˆgold medal*   (*Well that's a turn up for the books!*)

Although speakers often find it quite difficult to identify the specific type of tone on a syllable when studying language, all speakers are able to respond to the tones they hear and make accurate judgements about the implied meaning behind them.

So far, then, we have seen that in any utterance some syllables will be stressed while others will be unstressed. A stressed syllable may be gently prominent simply due to the natural rhythm of speech or it may be especially prominent because particular attention is being drawn to it. We use falling and rising tones, as well as fall-rise and rise-fall tones, to draw greater attention to a particular word as well as to indicate our stance or attitude towards what is said. For example, we can use a particular tone to indicate that we are asking a question or that we have nearly finished what we are saying or that we are doubtful about what we are saying. (Of course, the context of the utterance may also have a bearing on precisely how the meaning is interpreted). In any utterance, only some stressed syllables are marked with a noticeable change of pitch, namely with a tone. Such a syllable is referred to as a **tonic syllable** or **nucleus**.

A tonic syllable will normally, unless the utterance is simply a monosyllabic word (such as *yes* in reply to a question), occur within a **tone group** (or **tone unit**). This is best understood by looking at an example such as the following extract from a BBC documentary where an astronaut is talking about a mission to repair the Hubble space telescope:

> | *the Hubble symbolises man's quest for the bridge between cosmology and phiˎlosophy* | *and so when you go 'off to catch that thing* | *and it appears on*

the ho̲rizon | it's a powerful ˎmo̲ment | it is not any other ˎspace̲ship | Hubble ˎtou̲ches people | it touches ˎme̲ |

In this extract, the tone groups have been separated by vertical lines. The tonic syllables have been underlined and the symbol which precedes them indicates the type of tone on each tonic syllable. Tonic syllables, as we have already noted, are those stressed syllables which are particularly prominent because they carry a tone or noticeable pitch change. Most typically, a tonic syllable will occur towards the end of a tone group and often there is a relationship between the tone group and the grammatical structure of the utterance. In other words, there is some correlation between the tone group and grammatical completeness. Usually, the tonic syllable occurs close to a point of grammatical completeness (although this need not necessarily be a full clause) and it occurs on the last primary stress of the group. Sometimes, however, if a speaker wishes to draw attention to an element which occurs earlier in the group, then the tonic syllable will not necessarily be the last stressed syllable of the group. This can be seen in:

| Hubble ˎtou̲ches people |

The last stressed syllable in this group is the first syllable of *people* but here the speaker wants to give particular emphasis to the verb *touches* and so the falling tone occurs on the initial syllable of this verb. In the following group

| and so when you go 'o̲ff to catch that thing |

the position of the tonic syllable is even more noticeable because it falls on a syllable which, in the collocation *go off*, would normally be given slightly less stress than the verb *go*.

Since tonic syllables vary in position, this raises the question of how exactly you can identify where a tone group begins and ends. Sometimes, speakers will pause briefly or take a breath between tone groups. In addition, what often happens is that the pitch movement for the tonic syllable does not occur simply on that syllable but continues through the next syllable or syllables. When a new tone unit is then started there may be a sense of the speaker returning to what might be regarded as the 'normal' pitch for the utterance.

In most tone groups, then, the tonic syllable – or nucleus – is preceded by what we call the **pre-nucleus** and may be followed by the **post-nucleus**. Here is an example:

pre-nucleus	nucleus	post-nucleus
| it is not any other	*ˎspace̲*	*ship |*

Typically, the pre-nucleus will be longer than the post-nucleus. In the above example, the pre-nucleus contains some stressed syllables but none of them have the prominence of *space*. The post-nucleus here consists simply of *ship* and it is probable that this would be uttered with a slight return towards the normal pitch although the following tone group will begin on a noticeably more normal pitch. In the first tone group of the original example (| *the Hubble symbolises man's quest for the bridge between cosmology and phi\losophy* |), however, it is likely that the downward movement in pitch which begins on the second syllable of *philosophy* will continue through the unstressed syllables which make up the rest of this word. Although we can identify tonic syllables because they carry a noticeable change in pitch, this does not mean that the pitch of the rest of the tone group is constant. When making a statement, for example, speakers are likely to lower the pitch slightly as they move towards the tonic syllable. It is on the tonic syllable, however, that the listener would most notice a change in pitch.

11.5   SEMANTIC FUNCTIONS OF INTONATION

Intonation is part of the fabric of spoken language. Intonation can also serve two specific purposes. It can indicate the speaker's purpose or attitude towards what they are saying, and it can be used for a grammatical reason, something we will deal with in Section 11.6. We have already seen how the various tones can convey attitudes such as surprise or irony as well as other information such as the fact that the utterance is nearly complete. A speaker can also use intonation to draw attention to a particular element of an utterance, either for contrastive purposes or because the speaker wants to make sure the listener pays attention to something important.

We have also seen that intonation can indicate the particular function of a grammatical structure. (We touched on this point in Section 11.4.) If, for instance, you compare the tonic syllables in the following three examples you will see how intonation can indicate function even though each example takes the same declarative form:

1. *It's ˌcold in here*
2. *It's 'cold in here*
3. *It's ˎcold in here*

The falling tone on *cold* in Example 1 indicates that the declarative is functioning as a statement while the rising tone in Example 2 turns the declarative into a *yes-no* question. In Example 3, the fall-rise on *cold* could give the utterance a directive function, with the speaker implying that someone should do something about the cold.

Another important aspect of intonation is that certain intonation patterns are linked to different styles and genres. This is a complex area and we will only touch briefly on it here. To take one simple example, there are different ways of telling a story. We adopt one intonation pattern when we relate an anecdote spontaneously to a group of friends but a quite different pattern if we read a short story aloud. The latter would in turn differ depending on whether we are reading to children or to adults. Some varieties of English have very distinctive intonation patterns. Examples include the reading of the football results on radio or television, announcements at railway stations or airports, and sports commentaries.

11.6 GRAMMATICAL FUNCTIONS OF INTONATION

In contrast to the way in which intonation can convey meaning, some intonation features have a grammatical function. This is a salient example of the way in which language levels interact with each other. We have already seen that the positioning of stress can be related to word class. The position of a tonic stress can also signal the difference between a compound noun and a premodifier plus a head noun as in these *French teacher* examples:

> *Martin employed a <u>French</u> teacher*   compound noun
> *Martin employed a French <u>teacher</u>*   premodifier + head noun

Assuming the speaker did not want to assign any particular emphasis to either *Martin* or *employed* in the above examples, then the intonation pattern of the first example with the tonic stress on *French* would indicate that Martin employed a teacher of the French language. By contrast, the second example, with the tonic stress on *teacher* implies that Martin employed a teacher who was French. Many meanings which would be ambiguous in writing can be clarified in speech by the use of specific intonation patterns.

Another clear instance of how intonation can give grammatical information relates to relative clauses. You may remember from Chapter 6 that a relative clause postmodifies a head noun:

> *This is the picture <u>which I prefer</u>*

However, there are in fact two types of relative clause: **restrictive** and **non-restrictive**. Restrictive relative clauses distinguish one person, item or group from another whereas non-restrictive relative clauses simply give additional information about the noun in question. Compare the following examples:

> The students <u>who had completed their work</u> were given prizes
> The students, <u>who had completed their work</u>, were given prizes

The first example implies that prizes were only given to some students. The relative clause *who had completed their work* is restrictive here because it is separating the students with finished work from those with unfinished work. The second example, where the relative clause is more like an aside, implies that all the students had finished their work. The relative clause here is non-restrictive and functions as a means of providing additional information about all the students.

In the second example, the fact that the relative clause is non-restrictive is signalled by the use of commas. (An alternative way to show this would be to place the relative clause in brackets or between dashes.) In speech, we signal the difference between a restrictive and a non-restrictive relative clause by the way we organise the tone groups in the utterance:

> restrictive
> | *The students who had completed their ˌwork | were given ˌprizes |*
>
> non-restrictive
> *The ˌstudents | who had comˌpleted their work | were given ˌprizes |*

The non-restrictive relative clause is treated as a separate tone group while the restrictive relative clause occurs in the same tone group as the head noun which it postmodifies. Intonation is the means here by which the restrictive or non-restrictive status of a relative clause is indicated and thus the phonological level of language is operating in conjunction with the grammatical level.

☐ **compound words** ⇨ 3.5
☐ **noun phrases** ⇨ 5.2
☐ **relative clauses** ⇨ 6.13

11.7 OTHER SUPRASEGMENTAL FEATURES

Finally, we will consider some prosodic features which are more peripheral than stress, rhythm and intonation. These are **voice quality**, **volume** and **tempo**. Each of these aspects may have an effect on the meaning of what we say or they may be incidental to it. Since they are less central than the other prosodic features covered, we will discuss them only briefly.

Voice relates to the vibration of the vocal cords in the larynx. **Voice quality** refers to the various effects which are brought about depending on the state of the vocal cords and the extent to which the glottis is open or closed. This can lead to a contrast with the regular quality of our speaking voices since we may speak in a breathy voice or a creaky voice or a whispered voice, to name just three possibilities. Sometimes voice quality is irrelevant to what is being said: if, for example, you have a very sore throat and your vocal cords are swollen, this will inevitably affect the way you sound. On the other hand, you may choose to adopt a particular voice quality because it seems appropriate to what you are saying. For instance, if you are telling someone a secret you might speak in a whisper. If you are reading a child a horror story you might adopt a creaky voice.

Volume relates to how loudly or softly someone speaks. Some speakers are typically louder or quieter than the majority of speakers and the volume of the voice may also be related to physical size. We have already seen that one way to give prominence to a syllable is to give it greater volume. We often increase the general volume of our speech when we are angry or trying to get someone's attention. By contrast, we often decrease the volume if we are trying to be gentle or show sensitivity. Volume is measured in decibels and special equipment is of course required for this.

Finally, **tempo** is the speed at which we speak. We can measure tempo in words per minute although sometimes syllables per minute may be more appropriate. There is a contrast between regular spoken tempo and a tempo which is adopted for a particular purpose. For instance, a sports commentator describing a race is likely to increase their tempo as the race draws to a conclusion, whereas someone who is dictating or explaining something very carefully will normally decrease the speed of their speech. In unbroken speech, speakers can easily utter an average of one hundred and fifty words per minute. Some speakers will of course utter far more and others typically fewer.

☐ **variation in prosodic features** ⇨ 12.11

Phonological Frameworks: Exercises

Exercise 1: Describing consonants and vowels

Write descriptions for the sounds represented by the following phonetic symbols:

consonants: / θ, g, ŋ, ʤ, j, v /
vowels: / ɜː, e, uː, ɒ /

Exercise 2: Making phonetic transcriptions

Transcribe the following words using the phonetic alphabet. Begin by using the RP pronunciation, but if there are variations in your own accent, try to write this version too.

strength	*youth*	*justice*	*probability*	*vocation*
pleasure	*choice*	*praise*	*judgement*	*sexism*

Exercise 3: Syllable structures

Transcribe the given words into the phonetic alphabet and then work out the syllable structure using the template given in Chapter 10.

syllable							
onset (*optional*)			rhyme				
			peak	coda (*optional*)			
consonant(s)			vowel	consonant(s)			
pre-initial consonant	initial consonant	post-initial consonant	V	pre-final consonant	final consonant	post-final consonant	(post-final consonant)

spend, scratch, quilts, clasp, tubes

Exercise 4: Stress patterns

(1) Mark the primary stress as well as any secondary stress on the following disyllabic and polysyllabic words:

> *aroma*   *aromatic*
> *different* *differential*
> *envelop*   *envelope*
> *imagine*   *imagination*
> *portrait*   *portrayal*
> *suppose*   *supposition*

(2) Show the differing stress patterns in the following word-forms according to the two word classes they belong to. Is there any correlation between word class and stress pattern?

> *insult, contract, dictate, entrance, escort, frequent*

PHONOLOGICAL FRAMEWORKS: SUGGESTIONS FOR FURTHER READING

Language textbooks

Ashby, Patricia (2011) *Understanding Phonetics* (Abingdon: Hodder Education)
A general course which deals with both individual speech sounds and with suprasegmental aspects. There are plenty of exercises to help the reader develop their listening skills, and online resources are available too.

Collins, Beverley and Inger M. Mees (2008) *Practical Phonetics and Phonology: A Resource Book for Students,* 2nd edn (London: Routledge)
Covers a wide range of aspects, including pronunciation change. Includes 20 accents from Britain and beyond, and comes with an audio CD.

Johnson, Keith (2011) *Acoustic and Auditory Phonetics*, 3rd edn (Oxford: Blackwell)
Useful for readers wishing to learn about the two aspects of phonetics not covered here. Inevitably, involves a lot of physics.

McMahon, April (2001) *An Introduction to English Phonology* (Edinburgh: Edinburgh University Press)
A helpful introduction which provides basic tools and concepts.

Ogden, Richard (2009) *An Introduction to English Phonetics* (Edinburgh: Edinburgh University Press)
Another very helpful introductory text, which expands what has been covered in Chapter 9. A companion text to April McMahon's title above.

Roach, Peter (2009) *English Phonetics and Phonology*, 4th edn (Cambridge: Cambridge University Press)
Another standard course, with audio CDs to illustrate all key features. Aimed at both native and non-native speakers.

Tench, Paul (2011) *Transcribing the Sound of English* (Cambridge: Cambridge University Press)
A workbook in phonetic transcription which gives guidance on transcribing connected speech as well as individual words. It also contains material on accents other than RP.

Reference books

International Phonetic Association, The (1999) *The Handbook of the International Phonetic Association* (Cambridge: Cambridge University Press)
A comprehensive guide to phonetic symbols and the principles underlying them.

Pullum, Geoffrey K. and William A. Ladusaw (1996) *Phonetic Symbol Guide*, 2nd edn (Chicago: University of Chicago Press)
A useful reference book which lists and explains the whole range of phonetic symbols.

Internet resources

www.langsci.ucl.ac.uk/ipa/
The home site of the International Phonetic Association, which includes charts of the IPA symbols.

www.ling.mq.edu.au/speech/phonetics/topics.html
A comprehensive set of resources for the study of phonetics and phonology, originally designed for use by undergraduate students at Macquarie University, Sydney, Australia. Sound recordings are available on this site.

www.uvic.ca/ling/resources/ipa/charts/IPAlab/IPAlab.htm
A very useful resource from the University of Victoria in Canada which plays recordings of speech sounds when you click on the associated phonetic symbols.

www.ucl.ac.uk/psychlangsci/research/speech
The website of the Speech, Hearing and Phonetic Sciences department (part of the division of Psychology and Language Sciences) at University College London contains some excellent resources and advice for studying speech.

Part VI
BROADER PERSPECTIVES

12 Variation in English

12.1 BEYOND RP AND STANDARD BRITISH ENGLISH

As you have been reading the preceding chapters of this book, you will probably have formed an impression as to what extent the English described here
is similar to the English you speak yourself, or that you are learning to speak if
English is not your first language. Even if you are not a speaker of the Standard
British English dialect, you will probably be familiar with this 'benchmark'
variety through the media and through education, science or business, where
it has national and international communicative functions, especially in the
written mode. However, any linguist who sets out to describe English using
such 'representative' forms as Standard British English and the RP accent is
aware of the irony of the task: that they are describing an English spoken by
a small minority, particularly as far as RP is concerned. Arguably, however,
the number of people who speak the English outlined here is irrelevant: what
is important is that a set of reference points has been established with which
other accents and dialects can be compared.

   English is characterised not only by the vast number of people who
speak it, but also by the extent it is used globally. It is spoken in some capacity
by a significant number of people on every inhabited continent, as Figure 12.1
shows. Speakers fall into one of three groups: those who have English as a
native language (ENL), those who have it as a second language (ESL – where
speakers usually use a different language at home but English for more public
purposes), and then the large number of speakers across the world who have
learnt English as a foreign language (EFL). In countries where English is an
official language (whether constitutionally or simply in practice), the users
are either predominantly native speakers or ESL speakers, or a mixture of both.
At least 60 sovereign states in the world have English as an official language, far
more if we include dependencies. In countries such as Australia and the United
States of America, English is the only 'official' language, reflecting the fact
that the majority of the population are native speakers of English. This is not
to say that other languages are unimportant, be they spoken by a significant
percentage of the population (such as Spanish in the United States) or a tiny

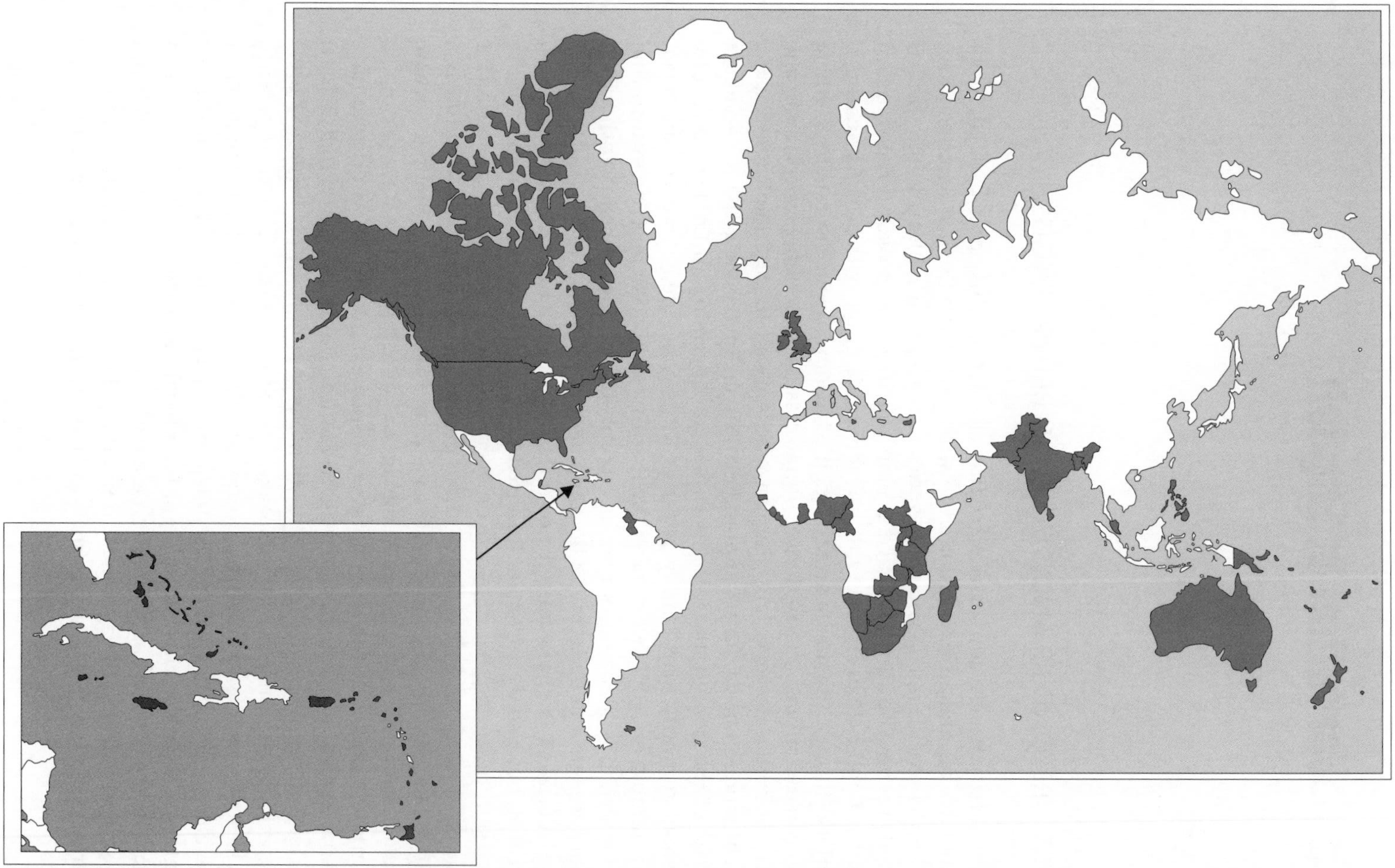

Figure 12.1 Countries where English is significant as an official, native or second language

minority (such as the Aboriginal languages of Australia). In other countries, English is a co-official language, sharing its status with other languages which also have a significant number of native speakers among the population, such as French in Canada or Afrikaans in South Africa (which has eleven official languages). Elsewhere, English may have the status of an official language, but its importance is as a *lingua franca* (a language used by speakers who do not share a native language). This is the case in India, where the primary official language is Hindi and where English is only spoken as a native language by a smallish minority. However, English is used by the majority as a second language and has considerable importance in government and education. There are also many countries where English is not classified or regarded as an official language but is used as a *lingua franca* (Cyprus and Malaysia, for example), or is widely spoken as a foreign language, as in Scandinavia.

Many linguists have attempted to calculate the number of speakers of English throughout the world. In doing so, it is usual to make a distinction between the native speakers, who are brought up speaking English at home, and non-native speakers, who learn English through other cultural, social and educational influences. Native speakers are characterised by their complete fluency in the language, and it is believed there are at least 350 million of them in the world. With regard to non-native speakers, as mentioned above, a further distinction is usually made between those who use English as a second language and those who speak it as a foreign language. Second language speakers may or may not be as fluent as native speakers (or some EFL speakers for that matter) but it is less likely they will speak English in a private, domestic context or regard English as their 'primary' language. The number of second language English speakers is believed to be comparable to the number of native speakers, and probably larger. In other words, around 700 million people worldwide have English as their primary or secondary language. With the global population now calculated at about seven billion inhabitants, this means at least one person in ten can be classified as speaking English. If we add the number of people who elect to learn English as a foreign language and are able to use it with a good degree of fluency, then this figure could easily double to a fifth or more of the global population being able to communicate in the same language.

Depending on their personal circumstances, speakers of English will use either a standard or a non-standard dialect of English. Although there is a high degree of commonality between them, Standard Englishes do vary across the globe. The non-standard varieties will differ from the standards a little or a great deal as a result of various social, regional and historical factors. Many speakers are bidialectal, typically using a non-standard variety at home or socially, and a more standard variety in work or education. Whereas standard varieties tend to be national and non-regional, non-standard dialects are often linked to a specific geographical region or community, and are likely to have associated accents, whereas standard varieties may be spoken with 'received' accents or with regional accents. Of all the non-standard varieties of English, the most marked in terms of their difference from any of the standards are the English-based pidgin and creole varieties found in the Caribbean, the Pacific and West Africa. These are hybrid languages originally formed for a specific purpose (such as trade) through contact between speakers of two dissimilar languages. A pidgin has no native speakers whereas a creole is a pidgin that has developed sufficiently to be learnt as a native language. Below is an extract from the biblical account of creation in Standard English, followed by a version in Tok Pisin, an English-based creole which is an official *lingua franca* in Papua New Guinea as well as having a growing number of native speakers.

from *Genesis* Chapter 1 in Standard English
(from the New Revised Standard Version, 1989)

verse 3   *Then God said, 'Let there be light'; and there was light.*
verse 4   *And God saw that the light was good; and God separated the light from the darkness.*
verse 5   *God called the light Day, and the darkness he called Night. And there was evening and there was morning, the first day.*

from *Genesis* Chapter 1 in Tok Pisin
(published by The Bible Society of Papua New Guinea in 1989)

verse 3   *Na God i tok olsem, 'Lait i mas kamap.' Orait lait i kamap.*
verse 4   *God i lukim lait i gutpela, na em i amamas. Na em i brukim tudak na tulait.*
verse 5   *Tulait em i kolim 'De', na tudak em i kolim 'Nait'. Nait i go pinis na moning i kamap. Em i de namba wan.*

As you can see, there is a significant difference between these two varieties, so much so that some linguists consider Tok Pisin should be regarded as a separate language. However, on closer inspection (and possibly reading aloud) of the Tok Pisin example, the common features become more apparent, particularly in terms of the lexis. Although mutual intelligibility may be a problem for the speakers of these two varieties, it is reasonable to say that the two versions above represent not two distinct languages but the extremes of a continuum within the same language.

12.2   VARIATION IN ENGLISH: AN OVERVIEW

The small band of settlers and invaders, initially numbering probably only a few thousand, who came from north-west Europe in the 5th century AD to live in what later came to be known as England, would have been somewhat surprised to learn that their language would one day be spoken throughout the world, especially since their understanding of 'the world' was of the European mainland where Latin was the *lingua franca*. Even then, *English* (the language of the *Angles*) was characterised by variation as different tribal groups (Angles, Saxons and Jutes) settled in different parts of the country, taking their distinct dialects with them. Over a period of many centuries, and helped by factors such as the development of printing and the growing strength of London as the capital, a standard form of the language emerged and existed alongside the traditional dialects which were the linguistic descendants of the speech of the original settlers. Today, those traditional dialects are in decline, and are largely spoken by older speakers who have remained all their lives in the region in which they were born. Younger speakers have increasingly gravitated towards the standard language, or at least the 'standard' of London and other major cities in England, although they retain features of their regional accents. In the last 60 years or so then, a process of levelling has seen an expansion of the urban varieties, particularly throughout the south-east of England (where it has given rise to the accent known as **Estuary English**). Immigration has also changed the linguistic character of England, particularly in towns and cities where new varieties show the influence of English from the Caribbean, Africa and Asia.

Historically, migration also accounts for the presence of English throughout the British Isles – in Scotland, Wales, Northern Ireland and the Irish Republic, although all these countries retain their indigenous languages to some degree. Globally, the spread of English is the result of trade and colonisation, a process that happened over several centuries and which resulted in English being spoken as a native language in the USA, Canada and parts of the Caribbean, in Australia and New Zealand, and also in South Africa, with the political and commercial influence of the USA being the primary reason for English gaining status as a global language during the 20th century. Elsewhere in Africa and in Asia, British colonial influence was the cause of English now having the role of an official language with a large number of ESL speakers, India being the predominant nation in terms of numbers.

English continues to grow in importance throughout the world, a beneficial process in terms of global communication but not necessarily in terms of cultural and ethnic identity. In July 2011, the war-torn African region of South Sudan, a former British territory with over 200 ethnic groups and languages, became an independent state recognised by the UN and decreed that English should be its official language and, despite the shortage of English teachers in South Sudan, should remain the medium of education. This example of a country whose official language reflects the hope of promoting internal unity and bringing international benefits to its people serves as a reminder that it is always desirable to be sensitive to the reasons why a specific variety has come into existence in the first place.

12.3   STUDYING AND ANALYSING VARIATION

Variation in English is, then, a vast topic. To describe the extent of accent and dialect variation in Britain alone is a daunting task. Add to that the variation represented by speakers across the planet, as well as the inevitable constant changes taking place in the language, and the task of mapping variation in English becomes effectively impossible. However, students who have acquired the set of frameworks presented here have, to all intents and purposes, acquired the tools they need for analysing and describing any other variety of English. When you are studying different accents and dialects, there are several helpful points to bear in mind.

As just mentioned, it is always useful to appreciate something of the background of the variety you are studying and its status in the place where it is spoken, particularly in terms of whether it is a standard or non-standard variety and whether it is mainly used by native or non-native speakers. Many varieties of English rub shoulders with other languages and these may well have affected it to a greater or lesser extent, particularly where English is used as a second language or as a *lingua franca*. Pidgin and creole varieties will need particular consideration in terms of their hybrid origins. Depending on the focus of your study, your data may be spoken or written. In either case, the contexts of production and reception as well as the purpose of the example in question will need to be considered. As far as individual speakers are concerned, personal and social aspects such as age, gender and social status are also important. Furthermore, speakers themselves are not always consistent in how they speak and may show variation within a short extract, as the example in Section 12.12 demonstrates.

Language varies – and changes – at every level. It is best, therefore, to organise your analysis systematically, using the levels of language outlined in the preceding chapters. You may be using the accent and dialect described here as the benchmark for your comparison, but sometimes other benchmarks would be more appropriate. For instance, if you are studying a regional accent/dialect of North America, it would make more sense to use the General American accent and Standard American English as your starting points. Although standard varieties are valuable for identifying key characteristics of non-standard varieties, it is possible that a comparison between non-standard varieties is more appropriate, for example if you were comparing the speech of inhabitants in neighbouring regions. Here, mapping may prove a useful way to represent variation as maps can show the boundary between an accent or dialect feature, a division known as an **isogloss**.

Despite the extent of variation among speakers of English globally, patterns emerge across the different levels of language as the following sections will show. Sections 12.4 to 12.11 illustrate some of the likely **variables** (features which are prone to variation) and the **variant** forms they might take in order to give you an idea of some of the features to focus on when you are studying a particular accent or dialect. The examples are drawn from both standard and non-standard varieties from the British Isles and across the globe, and have been selected in an attempt to provide a range of examples rather than to describe any specific accent or dialect in detail.

This chapter aims to help you identify linguistic variation, but any detailed linguistic or historical explanation for the features you find is well beyond its scope. The suggestions for further reading will, however, direct you to some helpful texts on this subject. Exploring variation increases awareness of the pull between the trend towards uniformity, which correlates with the status of English as a global language, and the value of diversity, which helps speakers and speech communities maintain their individual identity. And despite the diversity in the way English is used and spoken across the planet, it is possible to appreciate what it means to say that all these millions of speakers share a common language.

☐ **levels of language** ⇨ 1.2

12.4   LEXICAL VARIATION

All aspects of language are affected by change but vocabulary changes are the most rapid and far-reaching, particularly in our technological age, where new words or new usages can be easily transmitted – whether in spoken or written form – to a large number of speakers. This means that words readily spread from one variety to another, thus increasing uniformity between global varieties. Nevertheless, there is a considerable degree of lexical variation to be found in both standard and non-standard dialects, and there are social, historical and geographical reasons for this. In fact, every word has its own unique story. Lexical variation affects chiefly content words, particularly nouns and verbs. Function words are, inevitably, less affected, although prepositions show some variation. (Differences in pronouns and pronoun systems will be treated as grammatical, and are dealt with in Section 12.5.) Words can be said to be common to two (or more) varieties if they share not only their form but also their meaning, and the degree of lexical overlap will inevitably vary from dialect to dialect. The lexical items which fall outside this category can be analysed in a variety of ways.

One approach is to begin with the concept or object to which a word refers, namely its referent. When comparing dialects, there are many examples to be found of different words for the same referent, as the following examples illustrate:

| Standard British English | *tap* | *nappy* | *lift* | *to tick* |
| Standard American English | *faucet* | *diaper* | *elevator* | *to check* |

Synonymous examples like these are plentiful across standard dialects, although lexicons are changing all the time. As the culture of the USA has extended its influence on Britain, for instance, many American English synonyms have been adopted into British usage, examples including *movie* (for *film*), *cookie* (*biscuit*), and *buggy* (*pram*), although these are not used by all speakers, with the result that both items in the pairings are in current use in British English, not necessarily always with identical meanings.

Traditional non-standard regional dialects of England also contain such equivalents. For instance, a narrow passageway between buildings is referred to in various ways throughout the country. Some examples of this are shown in Figure 12.2, where the trace of an isogloss can be seen in the north-west. In the 2005 BBC Voices survey of regional speech, a small number of speakers reported using *jitty* and *jigger,* although neither of these examples are found in the Oxford English Dictionary (or OED; accessed online in April 2012 in relation to these and the other examples in this section), reflecting the fact that even the most extensive and prestigious dictionaries do not record the complete range of language in use. However, the OED does list *snicket, ginnel, jennel,* and *twitten,* which were also cited in the BBC Voices survey. As already mentioned, traditional dialect words are gradually falling out of use and are now predominantly used by older speakers native to the dialect region. Lexical changes reflect lifestyle changes, so geographical mobility affects regional speech as do other social changes as represented in the 'passageway' examples, where new styles of urban planning are effectively making these words redundant.

Many words exist in one variety and not another simply because their referent has no relevance to the culture of a particular speech community. They are likely therefore to relate to aspects such as wildlife, topography, food, customs and so on, and will often be drawn from local languages with which

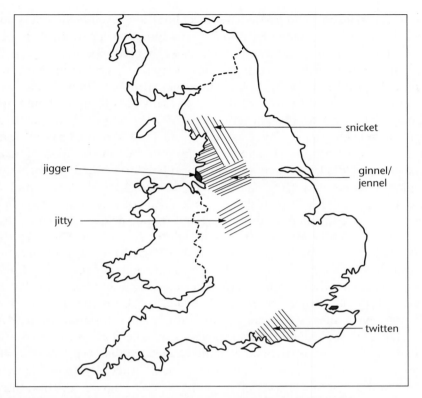

Figure 12.2   A selection of regional dialect words for 'narrow passageway'

English has come into contact. Australian English, for example, contains the following nouns adopted from Dharuk, an Aboriginal language spoken in the Sydney region of New South Wales:

gibber	a large stone or boulder
kipper	a young man who has been initiated into manhood
mundowie	a footprint
nannygai	a type of fish
nulla-nulla	a wooden club
potoroo	a type of kangaroo
wombat	a small bear-like mammal

Two of these examples have of course spread from Australian English to the northern hemisphere, with *wombat* now commonly known, and *potoroo* becoming better known. (The OED illustrates *potoroo* with a quotation from the 1997 *New Yorker* magazine.) *Mundowie* is distinctive in that, rather than replace the English word *footprint*, it is used in the context of tracking in the wild and is colloquial rather than formal. So a referent may have more than one associated lexeme in a particular dialect but these lexemes are not synonymous. In fact, as discussed in Section 3.9, true synonyms are unlikely to occur as the presence of one word would render the other redundant.

An alternative to exploring lexical variation by starting with word referents is to take an etymological approach. Although English itself is an amalgam of 'original' English words and of loanwords from a whole host of languages, many loanwords (particularly those derived from French, Latin and Greek) have been part of the language for so long that they are no longer considered to be 'foreign'. Therefore, returning to the British/American examples above, the *lift/elevator* pair are both considered to be English words, even though *elevator* is derived from Latin. *Faucet*, a word of French origin, probably seems 'foreign' to most British speakers but (with the meaning of 'a tap on a barrel') was once in standard use in England (hence its exportation to North America) and is still found in some regional British dialects. Speakers, then, develop a sense of what they perceive to be 'English' words and what they perceive to be 'foreign' words. As it has spread throughout the world, English has continued to absorb words from other languages with which it has had contact, particularly when those words relate to the life and culture of the region. We have already seen some borrowings from Aboriginal Dharuk into Australian English. The OED lists thousands of other loanwords from a vast array of languages across the globe. Some of these words have acquired widespread usage while others remain relatively local. Either way, these loanwords are gradually anglicised and accepted by speakers as 'English' words. Compare these two quotations from Indian publications which hint at this process:

| 1986 | from *Stardust* magazine, published in Bombay | 'It's true that Namrata like all other *bahus* is having a slight problem with her in-laws (and I can understand why).' |
| 2004 | from the *Times of India* newspaper | 'Some Indian homes—despite the modern facade they display—are strongly rooted in tradition. And mothers-in-law could always be influenced by the subservient bahus shown in every second television serial.' |

The Hindi word *bahu* is defined as 'a daughter-in-law, especially one who follows the tradition of living with her husband's family after marriage' so you can see it has a meaning distinct from *daughter-in-law* itself. In the 1986 example, the fact that '*bahus*' has been written in italics suggests an awareness by the writer that he or she is using a word that is 'foreign' to English. By comparison, the lack of italics in the 2004 example suggests that the word has now become fully assimilated into Standard Indian English.

The adoption of loanwords into English is one of the strategies by which new words find their way into global varieties. This leads us to a brief consideration of the morphology of lexical variants. Loanwords abound in English, most typically in their adopted form, or an anglicised version of that form. However, loanwords can also make up part of a **hybrid compound**, or can have an English affix (as in Indian English *box-wallah* and *babudom* respectively). In pidgin and creole varieties, which have a smaller range of morphemes than Standard English, compounding is often used to fill **lexical gaps**. In Tok Pisin, for example, 'toe' is *finga bilong fut* ('finger belong foot') and 'knee' is *nildaun* ('kneel down'). Multi-word verbs can vary quite considerably across dialects, either through a reduction of the multi-word verb to a simple verb (or an expansion in the other direction), or because the base verb combines with a different element. So, for instance, a British English speaker will *fill in* a form, while an American English speaker will *fill* theirs *out*. Specific word formation strategies (see Chapter 3) are particularly popular in some varieties, such as the fondness for clipping and/or affixing with *-o* (*journo*) or *-ie* (*truckie*) in Australia and New Zealand. We also noted in Chapter 3 that conversion is a highly productive strategy for new word creation and you will often find examples of this taking place in one dialect but not another. American English speakers, for example, use *gift*, *author* and *room* as verbs as well as nouns but their British counterparts currently use them only as nouns.

Lexical variation can also be approached by exploring variation in meaning. Needless to say, semantic differences can sometimes lead to confusion, as many travellers can attest. Most typically, a word form will have a different meaning in another dialect, although it can also have additional meanings. Here are some examples:

	word class	British English	other variety
school	noun	place of education for under-18s	American English: place of education for under-18s and a university
robot	noun	a machine with human abilities	South African English: a traffic light or signal
send	verb	to dispatch something or someone without going yourself	Singapore English: to accompany something or someone on its/their way (*send someone home*)

			Jamaican English:
carry	verb	to move or transport while holding	to take or escort (*carry someone home*)
			Welsh English:
tidy	adjective	neat	pleasing, attractive
			American English:
homely	adjective	domestic, simple	not very attractive

Differences in meanings or semantic coverage are particularly noticeable in creole varieties, which generally have a smaller lexicon than most other varieties, so one creole lexeme may be the semantic equivalent of more than one Standard English lexeme. In Tok Pisin, for instance, *tok* is equivalent to Standard English *talk* and *say*.

A final way to approach lexical variation is to consider usage. This can vary according to register, with a word being formal in one variety and informal in another. For example, *autumn* is in general use in British English but more poetic use in American English (where *fall* is the general word). In Tok Pisin, *bagarup* ('bugger up') is in general use for 'accident' or 'destroy', but has an informal, mildly offensive use as a verb in Standard British English. Frequency of use is another aspect to consider, since some speakers favour certain lexical items over other possible choices: for instance, Jamaican English speakers prefer *bawl* to British English *shout*. Variation in idioms and collocations often show a marked difference across dialects:

British English	*wait at tables*
American English	*wait tables*
British English	*turn on the light*
Philippine English	*open the light*
British English	*go to bed!*
Scottish English	*away to your bed!*

Interestingly, collocations and idioms become far more visible when two dialects are compared, and provide one of the key indicators as to whether a speaker of English as a foreign language sounds 'natural' in terms of the dialect they are speaking or writing.

☐ **morphemes** ⇨ 3.2
☐ **synonyms** ⇨ 3.9
☐ **register** ⇨ 8.11

12.5   GRAMMATICAL VARIATION: INFLECTIONS

As described in Section 4.1, grammar concerns two linguistic aspects: inflections and syntax. Inflections are the word endings which denote qualities such as singular and plural, or past and present tense, although we also included suppletion (the process by which a word changes its form to denote a different grammatical function) in our discussion of inflections. English has relatively few inflections. They occur on all the lexical word classes (nouns, verb, adjectives, adverbs). Pronouns are also inflected, but mainly through the process of suppletion.

Count nouns can be inflected to show plurality, and both count and non-count nouns can be inflected for possession. Variation can occur across dialects of English with regard to whether a noun has count or non-count status (in Indian English, for example, both *litter* and *furniture* can take plural inflections). In non-standard dialects plural nouns sometimes have a zero inflection when quantities are being denoted:

That cost me five pound

Very occasionally a noun will have a different plural form as in the irregular plural *een* for *eyes* and *sheen* for *shoes* found in the Lowland Scots dialect.

In Standard English verbs are inflected for third person singular present tense, the simple past tense, the *-ing* participle and the *-ed* participle. Many dialects regularise the present tense by omitting the *-s* inflection on the third person singular, or (less commonly) by adding it to all persons.

	Standard English	non-standard English	non-standard English
singular	*I walk*	*I walk*	*I walks*
	you walk	*you walk*	*you walks*
	he/she walks	*he/she walk*	*he/she walks*
plural	*we/you/they walk*	*we/you/they walk*	*we/you/they walks*

In England, the paradigm without the *-s* inflection is a particular feature of the East Anglia dialect while the paradigm with *-s* throughout is found in south-west England, although it is another traditional feature which is slowly dying out.

The formation of the past tense and the *-ed* participle varies mainly in relation to irregular verbs, which often use suppletion, and where various patterns occur in non-standard dialects, with a trend towards a reduction in the number of forms used:

		present tense	past tense	-ed participle
SEE	standard	*I see*	*I saw*	*I have seen*
	non-standard	*I see*	*I seen*	*I have seen*
COME	standard	*I come*	*I came*	*I have come*
	non-standard	*I come*	*I come*	*I have come*

Patterns like these reduce up to three verb forms to two, or even one. They are found in various parts of England and Northern Ireland. The examples above retain irregular forms in the process of reduction, but some irregular verbs show regularisation in the past tense and –*ed* participle, as in these examples:

		present tense	past tense	-ed participle
KNEEL	British English	*I kneel*	*I knelt*	*I have knelt*
	American English	*I kneel*	*I kneeled*	*I have kneeled*
CATCH	British English	*I catch*	*I caught*	*I have caught*
	Welsh English	*I catch*	*I catched*	*I catched*

Occasionally, different forms are to be found in the past tense, making a regular verb irregular, as in American English *dove* for *dived*, but it is far more common for irregular verbs to be affected by variation. The verb *be* is the most irregular verb in Standard English with three forms in the present tense (*am*, *are*, *is*) and two in the past tense (*was*, *were*), and it shows various patterns of regularisation in other dialects. For example, the West Midlands dialect of England uses only *be* in the present tense and *was* in the past tense, the latter also being a feature of the London dialect.

One of the features of natural language is a tendency towards redundancy. In other words, information may be marked on more than one element in a sentence. For instance, in the sentence *She walks her two dogs every day* third person singular is denoted by both the *she* pronoun and the inflected verb *walks*, while the plurality of *dogs* is also denoted by the numeral *two*. The information could be conveyed as accurately by *She walk her two dog every day*. In some instances, variation in the forms and uses of inflections has the effect of reducing redundancy, and this is particularly so in pidgins and creoles which barely use inflections at all.

In these varieties, then, there are normally no inflections on lexical words, although there are strategies available for avoiding confusion. In Jamaican Creole, for instance -*dem* can be used to show plurality:

di daag	the dog or the dogs
di daagdem	the dogs

With regard to the absence of a possessive inflection, possession is again inferred from context and the order of elements, so *di bwai niem* is *the boy's name*. Tense is usually deduced from context, but again there are ways to clarify meaning:

im waak	*he/she walks* or *walked*
im bin waak	*he/she walked*

As you can see, the addition of the element *bin* (*been*) is used to eliminate ambiguity.

In Standard English, related adjectives and adverbs of manner are usually distinct in form, as in *quick/quickly, slow/slowly*, whereas in non-standard dialects they typically take the same form:

Martin made a <u>quick</u> supper	standard or non-standard adjective
Martin made supper <u>quickly</u>	standard adverb
Martin made supper <u>quick</u>	non-standard adverb

This can also apply to irregular forms:

He did a <u>good</u> essay	standard or non-standard adjective
He did it <u>well</u>	standard adverb
He did/done it <u>good</u>	non-standard adverb

In some non-standard dialects, *more* is used with the comparative form, even when it already has the *-er* inflection, as in *She's <u>more</u> tall<u>er</u> than me*.

As we saw in Section 2.8 standard personal pronouns show person, number, grammatical function and, in the third person singular, gender. One of the marked features of Standard English (in comparison to other related languages) is that there is no longer any distinction in the second person between singular and plural. Many non-standard dialects do, however, make this distinction. Here are some examples:

	singular	plural
Standard English	*you*	*you*
Liverpool	*you*	*yous*
Glasgow	*youse*	*yese/yis*
Irish English	*you/youse*	*yiz*
Northern USA	*you*	*you-all/y'all*
Southern USA	*you*	*youse*
Barbadian English	*yu*	*wuhnuh*
Trinidadian English	*yu*	*all-you*
Tok Pisin	*yu*	*yupela*

Conversely, *thou/thee* remain as the singular pronoun in traditional English dialects in northern counties like Lancashire and County Durham. Traditional dialects of England also show other variants. For instance, in the West Midlands, *her* is used in both subjective and objective positions. Creoles show the most reduced pronoun systems. For example, Jamaican Creole uses *im* for both male and female in subjective and objective third person:

	subjective/ male	subjective/ female	objective/ male	objective/ female
Standard English	*he*	*she*	*him*	*her*
Jamaican Creole	*im*	*im*	*im*	*im*

It is interesting to note, though, that while creole varieties have fewer forms, they also make distinctions that Standard English lacks, not only in having singular and plural second person forms but sometimes also distinguishing between inclusive and exclusive *we*.

☐ **pronoun system** ⇨ 2.8
☐ **noun inflections** ⇨ 4.3
☐ **verb inflections** ⇨ 4.4
☐ **adverb inflections** ⇨ 4.5
☐ **pronoun inflections** ⇨ 4.6

12.6 GRAMMATICAL VARIATION: PHRASE STRUCTURE

Grammatical variation within phrases is most likely to occur in noun and verb phrases, because they typically contain more elements. In noun phrases, determiners and relative pronouns are particularly affected. For instance, the presence or absence of the definite article is one way in which the use of determiners may vary. With regard to relative pronouns, relative clauses in Standard English are introduced with *who* or *which*, or *that*:

The woman who helped me	or	*The woman that helped me*
The job which I applied for	or	*The job that I applied for*

In the London dialect, *what* is also used (*The woman what helped me*, *The job what I applied for*) while in Welsh English, *as* can be used as a relative pronoun (*The woman as helped me*).

Variation in verb phrases relates particularly to the way tenses and aspects are used and constructed. The relationship between the present tense and the present progressive aspect will be used here as an illustration of this. In terms of construction, creole varieties or varieties with a creole history often omit auxiliary verbs, as in this example of the present progressive aspect from Ebonics, a Black English dialect of the USA:

Standard English	*We are coming*
Ebonics	*We comin'*

Alternatively, the auxiliary may be retained but take a different form as this West African example shows:

Standard English:	*Mary is/was eating*
West African English:	*Mary de it ('Mary DO eat')*

In general, though, construction differs less than usage. In all dialects, there are constant, if subtle, shifts in the uses to which tenses and aspects are put. English is distinct from many other related languages in expressing current states and actions either through the simple present tense (*I go*) or the present progressive aspect (*I am going*). In French, for example, *je vais* is the equivalent of both these constructions. In Standard British English, the present tense is most typically used to express a current state or fact, or an habitual action:

I love your new car	current state
The earth orbits the sun	current fact
They visit the park every day	habitual action

A recent trend in Standard British English is towards using the progressive aspect to express current states, a feature possibly influenced by American usage:

'*Sergio Henao…is loving life in 2012 as a member of Team Sky*'
(from the Team Sky Pro Cycling website, posted 20 April 2012)

In Indian English (and other Asian dialects), the present progressive is the normal choice, a feature which is also found in Welsh English for the habitual present:

Mohan is needing a holiday	current state
Mohan is having two sons	current fact
Harry is visiting Cardiff every week	habitual action

Similarly, Indian English shows a preference for using the present progressive in contexts where Standard British English would use the perfect aspect. This and other variations illustrate how tense and aspect systems can differ quite considerably across some dialects of English.

Modal auxiliary verbs also vary in use across global dialects, where some modals are preferred above others. In Standard American English, for example, *shall* and *should* are rare, while *may* and *shall* are rare in Scottish English. In Irish and Scottish English, *will* is preferred over *shall* in first person interrogatives:

> English English   *Shall I cook the dinner?*
> Irish/Scottish English   *Will I cook the dinner?*

In some dialects (for example, in the north-east of England and the deep south of America) double modals are not uncommon, provided the second modal is *can* or *could*:

> *A fast worker would could do it by tonight*
> *If the weather's good, we might could arrive on time*

More subtle differences relate to the meaning of modal auxiliaries. For instance, *the machine mustn't be turned on* would be interpreted by a Standard English speaker as 'the machine needs to stay switched off' while a Tynesider would interpret it as meaning 'the machine has not yet been switched on'.

> ☐ **modal auxiliaries** ⇨ 2.10
> ☐ **noun phrase structure** ⇨ 5.2
> ☐ **verb phrase structure** ⇨ 5.3

12.7 GRAMMATICAL VARIATION: CLAUSES AND SENTENCES

Two of the most salient types of variation in clauses and sentences are the construction of negatives and questions. With regard to negation, multiple negation is common in many non-standard dialects. This is the process by which negation is marked on more than one element in a sentence:

	subject	verb	object	adverbial
standard	I	*don't like*	*any salt*	*on my chips*
non-standard	I	*don't like*	*no salt*	*on my chips*

In the non-standard example above, negation is marked on the object element as well as on the verb. It is also possible to apply multiple negation without making the verb negative:

standard	*He was left with<u>out</u> any choice*
standard	*He was left with <u>no</u> choice*
non-standard	*He was left with<u>out</u> <u>no</u> choice*

These three examples are grammatically affirmative but contain negation in the prepositional phrase. The first has a preposition with a negative meaning, while the second uses the negative determiner *no*. In the non-standard example, negative meaning is conveyed through both the preposition and the determiner.

In colloquial Standard English, where negation is only marked on the verb element, contraction usually occurs to avoid formality:

formal style	*I have not taken the dog for a walk*
colloquial style	*I haven't taken the dog for a walk*
colloquial style	*I've not taken the dog for a walk*

In the south of England, the tendency is to contract the auxiliary and the negative particle (*haven't*), whereas in the north it is more common to contract the subject and the auxiliary (*I've not*). The contraction *ain't* is commonly used in non-standard dialects in Britain (particularly in the London region) and the USA:

standard	non-standard
am not	*I ain't well today, I ain't going out today*
is not, are not	*Mick / Mick and Richard ain't happy / ain't training today*
has not, have not	*Dexter / the kids ain't been to school today*

The above examples show how *ain't* can be used for the lexical verb *be*, for the auxiliary verbs *be* and *have*, and for both singular and plural. Some non-standard dialects use *no* rather than *not* as the negative particle:

They canna come
Ah'm no comin'

These two examples are from Glaswegian English, with the spelling adapted (as it often is) to suggest the pronunciation.

In the formation of questions, some speakers show a preference for using rising intonation rather than inversion to indicate the question function, although of course this option is available in all varieties. In some dialects, such as Jamaican English and Indian English, there is no inversion in *wh-* questions:

> *Where you have been today?*
> *Why they are complaining?*

In Indian English, however, inversion does occur when the question is an embedded clause:

| Standard British English | *They asked her where she is living* |
| Indian English | *They asked her where is she living* |

In Standard English, question tags show a correspondence with the declarative clause to which they are attached:

> *They've been to France, haven't they?*

Here, the tag corresponds with the declarative in terms of the auxiliary and plural third person, as well as being negative while the initial clause is affirmative. In many varieties, a universal tag – *is it?* or *isn't it?* – is used:

> *They've been to France, is it?*

This can be found in Asian varieties and some creole-based varieties as well as in Welsh English.

☐ **negation** ⇨ 6.15
☐ **question formation** ⇨ 7.4

12.8   VARIATION IN DISCOURSE

We have already seen how lexical variation across dialects reveals something of the lifestyle, culture and values of the speakers of those dialects. When we move to the level of discourse, the notion of language as a reflection of culture comes more fully into play but in a very different way. Whereas lexical items most typically provide information about specific local features, variation in discourse reflects the communicative practices of a particular social group as played out through language use. A great deal of research has been done across different languages into what is termed the **ethnography of communication** and it has revealed significant variation in both written and spoken language.

Such variation can also be identified across dialects of English, particularly because of the use of English by so many different social and ethnic groups worldwide. In terms of spoken interaction, for example, speakers may have different expectations about turn-taking, how to conduct a telephone conversation, how to relay information, which topics are most acceptable in certain contexts, and the extent to which taboo language is offensive. In written language, there are often cultural differences relating to style and structure, for example a preference for a notably rhetorical style over a less ornate one.

We saw at the start of this chapter that many speakers of English are bilingual, and use English in their daily lives alongside another primary language. This often leads to the phenomenon of code-switching, where speakers move between their two languages, not just from interaction to interaction, but even within turns in a conversation. Code-switching can also occur within the same language if a speaker switches between two different dialects. There are various reasons why code-switching occurs. It can be related to the need for formality or informality, or to establish identity or solidarity. Code-switching can also help speakers express themselves more effectively, for example by selecting a language for the concept it expresses or because what they are talking about seems more closely related to that language.

The above is all part of the much bigger picture of studying discourse variation in English. More specific in terms of features is the way in which speakers use conversational discourse markers and there is considerable variation across dialects and regions. For instance, the affirmative adverb (*yes* in Standard English) has several variants, such as *sure* in American English (now finding its way into British English), *aye* in parts of northern England and in Scotland, and *I will* in Irish English. Boundary markers also vary, such as the use of *no* at the start of an utterance in South African English, or *lah* at the end of an utterance in Malaysian and Singaporean English. Speakers also show different preferences for fillers and monitoring devices. Welsh English speakers, for example, use *mind*, *look you* and *see* as monitoring devices at the completion of utterances. In London and elsewhere in England *innit* is commonly used as a monitoring device while the filler *like* has become very widespread, particularly among younger speakers.

☐ **discourse markers** ⇨ 8.10

12.9 PHONOLOGICAL VARIATION: CONSONANTS

So far we have explored aspects of variation which could occur in either spoken or written language, although in practice they are more likely to occur in speech. We now move on to look at phonological variation to see how the pronunciation and the prosodic features of English can vary from region to region and from speaker to speaker. We have already seen that a standard dialect of English could be spoken with, in theory, any accent, whereas regional forms of English usually have a specific accent associated with them.

Of the 44 phonemes of RP described in Chapter 9, some are more prone to variation than others, and vowels are more susceptible to variation than consonants, as might be expected by the difference in the manner of articulation, with mouth shape and tongue position being the means of articulation rather than some specific obstruction to the airflow. When speakers of English from different parts of the world encounter each other, it is their accents rather than their dialects which are more likely to cause comprehension difficulties. Accent features are sometimes predictable, sometimes not. For example, you can predict whether someone is likely to pronounce the <r> at the end of *butter*, but you could not predict the fact that *vase* is pronounced /vɑːz/ in RP and /veɪz/ in the General American accent. In this section we will concentrate on the most salient features which characterise accents rather than the random variations which also inevitably occur.

Of the six plosive consonants in RP, the voiceless phonemes are more susceptible to allophonic variation, with the alveolar plosive /t/ having the most variants. In the UK, in accents such as London, Glaswegian and Yorkshire, /t/ is often realised as a **glottal stop** [ʔ], a plosive sound which is made at the glottis rather than in the mouth. So *butter*, for example, might be pronounced [bʌʔə]. However, the glottal stop only occurs **postvocalically** (after a vowel) and so never replaces [t] word-initially. Although the glottal stop has often been stigmatised as 'lazy' or 'uneducated' speech, in certain contexts, it can also be heard in the prestigious RP accent when /t/ occurs before a syllable-initial consonant, as in *hat·stand* /hæʔ·stænd/. (The dot in this example represents a syllable boundary.) A variant of /t/ also occurs as one of the most distinctive features of the General American accent, where intervocalically /t/ is often voiced as a flapped 'd' sound [d̯] where only the tip of the tongue strikes the alveolar ridge as the tongue moves back to its resting position, a process known as ***t*-flapping**. Comparably, a distinctive feature of the Liverpool accent is the realisation of intervocalic /t/ as a flapped 'r' [ɾ]. Word-initially /t/ is constant apart from the possible variation in aspiration across accents (which can also occur in other positions and may also affect the voiceless plosives /p, k/). In Indian English and other South Asian varieties, both /t/ and its voiced counterpart /d/ tend to be **retroflex** [ʈ , ɖ] with the tip of the tongue curled up and back as it makes contact with the alveolar ridge.

We saw in Section 9.6 that the dental fricatives /θ/ and /ð/ are among the less common fricatives found in languages in general, so it is perhaps not surprising that among the fricative consonants in English, these are the most variable. In the Estuary English accent (which encompasses London and much of the south-east of England, continuing to spread further and further afield) some speakers will realise these sounds as [f] and [v] respectively (a process known as **th-fronting**), while in accents with a creole history speakers are likely to realise them as [t] and [d], a variant which is also found in Irish English and Indian English, usually with heavy aspiration. The process by which fricatives are realised as plosives is known as **stopping**. Here are some examples of /θ, ð/ variants:

	RP	Estuary English	British Black English	Irish English	Indian English
think	[θɪŋk]	[fɪŋk]	[tɪŋk]	[tʰɪŋk]	[tʰɪŋk]
that	[ðæt]	[ðæt]	[dæt]	[d̪ʰæt]	[d̪ʰæt]
brother	[brʌðə]	[brʌvə]	[brʌda]	[brʌd̪ə]	[brʌd̪ə]

In Estuary English, /θ/ can be [f] in any position, but /ð/ can only be [v] word-medially or word-finally. In Irish English, /t, d/ are usually dental plosives [t̪, d̪], with the tongue touching the upper teeth rather than the alveolar ridge.

The relatively marginal fricative /h/ is often dropped word-initially in various accents in England and parts of Wales, although it is a feature particularly associated with London English and the traditional Cockney accent where it is absent at the start of words such as *hat* and *house*. Like the use of the glottal stop, **h-dropping** is often frowned upon, despite being a widespread non-standard characteristic.

The nasals /m, n/ show very little variation but the more marginal velar nasal /ŋ/ is sometimes realised as [n] when it occurs in the -*ing* suffix, so *singing and dancing* could be pronounced [sɪŋɪn ən dɑnsɪn], where the pronunciation of /ŋ/ changes in the suffix, but not in the stem of *singing*. This feature can be found particularly in regional and social accents in the UK and in the USA. In England, speakers from the West Midlands and parts of Lancashire and Yorkshire will pronounce /ŋ/ as [ŋg], so singing becomes [sɪŋgɪŋg].

Of the four approximant sounds in English, /r/ has many variants, probably the most of all the consonants. There are two aspects to consider in relation to /r/, the first being how it is pronounced, and the second being whether it is pronounced at all in certain positions. With regard to allophonic variations of /r/, in RP and most English accents, as well as in Australian and New Zealand English, the tip of the tongue may be slightly raised, but far more so in General American, Canadian, and in some Irish and Scottish accents, where the /r/ is retroflex. This distinction may be represented by [ɹ] for the RP allophone and [ɻ] for its more retroflex counterpart. Other allophones of /r/

include the variant found in Indian English where /r/ is realised as an alveolar flap [ɾ] while in traditional accents of Scotland you might hear a trilled /r/ [r].

Of most significance as far as /r/ is concerned is whether an accent is **rhotic** or **non-rhotic**. All accents of English articulate /r/ word-initially and before or between vowels, but not all accents have /r/ after vowels when they occur at the end of a word or before another consonant (**non-prevocalic r**). Here are some examples, using RP and General American as the illustrative accents and a broad transcription to show the difference between them:

	RP	General American
red	/red/	/red/
bread	/bred/	/bred/
carry	/kæri/	/kæri/
board	/bɔːd/	/bɔːrd/
user	/juːzə/	/juːzᵊr/

As you can see, all the instances of /r/ pronounced in the rhotic General American accent are present in the spelling of the word. In the General American pronunciation of *user* the superscript ᵊ before the /-r/ indicates that the schwa vowel has very little prominence in this context, unlike in the RP pronunciation where it is slightly longer. **Rhoticity** is probably the most salient difference between accents of English, both in the UK and throughout the world. In the UK it is likely to be found in south-west England, as well as in parts of Scotland and Northern Ireland. The Geordie accent of north-east England has a residual quality of the rhotic /r/ in words such as *poor* [puə] and *here* [hiə] where the final vowel position moves towards the mouth shape of /r/. Elsewhere, rhotic /r/ is found in Ireland, and in much of the USA and Canada as well as parts of the Caribbean such as Barbados and Jamaica. Some Asian speakers also have a rhotic accent, particularly in the Philippines.

The approximant /l/, as we saw in Section 9.3, has two allophones in RP, with clear *l* occurring at the beginning of a syllable, dark *l* at the end. In other accents, /l/ is generally clear in both positions (Welsh English) or some degree darker (in other words, even more palatalised), as in Scottish English and also Australian English. In the London accent, and particularly in Cockney, final /l/ or /l/ preceding a consonant is often realised as a vowel (sometimes with a degree of lip rounding), so *meal* is [miʊʷ] and *milk* is [mɪʊk].

One final aspect of consonant variation is what can occur when two consonants combine in a cluster. Because the basic phonological template of syllables seems to favour CV or CVC structures, it is perhaps not surprising that in certain contexts, clusters of two (or possibly more) consonants are likely to be reduced, especially in the syllable coda. This happens as a natural part of connected speech (as we saw in Section 10.6), so all speakers reduce consonant clusters at times, and it would sound unnatural if they did not. For example, *fish and chips* is likely to be pronounced /fɪʃ ən ʧɪps/ rather than /fɪʃ ənd ʧɪps/, partly because *and* is an unstressed element, and partly because a sequence of /n, d, ʧ/ forms an awkward cluster of three consonants. However, there are some accents of English which reduce consonant clusters on a regular and system- atic basis, the most noticeable being the accents of speakers of pidgin and creole varieties, or the post-creole dialects derived from them. So, for a creole speaker, clusters are often reduced word-finally (for example /bes/ for *best* and /graʊn/ for ground), but word-initial clusters with /s-/ are also subject to reduc- tion to give *story* as /tari/ and *strong* as /traŋ/, a reduction which is reflected in the written form. Syllable-final reduction of consonants can also be found in other accents, such as in Glaswegian and in second language accents of Asia such as Malaysian English. A less common but alternative strategy to cluster reduction is to split the cluster by introducing an **epenthetic vowel**, so *skin* would become [səkɪn], a feature which is also found in some creole as well as in some Asian accents, and in Irish English [fɪləm] *film*, [wɑrəm] *warm*, and [ɑrəm] *arm*.

Consonant clusters which contain the approximant /j/ before /u/ are also subject to variation as this selection of examples shows:

	RP	Estuary English	General American	East Anglia
news	[njuːz]	[nuːz]	[nuːz]	[nuːz]
tune	[tjuːn]	[tuːn]/ [ʧuːn]	[tuːn]	[tuːn]
few	[fjuː]	[fjuː]	[fjuː]	[fuː]
music	[mjuːzɪk]	[mjuːzɪk]/[muːzɪk]	[mjuːzɪk]	[muːzɪk]

RP speakers will always pronounce the /j/ (often referred to as **yod**) in the above examples, while speakers of traditional East Anglian accents never will. General American speakers pronounce /j/ in some contexts, as do Estuary speakers. Sometimes an Estuary speaker will replace the C+/j/ combination with an affricate, causing /t/ + /j/ to become [ʧ] (as seen in [ʧuːn]) and /d/ + /j/ to become [ʤ], a process known as **yod coalescence**. The absence of /j/ in non-standard accents when it is present in the related standard is known as **yod-dropping**.

□ **RP consonants** ⇨ 9.6
□ **history of /ŋ/** ⇨ 10.2
□ **consonant clusters** ⇨ 10.4
□ **distribution of yod** ⇨ 10.4

12.10 PHONOLOGICAL VARIATION: VOWELS

Mapping vowel variation is a somewhat different task from mapping consonant variation given the more fluid relationship of one vowel to another and the way in which vowels result from a combination of features, chiefly tongue position, lip shape, and length. Despite this fluidity, it is possible to establish which vowels make up the vowel inventory of a particular accent and to identify allophonic variants of those vowel phonemes. We have already seen that RP has an inventory of 20 vowels, of which 12 are monophthongs and 8 are diphthongs. Other accents have fewer vowels than this, or have the same number but a different selection. For instance, the Newcastle accent (like several northern English accents) has no /ʌ/, nor does it have /ɜ/, but it does have /a/, which is a low front unrounded vowel. General American has a 15 vowel system, while Scottish English has 12. Accents with a creole or second language history are likely to have fewer than this. Complications in describing vowel variation arise not as a result of the different number or range of vowels in the inventory, but in their distribution.

Of the monophthong vowels of RP, as already mentioned, the short vowel /ʌ/ is absent from some northern accents in England and replaced by [ʊ], so *shut* and *tuck* are pronounced [ʃʊt] and [tʊk] respectively, with *tuck* becoming a homophone of *took*. In Welsh English, /ʌ/ is often realised as a schwa, so RP [bʌtə] will be [bətə]. In a variety of accents, the long vowel /ɑː/ is often realised as [æ], depending on the environment in which it occurs. In General American and in northern England, [æ] occurs before particular consonants or consonant clusters:

		RP	General American/ Northern England	Australian English
before /f, s, θ/	*laugh*	[lɑːf]	[læf]	[lɑːf]
	grass	[grɑːs]	[græs]	[grɑːs]
	path	[pɑːθ]	[pæθ]	[pɑːθ]
before /-n/+C	*grant*	[grɑːnt]	[grænt]	[grænt]

The above examples also show Australian speakers are likely to realise /ɑː/ as [æ] in some contexts. Other accents, such as Welsh English and Northern Irish English also show a tendency to reduce /ɑː/. We noted in Section 9.7 that there are five pairs of short/long vowels in RP, so in the above examples we can see that relationship at work, with the longer vowel often being reduced in the direction of the shorter one.

The short and long pair /ɒ/ and /ɔː/ show variation in several accents. In General American, for instance, /ɒ/ is absent so *cot* is pronounced with [ɑ], the unrounded counterpart of RP /ɒ/. However, this correspondence is not entirely consistent. In the first syllable of *coffee*, for example, the vowel could be [ɑ] or [ɔ]. Equally, the vowel in *caught* may be realised as [ɑ]:

	RP	GenAm
cot	[kɒt]	[kɑt]
coffee	[kɒfi]	[kɑfi] or [kɔfi]
caught	[kɔːt]	[kɔt] or [kɑt]

The last example above shows how General American *caught* might sound similar to RP *caught*, or may be a homophone of *cot*. Australian English and South African English realise the RP /ɒ, ɔː/ pair as [ɔ, o] while Welsh English and Scottish English realise both phonemes as [ɔ], in contrast to Irish English which has a [ɑ, ɑː] pair.

There is a comparable interplay between the short/long pair of /ɪ/ and /iː/. For example, a conservative RP speaker will have the short vowel at the end of *city*, whereas speakers of mainstream RP or Estuary English will have the longer vowel [i]. A similar pattern is noticeable in South African English in closed vowels where *bit* and *bin* will be [bit] and [bin] respectively. The short vowel /ɪ/ can occur in both stressed and unstressed syllables, but Australian and New Zealand speakers are likely to use schwa in unstressed syllables, so *damage* will be [dæməʤ] rather than [dæmɪʤ] and *carpet* [kɑːpət] rather than [kɑːpɪt].

Despite the degree of potential vowel variation, in many instances you could be forgiven for thinking that certain words have identical pronunciations across different accents. However, there may be additional subtle differences of articulation which will distinguish one accent from another. For instance, General American and Australian English speakers tend to have the tongue slightly closer to the roof of the mouth than speakers of mainstream RP, giving their vowels a different quality. Diphthongs also vary considerably across accents of English, and many accents have fewer in their inventory than RP. When comparing accents, four possible differences may occur. First, both accents may retain a diphthong, but there will be two variants: for instance, *take* is [teɪk] in RP but [tæɪk] for some speakers of Estuary English, particularly those with a strong Cockney influence. Sometimes a diphthong in one accent will have a monophthong elsewhere, so RP pair [pɛə] is a single vowel in Australian English [peː], Welsh English [pɛː] and Liverpudlian [pɜː]. By contrast, a diphthong may be articulated as two syllables as in the Welsh English pronunciation of *beer* as [bi·ə]. Less commonly, a vowel which is typically a monophthong is diphthongised. Some New Yorkers, for instance, will say [gɜɪl] for *girl* (RP [gɜːl]). Rhoticity can also affect the quality of a vowel, so *dear* is [dɪə] in non-rhotic RP but [dɪr] in rhotic General American.

☐ **RP vowels** ⇨ 9.7

12.11 PHONOLOGICAL VARIATION: PROSODIC FEATURES

In terms of prosodics, all speakers vary to some extent in terms of voice quality, and the tempo and volume of their speech. Having said that, some accents are particularly associated with a certain voice quality, the effect of the way the vocal tract is configured during speech. Conservative RP speakers, for instance, often seem to have a more 'tense' quality than speakers of mainstream RP. Liverpudlian speakers are particularly distinctive, their voice quality produced essentially by a tightening of the pharynx which draws the larynx into a higher position, although tongue position also plays its part. In addition, intonation preferences can also characterise an accent, most notably in speakers who favour rising intonation even when not asking a question, a central characteristic of Australian speech.

English accents in general can be divided between those which are stress-timed and those which are syllable-timed. As explained in Section 11.3, English is essentially a stress-timed language, in which the stressed syllables occur at roughly equal intervals. However, several varieties of English are more syllable-timed, with most syllables being of roughly equal duration and prominence. These varieties are used by ESL speakers whose first language is syllable-timed or by speakers of creole varieties which were originally influenced by syllable-timed languages. This means that the unstressed vowel schwa [ə] is largely absent in these accents. Instead, the vowel in this position has more prominence than in stress-timed accents of English. Syllable-timed accents of English include Caribbean creoles, African-American and Black African varieties, and are also a feature of speakers from the Indian subcontinent and the Far East.

☐ **rhythm** ⇨ 11.3
☐ **prosodic features** ⇨ 11.7

12.12 AN EXAMPLE

The status and history of London as a capital city and a commercial centre means it has a strong relationship with Standard English and the RP accent. However, London is a very good example of a geographical location where, as well as its own distinctive variety, a vast array of other English accents and dialects can be found due to the migrant backgrounds of many of its inhabitants. The speaker in the example below is Sterling Betancourt, who came to live in London from Trinidad in 1951. Betancourt is a musician who specialises in steelpan music. In this extract, he is talking to fellow musician Jools Holland, who is interviewing him for a BBC television documentary about the music of the capital.

Key

(.)	micropause
where are they going	underlining indicates passages of higher pitch and more varied intonation
dey, dere, dat	pronunciations of *they, there, that* with /ð/ realised as [d̪]
takin'	*-in'* indicates *-ing* participle ending realised as [-ɪn]

> *we (.) tried to give them a surprise cos we didn't paint the drums (.)*
> *we had it all rustic and rusty like (.) garbage (.) as as (.) a surprise you*
> *know so when the people saw us (.) takin'* [tekɪn] *out these (.) rusty*
> *oil drums they were laughing (.) they were saying* <u>where are dey goin'</u>
> 5 <u>with these (.) dustbins</u> [dʌsbɪnz] *they call us dustbin boys (.) but when*
> *(.) we finished played our first tune (.) everybody was applauded and*
> *you know was such a surprise they even say it was black* [blak] *magic*
> [madʒɪk] *be(.)cause they couldn't understand (.) how you can get music*
> *from these old rusty drums...*

> later *...in Archer Street (.) every Monday dey used to have a big crowd of*
> *musician dere (.) anybody wants to get a musician for a job you you*
> *go dere on a Monday (.) afternoon and the place is crowded you know*
> *people used to (.) say* <u>what's happ'nin' dere with all this crowd</u> *but*
> *dey seen the people with the notebook the musician and say listen*
> 15 *I'm lookin' for a trumpeter I want a bass guitar and everybody's goin'*
> *around* [araʊn] *but now dat don't happen*

Although Betancourt has lived in London for many years, his speech exhibits clear characteristics of his linguistic roots in Trinidad, where both Standard Trinidadian and Trinidadian Creole are significant varieties. With regard to consonantal variation, the interdental fricative /ð/ varies from its RP pronunciation by being stopped to a dental [d̪], a salient feature of West Indian speakers. Interestingly, this happens more frequently in the second part of the extract (as well as in the passages of direct speech) and suggests that as Betancourt becomes more relaxed in the interview, he is less concerned to use standard British pronunciation. Betancourt often realises the *-ing* participle ending as [-in] but this is as much a feature of Trinidadian English as London English. There is a degree of consonant cluster reduction, for example in *dustbins* [dʌsbɪnz] and *around* [araʊn] which again is a distinctive West Indian feature but of course also likely to occur in connected speech. Vowel differences in

Betancourt's accent are probably stronger indicators of his country of origin, for instance *taking* is pronounced [tekɪn] (as opposed to [teɪkɪn]), reducing the diphthong to a monophthong, while the /æ/ in *black* and *magic* is realised as [a] rather than [æ].

The prosodic features of Betancourt's speech also reveal his Trinidadian background. Typical of many West Indian speakers, there is a considerable degree of variation in pitch and intonation (most noticeable when he is imitating other speakers). As mentioned in Section 12.11, certain varieties of English, including Trinidadian English, are syllable-timed rather than stress-timed, and this extract shows traces of this in the pronunciation of some of the trisyllabic words:

		RP	Sterling Betancourt
line 8	*understand*	[ʌndəstænd]	[ʌndastænd]
line 11	*musician*	[mjuzɪʃən]	[mjuzɪʃɜn]
line 13	*happening*	[hæpənɪn]	[hap·nɪn]

In all three examples above, schwa is absent. In the first two examples, the vowel has a greater value in terms of length, which suggests the speaker is gravitating towards syllable-timing. This may also be reflected in the reduction of *happening* to two stressed syllables. Although this pronunciation would not be uncommon across a range of speakers, there is a clear break between the two syllables in Betancourt's pronunciation.

The grammar also displays some non-standard features, particularly in relation to verb forms:

line	Sterling Betancourt's dialect	Standard English
5	they <u>call</u> us dustbin boys	they <u>called</u> us dustbin boys
7	they even <u>say</u>	they even <u>said</u>
14	dey <u>seen</u> the people	they <u>saw</u> the people
16	dat <u>don't</u> happen	that <u>doesn't</u> happen
5–6	when we finished <u>played</u>	when we finished <u>playing</u>
6	everybody was <u>applauded</u>	everybody was <u>applauding</u>
10–11	a big crowd of <u>musician</u>	a big crowd of <u>musicians</u>
7	was such a surprise	<u>it</u> was such a surprise
11	anybody wants	<u>if</u> anybody wants

Betancourt shows a preference for present tense or base verb forms, with *call* (line 5) rather than *called* and *say* (line 7) rather than *said*, a common feature of West Indian creoles. The use of *seen* (line 14) rather than *saw* may reflect the preference for fewer verb forms in creole varieties, although this is also a feature of the London dialect, as is the regularisation of *doesn't* (*does not*) in line 16 to *don't* (*do not*). The use of the *-ed* participle is also of interest in line 6. It is hard to know how to analyse we *finished played* our first tune since in the broadcast it doesn't sound as if *played* is a self-correction. The construction may be analogous to we *done played*, the use of *done* to construct the perfect aspect being a common West Indian creole feature. Similarly, *everybody was applauded* is open to interpretation. It could of course mean *the musicians were applauded*, but it is less likely that the speaker would adopt the passive voice, and in the context it is more likely the story would focus on the audience who were so sceptical about the 'dustbins' as musical instruments. If *everybody was applauded* is equivalent to Standard English *everybody was applauding* then this is probably a noteworthy feature of Trinidadian grammar. There is some cross-over in West Indian dialects between active and passive meaning which could support this interpretation. Ideally, when there is uncertainty about how to analyse a specific feature, linguists consult the speakers themselves, but of course this is not always possible, as in this case.

With regard to noun forms, the noun *musician* in line 11 probably reflects West Indian creole usage in having a zero inflection on a plural noun. Interestingly, plural inflections are used elsewhere (in *dustbins, boys, drums*). *Notebook* could possibly be understood as a plural noun, but it is hard to be certain from the context. Finally, there is some evidence of the ellipsis of grammatical words in *Ø was such a surprise* and *Ø anybody wants*, again a characteristic of a dialect with a creole ancestry.

From this extract, it is possible to infer that, over the years, this speaker may well have been influenced by the London dialect, although the evidence is not conclusive. In addition, the alternation between standard and non-standard features (the pronunciation of <th> and the use of plural noun inflections) may be due in part to the purpose of the interview, which will be broadcast on national television. (The extent to which a speaker typically uses standard or non-standard features could of course be quantified by a comparison of more formal and less formal examples.) Overall, however, it is reasonable to conclude that Trinidadian features are the most salient aspect of Betancourt's speech, reflecting his sense of personal identity, particularly in relation to the story he tells in this extract.

☐ **creole varieties** ➪ 12.1
☐ **variation in inflections** ➪ 12.5
☐ **consonant variation** ➪ 12.9
☐ **vowel variation** ➪ 12.10
☐ **syllable-timed varieties** ➪ 12.11

BROADER PERSPECTIVES: EXERCISES

Exercise 1: Lexical variation in Australian English

The Macquarie Dictionary (www.macquariedictionary.com.au) describes itself as 'Australia's national dictionary online'. The dictionary is also linked with an online interactive project, the Australian Word Map, to record regional (and largely informal) Australian vocabulary. The following examples are all drawn from the Australian Word Map at http://www.abc.net.au/wordmap/ (accessed May 2012).

For each example below, identify the word class, formation strategy and/or etymology, the meaning(s) and the range of usage, as well as any variations in spelling. (The first example has been done for you.) The comments of the contributors to the Word Map will help you, although you may like to broaden the scope of your research. Through exploring this site, you may wish to add or research further examples of your own.

> *bluey*
> *chilax*
> *deadly treadly*
> *donga*
> *emu parade*
> *kylie*
> *lah*
> *sanga*
> *kindie*

word class	formation strategy and/or etymology	meaning(s)	usage
bluey			
noun	Suffixation of -*y* to the base, a strategy often found in Australian English. Meanings often have an association with the colour blue.	1 *a summons (on blue paper) issued for a parking offence* 2 *a type of jacket or coat* 3 *a bluebottle (type of fly)* 4 *a friend* 5 *a blue cattle dog* 6 *a bushman's bundle (typically wrapped in a blue blanket)*	Seems to be mainly used in the south-east of Australia and in Tasmania. Definitions 1, 2, 5 and 6 appear in the OED, suggesting usage may be more widespread.

Exercise 2: Variation in Standard Indian English grammar and discourse

The following extract was taken from the education section of the website of the Indian government, the National Portal of India, in June 2012.

1. Identify the grammatical differences between this extract and Standard British English.
2. Overall, how does this extract compare in terms of formality to British usage on a similar public information website?

Student's Corner

The most crucial, yet memorable days of one's life need the right kind of support and guidance to lead to a successful career and an enriching life. Though studies form a major part of a student's life, it will be unwise to be indifferent to numerous other potentials and talents that lie dormant in each of us. This section attempts to bring together elements to allow all round development of student life, exploring the limitless possibilities of extra-curricular stimulation, while giving due importance to academic pursuits.

This corner is exclusively designed for students (...) right from the primary education to the level higher secondary education. It also provides a list of **universities and institutions** spread across the country offering variety of courses including distance education streams to choose from. Sections such as **career guidance, scholarships and awards, professional courses, study abroad, etc.** will help students in numerous ways to pursue their career further. Now one need not visit pillar to post to know about their Exam Results, instead, one can view the detailed marksheets sitting in the comfort of their homes by visiting the section '**Results on the Net**'. Moreover, information on **Libraries, National Book Trust, National Bal Bhavan, NCC, Employment News** can also be browsed.

Exercise 3: Yod-dropping in American English

In RP, the following examples all contain the same segmental sequence of a consonant followed by /-juː/. However, in American English /j/ is sometimes absent from the sequence.

1. Using a dictionary which shows both British and American pronunciations or your own experience to help you, work out where in American English yod-dropping is likely to occur.
2. What do the affected preceding consonants have in common?

> *abuse, accuse, amuse, assume, beauty, cute, dew, duplex, ensue, few, fuse, huge, humour, music, news, nuisance, pew, puma, stew, tune, view, Zeus*

BROADER PERSPECTIVES: SUGGESTIONS FOR FURTHER READING

Language textbooks

Crystal, David (2003) *English as a Global Language*, 2nd edn (Cambridge: Cambridge University Press)
A highly readable account of how English became a global language which also provides a valuable assessment of the dangers and benefits associated with global linguistic status.

Hughes, Arthur, Peter Trudgill and Dominic Watt (2012) *English Accents and Dialects*, 5th edn (London: Hodder)
A clear and wide-ranging survey of social and regional varieties of English in the British Isles, with illustrative recordings which can be downloaded from the publisher's website. Written partly with foreign learners of English in mind.

Jenkins, Jennifer (2009) *World Englishes: A Resource Book for Students*, 2nd edn (Abingdon: Routledge)
A wide-ranging introduction to the subject of global variation, full of helpful examples and readings on the debates surrounding English as a world language. The book is also supported by an excellent website.

Kachru, Braj, Yamuna Kachru and Cecil L. Nelson (eds.) (2009) *The Handbook of World Englishes* (Chichester: Wiley-Blackwell)
Like its counterpart edited by Andy Kirkpatrick (below), this is a varied collection of essays on all key aspects of global English including a lot of historical background on the spread of English throughout the planet.

Kirkpatrick, Andy (ed.) (2012) *The Routledge Handbook of World Englishes* (Abingdon: Routledge)
An extremely expensive book to buy but a valuable one to access through libraries. Contains a wide collection of contributions on the linguistic features of global varieties as well as on their uses. It also explores some of the debates about the role of English in the world.

Melchers, Gunnel and Philip Shaw (2011) *World Englishes*, 2nd edn (London: Hodder)
Explores English in relation to Kachru's three circles of the inner, outer and expanding circles of English, so plenty of attention is given to historical and socio-political contexts.

Schneider, Edgar W. (2010) *English Around the World: An Introduction* (Cambridge: Cambridge University Press)
A lively and accessible introduction to the subject, with plenty of historical and geographical material as well as a range of examples for consideration. Also has a sociolinguistic perspective.

Trudgill, Peter and Jean Hannah (2008) *International English: A Guide to the Varieties of Standard English*, 5th edn (London: Hodder Education)
A comparative guide to the standard accents and dialects of global English, including an exploration of what is meant by 'Standard English'. The text is supported by a website from which audio files of examples can be downloaded.

Reference books

McArthur, Tom (2002) *The Oxford Guide to World English* (Oxford: Oxford University Press)
An authoritative reference book which surveys English continent by continent, indicating characteristic features of many global English varieties, and also discusses in some detail the historical and sociological aspects of the use of English worldwide.

Wells, John C. (2008) *Longman Pronunciation Dictionary*, 3rd edn (Harlow: Pearson Longman)
A really useful guide to English pronunciation in that it contains both British and American standard pronunciations, as well as frequently used non-RP variants. Contains over 225,000 examples, as well as guidance on stress and intonation.

Internet resources

http://accent.gmu.edu/
This is the Speech Accent Archive based at George Mason University. It enables users to listen to a wide variety of both ENL and ESL speakers reading the same paragraph, so is ideal for comparing accents. Phonetic transcriptions of the recordings are also provided.

www.bbc.co.uk/voices
As well as being an excellent site for exploring dialect variation, this site contains a wide variety of recordings of regional accents from different parts of the British Isles.

www.collectbritain.co.uk/collections/dialects
This British Library audio collection contains over 650 examples from around Britain of accents and dialects recorded between 1950 and the present day.

www.phon.ox.ac.uk/files/apps/IViE/
A University of Oxford site, which houses a collection of downloadable recordings of urban accents in the British Isles. The materials are useful for studying an individual accent or for comparative purposes.

Phonetic and Other Symbols

THE CONSONANTS AND VOWELS OF RECEIVED PRONUNCIATION

Consonants		Vowels			
		Monophthongs		**Diphthongs**	
/b/	bead	/æ/	bat	/aɪ/	buy
/d/	deed	/ɑ/	bard	/aʊ/	bough
/ʤ/	jet	/e/	bet	/eɪ/	bay
/f/	feed	/ɜ/	bird	/ɛə/	bear
/g/	get	/ə/	about	/əʊ/	beau
/h/	heed	/i/	bead	/ɪə/	beer
/j/	yet	/ɪ/	bit	/ɔɪ/	boy
/k/	keep	/ɒ/	bomb	/ʊə/	tour
/l/	let	/ɔ/	board		
/m/	met	/u/	food		
/n/	net	/ʊ/	book		
/ŋ/	ring	/ʌ/	but		
/p/	pet				
/r/	reed				
/s/	seed				
/ʃ/	shape				
/t/	tape				
/ʧ/	cheat				
/θ/	thin				
/ð/	then				
/v/	vet				
/w/	win				
/ʒ/	measure				
/z/	zone				

OTHER USEFUL SYMBOLS

Brackets

/ /   slant brackets are used for phoneme symbols and for broad transcriptions

[ ]   square brackets are used for narrow transcriptions (and for phrases)

< >   angled brackets are used for letters

Other consonant and vowel symbols

[ʔ]   a glottal stop, as might occur in *butter* where it replaces [t] (*bu'er*)

/ x /   a voiceless velar fricative, such as a Scots speakers might use at the end of *loch*

[l]   clear *l*

[ɫ]   dark *l*

/ o /   the vowel sound in the French *beau*

[r]   trilled *r*

[ɹ]   the *r* of RP

[ɻ]   retroflex *r*

[ɾ]   flapped *r*

[ʈ , ɖ]   retroflex *t* and *d*

Diacritics

~   above a vowel symbol indicates nasalisation, e.g. in [restərɔ̃n(t)] *restaurant*

ː   after a vowel symbol indicates that the vowel is long, e.g. in [kaː] *car*

ᵊ   superscript ᵊ shows that schwa has reduced prominence, e.g. in General American [juːzᵊr] *user*

ˌ   below a consonant symbol indicates a syllabic consonant, e.g. in [bʌtn̩] *button*

ʰ   superscript and after a consonant indicates that the consonant is aspirated, e.g. in [kʰʌp] *cup*

ⁿ   below a consonant symbol indicates the consonant is dental, e.g. in the Irish pronunciation of *that* [d̪ʰæt] [d] is pronounced with the tongue touching the upper front teeth rather than the alveolar ridge

⌒ below a consonant symbol indicates that the consonant is flapped, e.g. in the General American pronunciation of *water* [wɔd̯ᵊr] where the tip of the tongue briefly strikes the alveolar ridge

•   a dot can be used to indicate a syllable boundary as in *hat·stand* or /hæt·stænd/

Word stress

*a*ˈ*muse*   a superscript vertical line indicates that the following syllable is stressed

ˌ*contra*ˈ*dict*   a subscript vertical line indicates that the following syllable has secondary stress (in contrast to the primary stress of the other stressed syllable here)

Tones

-   a level tone

`   a falling tone

ʹ   a rising tone

ˆ   a rise-fall tone

ˇ   a fall-rise tone

Transcription symbols

(.)   micropause

(2.0)   pause measured in seconds

//   //   overlapping speech

=   latching on

some.   unfinished word (*something*)

Miscellaneous symbols

*   before an example indicates that the example would not normally occur in English

?   before an example indicates that the example might occur but it may not be accepted by all speakers

Ø   indicates ellipsis (the omission of a retrievable or understood item) or an empty position

C   before a vowel symbol indicates that it is a cardinal vowel

Answers to Exercises

LEXICAL FRAMEWORKS

Exercise 1: Lexemes

Identify the lexemes and group them into word classes using their dictionary citation form.

nouns	*Amsterdam, Schiphol Airport, step, terminal, sign, ceiling, way, arrival, hall, exit, transfer, desk*
verbs	*disembark, strike, hang, announce*
adverbs	*only*
pronouns	*I, that*
determiners	*a, few, the*
auxiliaries	*am*
prepositions	*on, at, inside, by, from, to*
conjunctions	*and*

The primary auxiliary *am*, although not a base form, is given in this form in dictionaries as it is an irregular part of the verb *be*.

Exercise 2: Homonymy and polysemy

Decide whether the two identical words are connected through homonymy or polysemy.

1	*high*	polysemy
2	*list*	homonymy
3	*beam*	debatable
4	*skip*	polysemy
5	*perch*	homonymy

When words are homonymous, they typically have different etymologies. In Example 3, both meanings of *beam* derive from the Old English *bēam* ('a tree'), from which 3a is an extended meaning, and 3b a figurative one. However, although The Oxford English Dictionary treats these two items as polysemous, The Longman Dictionary of Contemporary English gives them separate entries, effectively treating them as homonyms.

Exercise 3: Word classes

Identify which word classes each of the following word-forms can belong to:

well	noun, verb, adjective, adverb, interjection
slow	verb, adjective, (adverb – although *slowly* is more standard)
blast	noun, verb, interjection
better	noun, verb, adjective, adverb
whatever	pronoun, determiner, interjection
fast	noun, verb, adjective, adverb
if	noun, conjunction
round	noun, verb, adjective, adverb, preposition
rash	noun, adjective
will	noun, (lexical) verb, (modal) auxiliary verb

Exercise 4: Morphemes

Break the complex words down into morphemes, using an etymological dictionary if necessary.

percentage	per - cent - age
percolate	per - col - ate
periscope	peri - scope
permafrost	perma -frost
percher	perch - er
personal	person - al
Persian	Persi(a) - an
pernicious	per - nic - ious
perky	perk - y
perilous	peril - ous

Exercise 5: Latin roots

The groups of words share the same Latin root. Identify the root, and work out the primary meaning of the root.

1   root <vers> from Latin *vertere*, 'to turn'
2   root <fer>, from Latin *ferre*, 'to carry' or 'to bring'
3   root < duc(t)>, from Latin *ducere*, 'to lead'
4   root <ambul>, from Latin *ambulare*, 'to walk' or 'to go about'
5   root <cur(r)>, from Latin *currere*, 'to run'

Exercise 6: Word formation strategies

Identify the word class of the neologisms and the word formation strategies used to form them.

people-ready	a compound adjective
microbuffer(s)	a noun formed through affixation of the prefix *micro-* to the noun *buffer*
Rooneyesque	an adjective formed through affixation of the suffix *-esque* to the proper noun *Rooney*
volcanicity	a noun formed by affixation of the suffix *-ity* to the adjective *volcanic*
diplo language	debatable: either a noun formed by affixation, or a compound noun, depending whether you treat *diplo* as a new prefix or as a clipped noun, the latter being more likely
hairapy	a noun formed by blending *hair* with *therapy*, the effect being derived from the partial phonological similarity between *hair* and the first syllable of *therapy*
retweet	a noun or verb formed by adding the prefix *re-* to the base *tweet*
tweetheart	a compound noun formed from the nouns *tweet* and *heart*, and analogous both in structure and phonologically with the associated noun *sweetheart*
Merkozy	a blend of the proper nouns *Merkel* and *Sarkozy* (the <k> overlapping the two names) to form a proper noun
Arab Spring	a compound noun formed from an adjective and noun (probably analogous to the *Prague Spring* of 1968)

GRAMMATICAL FRAMEWORKS

Exercise 1: Noun plurals

(1)   Complete the table relating to irregular plurals:

Singular noun	Irregular plural	Type of plural	Can regular plural be used?
cactus	*cacti*	Latin plural	yes – *cactuses*
corona	*coronae*	Latin plural	yes – *coronas*
bacterium	*bacteria*	Latin plural	no – in fact the plural is used far more than the singular
goose	*geese*	vowel mutation	no – although a child might say *gooses*
criterion	*criteria*	Greek plural	no – speakers sometimes mistake the plural for a singular noun
syllabus	*syllabi*	Latin plural	yes – *syllabuses*
curriculum	*curricula*	Latin plural	yes – *curriculums* – although it sounds awkward
stigma	*stigmata*	Greek plural	yes – although *stigmas* is rare
louse	*lice*	vowel mutation	no – although, again, a child might say *louses*
appendix	*appendices*	Latin plural	yes – *appendixes*
kibbutz	*kibbutzim*	modern Hebrew plural	yes – *kibbutzes*

In some instances, speakers don't know the irregular plural forms. If they do, they might avoid them in contexts, particularly informal speech, where it might sound pretentious to use the irregular plural. Often the irregular plurals have a more specialised use than their regular counterparts. For instance, *stigmata* is used in a religious context to refer to Christ's wounds when crucified. Children often use regular plurals as they are unaware of irregular forms, and adults may adopt them in order to imitate children's language, or for humorous purposes.

(2)   The noun plurals are: *pleats* (regular), *legs* (regular), *jeans* (plural only – regular, but see following comment), *pairs* (regular). The use of *trouser* as a singular noun is unusual. (See the discussion of *trousers* in Section 4.3.) This is a specialised use of the noun, to talk about the item of clothing

genencally. In a fashion context, singular forms such as *trouser, jean* and *knicker* are often used.

Exercise 2: Irregular verb forms

Work out the *-ed* past tense form and the *-ed* participle form of the given bases. Group the verbs according to their patterns of irregularity.

An obvious categorisation is as follows:

Pattern	Base form	Past tense form	*-ed* participle form
• regular past tense	sew	sewed	sewn
• irregular *-ed* participle	swell	swelled	swollen
• irregular past tense and *-ed* participle	keep	kept	kept
• past tense and *-ed* participle the same	send	sent	sent
	teach	taught	taught
• irregular past tense and *-ed* participle	blow	blew	blown
• past tense and *-ed* participle different	go	went	gone
	take	took	taken
• all three forms the same	cut	cut	cut
	hit	hit	hit
	shut	shut	shut

In fact, linguists have divided irregular verbs into seven categories. You can find out more about these in Sidney Greenbaum's *The Oxford English Grammar*, Section 4.18.

Exercise 3: Phrase structures

From the conversational extract, identify the type of each underlined phrase, identify any pre- or postmodification in the phrase, and comment on the complexity of these phrases in this spoken extract.

Noun phrases

Most of the noun phrases are simply pronouns: [*that*] x 2, [*I*] x 7, [*it*] x 8, [*you*] x 3, [*nothing*] x 2, [*they*] x 3. The way these pronouns are used reflect the informality of the passage: for example, the use of *you* to mean 'someone', and the way *they* is used towards the end without specifying that the characters in *Lost* are being referred to. Of the other NPs, three of them are simple: [*the story*], [*next week*], [*the boy*]. [*The last episode*] is also simple, but contains both a central and postdeterminer. The only complex NP, which contains a considerable amount of embedding, is at the end and may be analysed thus (with *nfcl* standing for **non-finite clause**):

[*four episodes* [*of* [*them* [*trying* [*to get* [*into* [*that hatch thing* NP] PP] nfcl] nfcl] NP] PP] NP]

Adjective phrases

There are only three. Two of these are simple – [*good*] and [*honest*] – and in the third the head word *written* is premodified by the adverb phrase [*very cleverly*].

Prepositional phrases

Apart from the PPs which occur in the complex NP analysed above, the three remaining PPs all have simple NPs as the prepositional complement: [*on* [*E4* NP] PP], [*since* [*the last series* NP] PP], [*on* [*the raft* NP] PP]. Again, the simplicity of the PPs reflects the informal context of everyday speech.

Exercise 4: Verb tenses and aspects

Change the VP in *The students* <u>*protest*</u> *about funding in education* into the tense and/or aspect specified.

> present tense, progressive aspect: *are protesting*
> past tense, perfect aspect: *had protested*
> progressive aspect with modal *could*: *could be protesting*
> past tense, perfect progressive aspect: *had been protesting*
> simple past tense: *protested*

Exercise 5: Verb complementation

Decide if the verbs are intransitive and/or what obligatory complementation they take according to their different meanings.

arrive	intransitive
believe	intransitive; object
cook	intransitive; object
grow	intransitive; object; complement
hand	object (indirect) + object (direct)
make	object; object (indirect) + object (direct); object + object complement

shove	intransitive; object + adverbial
swear	intransitive; object
telephone	intransitive; object
weep	intransitive

Exercise 6: Active and passive clauses

Transform the active clauses into their passive counterparts, maintaining the agent.

1   *The thief was being chased down the road by the police*
2   either: *This beautiful wedding cake was made for Sara and Mick by Jo*
      or: *?Sara and Mick were made this beautiful wedding cake by Jo*
3   *The house has been tidied by William ready for their return*
4   *I'm told by Amy and Rebecca (that) you like cycling*
5   either: *Visitors have been being entertained here by the elephants for many years now*
      or: *Visitors have been being entertained here for many years now by the elephants*

Exercise 7: Clause structures

Identify the clause structure, as well as any embedded elements. The embedded elements have been underlined.

1   *Bradley Wiggins* (S) *has won* (V) *the most prestigious race <u>in cycling</u>* (O)
2   *Are* (V_{op}) *you* (S) *feeling* (V) *better* (C) *today* (A)
3   *I* (S) *think* (V) <u>*they've arrived by now*</u> (O)
4   *The pyramids <u>of Egypt</u>* (S) *are* (V) *much bigger <u>than I imagined</u>* (C)
5   *The woman <u>who lives next door</u>* (S) *showed* (V) *me* (O_i)
      her new computer (O_d)

(In Example 3, a clause is embedded as object. In the other examples, the embedded elements all postmodify head nouns, apart from in the complement in Example 4 where an adjective is head of the postmodified phrase.)

Exercise 8: Sentence types and structures

1   exclamative; simple
2   declarative; compound-complex

3 imperative; compound
4 interrogative; complex
5 declarative; simple
6 imperative; simple
7 exclamative; complex
8 declarative; simple
9 interrogative; compound
10 interrogative; simple

DISCOURSE FRAMEWORKS

Exercise 1: Cohesive devices

Identify the cohesive devices in the conversational extract between Daniel and Kate.

- Much of the cohesion is achieved through lexical and phrasal repetition. The participants repeat themselves (e.g. *tattoos*, *all the blueprints*, *his brother out*) as well as each other (e.g. *story*, *together*, *prison*, *brother*, *clever*).
- There are several interwoven semantic fields: crime and punishment (*death row*, *crime*, *commit*, *prison*); planning an escape (*get out*, *escape*, *plan of the prison*, *planned*, *layout of the prison*, *blueprints*); tattoos (*body*, *tattoos*, *needles and ink*).
- There is a considerable use of anaphoric reference using third person pronouns (*his*, *he*, *himself*) to refer to the man who is planning the escape (who presumably has been identified prior to the start of this extract) but in turn 3 the first use of *he* (*for a crime he didn't commit*) has the *brother* as its antecedent. This can be inferred from the semantic context. In turn 4 *they* refers to the man and his brother. In turns 8 and 9 *that* and *it* refer to the man having the tattoos done, and in turn 18 *this* refers to everything Daniel has told Kate about the plot of the programmme.

Exercise 2: Structure in spontaneous conversation

Are there identifiable conversational structures? Is the argument essentially orderly?

- Although there is quite a lot of overlapping speech, most of the turns are completed. Incomplete utterances occur at turns 4, 6, 12, 13, 14 and 16.

- Whether turns are complete or not, adjacency pairs (often with follow-up responses) are clearly identifiable, for example in turns 1 and 2 (accusation and denial pair) and in turns 20 (*you're so horrible I hate you*) and 21 (*I hate you too*) (statement and response pair). Very frequently, the turns begin with a brief follow-up (e.g. *yeah, exactly, whatever*) before initiating a new first pair part. Several of the turns begin with *yeah but* which functions both as a follow-up turn and as the start of an initiating utterance.

PHONOLOGICAL FRAMEWORKS

Exercise 1: Describing consonants and vowels

Write descriptions for the sounds represented by the given symbols.

/θ/	voiceless (inter-)dental fricative
/g/	voiced velar plosive
/ŋ/	velar nasal
/dʒ/	voiced palato-alveolar affricate
/j/	palatal approximant
/v/	voiced labio-dental fricative
/ɜː/	half-open central unrounded monophthong
/e/	half-close front unrounded monophthong
/uː/	close back rounded monophthong
/ɒ/	open back unrounded monophthong

Exercise 2: Making phonetic transcriptions

Transcribe the words using the phonetic alphabet to show the RP pronunciation.

strength	/streŋθ/
youth	/juːθ/
justice	/dʒʌstɪs/
probability	/prɒbəbɪləti/
vocation	/vəʊkeɪʃən/
pleasure	/pleʒə/
choice	/tʃɔɪs/
praise	/preɪz/
judgement	/dʒʌdʒmənt/
sexism	/seksɪzəm/ or /seksɪzm̩/

Exercise 3: Syllable structures

Using the phonetic alphabet, work out the syllable structure of the given words.

syllable							
onset (*optional*)			rhyme				
			peak	coda (*optional*)			
consonant(s)			vowel	consonant(s)			
pre-initial consonant	initial consonant	post-initial consonant	V	pre-final consonant	final consonant	post-final consonant	(post-final) consonant
s	p		e	n	d		
s	k	r	æ		tʃ		
	k	l	ɑː	s	p		
	k	w	ɪ	l	t	s	
	t	j	uː		b	z	

Exercise 4: Stress patterns

(1)   Mark the primary stress as well as any secondary stress on the following disyllabic and polysyllabic words.

a│roma   ˌaroˈmatic
ˈdifferent   ˌdiffeˈrential
enˈvelop   ˈenvelope
iˈmagine   iˌmagiˈnation
ˈportrait   porˈtrayal
suˈppose   ˌsuppoˈsition

(2)   Show the stress patterns in the word-forms according to word class.

noun: ˈinsult   verb: inˈsult
noun: ˈcontract   verb: conˈtract
noun: ˈdictate   verb: dicˈtate
noun: ˈentrance   verb: enˈtrance
noun: ˈescort   verb: esˈcort
adjective: ˈfrequent   verb: freˈquent

There is a clear pattern here, with the first syllable stressed in the nouns and adjective, and the second syllable stressed in the verbs.

BROADER PERSPECTIVES

Exercise 1: Lexical variation in Australian English

Identify the word class, and research the origin, meaning and usage of the given words.

(In the comments below, the Australian Word Map and the Oxford English Dictionary were accessed online in May 2012.)

word class	formation strategy and/or etymology	meaning(s)	usage
bluey			
noun	Suffixation of -*y* to the base, a strategy often found in Australian English. Meanings often have an association with the colour blue.	1 *a summons (on blue paper) issued for a parking offence* 2 *a type of jacket or coat* 3 *a bluebottle (type of fly)* 4 *a friend* 5 *a blue cattle dog* 6 *a bushman's bundle (typically wrapped in a blue blanket)*	Seems to be mainly used in the south-east of Australia and in Tasmania. Definitions 1, 2, 5 and 6 appear in the OED, suggesting usage may be more widespread.
chilax			
verb	Blend of the verbs *chill (out)* and *relax*. It may have its origins in a 2003 television talk show.	*(a more emphatic version of the verbs which form this blend)*	Seems mainly used in the Melbourne area.
deadly treadly (treddly)			
noun	Reduplication based on *treadly* (a bicycle), which is derived from the verb *treadle*.	*a bicycle, particularly a fast or unsafe one*	Fairly widely used.
donga			
noun	The word seems to have its origins in South Africa and/or New Guinea. Meaning 3 may have given rise to the idea of a *donga* as some kind of accommodation.	1 *the outback* 2 *open ground* 3 *a gully (where people could rest)* 4 *portable accommodation*	Meanings 1 and 2 are used in south Australia and in New South Wales. The last definition seems to be more widely used. Meaning 3 is recorded in the OED and may be more generally known.

emu parade			
noun	Compound of noun + noun. There is a metaphorical connection with the emu bird, which is indigenous to Australia.	*an organised collection of items left on the ground, for example by school children collecting litter or police officers searching for clues*	Fairly widely used although less common in the west of Australia. There are some varia-tions, such as *emu bob* and *emu walk*.
kylie (kylee, kiley, koilee)			
noun	A borrowing from the Aboriginal language Nyungar.	*a boomerang-like object made of tin and used for catching fish*	Found in south-west Australia around Perth.
lah			
interjection	A discourse marker which has migrated to Australia from Singaporean English.	*(used at the end of an utterance or comment for emphasis or to express the speaker's attitude)*	Found in the Perth area where a lot of Singaporean students attend university.
sanga			
noun	A clipping, analogous to British English *sarnie*.	*(an informal version of)* *sandwich*	Fairly widely used.
kindie (kindy)			
noun	The base is clipped from the noun *kindergarten* and then the *-ie* suffix has been added (as in *bluey* above).	*(an informal version of)* *kindergarten*	Fairly widely used.

Exercise 2: Variation in Standard Indian grammar and discourse

1. Identify the grammatical differences between this extract and Standard British English.

There are several significant variants. The use of determiners differs in relation to both the definite and indefinite articles:

> Indian English
> *from the primary education*
> *offering variety of courses*

> British English
> *from primary education*
> *offering a variety of courses*

Singular and plural forms also vary. The Indian extract states that *stud<u>ies</u> form a major part of a student's life* whereas British English is more likely to say *study/ studying forms*... Similarly, *potential* takes a plural form in this extract but is a non-count noun in British English. A different modal auxiliary is selected in *it <u>will</u> be unwise*: a British speaker is more likely to say *it <u>would</u> be unwise*. (On a lexical note, you may also have noticed the expression *visit pillar to post*. In British English, the collocation is <u>*to go from*</u> *pillar to post*.)

2. Overall, how does this extract compare in terms of formality to British usage on a similar public information website?

The passage adopts a more formal register than would be expected of a British counterpart. Most noticeably, the extract uses the pronoun *one* rather than *you* to refer to the reader, increasing the level of formality through the absence of direct address. The use of the passive voice in *information ... can also be browsed* is a formal feature, and seems particularly formal in that *browse* has connotations of everyday online activity. In the first paragraph in particular, lexical choices seem more formal, with a fairly high incidence of words derived from Latin, such as in <u>*numerous*</u> *other* <u>*potentials*</u> *and* <u>*talents*</u> *that lie* <u>*dormant*</u> *and* <u>*exploring*</u> *the* <u>*limitless*</u> <u>*possibilities*</u> *of* <u>*extra-curricular*</u> <u>*stimulation*</u>. Overall, formality is seen as a cultural marker of an educated person and reflects the value placed on education. This is in contrast to the British trend towards informality in public web-based texts.

Exercise 3: Yod-dropping in American English

1. Work out in which words yod-dropping occurs in American English.

assume, dew, duplex, ensue, news, nuisance, stew, tune, Zeus

2. What do the affected preceding consonants have in common?

They are all alveolar consonants: the plosives /t, d/, the nasal /n/ and the fricatives /s, z/.

Glossary

(All entries are nouns, unless stated otherwise)

A

absolute *(adjective)*
The absolute form of an adjective is its unmarked form, without comparative or superlative inflections.

abstract noun
A noun which refers to a concept or thing which has no material existence, e.g. *truth.*

accent
The pronunciation of a language or dialect.

accidental gap
A combination of sounds (such as /stw-/) which could occur but doesn't.

accusative case
In traditional grammar, the object role, which requires a particular inflection.

acronym
A word formed from the first letters of a sequence of words, e.g. *scuba* from *self-contained underwater breathing apparatus.*

active articulator
Any part of the vocal tract used in articulating speech sounds which can change position. The active articulators are the lips, the tongue and the velum.

active verb
A verb phrase whose subject is also the agent of the activity denoted by the verb.

active voice
The voice of a clause whose verb element is active.

adjacency pair
In spoken interaction, a paired sequence of turns which relate to each other, e.g. a question and answer sequence.

adjective
An open class word, usually having a descriptive function within a sentence, but normally identified grammatically by its ability to occur both attributively and predicatively, and in comparative and superlative forms.

adjective phrase (AdjP)
A phrase which has an adjective as its head word.

adjunct
A type of adverb or adverbial element. Adjuncts typically indicate manner, place, time or degree.

adverb
An open class word, but less central than nouns, verbs and adjectives. Adverbs perform a variety of functions: some indicate manner, place, time or degree (adjuncts) while others provide comment on a statement (disjuncts) or link sentences to each other (conjuncts).

adverb of degree
An adverb which indicates extent, e.g. *particularly, too.*

adverb of manner
An adverb which indicates how something is done or occurs, e.g. *carefully.*

adverb of place
An adverb which indicates location or direction, e.g. *abroad* or *backwards.*

adverb of time
An adverb which indicates when something occurred, how long it lasted or how often it happened, e.g. *tonight, forever, nightly.*

adverb phrase (AdvP)
A phrase which has an adverb as its head word.

adverbial clause
A clause which functions as an adverbial element of another, superordinate clause.

adverbial element
The least obligatory element of a clause and one which gives information in a comparable way to an adverb.

affected
The element of a clause (normally a noun phrase referent) on which the verb is performed. In an active clause, the affected is in object position, but in a passive clause it is in subject position.

affirmative clause
A clause whose truth or proposition is not denied, the opposite of a negative clause.

affix
A bound morpheme which is used to form a new word. Affixes can be subdivided into prefixes, infixes and suffixes.

affixation
The process of adding affixes to a base word-initially or word-finally to form a new word.

affricate
A speech sound which is produced with a plosive-fricative sequence. The two affricates in English are /ʧ/ and /ʤ/.

agent
The element of a clause (usually a noun phrase referent) which is carrying out the action of the verb. In an active clause, the agent will be in subject position. In a passive clause, the agent may be indicated with a *by*-phrase.

aggregate noun
A noun which refers to a collection of people (e.g. *police*) or things (e.g. *goods*) and which normally takes the plural form of the verb.

agreement
An alternative term for concord.

airstream
The flow of air through the vocal tract which is used in the production of speech sounds.

allomorph
The surface form which occurs in the realisation of a morpheme.

allophone
The surface form which occurs in the realisation of a phoneme.

alveolar (*adjective*)
Of a consonant, articulated with the tongue against the alveolar ridge.

alveolar ridge
The hard ridge which runs above and inside the upper teeth.

anaphor (*adjective*: **anaphoric**)
A linguistic element which refers back to another item already introduced, e.g. *he* in *Harry knew he was making a mistake.*

***and* coordination**
The joining together of several elements (usually clauses) using the coordinating conjunction *and.*

anglicise (*verb*)
To adapt a word derived from another language to an English form, e.g. *contemptuous* from Latin *contemptuus.*

antecedent
The linguistic element to which an anaphor refers. In the following example, *Harry* is the antecedent of *he: Harry knew he was making a mistake*

anticipatory assimilation
The assimilation of a speech sound to a following one in anticipation of a feature of that sound.

anticipatory *it*
The dummy item *it* when it signals the removal of a subject or object element to a position later in the clause or sentence.

antonym
A word whose meaning is opposite (usually by being at one extreme of a scale) to that of another word with which it might be paired, e.g. *black* is the antonym of *white*.

apposition
The placing of phrases of the same type, and with the same referent, side by side, e.g. the first two noun phrases in *Tony Blair, the Prime Minister, arrived in Geneva this evening.*

approximant
A speech sound which is produced by a partial closure of the vocal tract. The four approximant sounds in English are /w, l, r, j/.

arhythmic (*adjective*)
Without a regular rhythm.

articulator
Any part of the vocal tract which is used in the production of speech sounds.

articulatory phonetics
The branch of phonetics concerned with the production of speech sounds.

aspect
A feature of a verb phrase indicating whether the state or action referred to is complete (perfect aspect) or ongoing (progressive aspect), e.g. *I have read the book* is perfect aspect while *I am reading* is progressive.

aspirate
The speech sound /h/, which is a glottal fricative.

aspiration
The uttering of the aspirate sound /h/, particularly as a feature of a stop consonant preceding a vowel.

assimilation
The adjustment to a surface form of a phoneme which results in that form becoming more similar to another surface form.

attributive (*adjective*)
In a noun phrase, the attributive position is that immediately preceding the head noun (but following any determiners).

auxiliary
A type of verb, but belonging to a closed class and occurring in a verb phrase before the lexical verb. This very small class can be subdivided into modal auxiliaries and primary auxiliaries.

auxiliary verb
An alternative term for an auxiliary.

B

back vowel

A vowel whose articulation includes the raising of the back of the tongue towards the soft palate.

back-formation

A word-formation process in which an affix is removed from an existing word and the resulting word belongs to a different word class, e.g. *television* (noun) gives rise to *televise* (verb).

bare infinitive

The infinitive form of the verb without the particle *to*.

base

A unit to which another morpheme may be added to create a new word, e.g. *origin* is the base of *original* and *original* is the base of *originally*.

base form

The form of a verb without any inflections.

bilabial (*adjective*)

Of a consonant, articulated at the lips.

blend

A word formed through merging part of one word with part of another, e.g. *brunch* is formed from *breakfast* and *lunch*. Blends are also known as portmanteau words.

borrowing

An alternative term for a loanword.

bound morpheme

A morpheme which cannot stand alone and therefore is not a word in its own right.

British Black English

An urban variety of English spoken by British people of West Indian origin.

broad transcription

A phonetic transcription which does not provide detailed information about allophonic realisations.

***by*-phrase**

In a passive clause, a *by*-phrase can be used to indicate the agent of the verb, e.g. *Gill's garden was admired <u>by everyone</u>*.

C

cardinal numeral

A whole number in its counting form, e.g. *one, two, three*.

cardinal vowel

A member of a set of vowels used to map out tongue positions.

case

The role adopted by a noun (or pronoun) according to its clause function and normally indicated by an inflectional ending. Case is more relevant to highly inflected languages than to English.

cataphor (*adjective*: **cataphoric**)

A linguistic item which refers forward to another item not yet mentioned, e.g. *this* in *This is what I want you to do: go to the shops and buy some bananas.*

central adjective

An adjective which can occur in both attributive and predicative position.

central approximant

The approximant /r/, so-called because the air escapes down the centre of the mouth in its articulation.

central determiner

A member of the largest group of determiners, identified according to their inability to co-occur with other central determiners.

central vowel

A vowel whose articulation involves the tongue being flatter than it is for front and back vowels.

centring diphthong

A diphthong which glides towards schwa during its articulation.

citation form

The form of a word which is used for reference purposes or as a dictionary entry.

class-changing (*adjective*)

An affix is class-changing if, when added to a base, it creates a new word of a different class from the base, e.g. adding *-ly* to the adjective *kind* creates the adverb *kindly.*

class-preserving

An affix is class-preserving if, when added to a base, it creates a new word of the same class as the base, e.g. when *-dom* is added to the noun *king* a further noun *kingdom* is formed.

clause

A unit of syntactic structure larger than a phrase and normally containing an overt subject element, a verb element, and any verb complementation.

clear *l*

The allophonic form of the phoneme /l/ produced with the front of the tongue and which occurs before a vowel in RP.

cleft sentence

A restructured sentence consisting of the dummy subject *it,* followed by the verb *be* and then the focus of the sentence followed by a relative clause or a *that*-clause, e.g. *It is Terry who plays jazz piano.*

clipping
A word-formation strategy in which a new word (but of the same class as the original) is formed by shortening an existing one, e.g. *cred* from *credibility*. A word formed in this way is also termed a clipping.

close vowel
A vowel which is produced with a relatively small cavity between the tongue and the palate.

closed class
A class of words which is relatively small and changes very slowly. The closed classes are pronouns, determiners, auxiliaries, prepositions and conjunctions. The words of the closed classes are also known as grammatical words or function words.

closed syllable
A syllable which ends in at least one consonant.

closing diphthong
A diphthong whose finishing position has less distance between the tongue and the palate than its starting position.

closure
The process of blocking off the airstream in the articulation of a consonant sound.

coalescence
An alternative term for coalescent assimilation.

coalescent assimilation
Assimilation in which two speech sounds merge into one.

coda
In syllable structure, any consonant(s) which follows the vowel at the syllable peak.

cohesion
The process whereby a range of linguistic strategies signal that sentences belong together as a text and in a particular sequence.

collective noun
A noun which refers to a group but which can take both singular and plural forms, e.g. *family, herd*.

collocation
A typical or habitual combination of words or lexemes, or the process of combining words in this way, e.g. *rancid* collocates with *butter* but not with *wine*.

combining form
A unit of word-formation which is neither a typical affix nor a typical root or base, e.g. *technophobe* consists of the combining forms *techno-* and *-phobe*.

common case
A term used to refer to any noun, singular or plural, not in the possessive form.

common noun
A noun other than a proper noun, and which in isolation can be preceded by the definite article.

comparative
A form taken by adjectives and adverbs when they are used for purposes of comparison, e.g. *taller, faster.* The comparative inflection is *-er.*

comparative clause
A type of subordinate clause expressing comparison and typically introduced by the subordinators *than* or *as.*

complement element
The element of a clause which follows a copular verb such as *be* or *seem.*

complementary (*adjective*)
Two words whose meanings are mutually exclusive are complementary to each other, e.g. *dead/alive.*

complex preposition
A preposition consisting of two or three words, e.g. *according to, on behalf of.*

complex sentence
A sentence in which at least one of the elements of the superordinate clause is realised by a subordinate clause.

complex tone
A tone which involves at least one rise and at least one fall in pitch.

complex word
A word which is formed of at least two morphemes or, more specifically, through affixation. Complex words may be contrasted with simple words and compound words.

complex-transitive verb
A verb which is followed by both an object and an object complement.

compound sentence
A sentence in which at least two independent clauses are joined by a coordinating conjunction.

compound word
A word constructed from at least two free morphemes, e.g. *sketchpad.*

compound-complex sentence
A sentence which contains coordinated clauses and at least one subordinate clause functioning as a clause element.

compounding
The process of forming compound words.

concessive clause
A subordinate clause which normally begins with *although, though* or *while,* and expresses a qualification of the truth stated in the main clause.

concord
The agreement in singular or plural number which exists between a verb and its subject.

concrete noun
A noun which refers to something measurable or perceptible through the senses.

conditional clause
A subordinate clause which normally begins with *if* (or conjunctions such as *provided, unless*) and expresses a condition.

conditional *wh*-pronoun
A pronoun belonging to the subset of *wh*-pronouns and which is used to introduce a *wh*-conditional clause.

conjugation
A set of verb forms consisting of the 1st, 2nd and 3rd person both singular and plural, and in present or past tense.

conjunct
A type of adverb or adverbial element which performs the function of linking one sentence to another, e.g. *however, nevertheless.*

conjunction
A closed class word with either coordinating or subordinating properties.

connected speech
Speech which consists of strings of words as opposed to words uttered in isolation.

connotation (*adjective:* **connotative**)
The association (positive or negative) of a particular word, e.g. *darkness* could have a positive or negative connotation depending on context.

conservative RP
The variety of Received Pronunciation associated with older royals and the upper classes.

consonant
A speech sound which is produced through a temporary closure (partial or complete) of the vocal tract.

consonant cluster
A sequence of at least two consonants.

content word
Any word which belongs to an open class (in contrast to a function word).

context

The situation in which discourse is composed or received, and which influences both the linguistic choices made and the way meaning is constructed.

continuum

A linguistic scale.

contraction

The form resulting from the shortening of a word as part of the process of being joined to a preceding word, e.g. *n't* from *not,* or the form of the two elements together, e.g. *can't.*

contrastive stress

Stress which is placed on a syllable or word which is greater than the natural stress and serves the purpose of emphasising that syllable or word.

converse (*adjective*)

A converse relationship exists between the meanings of pairs of words such as *lend/borrow* and *learn/teach.*

conversion

A strategy for creating a new word by changing the class of an existing word, e.g. the noun *access* has given rise to the verb *access.*

coordinating conjunction

A conjunction which joins two elements of equal status. The three main coordinating conjunctions are *and, but* and *or.*

coordination

The process of joining linguistic elements of an equal status with a coordinating conjunction.

coordinator

An alternative term for a coordinating conjunction.

copula

A copular verb, particularly the verb *be.*

copular verb

A verb which is followed by a complement element. There are only a few copular verbs, e.g. *be, seem, appear, become.*

co-referential (*adjective*)

Of two linguistic items, denoting the same referent.

correlative (*adjective*)

Of conjunctions, operating in pairs, e.g. *either/or.*

count noun

A noun which can refer to more than one and which therefore has a plural form.

D

dark *l*

The palatalised allophonic form of the phoneme /l/ produced with the back of the tongue and which occurs at the end of a syllable in RP.

declarative (*noun & adjective*)
The sentence type whose order is subject, verb, and then any verb complementation.

definite article
A specific term for the central determiner *the*.

deixis (*adjective:* **deictic**)
The use of a word whose meaning is relative to the speaker or to the context of utterance, e.g. *mine* and *yours, here* and *there, this* and *that*.

demonstrative pronoun
Any of the pronoun set which consists of *this, that, these* and *those*.

denotation (*adjective:* **denotative**)
The meaning or referent of a word (as opposed to any connotation it may possess).

dental (*adjective*)
Of a consonant, articulated with the tip of the tongue touching the teeth, usually the upper front teeth.

deontic modal auxiliary
A modal auxiliary which expresses the degree of obligation in the meaning of the lexical verb, e.g. *I should go*

dependent clause
A clause which cannot stand alone. This is an alternative term for a subordinate clause.

dependent form
The form of possessive pronouns which cannot stand alone but must qualify a following noun, e.g. *my, their*.

derivational morphology
The branch of morphology concerned with the formation of new words, particularly through affixation. Derivational morphology is sometimes used as an alternative term for lexical morphology.

derived word
A word formed through the process of affixation.

descriptive (*adjective*)
A descriptive approach to language study is one which is concerned with open-mindedly describing a language and how it is used (rather than prescribing or judging use).

determiner
A closed class word which occurs only at the beginning of noun phrases and which has a function distinct from that of other noun premodifiers.

deverbal adjective
An adjective derived from a verb by the addition of the suffix *-ed* or *-ing*, e.g. *confused, confusing*. A deverbal adjective is sometimes referred to as a participle.

deverbal noun
A noun derived from a verb by the addition of the suffix *-ing,* e.g. *dancing.* A deverbal noun is sometimes referred to as a participle.

diacritic
A mark used in phonetic transcription to give additional information about the pronunciation of speech sounds.

dialect
The vocabulary and grammar of a language variety, be it regional or non-regional.

diminutive
A suffix which, when added to a base, creates a word denoting a smaller version of the original, e.g. *-ette, -ling.* A word formed in this way may also be termed a diminutive.

diphthong
A vowel sound which is produced by gliding from one vowel position to another.

direct object
The object element which complements a ditransitive verb and is distinct from the indirect object, e.g. *a present* in *Judith promised Matthew a present.*

directive
The typical function of an imperative sentence.

discourse
The largest unit of language construction in that it consists of one sentence or more. Text is an alternative term. Sometimes, discourse is used specifically to refer to conversation.

discourse markers
Lexical items which primarily indicate the relationship of one section of text to another.

disjunct
A type of adverb or adverbial element whose function is to comment on the content of a sentence or to indicate the 'voice' in which it is said, e.g. *fortunately, frankly.*

disyllabic (*adjective*)
Consisting of two syllables.

ditransitive verb
A verb which is followed by both a direct object and an indirect object.

dummy subject
It or *there* in subject position but when they have no co-reference.

dyadic (*adjective*)
A dyadic conversation is one which takes place between two participants.

dynamic modal auxiliary
A modal auxiliary which states a fact (rather than degree of obligation or certainty). Dynamic modal auxiliaries are able to refer to past actions, e.g. *I could ride a bike when I was four.*

dynamic verb
A verb which refers to an action or physical process, as opposed to a stative verb which refers to a state or condition.

E

-*ed* participle
A non-finite verb form which in regular verbs consists of the base plus an *-ed* inflection but which has an equivalent form in irregular verbs, e.g. *summoned, taken.*

egressive pulmonic airstream
An airstream which flows outwards from the lungs.

elision
In connected speech, the omission of one or more speech sounds.

ellipsis
The omission of a phrase or clause element whose existence can be inferred from the semantic and grammatical context.

embedding
The occurrence of one linguistic unit in a dependent position within another unit, e.g. the prepositional phrase *of the journey* is embedded in the noun phrase *the end of the journey.*

end focus
The positioning of the part of a sentence whose content is of most importance at the end of that sentence.

endophoric reference
Anaphoric or cataphoric reference which relates to another linguistic item as opposed to the context of use.

end-shift
The removal of a subject element to the end of its clause or sentence.

epenthetic vowel
A vowel inserted into a word, typically to break up a consonant cluster, as in Irish English 'arum' for *arm.*

epistemic modal auxiliary
A modal auxiliary which expresses the degree of certainty in the meaning of the lexical verb, e.g. *I will go*

eponym
An open class word derived from a proper noun, e.g. *hoover.*

eponymy
The use of a proper noun to refer to an object or action.

Estuary English
The supposedly classless accent which is associated with London and the south-east of England.

ethnography of communication
The study of the ways in which language use varies across different cultures.

etymology (*adjective:* **etymological**)
The historical origin of a word or words, or the study of word origins.

exclamation
The typical function of an exclamative sentence.

exclamative
A sentence form which begins with *what* or *how,* and in which this *wh-*word is attached to a clause element (and fronted if necessary), e.g. *What a lovely day it is.*

existential *there*
The dummy subject *there* when used to state the existence of whatever is referred to by a noun phrase in complement position, e.g. in *There is a raven flying towards us.*

exophoric reference
A reference which relates to the context or situation and not to another linguistic element.

explicit (*adjective*)
Explicit (as opposed to implicit) knowledge about language is conscious, and usually achieved through studying the language.

extraposition
The moving of a linguistic item (normally a subordinate clause in subject position) out of its normal clause position and the placing of it later in the clause or sentence.

F
falling tone
A tone which falls from a higher to a lower pitch.

fall-rise tone
A tone which falls from a higher to a lower pitch and then rises again.

false start
In spoken language, a false start occurs when a speaker abandons a structure in favour of a new one.

field
The subject matter and/or situational use of a text.

final consonant position
In syllable structure, one of the consonant positions following the vowel and which can be filled by the greatest number of singly occurring consonants.

finite clause
A clause in which the verb phrase is marked for tense.

finite verb
A verb or verb phrase which is marked for tense.

first pair part
The first turn in an adjacency pair sequence.

focus
The part of a sentence whose content is of most importance.

follow-up turn
In spoken interaction, an additional third turn which follows an adjacency pair.

form
The shape or structure taken by a linguistic unit.

formal approach
An approach to discourse which focuses on internal structural aspects.

formal register
The register associated with more overtly polite usage, often adopted where there is inequality of status between participants.

fraction
A numeral which refers to a number which is not whole, e.g. *half, three-quarters.*

framework
A systematic structure or model used in the study of language.

free morpheme
A morpheme which can stand alone as a word.

fricative
A speech sound which is produced through friction at the place of articulation.

front vowel
A vowel whose articulation involves the raising of the front of the tongue towards the alveolar ridge and the hard palate.

fronting
The process of moving an element to the beginning of a clause or sentence in order to draw greater attention to it.

full verb
An alternative term for a lexical verb.

function
The role or purpose of a linguistic unit, as distinct from its form.

function word
An alternative term for a closed class word.

functional approach
An approach to discourse which focuses on how external aspects influence language choices and the construction of meaning.

G

generic pronoun
A pronoun which refers to people in general as opposed to a specific person or sex, e.g. *one, they.*

genitive case
In traditional grammar, a particular role and form of a noun (or pronoun) used primarily to show possession. In modern grammar, genitive case is sometimes used to refer to a noun in its possessive form.

genre
The type of a particular text, e.g. letter, news article, voicemail.

glide
A vowel sound which is produced by gliding from one vowel position to another. Glide is an alternative term for a diphthong.

glottal (*adjective*)
Of a consonant, articulated at the vocal cords and the glottis.

glottal stop
A voiceless plosive sound, articulated at the glottis, often as a realisation of /t/.

glottis
The opening between the vocal cords.

gradable (*adjective*)
Adjectives and adverbs are gradable if they can be preceded by intensifiers or take comparative and superlative forms.

grammar
The set of rules in a language which enable a speaker to construct any well-formed sentence in that language. Grammar is subdivided into syntax and inflections.

grammatical word
Any word which belongs to a closed class (in contrast to a lexical word).

group
Usually, an alternative term for a phrase, although some approaches make a distinction between phrase and group.

group genitive
An alternative term for a group possessive.

group possessive
A coordinated or complex noun phrase where the possessive inflection applies to the whole group, not just the noun to which it is attached, as in *Chris and Jonathan's mother*, meaning 'the mother of Chris and Jonathan'.

H

***h*-dropping**
In speech, the omission of /h/ at the start of a word like *hat* or *house*.

half-close vowel
A vowel which is articulated with the tongue a little less close to the palate than it is for a close vowel.

half-open vowel
A vowel which is articulated with the tongue a little less low in the mouth than it is for an open vowel.

hard palate
The roof of the mouth.

head word
The pivotal or only word in a phrase. The class of the head word typically correlates with the phrase type, e.g. the head of an adjective phrase is an adjective.

homograph
A word which takes the same written form as another word, but may have a different pronunciation, e.g. *row* ([raʊ] 'argument', [rəʊ] 'line').

homonym
A word which takes the same word-form as another word but has a different, unrelated meaning, e.g. *rent* ('payment' and 'rip').

homophone
A word which has the same sound as another word but a different meaning and written form, e.g. *dough* and *doe*.

hybrid compound
A compound word formed from two different languages, e.g. *box-wallah*

hypernym
A name for an overarching category, e.g. *fruit* is the hypernym of *apple, pear, banana* etc.

hyponym
A member of a lexical set or category, e.g. *apple* is a hyponym of the lexical set of *fruit*.

I

idiom
An expression or group of words whose meaning is not retrievable from the individual elements in the idiom, e.g. *pay through the nose*.

idiomatic (*adjective*)
Containing lots of idioms. Idiomatic English could more generally refer to the natural language use of a native speaker.

imperative
A sentence form which usually lacks an overt subject and in which the verb takes the base form. An imperative typically functions as a directive, e.g. *Stop!*

implication
The way in which meaning is hinted at rather than stated explicitly.

implicit (*adjective*)
Implicit (as opposed to explicit) knowledge about language is subconscious, and is possessed by all speakers.

indefinite pronoun
A pronoun which typically does not have an identifiable referent and is not therefore functioning as a noun or noun phrase substitute.

independent clause
A clause whose verb element is marked for tense and which can stand alone. This is an alternative term for a main clause.

independent form
The form of possessive pronouns which can stand alone as a noun phrase, e.g. *mine, theirs.*

indicative mood
The normal mood of a verb phrase in English, as opposed to the subjunctive mood.

indirect object
The object element which occurs first after a ditransitive verb and which can be restructured into a prepositional phrase with *to* or *for,* e.g. *Matthew* in *Judith promised Matthew a present.*

inference
The process by which meaning is deduced, especially when the meaning is implicit.

infinitive
The uninflected form of a verb, sometimes preceded by the infinitive particle *to,* e.g. *to go.* This is an alternative term for the base form of a verb.

infinitive particle
The linguistic item *to* when combined with the base or uninflected form of the verb.

infix
An affix which occurs word-medially, although this is not found in English.

inflection
A grammatical word ending which indicates features such as number, possession, person and tense.

inflectional morphology
The branch of morphology concerned with grammatical word endings or inflections.

informal register
The register employed for relaxed, often colloquial usage.

-*ing* participle
A non-finite verb form which consists of the base plus the inflection -*ing*.

ingressive pulmonic airstream
An airstream which is drawn inwards to the lungs.

initial consonant position
In syllable structure, one of the positions preceding the vowel and which can be filled by almost every consonant of English.

initialism
A word which, like an acronym, is formed from the first letters of a sequence of words but the letters themselves are pronounced, e.g. *BBC*.

insertion sequence
In spoken interaction, the process by which one adjacency pair is embedded within another.

intensifier
A type of adverb (belonging to a subset of adverbs of degree) which premodifies another adverb or an adjective and which indicates a point on an imagined scale, e.g. *slightly, very*.

interaction
The process by which two or more speakers converse.

interjection
A member of a minor word class consisting of emotive or spontaneous words which do not enter into syntactic structures, e.g. *wow, gosh, oh*.

International Phonetic Alphabet
An alphabet used for transcribing speech in which one symbol is assigned to each speech sound.

International Phonetic Association
An association formed in 1886 for the purpose of improving the teaching and learning of foreign languages.

interrogative
A sentence form in which the subject and the first element in the verb phrase are inverted and which is typically used to ask a question.

interrogative pronoun
A pronoun belonging to the subset of *wh*-pronouns and which is used to form a question.

intonation
The way in which pitch rises and falls in speech.

intransitive verb
A verb which requires no complementation.

intrusive *r*
The speech sound /r/ when it appears between two words, where the first word doesn't end in /r/ nor does the second word begin with it.

IPA
The International Phonetic Association, or the International Phonetic Alphabet which this association devised.

isogloss
A geographical boundary between two linguistic variants or the boundary of an area of specific usage.

L

labio-dental (*adjective*)
Of a consonant, articulated with the upper front teeth placed against the lower lip.

larynx
The voice box, or section of the trachea which contains the vocal cords.

lateral approximant
The speech sound /l/, so-called because the air escapes down the side of the mouth in its articulation.

length
A feature of some vowels, particularly those which can occur in open syllable structure.

level tone
A tone which retains a constant pitch.

levels of language
The various layers of linguistic construction, such as lexis, grammar and discourse.

lexeme
The abstract, representative form of a word.

lexical cohesion
Cohesion produced by the related meanings of words.

lexical gap
The absence in a language or dialect of an equivalent word to one which occurs in another language or dialect.

lexical item
An alternative term for a lexeme.

lexical level
The layer of language structure related to the lexis or vocabulary of that language.

lexical morphology
The branch of morphology concerned with strategies for the formation of lexical words.

lexical set
A group of words belonging to the same word class and closely related by their meanings, e.g. the names of fruits.

lexical verb
A verb other than an auxiliary verb.

lexical word
Any word which belongs to an open class (in contrast to a grammatical word).

lexicon
The full set of words or lexemes in a language. Lexicon can also refer to a type of dictionary.

lexis (*adjective*: **lexical**)
An alternative term for vocabulary, or the words of a language.

liaison
The appearance or addition of speech sounds (usually /r/ in English) at word boundaries.

lingua franca
A language used by speakers who do not share a native language.

linking *r*
In a non-rhotic accent, the articulation of /r/ at the end of a word where it would not normally be pronounced but it surfaces because it precedes a vowel.

lips
Active articulators used in the production of bilabial and labio-dental consonants, and which affect the production of vowels depending on whether they are rounded or unrounded.

liquid approximant
Either of the consonants /l/ and /r/.

loanword
A word which is brought wholesale into one language from another, e.g. *tortilla, feng-shui.*

lungs
The organs which are crucial to voice production in that the airstream flows from them.

M
main clause
In a sentence, a clause whose verb element is marked for tense and which, in contrast to a subordinate clause, can stand alone.

main verb
An alternative term for a lexical verb.

mainstream RP
The less class-based variety of Received Pronunciation, the variety more likely to be heard in the media.

manner of articulation
The way in which a consonant sound is produced, e.g. a plosive or fricative.

meronym
The use of a word whose referent denotes part of something to stand for the whole, e.g. using *wheels* to refer to a car.

metalanguage (*adjective*: **metalinguistic**)
Language which itself refers to language and language use.

metonym
A word used to refer to something with which that word is associated, e.g. *palace* to refer to the British royal family.

minimal free form
The smallest unit of language which can stand alone and still be meaningful.

minor sentence
A semantically complete unit but one which is incomplete as far as clause elements are concerned, e.g. *Pint of bitter* said to a barman is complete in meaning although it is just a noun phrase.

modal auxiliary
One of nine possible auxiliary verbs from the set *can, could, shall, should, will, would, may, might, must*. Modals have a range of meanings and functions in verb phrases.

mode
The medium of discourse, normally speech or writing, but signing is also a mode.

monitoring devices
Utterances such as *I mean* and *you know* which enable a speaker to regulate their own or their addressee's position towards a piece of discourse.

monophthong
A vowel which involves no change in mouth shape in its articulation, unlike a diphthong.

monosyllabic (*adjective*)
Consisting of one syllable only.

monotransitive verb
A verb which, in contrast to a ditransitive verb, is followed by one object element only.

morpheme
A minimal and abstract unit of word construction.

morphology
The formation of words or the study of the formation of words.
multi-party talk
Spoken interaction which takes place between three or more participants.
multiple negation
The use of more than one negative element to make a clause negative, as in
I never did nothing to upset her. This structure is often found in non-standard
dialects of English and is one of the features that prescriptive linguists view as
incorrect or 'poor' English.
multi-word verb
A lexical verb which consists of two or three elements and whose meaning is
usually partly or wholly idiomatic, e.g. *run up, play down*.

N
narrow transcription
A phonetic transcription which provides detailed information about allophonic realisations.
narrowing
The degrees of closure involved in the articulation of speech sounds.
nasal
A type of stop consonant in which air is released through the nasal as well as
the oral cavity during articulation.
nasal cavity
The section of the vocal tract from the velum to the nostrils.
nasalisation
The release of air through the nasal cavity during the articulation of a vowel,
giving that vowel a nasal quality.
negative clause
A clause in which a negative particle (usually *not*) denies the truth asserted.
neologism
A new word.
nominal clause
A clause which occurs in a position normally occupied by a noun phrase, typically as a subject or object.
nominal relative clause
A clause which occurs pronominally and which begins with a *wh*-word for
which the antecedent is implicit, e.g. *Where to go was quite a problem*.
nominal relative pronoun
A pronoun belonging to the subset of *wh*-pronouns and which is used to introduce a nominal relative clause.

nominative case
In traditional grammar, the subject role, which requires a particular noun (or pronoun) inflection.

non-count noun
A noun which cannot refer to more than one of its referent and so has no plural form, e.g. *hockey, music, furniture.*

non-finite clause
A clause in which the verb element is not marked for tense.

non-finite verb
A verb which is not marked for tense.

non-fluency features
Features of spoken language such as hesitations and false starts which interrupt the flow of speech and are superfluous to it.

non-fluent repetition
In spoken language, the unintentional repetition of a word or phrase.

non-prevocalic *r*
In rhotic accents, the articulation of /r/ after a vowel when it occurs at the end of a word or before another consonant, e.g. the pronunciation of *car* as [kɑːr] and *card* as [kɑːrd].

non-restrictive relative clause
A relative clause which gives additional information about the referent(s) of the noun which it postmodifies.

non-rhotic (*adjective*)
An accent like RP in which /r/ is not articulated in words such as *car* and *card.*

noun
An open class word characterised by its naming function and normally possessing the property of being able to be preceded by *the.*

noun phrase (NP)
A phrase which has a noun (or pronoun) as its head.

noun phrases in apposition
Adjacent noun phrases which have the same referent.

nucleus
An alternative term for the tonic syllable in a tone group.

number
The grammatical distinction between singular and plural.

numeral
A word which refers to a number, be it a pronoun, a determiner or a noun.

O

object complement
A complement which gives more information about the object of the clause, e.g. *unhappy* in *She made her friend unhappy.*

object element
The element of a clause which follows a transitive verb and which is typically the affected element in the clause, e.g. *three eggs* in *Julia broke three eggs*.

object predicative
An alternative term for an object complement.

objective form
The form a pronoun normally takes when it is in the object position in a clause, e.g. *me, him, us.*

obligatory (*adjective*)
An obligatory linguistic element is one that cannot be omitted from a particular structure without causing it to be ill-formed.

of-**construction**
A prepositional phrase with *of* as its head used to indicate possession or association, e.g. *the end of a journey*.

official language
A language designated by a nation or organisation to be used for official and public purposes.

Old English
The earliest phase of English, dating from approximately AD 450–1100.

onomatopoeia (*adjective:* **onomatopoeic**)
The mimicking of a sound by a word, although the representation is only approximate.

onset
In syllable structure, any consonant(s) which occurs before the vowel.

open class
A class of words which is too large to quantify and is constantly changing. Nouns, verbs, adjectives and adverbs are all open class words.

open syllable
A syllable whose vowel is not succeeded by a consonant.

open vowel
A vowel which is articulated with a relatively large cavity between the tongue and the palate.

operator
The first (or only) auxiliary in a verb phrase.

oral cavity
The section of the vocal tract from the larynx to the lips, and excluding the nasal cavity.

ordinal numeral
A numeral which is used to count in rank order, e.g. *first, second, third.*

P

palatal (*adjective*)

Of a consonant, articulated with the tongue against the hard palate.

palato-alveolar (*adjective*)

Of a consonant, articulated with the tip of the tongue against the alveolar ridge, while the front of the tongue is raised towards the hard palate.

paradigm

A systematic set of inflected forms, especially of nouns and verbs.

parallelism

The repetition of a grammatical structure, e.g. subject and past tense verb in *I came, I saw, I conquered.*

part of speech

A traditional term for a word class.

participle

A non-finite verb form ending in either *-ed* (or taking an equivalent form in irregular verbs) or *-ing.*

particle

A member of a very small and minor word class, which includes the negative particle *not* and the infinitive particle *to.*

passive articulator

Any part of the vocal tract used in articulating speech sounds which cannot change position. The passive articulators are the teeth, the alveolar ridge and the hard palate.

passive verb

A verb phrase whose subject is the affected element of the lexical verb and which is constructed by using a form of the verb *be* as an auxiliary, e.g. *was surrounded* in *The castle was surrounded.*

passive voice

The voice of a clause whose verb element is passive.

past perfect

The tense and aspect combination constructed using the auxiliary *have* in the past tense and by placing the lexical verb in its *-ed* participle form, e.g. *had walked.*

past perfect progressive

The tense and aspect combination constructed using the auxiliary *have* in the past tense, the auxiliary *be* in its *-ed* form, and by adding *-ing* to the lexical verb, e.g. *had been walking.*

past progressive

The tense and aspect combination constructed using the auxiliary *be* in the past tense and by adding *-ing* to the lexical verb, e.g. *was walking.*

past tense
One of the two tenses in English (the other being the present), signalled in regular verbs by an *-ed* inflection, e.g. *walked* in *Rasheed walked to college.*

patient
An alternative term for affected.

peak
The vowel at the heart of a syllable.

perfect aspect
An aspect constructed using the auxiliary *have* and denoting completion of the activity referred to by the lexical verb in its *-ed* form, e.g. *has read* in *She has read this book.*

performative verb
A verb which, in the first person present tense, performs the action to which it refers through the actual speaking or writing of the verb, e.g. *promise* in *I promise.*

perseverative assimilation
Assimilation in which a feature of one speech sound continues into the next sound.

person
A grammatical category distinguishing between 1st, 2nd and 3rd person.

personal pronoun
A member of the set of pronouns distinguishing between 1st, 2nd and 3rd person (singular and plural) and taking either a subjective or an objective form, e.g. *I, me, you, they, them.*

pharynx
The section of the vocal tract between the uvula and the larynx.

phoneme
A distinct speech sound in its representative, abstract form.

phoneme inventory
The set of phonemes which represents all the distinct speech sounds of a particular language.

phonetic transcription
The writing down of speech using the phonetic alphabet to indicate pronunciation.

phonetics
The study of speech sounds.

phonology
The sound system of a language or the study of that system.

phonotactics
The systematic possibilities for combining distinct speech sounds in a particular language.

phrasal verb
An alternative term for a multi-word verb or, more specifically, a multi-word verb consisting of the lexical verb and an adverb, e.g. *give away.*

phrase
A unit of linguistic construction smaller than a clause, consisting of a head word and any other words dependent on that head word, and having the capacity to fill a clause element slot.

pitch
The apparent height of the voice, ranging from low to high.

place of articulation
The point in the vocal tract where complete or partial closure occurs in the articulation of a consonant.

plosive
A consonant which is produced by a complete closure at some point in the oral cavity and the sudden release of the pressurised air at this point.

plural form
The form taken by a noun, usually through adding an inflection, when it refers to more than one of its singular referent, e.g. *books, addenda.*

politeness marker
A linguistic element which is often peripheral to a clause but which is used to show respect for the addressee, e.g. *please.*

polysemy (*adjective:* **polysemous**)
With regard to a word, the state of having more than one meaning, e.g. *mouse.*

polysyllabic (*adjective*)
Consisting of three or more syllables.

portmanteau word
An alternative term for a blend.

possessive form
The form taken by a noun when an inflection has been added to indicate possession or association, e.g. *Susan's* in *Susan's brother* or *journey's* in *the journey's end.*

possessive pronoun
Any pronoun used to indicate possession, whether it is in the dependent or independent form (although those in the dependent form are sometimes classified as determiners), e.g. *my, mine, your, yours.*

postdeterminer
One of a handful of determiners which succeed any central determiner in a noun phrase.

post-final consonant
In syllable structure, any consonant(s) (one or two) which follows a final consonant.

post-initial consonant
In syllable structure, any consonant which follows an initial consonant.
postmodification
In phrases, modification which follows the head word.
postnominal (*adjective*)
Occurring after a noun.
post-nucleus
The part of a tone group which follows the nucleus, usually shorter than the pre-nucleus.
postvocalic (*adjective*)
Occurring after a vowel.
pragmatics
The branch of linguistics which deals with language use and the interpretation of meaning which is not explicit.
predeterminer
One of a handful of determiners which precede any central determiner in a noun phrase.
predicate
In a clause, the verb element and any obligatory elements which follow it.
predicative (*adjective*)
The predicative position is the one following a copular verb where a complement element occurs.
predicator
An alternative term for the verb element in a clause.
pre-final consonant
In syllable structure, any consonant which precedes a final consonant.
prefix
An affix which occurs word-initially or at the beginning of a base.
pre-initial consonant
In syllable structure, any consonant which precedes an initial consonant.
premodification
In phrases, modification which precedes the head word.
pre-nucleus
The part of a tone group which precedes the nucleus, usually longer than the post-nucleus.
preposition
A closed class word often used to express the relationship between two elements and typically complemented by a noun phrase to form a prepositional phrase.
prepositional complement
The phrase or clause which follows a preposition and which, together with that preposition, forms a prepositional phrase.

prepositional phrase (PP)
A phrase which has a preposition as its head. The preposition occurs at the beginning of the PP and is followed by the prepositional complement, which is most typically a noun phrase.

prescriptive (*adjective*)
A prescriptive approach to language study is one which is concerned with prescribing how a language should be used and often leads to judgemental attitudes towards users of the language.

present perfect
The tense and aspect combination constructed using the auxiliary *have* in the present tense and by placing the lexical verb in its *-ed* participle form, e.g. *have walked*.

present perfect progressive
The tense and aspect combination constructed using the auxiliary *have* in the present tense, the auxiliary *be* in its *-ed* form, and by adding *-ing* to the lexical verb, e.g. *have been walking*.

present progressive
The tense and aspect combination constructed using the auxiliary *be* in the present tense and by adding *-ing* to the lexical verb, e.g. *is walking*.

present tense
One of the two tenses in English (the other being the past) indicated normally by a zero inflection on the verb but with an *-s* inflection in the 3rd person singular.

primary auxiliary
Any of the verbs *be, have* or *do* when functioning as an auxiliary rather than a lexical verb.

primary cardinal vowel
One of a set of eight vowels used to map out tongue positions and moving from spread to rounded lips through the sequence.

primary pronoun
A member of the group which includes personal, possessive and reflexive pronouns.

primary stress
The most prominent stress in a word, in contrast to any secondary stress.

productive (*adjective*)
Of any linguistic process, leading to new forms.

progressive aspect
An aspect constructed using the auxiliary *be* and denoting that the activity referred to by the lexical verb is continuous or ongoing, e.g. *is reading* in *She is reading her book*.

pronominal (*adjective*)
Occurring in place of a noun.

pronoun
A closed class word which occurs in the same position as a noun and which sometimes acts as a co-referent with a noun or noun phrase.

proper noun
A noun which names someone or something which is unique, e.g. *Jane, London*. Proper nouns are conventionally written with a capital letter at the beginning.

prosodic features
The features of speech covered by prosodics.

prosodics
The suprasegmental aspects of speech, namely pitch, intonation, stress, volume, tempo and voice quality.

purpose clause
A subordinate clause normally introduced by *so that* or *in order that* and expressing motive.

Q

question
The typical function of an interrogative sentence.

question tag
A unit formed from an auxiliary verb followed by a pronoun, and which is added to a declarative sentence to form a tag question, e.g. *isn't it* in *It's hot, isn't it?*

R

reason clause
A subordinate clause normally introduced by *as, because, for* or *since* and providing explanation.

Received Pronunciation (RP)
The non-regional accent which is taken to typify British English, and which is often taught to foreign learners. Mainstream RP is used in British dictionaries to illustrate pronunciation.

recursion
The occurrence more than once of a structural pattern, particularly as seen in embedded structures.

recycling
In spoken language, recycling occurs when a speaker takes several attempts to articulate a word.

reduced relative clause
A postmodifying non-finite clause which has the potential to be expanded to a full relative clause, e.g. *the storm <u>brewing at sea</u>* could become *the storm <u>which is brewing at sea</u>*.

reduplication
A word formation strategy involving the total or partial repetition of an element, e.g. *no-no, flip-flop.*

referent
The person(s) or thing(s) to which any linguistic item refers.

reflexive pronoun
A member of a set of pronouns formed from a personal or possessive pronoun and *self* (singular) or *selves* (plural), e.g. *myself, themselves.*

register
In discourse, the configuration of textual features and meanings as determined by a range of contextual factors, namely field, tenor and mode.

relative clause
A type of subordinate clause which postmodifies a noun and is introduced by a relative pronoun, adverb or determiner.

relative pronoun
A pronoun belonging to the subset of *wh*-pronouns and which is used to introduce a relative clause, or the pronoun *that* when it fulfils the same function.

repetition
The recurrence of any linguistic feature.

restrictive relative clause
A relative clause which distinguishes the referents of the noun it modifies from another person, item, or group.

result clause
A subordinate clause normally introduced by *so* and expressing outcome.

retroflex (*adjective*)
A retroflex consonant is articulated by curling the tip of the tongue towards the back of the mouth.

rhotic (*adjective*)
A rhotic accent is one where /r/ is pronounced where it would not be realised in RP, e.g. in *car* and *card.*

rhoticity
The characteristic possessed by a rhotic accent.

rhyme
The part of a syllable containing the vowel (which is the peak), and any following consonants (which make up the coda).

rhythm
The pattern of stressed and unstressed syllables in connected speech.

rise-fall tone
A tone which rises from a lower to a higher pitch and then falls again.

root
The part of a word which is at the heart of its construction and meaning, e.g. *-pel* in *impel, expel* and *compel.*

root morpheme
An alternative term for a root.
RP
The abbreviation for Received Pronunciation.

S
-*s* plural
The regular plural form occurring on nouns.
schwa
The neutral vowel which is represented in the IPA by the symbol /ə/.
second pair part
The second turn in an adjacency pair sequence.
secondary cardinal vowel
One of a set of eight vowels used to map out tongue positions and, in contrast to the primary set, moving from rounded to spread lips through the sequence.
secondary stress
A degree of syllable prominence greater than that of an unstressed syllable but less than primary stress.
segment
A distinct speech sound.
segmental phonology
The branch of phonology that deals with the distribution of phonemes in a language.
semantic field
A theme or topic created by the occurrence of words of associated meanings within a text.
semantics
The meaning of linguistic elements, or the study of meaning.
semi-consonant
An alternative term for an approximant, also known as a semi-vowel.
semi-vowel
An alternative term for an approximant, also known as a semi-consonant.
sentence
The largest unit of syntactic construction, consisting of one or more clauses.
simple preposition
A single-word preposition, e.g. *under, through, into.*
simple sentence
A sentence which has no elements realised by a subordinate clause.
simple tone
A level, rising or falling tone.
simple word
A word constructed from one free morpheme only.

slang
Vocabulary which has a short linguistic shelf-life and which is used very informally, often by specific groups of users.

soft palate
The back part of the roof of the mouth, also known as the velum.

sonority
The volume of speech, often greatest in connected speech at a syllable peak.

speech sound
A distinct sound realising any of the phonemes of a language.

Standard British English
The standard dialect of English used in the British Isles. Socially, it is prestigious, and associated with a good education. There are some lexical and grammatical differences between this standard and that of other English-speaking countries, as well as some variation within the British Isles.

Standard English
The non-regional dialect of English which is regarded as typifying the language in terms of vocabulary and grammar.

statement
The typical function of a declarative sentence.

stative verb
A verb which refers to a state or condition, in contrast to a dynamic verb which refers to an action or physical process.

stop
A nasal or a plosive sound, both of which involve momentary total closure in the vocal tract.

stopping
The replacement of a fricative sound by a plosive or nasal sound.

stress
In speech, the means by which some syllables are given prominence.

stressed syllable
Any syllable in a word or in connected speech which is given prominence (in contrast to an unstressed syllable).

stress-timed language
A language such as English where the stressed syllables occur at roughly equal intervals.

stricture
The process of blocking off the airstream in the articulation of a consonant sound. An alternative term for closure.

strong form
The stressed pronunciation of a grammatical word which in other contexts is unstressed.

subject complement
A complement which gives more information about the subject of the clause.
subject element
The element of a clause which precedes the verb and which is typically the agent of an active clause, e.g. *Julia* in *Julia has broken three eggs*.
subject position
The clause position in front of the verb element which is filled by the subject.
subject predicative
An alternative term for a subject complement.
subjective form
The form a pronoun normally takes when it is in the subject position in a clause, e.g. *I, he, we, they*.
subject-operator inversion
The inversion of the subject element and the first auxiliary of a verb phrase which occurs in the formation of an interrogative sentence.
subject-specific lexis
Lexis which relates to a specific field or topic.
subject-verb inversion
An alternative term for subject-operator inversion or, more specifically, the inversion of the subject element and the verb *be* when *be* is the lexical verb and there are no auxiliaries in the verb phrase, e.g. *Is he ready?*
subjunctive mood
A feature of a verb phrase (rare in English) which may be contrasted with the indicative mood. It is found chiefly when the base form of the verb occurs instead of an inflected form, e.g. *be* in *The police are anxious that the criminal be caught*.
subordinate clause
A clause which cannot stand alone and is therefore subordinate to or dependent on some other element(s).
subordinating conjunction
A conjunction which introduces a subordinate clause.
subordinator
An alternative term for a subordinating conjunction.
substitute pronoun
Any pronoun when it is used to replace a noun or noun phrase.
suffix
An affix which occurs word-finally or at the end of a base.
superlative
A form taken by adjectives and adverbs when they indicate the most of something, e.g. *tallest, fastest*. The superlative inflection is *-est*.

superordinate clause
In a complex sentence, the independent clause on which the subordinate clause(s) is dependent.

suppletion
The process by which a particular word-form is supplied by a seemingly unrelated form rather than by an inflectional ending, e.g. *went* as the past tense of *go*.

suprasegmental phonology
The aspect of phonology concerned with prosodic features such as stress, pitch and intonation.

syllabic consonant
A consonant which functions as the peak of a syllable in place of a vowel.

syllabification
The way in which a word divides into syllables.

syllable
A unit of a word's pronunciation with a vowel at its peak.

syllable template
The internal structure of a syllable.

syllable-timed language
A language such as French where the syllables have approximately equal duration. Some varieties of English are closer to syllable-timing than stress-timing.

synonym (*adjective:* **synonymous**)
A word which has the same meaning as another word in the same language, e.g. *sight* meaning the same as *vision,* although it is arguable that there are no true synonyms.

syntactic rule
A rule relating to word order.

syntax
Word order, or the rules which govern word order. Syntax is one of the two aspects of grammar, the other being inflections.

T

tag question
A question formed from a declarative sentence followed by a question tag.

tempo
The speed of speech, usually measured in words per minute.

tenor
In discourse, the relationship between the participants (speaker/writer and audience) in a text and the way this affects linguistic choices, particularly in terms of formality.

tense

A grammatical feature of verbs, indicated by inflections and having both a present and a past form in English.

text

An alternative term for discourse.

textuality

The fact of being a cohesive text, spoken or written.

***t*-flapping**

The process by which /t/ is articulated by striking the tip of the tongue against the alveolar ridge as the tongue moves back to its resting position.

***th*-fronting**

The realisation of /θ/ as [f], and of /ð/ as [v].

***that*-clause**

A subordinate clause introduced by *that* and having a pronominal function or postmodifying a noun.

***to*-infinitive**

The infinitive form of the verb preceded by the particle *to,* e.g. *to write.*

tone

The pitch contour on a single syllable, although this may extend to adjacent syllables.

tone group

A unit of connected speech which contains a tonic syllable or nucleus, usually towards the end of the group, and usually a pre-nucleus and post-nucleus as well. A tone group is likely to have some degree of grammatical completeness.

tone unit

An alternative term for a tone group.

tongue

The most important active articulator, comprising the tip, blade, front, back and sides.

tonic syllable

The syllable in a tone group on which there is the most noticeable change in pitch.

topic-comment structure

A structure which begins by specifying one of the sentence elements, and then follows it with a full clause containing reference to that element e.g *one of the part-timers Steve...he came over to me.*

trachea

The windpipe, which carries air from the lungs to the mouth.

transitive verb

A verb which requires an object element to follow it.

tree diagram
A method of representing a linguistic analysis diagrammatically using vertical and diagonal lines to show branching.
triphthong
A vowel sequence in which a diphthong is followed by a further vowel, usually schwa. Speakers may realise triphthongs as one syllable or two.
trisyllabic (*adjective*)
Consisting of three syllables.

U
unstressed syllable
A syllable which is given no prominence and in which the vowel is often realised as /ə/ or /ɪ/.
upper teeth
The passive articulators used in the production of labio-dental sounds.
uvula
The piece of flesh at the tip of the velum which hangs down at the back of the mouth.

V
variable
A linguistic feature which has more than one surface form.
variant
One of the surface forms taken by a linguistic variable.
velar (*adjective*)
Of a consonant, articulated with the back of the tongue against the soft palate.
velum
The soft palate.
verb
The most central type of open class word, identified by its ability to make a contrast of present and past tense.
verb complementation
The obligatory element(s) which follows a particular lexical verb.
verb element
The most obligatory element of a clause and which is always a verb phrase.
verb phrase (VP)
A phrase which has a lexical verb as its head.
verbless clause
A linguistic unit which does not contain a verb element but resembles a full clause, particularly in its potential to be expanded into a clause, e.g. *if available* could be expanded to *if it is available.*

vocabulary
An everyday term for the words in a language, or a subset of those words.
vocal cords
The two muscles situated in the larynx which are essential for speech.
vocal folds
An alternative term for the vocal cords.
vocal tract
The oral and nasal cavities, and the upper section of the trachea as far as the larynx.
voice
The contrast in verb phrases between active and passive.
voice box
The section of the trachea which contains the vocal cords. It is also known as the larynx.
voice quality
A type of spoken voice, e.g. creaky or husky.
voicing
The vibration of the vocal cords in the articulation of a speech sound.
volume
The degree of softness or loudness with which speech is produced.
vowel
A speech sound which is articulated without any closure of articulators in the vocal tract so that the airstream flows through freely.
vowel mutation
A vowel change for grammatical purposes and occurring instead of the addition of an inflection, e.g. *sang* as the past tense of *sing*.

W
weak form
The unstressed pronunciation of a grammatical word which in some contexts may have full stress.
***wh*-pronoun**
A pronoun beginning with *wh-*, one member of a larger set of *wh*-words.
***wh*-question**
A question formed with a *wh*-word at the beginning.
***wh*-word**
An adverb, determiner or pronoun which begins with *wh-* (although *how* is also a *wh-* word).
word class
A category of words whose members are identified by their grammatical similarities.

word formation
The process of forming or creating words.
word stress
The pattern of stressed and unstressed syllables in a word.
word-final (*adjective*)
Occurring at the end of a word.
word-form
The form a lexeme takes when it is realised in speech or writing.
word-initial (*adjective*)
Occurring at the beginning of a word.
word-medial (*adjective*)
Occurring in the middle of a word.

Y

yes-no question
A question formed through subject-verb inversion without the addition of a *wh*-word, and which could be answered simply with yes or no.
yod
The approximant /j/.
yod coalescence
The process by which a consonant merges with a following /j/ resulting in a single speech sound, e.g. when /t/ + /j/ in *tune* [tjuːn] become [ʧ] to give [ʧuːn].
yod-dropping
The dropping of /j/ in the pronunciation of a word where it is normally present, e.g. pronouncing *tune* as [tuːn].

Z

zero inflection
An absent inflection where an inflection would normally occur, e.g. the plural of *sheep* has a zero inflection.
zero relative pronoun
A relative pronoun absent from a relative clause but understood, e.g. in *the man Ø I saw*.

Index

abstract nouns, *see* nouns
accent, 8, 222, 246, 296, 297, 346
   variation in, 9, 227, 252, 253, 314–19, 320
   see also Received Pronunciation; rhotic
     accents
accidental gap, 258, 346
accusative case, *see* case
acronyms, 62, 346
active articulators, *see* articulators
active verbs, *see* verbs
adjacency pairs, 200ff, 346
   first pair part, 200, 360
   follow-up turn, 201, 360
   insertion sequence, 203, 364
   second pair part, 200, 378
adjective phrases, *see* phrases
adjectives, 20, 22, 27–8, 89–90, 97, 307, 346
   absolute form of, 90, 346
   central, 27, 28, 351
   comparative, 90, 353
   deverbal, 57, 356
   gradable, 28, 89–90, 97, 361
   postnominal, 99, 374
   pronominal, 100, 375
   superlative, 90, 380
adjuncts, 29–31, 171, 347
adverb phrases, *see* phrases
adverbial clauses, *see* clauses
adverbial element, *see* clause elements
adverbs, 20, 22, 29–32, 45, 46, 89–90,
     110, 347
   absolute form of, 90
   comparative, 90, 353
   degree, 30–1, 347, 364
   formation of, 29
   gradable, 89–90, 361
   manner, 30, 307, 347
   place, 30, 347
   relative, 137
   superlative, 90, 380
   time, 30, 347

wh-, 31, 46–7
   see also adjuncts; conjuncts; disjuncts;
     intensifiers
affected role, 128–9, 347
affirmative clauses, *see* clauses
affixation, 52, 53–7, 68, 347
affixes, 53, 56, 68, 303, 347
   class-changing, 53, 56, 351
   class-preserving, 53, 56, 351
   see also infixes; prefixes; suffixes
affricates, *see* consonants, manner of
     articulation of
agent role, 128–9, 348
aggregate nouns, *see* nouns
agreement, 86, 348
   see also concord
airstream, 227, 348
   egressive pulmonic, 227, 358
   ingressive pulmonic, 227, 364
allomorphs, 52, 348
allophones, 224, 225, 247, 248, 252, 314–17,
     318–19, 348
alveolar consonants, *see* consonants, place
     of articulation of
alveolar ridge, 229ff, 348
   see also articulators
American English, 8, 223, 252, 293, 300,
     303ff, 310, 314ff, 318–19
anaphors, 194–5, 348
and coordination, 188, 348
anglicising of words, 63, 302–3, 348
antecedents, 136–7, 140, 194–5, 348
anticipatory assimilation, *see* assimilation
anticipatory *it*, 153, 348
antonyms, 67, 349
apposition, 117, 349, 369
approximants, 231, 232, 249, 252, 258,
     315–7, 349
   central, 232, 351
   lateral, 232, 365
   liquid, 232, 366

28/10/17

Printed in China